# Commerce and Community

Since the end of the Cold War, the human face of economics has gained renewed visibility and generated new conversations among economists and other social theorists. The monistic, mechanical "economic systems" that characterized the capitalism vs. socialism debates of the mid-twentieth century have given way to pluralistic ecologies of economic provisioning in which complexly constituted agents cooperate via heterogeneous forms of production and exchange. Through the lenses of multiple disciplines, this book examines how this pluralistic turn in economic thinking bears upon the venerable social–theoretical division of cooperative activity into separate spheres of impersonal *Gesellschaft* (commerce) and ethically thick *Gemeinschaft* (community).

Drawing resources from diverse disciplinary and philosophical traditions, these essays offer fresh, critical appraisals of the *Gemeinschaft / Gesellschaft* segregation of face-to-face community from impersonal commerce. Some authors issue urgent calls to transcend this dualism, while others propose to recast it in more nuanced ways or affirm the importance of treating impersonal and personal cooperation as ethically, epistemically, and economically separate worlds. Yet even in their disagreements, our contributors paint the process of voluntary cooperation – the space of commerce and community – with uncommon color and nuance by traversing the boundaries that once separated the thin sociality of economics (as science of commerce) from the thick sociality of sociology and anthropology (as sciences of community).

This book facilitates critical exchange among economists, philosophers, sociologists, anthropologists, and other social theorists by exploring the overlapping notions of cooperation, rationality, identity, reciprocity, trust, and exchange that emerge from multiple analytic traditions within and across their respective disciplines.

**Robert F. Garnett, Jr.** is Professor of Economics at Texas Christian University, USA.

**Paul Lewis** is Reader in Economics and Public Policy at King's College London, UK.

**Lenore T. Ealy** is President of The Philanthropic Enterprise, USA.

"The editors of this path-breaking collection have assembled a veritable all-star list of interdisciplinary scholars to investigate the role of exchange in the development of cooperative behavior, how commerce affects our ability to form or reform meaningful human associations, and the extent to which commerce complements or hinders other important social institutions. This work is vitally necessary. We need to know, now more than ever, how – indeed, whether – market-based commercial societies can contribute to humane and just societies, and how – and whether – they contribute to human happiness. These essays broaden and deepen our understanding of human nature, of the nature of human social institutions, and of the effects of markets on human well-being. They deserve, and repay, serious attention."

James R. Otteson, Wake Forest University, USA

"This is a profound collection, addressing the relative and interacting roles of community and market in society. The conventional separation between communal gift-giving and impersonal commerce is effectively challenged. The authors, from various disciplines and perspectives, are unified in trying to see the inter-relations between community and market. The results of their research provide us with new and promising frameworks that could transform the study of economy and society."

Mario Rizzo, New York University, USA

"This important collection of essays represents a milestone in breaking down the separation between market-based forms of coordination principally associated with economics, and communal modes of cooperation principally associated with sociology and anthropology. The contributions, mostly by economists but also by representatives from other disciplines, provide a fascinating window into the many ways in which the commercial and the communal intertwine and in many cases presuppose one another."

Jochen Runde, University of Cambridge, UK

# Economics as Social Theory
Series edited by Tony Lawson
*University of Cambridge*

Social Theory is experiencing something of a revival within economics. Critical analyses of the particular nature of the subject matter of social studies, and of the types of method, categories and modes of explanation that can legitimately be endorsed for the scientific study of social objects, are re-emerging. Economists are again addressing such issues as the relationship between agency and structure, between economy and the rest of society, and between the enquirer and the object of enquiry. There is a renewed interest in elaborating basic categories such as causation, competition, culture, discrimination, evolution, money, need, order, organization, power probability, process, rationality, technology, time, truth, uncertainty, value etc.

The objective for this series is to facilitate this revival further. In contemporary economics the label "theory" has been appropriated by a group that confines itself to largely asocial, ahistorical, mathematical "modelling". Economics as Social Theory thus reclaims the "Theory" label, offering a platform for alternative rigorous, but broader and more critical conceptions of theorizing.

Other titles in this series include:

1. **Economics and Language**
   *Edited by Willie Henderson*

2. **Rationality, Institutions and Economic Methodology**
   *Edited by Uskali Mäki, Bo Gustafsson, and Christian Knudsen*

3. **New Directions in Economic Methodology**
   *Edited by Roger Backhouse*

4. **Who Pays for the Kids?**
   *Nancy Folbre*

5. **Rules and Choice in Economics**
   *Viktor Vanberg*

6. **Beyond Rhetoric and Realism in Economics**
   *Thomas A. Boylan and Paschal F. O'Gorman*

7. **Feminism, Objectivity and Economics**
   *Julie A. Nelson*

8. **Economic Evolution**
   *Jack J. Vromen*

9. **Economics and Reality**
   *Tony Lawson*

10. **The Market**
    *John O' Neill*

11. **Economics and Utopia**
    *Geoff Hodgson*

12. **Critical Realism in Economics**
    *Edited by Steve Fleetwood*

13. **The New Economic Criticism**
    *Edited by Martha Woodmansee and Mark Osteeen*

14. **What do Economists Know?**
    *Edited by Robert F. Garnett, Jr.*

15. **Postmodernism, Economics and Knowledge**
    *Edited by Stephen Cullenberg, Jack Amariglio and David F. Ruccio*

16. **The Values of Economics**
    An Aristotelian perspective
    *Irene van Staveren*

17. **How Economics Forgot History**
    The problem of historical specificity in social science
    *Geoffrey M. Hodgson*

18. **Intersubjectivity in Economics**
    Agents and structures
    *Edward Fullbrook*

19. **The World of Consumption**
    The material and cultural revisited
    2nd edn
    *Ben Fine*

20. **Reorienting Economics**
    *Tony Lawson*

21. **Toward a Feminist Philosophy of Economics**
    *Edited by Drucilla K. Barker and Edith Kuiper*

22. **The Crisis in Economics**
    *Edited by Edward Fullbrook*

23. **The Philosophy of Keynes' Economics**
    Probability, uncertainty and convention
    *Edited by Jochen Runde and Sohei Mizuhara*

24. **Postcolonialism Meets Economics**
    *Edited by Eiman O. Zein-Elabdin and S. Charusheela*

25. **The Evolution of Institutional Economics**
    Agency, structure and Darwinism in American institutionalism
    *Geoffrey M. Hodgson*

26. **Transforming Economics**
    Perspectives on the Critical Realist Project
    *Edited by Paul Lewis*

27. **New Departures in Marxian Theory**
    *Edited by Stephen A. Resnick and Richard D. Wolff*

28. **Markets, Deliberation and Environmental Value**
    *John O'Neill*

29. **Speaking of Economics**
    How to get in the conversation
    *Arjo Klamer*

30. **From Political Economy to Economics**
    Method, the social and the historical in the evolution of economic theory
    *Dimitris Milonakis and Ben Fine*

31. **From Economics Imperialism to Freakonomics**
    The shifting boundaries between economics and other social sciences
    *Dimitris Milonakis and Ben Fine*

32. **Development and Globalization**
    A Marxian class analysis
    *David Ruccio*

33. **Introducing Money**
    *Mark Peacock*

34. **The Cambridge Revival of Political Economy**
    *Nuno Ornelas Martins*

35. **Understanding Development Economics**
    Its challenge to development studies
    *Adam Fforde*

36. **Economic Methodology**
    An historical introduction
    *Harro Maas, Translated by Liz Waters*

37. **Social Ontology and Modern Economics**
    *Stephen Pratten*

38. **History of Financial Crises**
    Dreams and follies of expectations
    *Cihan Bilginsoy*

39. **Commerce and Community**
    Ecologies of social cooperation
    *Edited by Robert F. Garnett, Jr., Paul Lewis and Lenore T. Ealy*

# Commerce and Community
Ecologies of social cooperation

Edited by Robert F. Garnett, Jr.,
Paul Lewis and Lenore T. Ealy

Routledge
Taylor & Francis Group
LONDON AND NEW YORK

First published 2015
by Routledge
2 Park Square, Milton Park, Abingdon, Oxon OX14 4RN

and by Routledge
711 Third Avenue, New York, NY 10017

*Routledge is an imprint of the Taylor & Francis Group, an Informa business*

© 2015 selection and editorial material, Robert F. Garnett, Jr., Paul Lewis and Lenore T. Ealy; individual chapters, the contributors.

The right of the editors to be identified as the author of the editorial material, and of the authors for their individual chapters, has been asserted in accordance with sections 77 and 78 of the Copyright, Designs and Patents Act 1988.

All rights reserved. No part of this book may be reprinted or reproduced or utilised in any form or by any electronic, mechanical, or other means, now known or hereafter invented, including photocopying and recording, or in any information storage or retrieval system, without permission in writing from the publishers.

*Trademark notice*: Product or corporate names may be trademarks or registered trademarks, and are used only for identification and explanation without intent to infringe.

*British Library Cataloguing in Publication Data*
A catalogue record for this book is available from the British Library

*Library of Congress Cataloguing in Publication data*
Commerce and community : ecologies of social cooperation / edited by Robert F. Garnett, Jr., Paul Lewis and Lenore T. Ealy.
   pages   cm – (Economics as social theory)
Includes bibliographical references and index.
1. Cooperation.  2. Economics–Sociological aspects.  I. Garnett, Robert F.
HD2961.C6534 2014
306.3–dc23
2014024749

ISBN: 978-0-415-81009-8 (hbk)
ISBN: 978-0-415-81010-4 (pbk)
ISBN: 978-1-315-73717-1 (ebk)

Typeset in Palatino
by Out of House Publishing

Printed and bound in Great Britain by
TJ International Ltd, Padstow, Cornwall

For Richard C. Cornuelle (1927–2011),
our provocateur, champion, and friend

# Contents

*List of contributors* xiv
*Acknowledgments* xxii

Introduction 1
ROBERT F. GARNETT, JR., PAUL LEWIS, AND LENORE T. EALY

**PART I**
**Social cooperation** 11

1  The evolution of human cooperation 13
   SAMUEL BOWLES AND HERBERT GINTIS

2  The theory of social cooperation historically and robustly
   contemplated 38
   PETER J. BOETTKE AND DANIEL J. SMITH

3  Commerce and beneficence: Adam Smith's
   unfinished project 56
   ROBERT F. GARNETT, JR.

4  Comment: Entering the "great school of self-command": the
   moralizing influence of markets, language, and imagination 77
   SANDRA J. PEART

**PART II**
**Identity and association** 83

5  Commerce, reciprocity, and civil virtues:
   the contribution of the Civil Economy 85
   LUIGINO BRUNI

6  What does true individualism really involve? Overcoming market–philanthropy dualism in Hayekian social theory  101
PAUL LEWIS

7  Methodological individualism and invisible hands: Richard Cornuelle's call to understand associations  122
STEVEN GROSBY

8  Comment: Don't forget the barter in "truck, barter and exchange"!  146
SHAUN P. HARGREAVES HEAP

## PART III
## Human(e) economics  155

9  Between *Gemeinschaft* and *Gesellschaft*: the stories we tell  157
EMILY CHAMLEE-WRIGHT AND VIRGIL HENRY STORR

10  Community, the market, and the state: insights from German neoliberalism  177
SAMUEL GREGG

11  Bourgeois love  195
DEIRDRE MCCLOSKEY

12  Comment: Behind the veil of interest  214
LAURENT DOBUZINSKIS

## PART IV
## Entangled spheres  219

13  How is community made?  221
COLIN DANBY

14  Commerce, community, and digital gifts  236
DAVE ELDER-VASS

15  Classical liberalism and the firm: a troubled relationship  253
DAVID ELLERMAN

16  Comment: Exploring the liminal spaces between commerce and community  274
MARTHA A. STARR

## PART V
## Not by commerce alone — 279

17  Reciprocity, calculation, and non-monetary exchange — 281
    STEVEN HORWITZ

18  Kidneys, commerce, and communities — 303
    NEERA K. BADHWAR

19  Banks and trust in Adam Smith — 322
    MARIA PIA PAGANELLI

20  Comment: Bankers, vampires, and organ sellers: who can you trust? — 336
    JOHN THRASHER AND DAVID SCHMIDTZ

    Envoi
    *The Apologia of Mercurius* — 342
    FREDERICK TURNER

    *Index* — 347

# Contributors

**Neera K. Badhwar** is Professor Emerita of Philosophy at the University of Oklahoma, where she taught from 1987–2010, and is affiliated with the Department of Economics and the Department of Philosophy at George Mason University. Her articles on moral psychology, ethical theory, and political theory have appeared in *Ethics, Journal of Philosophy, Nous, Philosophy and Phenomenological Research, Social Philosophy and Policy, Politics, Philosophy & Economics, American Philosophical Quarterly*, and other journals. She is the author of *Well-Being: Happiness in a Worthwhile Life* (2014), and editor of *Friendship: A Philosophical Reader* (1993). She has held fellowships at the University Center for Human Values, Princeton University (1996–7); Social Philosophy and Policy Center (Spring 1994 and 2008); and Dalhousie University (1986–7). In fall 1999 she was NEH Visiting Professor at SUNY Potsdam, and in 2002 a Visiting Scholar at Liberty Fund.

**Peter J. Boettke** is University Professor of Economics and Philosophy at George Mason University, where he is also the Director of The F. A. Hayek Program for Advanced Study in Philosophy, Politics, and Economics at the Mercatus Center. Boettke is also the BB&T Professor for the Study of Capitalism at the Mercatus Center. He is the editor of *The Review of Austrian Economics*. His most recent book is *Living Economics* (2012).

**Samuel Bowles** heads the Behavioral Sciences Program at the Santa Fe Institute. He earned his PhD in Economics from Harvard University and taught economics at Harvard from 1965 to 1973. He also taught at the University of Massachusetts and at the University of Siena from 2002 to 2010. His papers have appeared in *Science, Nature, New Scientist, American Economic Review, Theoretical Population Biology, Games and Economic Behavior, Journal of Theoretical Biology, Journal of Political Economy, Quarterly Journal of Economics, Behavioral and Brain Science,* and *Philosophy and Public Affairs*. His next book, *Machiavelli's Mistake: Why good laws are no substitute for good citizens*, will explore how organizations, communities, and nations could be better governed in light of the fact that altruistic and ethical motives are common in most populations. Bowles also studies political hierarchy and wealth inequality and their evolution over the very long run. He has served as an economic advisor to the governments of Cuba, South Africa, and Greece, to presidential candidates Robert F. Kennedy and Jesse Jackson, to the New Mexico House of Representatives, to the Congress of South African Trade Unions, and to South African President Nelson Mandela.

**Luigino Bruni** is Professor of Economics at the University of Lumsa (Rome). He earned a PhD in the History of Economics at the University of Florence in Italy in 1998 and a PhD in Economics at the University of East Anglia in 2006. His research interests include microeconomics, ethics and economics, the history of economic thought, economic methodology, sociality and happiness, and economics and theology. His most recent work examines the Civil Economy, reciprocity, the nature of the gift, and the role of intrinsic motivation in economic and civil life. His English-language books include: *Civil Happiness* (2006), *Reciprocity, Altruism and Civil Society* (2008), the *Handbook on The Economics of Happiness* (edited with P. Porta, 2007), *Civil Economy* (with S. Zamagni, 2007), *Ethos and Genesis of the Market* (2012), and *The Wound and the Blessing* (2012).

**Emily Chamlee-Wright** is Provost and Dean of the College at Washington College on Maryland's Eastern Shore. Her research investigates the confluence of cultural and economic processes. She is the author of *The Cultural and Political Economy of Recovery: Social Learning in a Post-Disaster Environment* (2010), *Culture and Enterprise: The Development, Representation, and Morality of Business*, with Don Lavoie (2000), and *The Cultural Foundations of Economic Development* (1997), and co-editor of *The Political Economy of Hurricane Katrina and Community Development* (2010) with Virgil Storr. Her current book project is entitled *Liberal Learning and the Art of Self-Governance* (forthcoming).

**Colin Danby** is Professor of Interdisciplinary Arts and Sciences at the University of Washington, Bothell. His publications have drawn on post-Keynesian economics to critique splits between gift and exchange in anthropology and philosophy, and examine their consequences for feminist thought. His writings on the history of Latin American economic thought also address the contributions of trans-disciplinary social science to money and credit. His recent work examines the politics of economic representation.

**Laurent Dobuzinskis** teaches Political Science at Simon Fraser University (Canada). His current interests bear on the history of political and economic thought, with special emphasis on eighteenth- and nineteenth-century French political economists and philosophers. He has written many papers and co-edited books on such topics, as well as on the

Austrian School of economics, policy analysis, and the philosophy of social science.

**Lenore T. Ealy** is President of The Philanthropic Enterprise, an independent scholarly research institute that seeks to strengthen understanding of how philanthropy and voluntary social cooperation promote human flourishing. She also founded and serves as editor of *Conversations on Philanthropy*, the institute's annual journal. Author of numerous articles on philanthropy, Ealy is also co-editor, with Steven Klugewicz, of *History, on Proper Principles: Essays in Honor of Forrest McDonald* (2010) and co-editor, with Robert C. Enlow, of *Liberty and Learning: Milton Friedman's Voucher Idea at Fifty* (2006). She earned her PhD in history and early modern moral and political thought at The Johns Hopkins University.

**Dave Elder-Vass** is a senior lecturer in sociology at Loughborough University, UK. His writing on social ontology and social theory includes two recent books: *The Causal Power of Social Structures* (2010) and *The Reality of Social Construction* (2012). Currently, he is working on issues in the social ontology of economic phenomena, on the nature of cultural communities, and on giving as an alternative to market exchange.

**David Ellerman** returned to academia as a visiting scholar at University of California-Riverside after ten years at the World Bank, where he was the Economic Advisor to the Chief Economist, Joseph Stiglitz. He worked on transitional economies, labor issues, knowledge management, and strategies of development. In his prior university teaching, he taught over a twenty-year period in the Boston area in five disciplines: Economics, Mathematics, Computer Science, Operations Research, and Accounting. He was educated at MIT and at Boston University, where he has two Master's degrees, one in Philosophy and one in Economics, and a doctorate in Mathematics. He has published over fifty articles in scholarly journals in economics, mathematics, philosophy, and law (see http://www.ellerman.org) and he has published five books, the most recent ones being: *Helping People Help Themselves: From the World Bank to an Alternative Philosophy of Development Assistance* (2005), *Intellectual Trespassing as a Way of Life: Essays in Philosophy, Economics, and Mathematics* (1995), and *Property and Contract in Economics: The Case for Economic Democracy* (1992).

**Robert F. Garnett, Jr.** is Professor of Economics at Texas Christian University. He earned his BA in Economics (with Highest Honors) from the College of William and Mary in 1984 and his PhD in Economics from the University of Massachusetts, Amherst, in 1994. Before coming to TCU in 1996, he held full-time positions at the University of Southern Maine, Denison University, and the University of Texas at Arlington. His research over the past decade has explored the goals and methods of liberal learning in undergraduate economics education, the meaning and value of pluralism in economic inquiry, and the role of gifts and philanthropy in economic life. He is currently working on two books, *Adam Smith and the Strength of Weak Duties* and *After Samuelson: Liberal Education and the Future of Econ 101*.

**Herbert Gintis** is External Professor at the Santa Fe Institute (Santa Fe, NM) and Professor of Economics, Central European University (Budapest, Hungary). He earned an MA in Mathematics and a PhD in Economics at Harvard University (1969). He recently published, with Samuel Bowles, *A Cooperative Species: Human Reciprocity and Evolution* (2011). He is also author of *The Bounds of Reason: Game Theory and the Unification of the Behavioral Sciences* (2009), translated into Chinese and Japanese in 2011; *Game Theory Evolving* (2009); with Joe Henrich, Robert Boyd, Samuel Bowles, Colin Camerer, and Ernst Fehr, *Foundations of Human Sociality: Economic Experiments and Ethnographic Evidence from Fifteen Small-scale Societies* (2004); with Samuel Bowles, Robert Boyd, and Ernst Fehr, *Moral Sentiments and Material Interests: On the Foundations of Cooperation in Economic Life* (2005). His recent work on market dynamics includes "The Emergence of a Price System from Decentralized Bilateral Exchange," *Contributions to Theoretical Economics* 6,1,13 (2006); "The Dynamics of General Equilibrium," *Economic Journal* 117 (2007): 1289–1309; and "The Stability of General Equilibrium with Networked Traders," *Complexity Economics* (forthcoming). Professor Gintis lives in Northampton, Massachusetts, USA.

**Samuel Gregg** is director of research at the Acton Institute. He has written and spoken on questions of political economy, ethics in finance, and natural law theory. He has a Doctor of Philosophy degree in moral philosophy and political economy from the University of Oxford. He is the author of several books, including *Morality, Law, and Public Policy* (2000), *Economic Thinking for the Theologically Minded* (2001), *On Ordered Liberty* (2003), his prize-winning *The Commercial Society* (2007), *The Modern Papacy* (2009), *Wilhelm Röpke's Political Economy* (2010), and *Becoming Europe: Economic Decline, Culture and America's Future* (2012). He has also co-edited books such as *Christian Theology and Market Economics* (2008), *Profit, Prudence and Virtue: Essays in Ethics, Business and Management* (2009), and *Natural Law, Economics and the Common Good* (2012). He also publishes in journals such as the *Journal of Markets & Morality*, *Harvard Journal of Law and Public Policy*, *Law and Investment Management*, *Journal des Economistes et des Etudes Humaines*, *Notre Dame Journal of Law, Ethics and Public Policy*, *Economic Affairs*, *Communio*, and *Journal of Scottish Philosophy*. In 2001, he was elected a Fellow of the Royal Historical Society.

**Steven Grosby** is Professor of Religion at Clemson University. He received his PhD from the Committee on Social Thought of the University of

Chicago. His areas of research include the ancient Near East, the Hebrew Bible, the relation between religion and nationality, social and political philosophy, and philanthropy. His works include *Nationalism: A Very Short Introduction* (2005), *Biblical Ideas of Nationality: Ancient and Modern* (2002), and the editing and translation of Hans Freyer, *Theory of Objective Mind: An Introduction to the Philosophy of Culture* (Series in Continental Thought No. 25 1998). He has also edited three volumes of the selected writings of Edward Shils, *A Fragment of a Sociological Autobiography: The History of My Pursuit of a Few Ideas* (2007), *The Virtue of Civility* (1997), and *The Calling of Education* (1997). His many articles have appeared in journals such as *Zeitschrift für die alttestamentliche Wissenschaft*, *History of Religions*, *Journal of the Economic and Social History of the Orient*, *Archives Européennes de Sociologie*, *Hebraic Political Studies*, *Azure*, *Nations and Nationalism* and *Conversations on Philanthropy*. He is currently working on the book-length manuscript, *Hebraism in Religion, History, and Politics: The Third Culture*.

**Shaun P. Hargreaves Heap** teaches at King's College London. He has also held positions at the University of East Anglia, Concordia University, and Sydney University. He was an undergraduate at Oxford and did his PhD at UC Berkeley. His current research is on decision making in a social and historical context and uses experiments to investigate decision making. His early research was in macroeconomics and labor economics, particularly on hysteresis in unemployment, and he is developing a research interest in tax reform for improving macroeconomic performance.

**Steven Horwitz** is the Charles A. Dana Professor of Economics and department chair at St. Lawrence University in Canton, NY. An Affiliated Senior Scholar at the Mercatus Center in Arlington, VA, and a Senior Fellow of the Fraser Institute in Vancouver, BC, Horwitz completed his MA and PhD in economics at George Mason University and received his BA in economics and philosophy from The University of Michigan. He is the author of two books, *Microfoundations and Macroeconomics: An Austrian Perspective* (2000) and *Monetary Evolution, Free Banking, and Economic Order* (1992), and he has written extensively on Austrian economics, monetary theory and history, macroeconomics, and the social thought of F. A. Hayek. In addition to several dozen articles in numerous academic journals, he has also done nationally recognized public policy work on the role of the private sector during the recovery from Hurricane Katrina. The author of numerous op-eds, Horwitz is also a frequent guest on TV and radio programs. He was awarded the Hayek Prize in 2010 by the Fund for the Study of Spontaneous Order for his work on the economics of the family, among other contributions. A member of the Mont Pelerin Society, his current research is on the economics and social theory of the family, and he has a forthcoming book on *Hayek, the Family, and Classical Liberalism*, due out in 2015.

Contributors xix

**Paul Lewis** was educated at Peterhouse, Cambridge, and Christ Church, Oxford, after which he became a Newton Trust Lecturer in the Faculty of Economics and Politics, and the Faculty of Social and Political Sciences, Cambridge University, and a Fellow of Emmanuel and Selwyn Colleges. He is currently Reader in Economics and Public Policy at King's College London. His research interests include the Austrian School of economics, social ontology, and the political economy of vocational education and training. He is a member of the Cambridge Social Ontology Group and a Visiting Scholar at the Mercatus Center at George Mason University, USA. He was a Visiting Fellow of Peterhouse, Cambridge, and the Shackle Scholar at St Edmund's College, Cambridge, in the Easter Term 2013.

**Deirdre McCloskey** teaches economics, history, English, and communication at the University of Illinois at Chicago. A well-known economist, historian and rhetorician, she has written sixteen books and around 400 scholarly pieces on topics ranging from technical economics and statistics to transgender advocacy and the ethics of the bourgeois virtues. Her latest book, *Bourgeois Dignity: Why Economics Can't Explain the Modern World* (2010), is the second in a series of four on the Bourgeois Era. With Stephen Ziliak she wrote *The Cult of Statistical Significance*, in 2008, which criticizes the proliferation of tests of "significance."

**Maria Pia Paganelli** is Associate Professor of Economics at Trinity University. She works on Adam Smith, David Hume, and eighteenth-century monetary theories. She won the 2009 European Society of the History of Economic Thought's Best Article of the Year award, and she is the book review editor for the *Journal of the History of Economic Thought*.

**Sandra J. Peart** is Dean of the Jepson School of Leadership Studies at the University of Richmond. She obtained her PhD in economics at the University of Toronto. Before coming to the Jepson School, she taught at Baldwin-Wallace College and at the College of William and Mary. She is President of the International Adam Smith Society, a former president of the History of Economics Society, and co-director of the Summer Institute for the History of Economic Thought. Peart has written more than fifty refereed journal articles on ethics and economics, rationality, utilitarianism, race and eugenics, the transition to "modern" economics, and leadership in public goods experiments. She has also written or edited eight books, many with David M. Levy, a professor of economics at George Mason University, including: *Hayek on Mill: The Mill–Taylor Friendship and Related Works; F. A. Hayek and the Modern Economy: Economic Organization and Activity; The Street Porter and the Philosopher: Conversations on Egalitarian Economics;* and *The "Vanity of the Philosopher": From Equality to Hierarchy in Post-Classical Economics.*

**David Schmidtz** is Kendrick Professor at the University of Arizona. He is editor of *Social Philosophy and Policy*, and founding Director of the Center for Philosophy of Freedom at the University of Arizona. He is author of *Rational Choice and Moral Agency* (1996), *Elements of Justice* (2006), *Person, Polis, Planet* (2008), and co-author, with Bob Goodin, of *Social Welfare and Individual Responsibility* (1998) and with Jason Brennan, *Brief History of Liberty* (2009). He currently is working on *Markets in Education* with Harry Brighouse. His articles have appeared in journals such as *Political Theory*, *Journal of Philosophy*, and *Ethics* (most recently on the topic of non-ideal theory). Essays of his have been reprinted seventy-three times as of 2014 (including Spanish, Portuguese, Italian, Mandarin, simplified Chinese, German, Romanian, Slovak, Czech, and Turkish translations). His thirteen former doctoral students all occupy faculty positions.

**Daniel J. Smith** is Assistant Professor of Economics in the Johnson Center at Troy University. He has published articles in a variety of professional journals and as chapters in books. He received his PhD in Economics from George Mason University in 2011. He is the book review editor of *The Review of Austrian Economics*.

**Martha A. Starr** is a member of the economics faculty at American University in Washington, DC, prior to which she was a senior economist at the Federal Reserve Board of Governors. Her research is centrally concerned with issues of social values in economic life, and has covered such subjects as lifestyle norms and saving patterns, socially responsible investment, ethical consumption, healthcare spending, distributional effects of housing bubbles and business cycles, and anti-consumer effects of pay-for-delay patent settlements. Her work has appeared in a wide range of journals, with recent articles having appeared in *Economic Inquiry*, *Review of Economics of the Household*, and *Health Affairs*. She is a past president of the Association for Social Economics and former co-editor of the *Review of Social Economy*.

**Virgil Henry Storr** is a Senior Research Fellow and the Director of Graduate Student Programs at the Mercatus Center, George Mason University. He is also a Research Associate Professor of Economics in the Department of Economics and the Don C. Lavoie Research Fellow in the F. A. Hayek Program in Philosophy, Politics and Economics at George Mason University. He is the author of *Enterprising Slaves and Master Pirates* (2004) and *Understanding the Culture of Markets* (2012). His writings on community recovery and redevelopment, comparative political economy, culture and markets, and Bahamian studies have been published or are forthcoming in *Rationality and Society*, *Public Choice*, the *Journal of Urban Affairs*, the *Cambridge Journal of Economics*, the *American Journal of Economics and Sociology*, the *Review of Austrian Economics*, and several other scholarly publications. He holds a PhD in Economics from

George Mason University and a BA in Economics and Management from Beloit College.

**John Thrasher** is a Lecturer in Philosophy at Monash University in Melbourne, Australia. Before that, he was a Research Fellow at the Center for the Philosophy of Freedom at the University of Arizona, where he also earned his PhD in philosophy in 2013. His work centers on the relationship between rationality and social rules. Much of his recent work is on contractarian political and moral philosophy. He has also written on the history of political and moral thought, specifically on Epicurus and Adam Smith. He has published work in *Philosophical Studies, The Journal of Moral Philosophy, The European Journal of Philosophy, Ethical Theory and Moral Practice, The Adam Smith Review*, as well as in several other journals and as chapters in collected volumes. He also co-edited with David Schmidtz the textbook *Creating Wealth: Ethical and Economic Perspectives* (2nd edition).

**Frederick Turner,** Founders Professor of Arts and Humanities at the University of Texas at Dallas, was educated at Oxford University. A poet, critic, interdisciplinary scholar, public intellectual, translator, and former editor of *The Kenyon Review*, he has authored over 30 books, including: *The New World Beauty: The Value of Values, The Culture of Hope Genesis: An Epic Poem; Hadean Eclogues, Shakespeare's Twenty-First Century Economics, Paradise: Selected Poems 1990–2003, Two Ghost Poems,* and *Epic: Form, Content, History*. His many honors include the Levinson prize for poetry and the Milan Fust Prize, Hungary's highest literary honor.

# Acknowledgments

Chapter 1 draws from *A Cooperative Species: Human Reciprocity and its Evolution* by Samuel Bowles and Herbert Gintis (Princeton University Press, 2011), pages 15–31 and 209–213. We are grateful to Princeton University Press for their permission to republish these pages.

Chapter 11 draws from *The Bourgeois Virtues: Ethics for an Age of Commerce* by Deirdre N. McCloskey (University of Chicago Press, 2006), pages 108–125. We are grateful to Professor McCloskey and the University of Chicago Press for their permission to republish these pages.

# Introduction

*Robert F. Garnett, Jr., Paul Lewis, and Lenore T. Ealy*

*Gesellschaft* and *Gemeinschaft*, Ferdinand Tönnies' juxtaposition of impersonal and personal modes of thought, action, and social organization is a perennial *topos* in ancient and modern philosophy. Confucius, Plato, Aristotle, Cicero, Augustine, Aquinas, Khaldun, and Hegel all posited similar distinctions (Sorokin 1955). In the twentieth century, a widening division of labor within social science – particularly between the disciplines of economics and anthropology – turned the impersonal/personal contrast into a reified, reductive dualism (Joy 1967; Gregory 1982).

Economists claimed the mantle of *Gesellschaft*. Leading economists defined their discipline as a science of market exchange (Schumpeter 1954, 827; Hahn 1984), with exchange understood as impersonal "spot transactions in which one thing is instantaneously swapped for something else by transactors who may never meet again" (Danby 2002, 15). Anthropologists meanwhile made *Gemeinschaft* the focus of their work, defining their fundamental category of gift exchange as the obverse of Walrasian exchange: reciprocal transactions that occur over time between parties who share an ongoing relationship (Malinowski 1922; Mauss 1925 [1966]; Cheal 1988; Kranton 1996; Negru 2009; see also Danby 2002).

Tracing its provenance to Adam Smith's celebration of commercial exchange as an engine of extensive, impersonal cooperation (Smith [1776] 1981) and his alleged focus on small rather than large-group cooperation in *The Theory of Moral Sentiments* ([1790] 1984), the disciplinary image of economics as the *Gesellschaft* science became entrenched after World War II (Hodgson 2006). Inspired by Gerard Debreu's *Theory of Value* (1959), many microeconomists came to regard "the model of Walrasian equilibrium" as "the root structure from which all further work in economics would eventuate" (Weintraub 2002, 121), while prominent macroeconomists such as Paul Samuelson and Robert Solow spoke of their Walrasian–Keynesian synthesis as if it were the final chapter in the history of macroeconomic thought:

> Most economists [now] feel that short-run macroeconomic theory is pretty well in hand. ... The basic outlines of the dominant theory have

not changed in years. All that is left is the trivial job of filling in the empty boxes, and that will not take more than 50 years of concentrated effort at maximum.

(Solow, cited in Hahn and Brechling 1965, 146)

Notwithstanding deep disagreements over the proper role of government, mainstream economists circa 1965 shared a common image of the national economy as a machine-like system of markets supplemented by corrective government policies (Leonard 2009). As economists, citizens, and government officials became enchanted with the notion of a *Gesellschaft* economy – a programmable, Progressive machine – the perceived roles of commercial and communal forms of cooperation became more rigidly stratified. The mid-twentieth-century economist likely would have seen markets as the generative if amoral core of economic life (potent, systemic, efficient), in contrast to the ethically inspired but antiquated world of gifts, philanthropy, and non-commercial collaboration.

In other branches of post-war social science, critics of "*Gesellschaft*-only" economics took up the *Gemeinschaft* end of the classic binary. Anthropologists and sociologists focused on the thick sociality of reciprocity, altruism, and solidarity within and among human communities. Similar positions were carved out by economists who focused on neglected social and ethical dimensions of exchange and provisioning, including mainstream mavericks such as Kenneth Boulding (1969, 1970) and Amartya Sen (1977, 1987), and heterodox economists of the institutionalist, Marxian, Austrian, feminist, social, and post-Keynesian Schools (Harvey and Garnett 2008; Lee 2009).

These intra- and inter-disciplinary differences could have been scientifically productive if specialists within the various branches had been able and willing to learn from one another (McCloskey 2000). Yet decades of limited communication and trade among *Gesellschaft*-only economists and their *Gemeinschaft*-focused critics gave rise to ossified divisions between thick and thin social-economic theories. Across a broad spectrum of social-scientific thought, the categories of commerce and community became oddly segregated, with "homely *Gemeinschaft*" exalted as "the exclusive site of virtue" and "businesslike *Gesellschaft*" cast as "an ethical nullity" (McCloskey 2006, 254).

After the official end of the Cold War in 1989, new lines of thought and exchange began to emerge among social theorists of diverse methodological and ideological orientations (Garnett *et al.* 2009). The narrowly conceived motives, behaviors, and institutional structures that characterized mid-twentieth-century thinking about comparative economic systems (e.g., market vs. plan, capitalism vs. socialism) were steadily supplanted by pluralistically conceived ecologies of provisioning in which agents with varied motives cooperate via heterogeneous forms of production and exchange. As detailed in the chapters below, this pan-paradigmatic shift was effected by a growing number of thinkers within and beyond the discipline of economics who share a broadly convergent aim: to re-inscribe the social science of human cooperation within analytic structures that recognize the plurality of (1) self- and other-regarding motives that shape human action and (2) cooperation-inducing processes – including but not limited to commercial trade – through which social learning and coordination occur.

The contributors to this volume explore multiple ways in which this pluralistic turn in economic and social thought bears upon the ingrained segregation and stigmatization of commercial and communal forms of cooperation: the ritual praise of one and suspicion of the other as *the* fertile nexus of human flourishing and its corrosive antithesis. We invited all contributors to consider whether overcoming commerce/community dualisms in their areas of research might promote an improved understanding of the humane ecology of modern commercial societies. By encouraging mature scholars to tackle this broad question through the lenses of varied perspectives on cooperation, rationality, identity, reciprocity, trust, and exchange, we seek to facilitate broader dialogue on the commerce/community relationship.

The twenty essays that follow offer fresh, critical responses to the political economy of *Gemeinschaft/Gesellschaft*, drawn from diverse disciplinary and philosophical traditions. Some authors issue urgent calls to desegregate the separate spheres, to recognize how communal mutuality and impersonal trade coexist in symbiotic and antagonistic ways in every corner of economic life (Gudeman 2008). Others affirm the importance of treating impersonal and personal cooperation as ethically, epistemically, and economically separate worlds. Yet even in their disagreements, these humane thinkers all portray the space of commerce and community with uncommon color and nuance, crisscrossing the erstwhile boundaries between the thin sociality of economics (qua science of commerce) and the thick sociality of sociology and anthropology (qua sciences of community).

## New work for invisible hands

The work of one pioneering figure, Richard Cornuelle, has been an important catalyst for each of the editors of this volume, as well as for many of our contributors. Cornuelle is not widely known among academic writers today, but many of the questions being addressed in this volume take up themes running throughout Cornuelle's written and philanthropic work. Cornuelle had a varied and highly practical intellectual career, including: graduate study with Ludwig von Mises at New York University; helping resource the nascent field of Austrian economics as a program officer with the William Volker Fund; working for a stint with the National Association of Manufacturers; advising politicians and policymakers; and publishing numerous articles and books. Increasingly puzzled that market-minded economists paid such little attention to America's diverse landscape of not-for-profit entities, Cornuelle wrote *Reclaiming the American Dream: The Role of Private Individuals and Voluntary Associations* ([1965] 1993) and coined the term "independent sector" to describe and encourage attention to the pluralistic array of non-commercial institutions and social processes that "takes a thousand forms and works in a million ways" and "functions at any moment when a person or group acts directly to serve others" (Cornuelle [1965] 1993, 38).

Cornuelle sought to rebuild the classical liberal case for voluntary cooperation and limited government based on a robust theory of community, drawing jointly from his Misesean understanding of economics as the science of human action, his Tocquevillean reading of American history, and his first-hand observations of Americans' vibrant volunteerism and giving ([1965] 1993, 1991, 1992). In Cornuelle's view, the economists' *Gesellschaft*-only image of modern society, with no civic institutions and processes other than commercial trade, had contributed to the "radical constriction of the definition of the citizens' role" and consequent "systematic, irrational disconnection of ordinary people from the business of the society" (1996, 11). He cited numerous ways in which citizens' expectations and experiences of public life are diminished by conventional markets-and-governments-only conceptions of commercial society, recalling the reflections of a veteran social worker, who lamented,

> The average American today has no twinge of conscience when he passes the sick man on the road ... He knows he has paid the Good Samaritan to come along after him and take care of this rather unpleasant social obligation.
> (Cited in Cornuelle [1965] 1993, 137)

For almost five decades, Cornuelle would continue to expose troubling gaps in the social thought of classical liberals. The salience of his critique was not confined to libertarian thought; he presciently marked a lacuna in modern economic theory at large. To illustrate Cornuelle's insight, consider a textbook economic model of "perfect competition" (Mankiw 2007, 289–307). Each agent exists in an ethical vacuum, interacting with a faceless, generic Other ("the market") but exerting no influence upon anyone in particular except the agent himself. Ethical responsibility vanishes as the assumed number of market participants approaches infinity. In Chicago School (Stiglerian) versions of the story, market prices summarize the choices and circumstances of all traders. By choosing optimal production and consumption levels in response to these efficient signals, individuals maximize their contributions to all others. In Samuelsonian versions, market imperfections such as externalities or monopoly power cause individual and social optima to diverge but government actions (such as antitrust regulations or Pigovian taxes and subsidies) are able to bring prices to efficient levels, enabling individuals to achieve maximum social cooperation (Mankiw 2007, 203–222, 311–371). Either way, the roles of neighbor and citizen and all manner of positive-sum interactions among non-commercial actors are suppressed by reductive representations of "the economy" as an amalgam of impersonal economic, political, or bureaucratic processes.

Cornuelle took a broad view of the scope of human action and the indispensability of ethical responsibility. The good society he envisioned is not just a market economy but a commercial society in which the average citizen "works and votes and pays his taxes" *and* responsibly undertakes "independent action on public problems" (1993 [1965], 62 and 180). He theorized independent action as a self-renewing process whose by-products include new desires, knowledge, and corrective feedback to inform engagement in further acts of voluntary cooperation. In Cornuelle's vision of voluntary community as a decentralized, polycentric order, the Tocquevillean hues are unmistakable ([1965] 1993, 21). He saw 'market' and 'community' as terms historically identified with localized, face-to-face modes of interaction but ripe for reclaiming as a species of voluntary spontaneous order – emerging from the very processes of association and exchange, as "people come together to accomplish things that are important to them and succeed" (32). He memorably observed:

> In the end, a good society is not so much the result of grand designs and bold decisions, but of millions upon millions of small caring acts, repeated day after day, until direct mutual action becomes second nature and to see a problem is to begin to wonder how best to act on it.
> (1983, 196)

The end of the Cold War found Cornuelle, in "New Work for Invisible Hands" (1991), calling for classical liberal scholars to take seriously the challenges of the regimentation of work by modern corporations and to redouble their efforts to document, analyze, and energize the mislaid voluntary sector. Despite his optimism about the potential of the voluntary community, Cornuelle was cognizant of the fact that good intentions do not always produce good results, especially in non-price environments (cf. Boulding [1965] 1974). He encouraged scholars to address these problems, in the hope that we could come to better understand the comparative possibilities, limits, and synergistic operations of non-commercial and commercial exchange.

The ideologically broad dialogue represented in this volume is a fitting tribute to and extension of Cornuelle's aims and vision. Cornuelle sought to "find an alternative path to the good society other than those of the doctrinaire conservatives or the dogmatic liberals of the Cold War era," and, like Boulding, believed in the transformative liberality of conversation itself (Ealy 2002, 2; also Cornuelle [1965] 1993, 3–19 and Boulding 1981, 112). Upon completion of *Reclaiming the American Dream* in 1965, Cornuelle confessed with characteristic wit and modesty that he was "astonished at how many other people are earnestly exploring the same unmapped region," likening himself to "someone who struggled to climb the highest mountain, and, arriving, blundered into a Sunday school picnic" ([1965] 1993, 52–53). The record shows that Cornuelle had himself given voice to an unease that spanned partisan, ideological, and disciplinary boundaries, and yet he answered that unease with encouragement and his characteristic optimism that people who believe they can solve problems can certainly make a start. The raft of new work across the social sciences detailing the varied behavioral and institutional ways in which voluntary cooperation occurs suggests that the behavioral-institutional core of Cornuelle's work is even more germane to the current generation of thinkers than it was to his contemporaries half a century ago.

## The essays to follow

The papers contributed to this volume have been written mostly by economists drawn from multiple theoretical traditions but also by scholars from philosophy, sociology, history, religious studies, evolutionary biology, and literature. Interdisciplinary "paradigm shifts" can be jarring, even to those of us who work frequently in such cross-disciplinary spaces. To help the reader take up the polyvalent concepts and ideas presented here, we have organized the essays into five groups, each consisting of three core essays and a respondent's reflections. This arrangement is merely indicative, and we hope readers will identify and pursue the multiple and overlapping threads of dialogue and inquiry among these chapters in whatever directions they see fit.

### *Part I: "Social cooperation"*

All three essays in Part I address the fundamental role of exchange in the development of cooperative behavior, and the ways in which this important role is obscured by received economic theories of exchange. Yet, as Sandra J. Peart notes in her comment, the authors present conflicting views of social cooperation and the range of institutions that induce it. In "The theory of social cooperation historically and robustly contemplated," Peter J. Boettke and Daniel J. Smith defend a Hayekian view in which social cooperation is coterminous with the extended order of commercial specialization and trade. In contrast, Samuel Bowles and Herbert Gintis's "The evolution of human cooperation" and Robert Garnett's "Commerce and beneficence: Adam Smith's unfinished project" define cooperation as any form of mutually beneficial activity, commercial or non-commercial. Their differences notwithstanding, all three essays illuminate the ways in which commercial and non-commercial exchange helps people to develop their capacity for cooperation.

*Part II: "Identity and association"*

The three essays in Part II focus on existing alternatives to the commerce/community dualism. In "Commerce, reciprocity, and civil virtues: the contribution of the Civil Economy," Luigino Bruni sketches the history and philosophy of the Italian Civil Economy tradition. Paul Lewis discusses the rich concept of 'we-intentionality' in "What does true individualism really involve? Overcoming market–philanthropy dualism in Hayekian social theory." Steven Grosby seeks to move us further toward a more robust understanding of associations, especially those beyond the market, in "Methodological individualism and invisible hands: Richard Cornuelle's call to understand associations." Commentator Shaun Hargreaves Heap suggests that, in striving to show how the commerce/community dualism can be overcome, these three papers nevertheless do succeed in resolving the conflict between commitment to a principle of mutual benefit and to a principle of equal treatment.

*Part III: "Human(e) economics"*

The papers in Part III propose a variety of new insights that can help us look anew at the heterogeneous ways in which human beings cooperate socially. In "Between *Gemeinschaft* and *Gesellschaft*: The stories we tell," Emily Chamlee-Wright and Virgil Storr show how the lines between the intimate order and the extended order can become blurred in a post-disaster context. In "Bourgeois love," Deirdre McCloskey considers the shortcomings that arise from modern economics' commitment to the view that all human motivations can be reduced to utility. Samuel Gregg explains how German neoliberalism sought to distinguish the functions of "Community, the market, and the state" without extinguishing any of these important social institutions. As Laurent Dobuzinskis observes in his comment, "the three papers discussed here illustrate the empirical limitations and philosophical shallowness of views that reduce the real-life complexities of free markets and liberal democracies to Tönnies' abstract model of the *Gesellschaft*." He also notes, however, that much more work is required to ascertain whether *Gemeinschaft* is a preferable alternative or whether the dualism itself is obsolete.

*Part IV: "Entangled spheres"*

The main focus of Part IV is rethinking community and its institutions. Colin Danby's "How is community made?" explores the nascent complexity – the cosmos-like character – of Cornuelle's notion of "community." Dave

Elder-Vass ("Commerce, community, and digital gifts") discusses how old barriers between commerce and community are breaking down in the era of internet "commerce." In "Classical liberalism and the firm: A troubled relationship," David Ellerman follows one of Cornuelle's signposts and offers a deeper conception of the firm as a locus of both commercial and communal responsibility. Martha Starr's comment notes that the fascinating intertwinements of commerce and community explored in these papers nevertheless leave us short of solving "the contentious academic and public debates over the economic consequences" of favoring either commerce or community as the primary sphere of social provisioning.

## Part V: "Not by commerce alone"

In commenting on the essays in Part V, John Thrasher and David Schmidtz pose an incisive and arresting question: Is commerce (at its best) coterminous with community, and vice versa? The three papers in this section tacitly raise this question in entirely different ways. In "Reciprocity, calculation and non-monetary exchange," Steven Horwitz explores the dynamics of non-monetary exchange of social and economic goods in a cash-poor neighborhood. Neera Badhwar's "Kidneys, commerce, and communities" considers how opportunities for mutually beneficial exchange or exploitation in the realm of organ transplants can be affected by institutional frameworks that favor or disfavor markets. In "Banks and trust in Adam Smith," Maria Pia Paganelli shows how attention to personal trust and impersonal trust as complements began to figure in early modern financial markets.

## Envoi

In closing this volume, we have the pleasure of publishing Frederick Turner's poem, "The Apologia of Mercurius." Where prose clouds, poetry can sometimes reveal. Turner does not let us off that easily, however, introducing us to Mercurius, the hermaphroditic god of messages, money, markets, commerce, and information. In Mercurius' song we find identity and diversity; personal agency and impersonal process; difference and continuity in nature extending from the physics of the subatomic to the plant and animal kingdoms to the kingdoms of man and to the cosmic realms; and the ironies of gift as a form of robbery and exchange as a form of gift. As Turner puts it in prose, "S/he is the agent of liberation, progress, collective knowledge, selfhood: the openness of time, not the fixity of eternity."

It is our hope that in coming to the end, the reader will be reminded where we began and will gain anew an appreciation for the natural miracles of voluntary cooperation that continually take place around us in numerous forms as people truck, barter, and trade to improve their own lives but also reach more deeply into their human capacities for sympathy, for openness, generosity, and liberality. Without such sociality and liberality, this volume would not have been conceived nor now be in your hands.

## References

Boulding, Kenneth E. [1965] 1974. "The Difficult Art of Doing Good." In *Collected Papers of Kenneth Boulding*, vol. IV, edited by Larry D. Singell, 247–261. Boulder, CO: Colorado Associated University Press.
Boulding, Kenneth E. 1969. "Economics as a Moral Science." *American Economic Review* 59 (1): 1–12.
Boulding, Kenneth E. 1970. *Economics as a Science*. New York: McGraw-Hill.
Boulding, Kenneth E. 1981. *A Preface to Grants Economics: The Economy of Love and Fear*. New York: Praeger.
Cheal, David J. 1988. *The Gift Economy*. London: Routledge.
Cornuelle, Richard C. [1965] 1993. *Reclaiming the American Dream: The Role of Private Individuals and Voluntary Associations*. New Brunswick, NJ: Transaction Publishers.
Cornuelle, Richard. C. 1983. *Healing America*. New York: G. P. Putnam's Sons.
Cornuelle, Richard. C. 1991. "New Work for Invisible Hands: A Future for Libertarian Thought." *The Times Literary Supplement*, April 5.
Cornuelle, Richard. C. 1992. "The Power and Poverty of Libertarian Thought." *Critical Review* 6 (1): 1–10.
Cornuelle, Richard. C. 1996. "Denationalizing Community." *Philanthropy Roundtable* (Spring): 10–11 and 32–33.
Danby, Colin. 2002. "The Curse of the Modern: A Post-Keynesian Critique of the Gift/Exchange Dichotomy." In *Research in Economic Anthropology*, vol. XXI, edited by Norbert Dannhaeuser and Cynthia Werner, 13–42. Amsterdam: JAI.
Debreu, Gerard. 1959. *Theory of Value*. New York: Wiley.
Ealy, Lenore T. 2002. "Richard Cornuelle Bibliographic Essay." Unpublished manuscript. Indianapolis, IN: Donors Trust.
Garnett, Robert F., Erik Olsen, and Martha Starr. 2009. *Economic Pluralism*. London: Routledge.
Gregory, Chris A. 1982. *Gifts and Commodities*. London: Academic Press.
Gudeman, Stephen. 2008. *Economy's Tension: The Dialectics of Community and Market*. New York and Oxford: Berghahn Books.
Hahn, Frank H. 1984. *Equilibrium and Economics*. Oxford: Blackwell.
Hahn, Frank H. and Frank P. R. Brechling, eds. 1965. *The Theory of Interest Rates*. London: Macmillan.
Harvey, John T. and Robert F. Garnett. 2008. *Future Directions for Heterodox Economics*. Ann Arbor, MI: University of Michigan Press.
Hodgson, Geoffrey M. 2006. *Economics in the Shadows of Darwin and Marx*. Northampton, MA: Edward Elgar.
Joy, Leonard. 1967. "One Economist's View of the Relationship between Economics and Anthropology." In *Themes in Economic Anthropology*, edited by Raymond Firth, 29–46. London: Tavistock.
Kranton, Rachel E. 1996. "Reciprocal Exchange: A Self-Sustaining System." *American Economic Review* 86 (4): 830–851.

Lee, Frederic. 2009. *A History of Heterodox Economics: Challenging the Mainstream in the Twentieth Century*. London: Routledge.

Leonard, Thomas C. 2009. "American Economic Reform in the Progressive Era: Its Foundational Beliefs and Their Relationship to Eugenics." *History of Political Economy* 41 (1): 109–141.

Malinowski, Bronisław. [1922] 1961. *Argonauts of the Western Pacific*. New York: Dutton.

Mankiw, N. Gregory. 2007. *Principles of Microeconomics*, 4th edition. Mason, OH: Thomson South-Western.

Mauss, Marcel. [1925] 1966. *The Gift: Forms and Functions of Exchange in Archaic Societies*. London: Routledge & Kegan Paul.

McCloskey, Deirdre N. 2000. "Kelly Green Golf Shoes and the Intellectual Range from M to N." In *How to be Human* *Though an Economist*, D. N. McCloskey, 149–154. Ann Arbor, MI: University of Michigan Press.

McCloskey, Deirdre N. 2006. *The Bourgeois Virtues: Ethics for an Age of Commerce*. Chicago: University of Chicago Press.

Negru, Ioana. 2009. "The Plural Economy of Gifts and Markets." In *Economic Pluralism*, edited by Robert Garnett, Erik Olsen, and Martha Starr, 194–204. London: Routledge.

Schumpeter, Joseph. A. 1954. *History of Economic Analysis*. New York: Oxford University Press.

Sen, Amartya K. 1977. "Rational Fools: A Critique of the Behavioral Foundations of Economic Theory." *Philosophy and Public Affairs* 6 (4): 317–344.

Sen, Amartya K. 1987. *On Ethics and Economics*. Oxford and New York: Basil Blackwell.

Smith, Adam. [1776] 1981. *An Inquiry into the Nature and Causes of the Wealth of Nations*. Glasgow edition, vols. 1 and 2. Edited by Roy H. Campbell and Andrew S. Skinner with assistance from W. B. Todd. Indianapolis, IN: Liberty Fund.

Smith, Adam. [1790] 1984. *The Theory of Moral Sentiments*. Glasgow edition. Edited by David D. Raphael and Alec L. Macfie. Indianapolis, IN: Liberty Fund.

Sorokin, Pitirim A. 1955. "Foreword." In *Community and Association*, Ferdinand Tönnies, Translated by Charles P. Loomis, v–vii. London: Routledge & Kegan Paul.

Weintraub, E. Roy. 2002. *How Economics Became a Mathematical Science*. Durham, NC: Duke University Press.

# Part I
# Social cooperation

# 1 The evolution of human cooperation

*Samuel Bowles and Herbert Gintis*

## Theories of cooperation

Cooperation was prominent among the suite of behaviors that marked the emergence of behaviorally modern humans in Africa. Those living 75,000–90,000 years ago at the mouth of what is now the Klasies River near Port Elizabeth, South Africa, for example, consumed eland, hippopotamus, and other large game (Singer and Wymer 1982). Among the slaughtered remains found, there is a now-extinct giant buffalo *Pelovoris antiquus*, which weighed almost 2,000 kilograms and whose modern-day (smaller) descendant is one of the most dangerous game animals in Africa (Milo 1998). The Klasies River inhabitants, and their contemporaries in other parts of Africa, almost certainly cooperated in the hunt and shared the prey among the members of their group. Even earlier evidence of trade in exotic obsidians extending over 300 kilometers in East Africa is another unmistakable footprint of early human cooperation.

Like those living at the Klasies River mouth, other "hunting apes" quite likely cooperated in the common projects of pursuing large game, sharing the prey, and maintaining group defense. Both *Homo neanderthalensis* and the recently discovered *Homo floresiensis* survived well into the Late Pleistocene (meaning the period from between about 126,000 and 12,000 years before the present) and hunted large game, the latter targeting the pygmy (but nonetheless substantial) elephants that had evolved on the island environment of Flores, off the coast of Indonesia.

Other primates engage in common projects. Chimpanzees, for example, join boundary patrols and some hunt cooperatively. Male Hamadryas baboons respect proximity-based property rights in food and mates. Many species breed cooperatively, with helpers and baby sitters devoting substantial energetic costs to the feeding, protection, and other care of non-kin (Hrdy 2009). Social insects, including many species of bees and termites, maintain high levels of cooperation, often among very large numbers of individuals. Other common forms of cooperation among non-human animals, summarized by Kappeler and van Schaik (2006), are "grooming and other forms of body care, alarm calling, predator inspection, protection against attacks by predators or conspecifics, supporting injured group members ... [and] egg-trading among hermaphrodites."

While cooperation is common in many species, Homo sapiens is exceptional in that in human cooperation extends beyond close genealogical kin to include even total strangers, and occurs on a much larger scale than other species except for the social insects.

## What is cooperation?

By cooperation we mean engaging with others in a mutually beneficial activity. Examples include the joint pursuit of political and military objectives as well as the more prosaic foundations of everyday life: collaboration among employees in a firm, exchanges between buyers and sellers, and the maintenance of local amenities among neighbors.

Cooperative behavior may confer benefits net of costs on the individual cooperator, and thus could be motivated entirely by self-interest. Market exchange is an example. In this case, cooperation is a form of *mutualism*, namely an activity that confers net benefits both on the actor and on others. But cooperation may also impose net costs upon individuals in the sense that not cooperating would increase their fitness or other material payoffs. In this case, cooperative behavior constitutes a form of *altruism*.

The evolution of cooperation that is mutualistic or that involves only close family relatives is easily explained. Cooperation among close family members could have evolved by natural selection because the benefits of cooperative actions are conferred on the close genetic relatives of the cooperator, thereby helping to proliferate alleles ("genes") associated with the cooperative behavior. Cooperation could also have evolved because one individual's costly contribution to the welfare of another individual is reliably reciprocated at a future date, thereby making cooperation mutualistic. Models of altruism toward close family members and reciprocal altruism (which really should be called "enlightened self-interest") are popular among biologists and economists alike and explain many forms of human cooperation, particularly those occurring in families or in frequently repeated dyadic (two-person) or other very small group interactions.

But these models fail to explain two facts about human cooperation: that it takes place in groups far larger than the immediate family, and that both in real life and in laboratory experiments, it occurs in interactions that are unlikely to be repeated, and where it is impossible to obtain reputational gains from cooperating.

The most parsimonious proximal explanation of cooperation, one that is supported by extensive experimental and other evidence, is that people gain pleasure from or feel morally obligated to cooperate with like-minded people. People also enjoy punishing those who exploit the cooperation of others, or feel morally obligated to do so. Free riders frequently feel guilty, and if they are sanctioned by others, they may feel ashamed. We term these feelings *social preferences*. Social preferences include a concern, positive or negative, for the well-being of others, as well as a desire to uphold ethical norms.

In many human groups, these motives are sufficiently common to sustain social norms that support contributions to projects of common benefit, even when cooperators bear costs in order to benefit others. The forms of cooperation and the behaviors that elicit punishment by peers differ from society to society, but the critical role of social preferences in sustaining altruistic cooperation is ubiquitous.

## The roots of human cooperation

Because we are convinced that most people enjoy cooperating at least in some situations and dislike people who do not, the task we will set for ourselves is not that typically addressed by biologists and economists, namely to explain why people cooperate despite being selfish. Rather, we seek to explain why we are not purely selfish – why the social preferences that sustain altruistic cooperation are so common. Proximate answers to this question are to be found in the way that our brains process information and induce the behavioral responses that we term cooperation. But how did we come to have brains that function in this manner?

Early human environments are part of our answer. Our Late Pleistocene ancestors inhabited the large-mammal-rich African savannah and other environments in which cooperation in acquiring and sharing food yielded substantial benefits at relatively low cost. The slow human life history with prolonged periods of dependency of the young also made the cooperation of non-kin in child rearing and provisioning beneficial. As a result, members of groups that sustained cooperative strategies for provisioning, child rearing, punishing non-cooperators, defending against hostile neighbors, and truthfully sharing information had significant advantages over members of non-cooperative groups.

In the course of our subsequent history we created novel social and physical environments exhibiting similar, or even greater, benefits of cooperation, among them the division of labor coordinated by market exchange and respect of rights of property, systems of production characterized by increasing returns to scale (irrigated agriculture, modern industry, information systems with network externalities), and warfare. The impressive scope of these modern forms of cooperation was facilitated by the emergence in the last seven millennia of governments capable of enforcing property rights and providing incentives for the self-interested to contribute to common projects.

But prior to the emergence of governments and since, cooperation has been sustained also by motives that led some people to bear costs on behalf of others, contributing to common projects, punishing transgressors, and excluding outsiders. We advance three reasons why these altruistic social preferences supporting cooperation confer competitive advantage over unmitigated and amoral self-interest.

First, human groups have devised ways to protect their altruistic members from exploitation by the self-interested. Prominent among these is the public-spirited shunning, ostracism, and even execution of free riders and others who violate cooperative norms. Other group activities protecting altruists from exploitation are leveling practices that limit hierarchy and inequality, including sharing food and information.

Second, humans adopted prolonged and elaborate systems of socialization that led individuals to internalize the norms that induce cooperation, so that contributing to common projects and punishing defectors became objectives in their own right rather than constraints on behavior. Together, the internalization of norms and the protection of the altruists from exploitation served to offset, at least partially, the competitive handicaps borne by those who were motivated to bear personal costs to benefit others.

Third, between-group competition for resources and survival was and remains a decisive force in human evolutionary dynamics. Groups with many cooperative members tended to survive these challenges and to encroach upon the territory of the less cooperative groups, thereby both gaining reproductive advantages and proliferating cooperative behaviors through cultural transmission. The extraordinarily high stakes of intergroup competition and the contribution of altruistic cooperators to success in these contests meant that sacrifice on behalf of others, extending beyond the immediate family and even to virtual strangers, could proliferate. Modern-day nationalism is an example.

This is part of the reason why humans became extraordinarily group-minded, favoring cooperation with insiders and often expressing hostility toward outsiders. Boundary maintenance supported within-group cooperation and exchange by limiting group size and within-group linguistic, normative, and other forms of heterogeneity. Insider favoritism also sustained the between-group conflicts and differences in behavior that made group competition a powerful evolutionary force.

In short, humans became the cooperative species that we are because cooperation was highly beneficial to the members of groups that practiced it, and we were able to construct social institutions that minimized the disadvantages of those with social preferences in competition with fellow group members, while heightening the group-level advantages associated with the high levels of cooperation that these social preferences allowed. These institutions proliferated because the groups that adopted them secured high levels of within-group cooperation, which in turn favored the groups' survival as a biological and cultural entity in the face of environmental, military, and other challenges.

Early humans were not alone in occupying territory and a feeding niche that made cooperation among group members highly advantageous. Indeed, our ancestors competed with lions, hyenas, wild dogs, and possibly other hominid cooperative hunters for the very same ungulates and other large mammals. Nor were our ancestors exceptional in the kinds of group competition for territory and other valued resources that made cooperation so essential to survival. Chimpanzees, too, engage in lethal contests between troops, where winners gain territory and reproductive advantages. The same is true of species as diverse as meerkats and fire ants. Nor are humans exceptional in constructing our own physical and social environments. Beavers build dams, birds build nests, and burrowing animals build underground catacombs. Why then did humans, rather than chimps, lions, or meerkats, develop such exceptional forms of cooperation?

Central to our reply are the human cognitive, linguistic, and physical capacities that made us especially good at all of the above, and more. These capacities allow us to formulate general norms of social conduct, to erect social institutions regulating this conduct, to communicate these rules and what they entail in particular situations, to alert others to their violation, and to organize coalitions to punish the violators. No less important is the psychological capacity to internalize norms, to experience such social emotions as shame and moral outrage, and to base group membership on such non-kin characteristics as ethnicity and language, which in turn facilitates costly conflicts among groups. Equally essential was the developmental plasticity of humans and our long period of maturation, the latter initially a result of the particular feeding niche that early humans occupied. Also important is the unique human capacity to use projectile weapons, a consequence of which is to lower the cost of coordinated punishment of norm violators within a group, to reduce the costs of hunting large animals, with concomitant benefits accruing to groups with widely endorsed sharing norms, and to render intergroup conflicts more lethal. A result was to elevate group-level competition to a more powerful evolutionary force.

These exceptional aspects of human livelihoods and social interactions, we will show, have favored the evolution of an individual predisposition to cooperate with others and to punish those who exploit the cooperation of others. But more than individual-level motivation is involved. The regulation of social interactions by group-level institutions plays no less a role than altruistic individual motives in understanding how this cooperative species came to be. Institutions affect the rewards and penalties associated with particular behaviors, often favoring the adoption of cooperative actions over others, so that even the self-regarding are often induced to act in the interest of the group. Of course, it will not do to posit these institutions a priori. Rather, the historical evidence indicates that they could

## Cooperation and competition

Cooperation is not an end, but rather a means. In some settings, competition, the antithesis of cooperation, is the more effective means to a given end. Similarly, the individual motives and group-level institutions that account for cooperation among humans include not only the most elevated, including a concern for others, fair-mindedness, and democratic accountability of leaders, but also the most wicked, such as vengeance, racism, religious bigotry, and hostility toward outsiders.

Price-fixing by cartels and other baleful economic effects of collusion motivated Adam Smith to advocate a competitive economic system under which such forms of antisocial collusion would unravel. In its stead he advocated an "invisible hand" that would guide the efforts of countless self-interested producers to coordinate a modern division of labor in the interest of all, a stunning example of mutualistic cooperation.

But if the late eighteenth century gave us this evocative metaphor for the beneficial effects of the pursuit of individual gain, the mid-twentieth century invented two no less riveting metaphors for the dark side of self-interest: the prisoner's dilemma and the tragedy of the commons. Their logic inverted Adam Smith's invisible hand, showing that even where cooperation was essential to the pursuit of common ends, it would falter in the face of self-interest. Garrett Hardin's tragedy of the commons (1968) was rapidly assimilated by scholars, as it embraced a model of self-interest that was already well established in both economics and the neo-Darwinian synthesis in biology. Social preferences, Hardin made clear, were powerless to counter the "remorseless" degradation of the environment:

> The tragedy cannot be solved by an appeal to conscience, for those who heeded the appeal would have fewer children, and by the heritability of capacity of conscience, this would lead to a less moral population.
>
> (Hardin 1968, 1246)

Because "freedom in a commons means ruin for all," he advocated a modern version of Thomas Hobbes' *Leviathan*, which he termed "mutual coercion mutually agreed upon." Hardin termed his contribution a "rebuttal to the invisible hand." In like manner, Mancur Olson's no less ineluctable "logic of collective action" in $n$-person prisoner's dilemmas demonstrated the inevitability of a passive citizenry and the impossibility of cooperation, due to ubiquitous free riders (Olson 1965).

But as the prisoner's dilemma and the tragedy of the commons were becoming staples of undergraduate instruction, field evidence from anthropologists and micro-historical studies of social movements pointed in an entirely different direction. Herders in high Alpine and Andean common summer pastures had averted tragedy without government regulation for centuries, possibly millennia (Netting 1989). Workers and democrats had for centuries risked their lives in collective actions that plainly defied Olson's logic (Moore 1978; Hobsbawm 1983). The work of Elinor Ostrom and her collaborators documented literally hundreds of decentralized tragedy-averting commons governance systems around the world, bringing to a head this collision of empirical observation and the logic of self-interest (Ostrom 1990).

The tension between the relentless logic of self-interest and the ubiquity of collective action in real-world settings was eventually resolved by a series of experiments by psychologists and economists, most notably by Ernst Fehr and his colleagues (Fehr and Gächter 2000; Herrmann *et al.* 2008). The experiments confirmed that self-interest is indeed a powerful motive, but also that other motives are no less important. Even when substantial sums of money are at stake, many, perhaps most, experimental subjects were found to be fair-minded, generous toward those similarly inclined, and nasty toward those who violate these prosocial precepts. In light of these results, the evidence that the tragedy of the commons is sometimes averted and that collective action is a motor of human history is considerably less puzzling. The puzzle, instead, is how humans came to be like this.

Biological classics such as Konrad Lorenz' (1963) *On Aggression* and Richard Dawkins' (1976) *The Selfish Gene* have now been joined by works whose titles signal the shift in attention: *Good Natured*, by Frans de Waal (1997), *Mother Nature*, by Sarah Hrdy (2000), *The Moral Animal*, by Robert Wright (1995), *Origin of Virtue*, by Matt Ridley (1998), *Unto Others*, by Elliot Sober and David Sloan Wilson (1998), *Altruistically Inclined?* by Alexander Field (2004), *The Genial Gene: Deconstructing Darwinian Selfishness*, by Joan Roughgarden (2009), and *Moral Origins: Social Selection and the Evolution of Virtue, Altruism, and Shame*, by Christopher Boehm (2011). These recent works are reminiscent of Pyotr Kropotkin's *Mutual Aid* a century earlier (1989 [1903]), a book that had advanced a kinder, gentler view of the evolutionary process in opposition to the then popular dog-eat-dog Social Darwinist claims about what natural selection entails for human behavior. The moral, generous, and civic-minded predispositions documented in these works and in the pages that follow show that evolution can not only foster self-interest but also promote the generous and ethical behaviors that help us escape the prisoner's dilemma and avert the tragedy of the commons, and that permit us to sustain the hope for a society committed to freedom and justice for all. However, we will see that this is true not despite the fact that, but in important measure because, evolutionary processes are "red in tooth and claw," in Alfred, Lord Tennyson's famous words.

## Preferences, beliefs, and constraints

We explore the proximal influences on an individual action such as helping using the *beliefs, preferences, and constraints* approach common to economics and decision theory. According to this approach, what individuals do when restricted to a specific set of feasible actions depends on their desires and goals on the one hand, and their beliefs on the other. The term *constraints* represents the limitations placed on the feasible actions an individual may take in a given situation. *Beliefs* are an individual's representation of the causal structure of world, including the relationship between the individual's actions and the probabilities of the various possible resulting outcomes. *Preferences* are the pro or con sentiments that make up the individual's valuation of the various possible outcomes of taking an action.

Preferences may be described as an ordering (technically, a preference function) of the states of the world that may result from one's actions. We assume preferences satisfy two conditions: they are complete (any two states can be compared) and transitive; that is, consistent, so that if one prefers A to B and B to C, one then prefers A to C. Preferences are the results of a variety of influences: tastes (food likes and dislikes, for example), habits, emotions (such as shame or anger) and other visceral reactions (such as fear), the manner in which individuals construe situations (or more narrowly, the way they frame decisions), commitments (like promises), internalized norms of ethical behavior, psychological propensities (for aggression, extroversion, and the like), and affective relationships with others.

We can succinctly and analytically summarize the individual's behavior as maximization of a preference function, even though this by no means describes the underlying psychological processes (Savage 1954). To say that individuals act on their preferences means that a knowledge of these preferences provides a concise and accurate account of their actions, given their beliefs and constraints. Of course, this analytical account will not generally coincide with the account that individuals would give of their own behavior.

The preferences, beliefs, and constraints approach is silent on the cognitive and other processes determining individual action. In some situations, buying a car, for example, individuals may deliberately optimize, while in others, diet or ethical behavior, for example, they may follow rules of thumb that have been adopted without conscious optimization. Optimizing models are commonly used to describe behavior not because they mimic the cognitive processes of the actors, which they rarely do, but because they capture important influences on individual behavior in a succinct and analytically tractable way.

A version of the beliefs, preferences, and constraints model, incorporating the behavioral assumptions sometimes summarized as *Homo economicus*, has become standard not only in economics but throughout the human behavioral sciences. F. Y. Edgeworth, a founder of neoclassical economics, expressed this view in his *Mathematical Psychics*: "The first principle of economics is that every agent is actuated only by self-interest" (1881, 104). But self-interest need not be part of the preferences, beliefs, and constraints approach. Preferences could be altruistic or even masochistic. Nevertheless, while self-interest is not formally implied by the conventional approach, it is generally assumed in practice. The assumption allows precise predictions in strategic situations, where it takes the form of what we term the *self-interest axiom*, namely that people seek to maximize their expected payoffs and believe that others do the same.

But predictions based on Edgeworth's self-interest axiom often fail to describe the actions people take. Indeed, the axiom was never intended to be taken literally. Edgeworth followed the statement above with the caveat that the axiom was strictly true only in "contract and war." But even in these areas, exceptions to the canon are glaring and increasingly well documented, as is shown by Truman Bewley's (2000) finding that firms do not cut wages during recessions because wage cuts demoralize workers, who consider them unfair. Similarly, Jessica Stern's (2003) finding that terrorist violence is motivated as a reaction against perceived injustice, and the case of kamikaze pilots (Hagoromo Society 1973), who volunteer to sacrifice their lives out of a sense of honor and duty, are dramatic indications that people are often motivated by non-selfish principles.

The economist's usual defense of the self-interest axiom is that it is self-evident, with the fallback assertion being that natural selection could not have produced any other kind of preferences. But, as the evidence to follow suggests, the assertion is far from self-evident, and in fact is simply false.

The importance of fairness considerations in wage setting and other exchanges just noted is an example (see also Blinder and Choi 2000). Equally at variance with self-evident self-interest is the fact that individuals bother to vote, given the vanishingly small likelihood that their vote is decisive, as well as their extensive support, when they do vote, for tax-financed income transfers to the poor even among those sufficiently rich and upwardly mobile to be very unlikely ever to benefit directly from these transfers (Gilens 1999; Fong 2001; Fong et al. 2005). Also telling against the self-evident status of the self-interest axiom are studies at Continental Airlines, Nucor Steel, and other companies that have found group incentives to be effective even where gain-sharing is distributed among such a large number that the additional income resulting from one's own effort is negligible (Hansen 1997; Knez and Simester 2001). Other examples include volunteering for dangerous military and other tasks, tax compliance far in excess of that which would maximize expected incomes (Andreoni et al. 1998), participating in various forms of collective action with little expectation of personal benefit (Moore 1978; Wood 2003), and conforming to norms and laws in cases where one's transgression would be personally advantageous and would not be detected or, as H. L. Mencken would say, when no one is looking.

## Social preferences and social dilemmas

Recall that *social preferences* are a concern for the well-being of others and a desire to uphold ethical norms. By contrast with *self-regarding* preferences, which are based on states concerning oneself alone, we stress *other-regarding* and *ethical* preferences, the former defined as valuations based at least in part on states that occur to others. Social preferences include not only generosity toward others and a preference for "fair" outcomes, but also what Thomas Hobbes called the desire for "eminence," Thorstein Veblen's "pecuniary emulation" exemplified by a desire to "keep up with the Joneses" (Veblen 1899), Charles Horton Cooley's "looking-glass self," according to which our self-esteem is dependent in part upon what others think of us, so we attempt to favorably impress others as a means of raising our subjective self-esteem (Cooley 1902; Brennan and Pettit 2004), and Aristotle's character virtues, such as honesty and courage, which are personal values that promote prosocial behavior (Aristotle 2002 [350 BC]).

Social preferences may be self-regarding. Ethical commitments may reflect a concern for the states experienced by others, but need not. One can be honest because one seeks to avoid imposing costs on others by deceiving them. But honesty could be entirely self-regarding, practiced in order to be the kind of person one wants to be. Thus the textbook "economic man" would be described not only as self-regarding, but as amoral as well, though we will frequently use the simpler description – self-regarding – when the meaning is clear.

Social preferences assume special importance in interactions termed *social dilemmas*, that is, interactions in which the uncoordinated actions of individuals result in an outcome that is *Pareto inefficient*, meaning that there exists some other feasible outcome such that at least one member could be better off while no member would be worse off. Examples of social dilemmas modeled by game theorists are the prisoner's dilemma, the public goods game, sometimes termed an $n$-person prisoner's dilemma, the so-called war of attrition and other so-called arms race interactions, the tragedy of the commons, and the common pool resource game in which contributing to the common project takes the form of forgoing the over-exploitation of a jointly utilized resource such as a fishery, water supply, or forest. We say a person *free rides* if he benefits from the contributions of other group members while himself contributing less or nothing at all.

Here is an example. The most famous of all experimental games is the *prisoner's dilemma*, with payoffs (the row player's first) shown in Figure 1.1. In this game, Alice and Bob will interact only once and cannot make any binding agreements about how they will play the game. This is an example

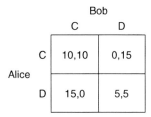

*Figure 1.1* The prisoners' dilemma game. Here, and in other payoff matrices, the row player's payoff is first (Alice in this case), and the column player's payoff is second

of an anonymous, non-repeated *non-cooperative game* (the latter term refers to the no-binding-agreements condition, not to the interests of the party or the outcomes of the game). The experimenter explains to Alice and Bob that each can take one of two actions without knowing the action taken by the other: cooperate (C) or defect (D). If both choose to cooperate, each receives $10 (the intersection of the C row and the C column in Figure 1.1), and if both defect, each receives $5 (the intersection of the D row and the D column). Moreover, if one cooperates and the other defects, the defector gets $15 and the cooperator gets nothing (the off-main-diagonal payoffs in Figure 1.1).

We assume both Alice and Bob do not have social preferences, and hence only care about their own payoffs. Alice reasons as follows. "If Bob cooperates, I get $15 by defecting and $10 by cooperating, so I should defect. If Bob defects, I get $5 by defecting and nothing by cooperating, so I should still defect. Thus I should defect no matter what Bob does." Bob of course comes to the same conclusion. Thus both defect, and each gets $5, which is half of what each could have got by cooperating. Thus, for Bob and Alice, defecting is a *dominant strategy*; that is, it is a *best response* (i.e., a payoff-maximizing strategy) regardless of what the other does. Because this is true for both Alice and Bob, mutually defecting is a *dominant strategy equilibrium* and is the predicted outcome for players without social preferences.

An other-regarding player cares about not only his own payoff, but that of his partner as well. Such a player might reason as follows. "I feel sufficiently positive toward a partner who cooperates that I would rather cooperate even if by doing so I forgo the larger payoff ($15) I could have had by defecting. If my partner defects, I, of course, prefer to defect as well, both to increase my earnings, and to decrease the earnings of a person who has behaved uncharitably toward me." If Bob and Alice reason in this manner, and if each believes the other is sufficiently likely to cooperate, both will cooperate. Thus, both mutual cooperate and mutual defect are equilibria in this new game, transformed from the old by augmenting the material payoffs with the players' concerns about one another.

A choice of strategies by players is a *Nash equilibrium* if each player's choice is a best response to the choice of the others. Note that a dominant strategy is always a Nash equilibrium because it is a best response whatever the other players do, but the reverse is not true. Social preferences may thus convert a prisoner's dilemma material payoff structure into what is called an *assurance game* payoff structure – each player will cooperate if assured that the other will cooperate as well, and will not if not. Thus mutual cooperation and mutual defection are both Nash equilibria. Which of the two Nash equilibria will obtain depends on the players' beliefs about what the other will do.

Despite the strong temptation to defect out of either selfishness or fear of being exploited by the other player, many experiments have found that a considerable fraction of subjects prefer to cooperate rather than defect in the prisoner's dilemma (Sally 1995). One famous real-life, high-stakes example is the popular TV show *Friend or Foe*, where contestants play a prisoner's dilemma with stakes varying between $200 and $22,000. About half the contestants choose to cooperate even though they are guaranteed to earn more money by defecting, no matter what their partner does. Even more striking, contestants are no more likely to defect when the stakes are higher (List 2006; Oberholzer-Gee *et al.* 2010).

Similar behavior is observed in the laboratory. Kiyonari *et al.* (2000) had Japanese university students play the prisoner's dilemma with real monetary payoffs. The experimenters ran three distinct treatments. The first treatment was a standard simultaneous prisoner's dilemma in which both players choose whether to cooperate or defect without knowing the partner's choice. The second was a sequential "second player" prisoner's dilemma in which one player had to choose between cooperating and defecting after being informed that the partner had already chosen to cooperate. The third was again a prisoner's dilemma, which we will call a "first player" prisoner's dilemma, in which a player was told that he would choose first, but his decision to cooperate or defect would be transmitted to his partner before the latter made his own choice. The experimenters found that 38 percent of the subjects cooperated in the standard simultaneous treatment, 62 percent cooperated in the second player treatment, and 59 percent cooperated in the first player treatment. The decision to cooperate in each treatment cost the subject about $5 (600 yen). This shows unambiguously that a majority of subjects (62 percent) were conditional altruistic cooperators. Almost as many (59 percent) were not only cooperators, but were also willing to bet that their partners would be, provided the latter were assured of not being defected upon, although under standard conditions, without this assurance, only 38 percent would in fact cooperate. Experiments conducted by Watabe *et al.* (1996), Morris *et al.* (1998), Hayashi *et al.* (1999), McCabe *et al.* (2000), and Clark and Sefton (2001) found similar subject behavior.

## Genes, culture, groups, and institutions

We define *culture* as the ensemble of preferences and beliefs that are acquired by means other than genetic transmission. Culture is an evolutionary force in its own right, not simply an effect of the interaction of genes and natural environments.

An alternative, but we think incorrect, approach holds that while preferences and beliefs that are transmitted culturally may constitute the proximate causes of behavior, they in turn are entirely explained by the interaction of our genetic makeup and the natural environment. It is of course true that natural environments and genes affect the evolution of culture. But it is also true that culture affects the relative fitness of genetically transmitted behavioral traits. C. J. Lumsden and Edward O. Wilson (1981), Luigi Luca Cavalli-Sforza and Marcus Feldman (1981), Robert Boyd and Peter Richerson (1985), William Durham (1991), Richerson and Boyd (2004), and others have provided compelling instances of these cultural effects on genetic evolution.

Recognizing the intimate interactions between genes and culture in humans, Edward Wilson, Charles Lumsden, Robert Boyd, Peter Richerson, Luigi Luca Cavalli-Sforza and Marcus Feldman began working in the 1970s on the parallels between genetic and cultural evolution and their interactions, their work initiating the modeling of *gene-culture coevolution*, the second concept underpinning our explanation of the origins and distinctive nature of cooperation among humans. According to gene-culture coevolution, human preferences and beliefs are the product of a dynamic whereby genes affect cultural evolution and culture affects genetic evolution, the two being tightly intertwined in the evolution of our species.

To see how gene-culture coevolution works, think about the ways that an organism may acquire information. The genome encodes information that is used to construct a new organism, to instruct the new organism how to transform sensory inputs into decision outputs (i.e., to endow the new organism with a specific preference structure), and to transmit this coded information virtually intact to the new organism. Since learning about one's environment is costly and error-prone, efficient information transmission is likely to ensure that the genome encodes information relevant not to ephemeral aspects of the organism's environment but rather to those that are constant, or that change only very slowly through time and space. Environmental conditions that vary more rapidly can be dealt with by providing the organism with the capacity to learn from one's environment, and hence phenotypically adapt to specific conditions.

For most animals, genetic transmission and individual learning are about all there is as far as information acquisition is concerned. Humans, by contrast, also acquire information from one another through a process of social learning. To see just how inadequate individual learning and genetically transmitted information would be in supporting human life in the absence of social learning, consider this sad story. Four hapless Europeans in 1860 attempted to cross the Australian continent from south to north and back, armed only with their ability to devise ways of living in an unfamiliar environment with the help of then-sophisticated equipment and ample stocks of food, carried on imported camels (Henrich and McElreath 2003). After a series of reverses, and having eaten the unfortunate camels, they resorted to foraging, attempting vainly to learn how to trap rats and birds and to catch fish in the occasional well-watered spot. Despite the generous gifts of food from the aboriginal groups they encountered as they struggled on, three perished. The last was saved by a community of Yantruwanta people living in the desert, where he fully recovered and was eventually found by a European search party.

Thus there is a distinctively human intermediate case that is not well handled by either genetic encoding or learning from one's environment *de novo* in each generation. When environmental conditions are positively but imperfectly correlated across generations, each generation acquires valuable information through learning that it cannot transmit genetically to the succeeding generation, because such information is not encoded in the germ line. In such environments, an animal could benefit from the transmission of information concerning the current state of the environment through some non-genetic information channel. Such information, called epigenetic by biologists, is quite common (Jablonka and Lamb 1995) and achieves its highest and most flexible form in cultural transmission in humans and to a considerably lesser extent in other primates (Bonner 1984; Richerson and Boyd 1998). *Cultural transmission,* also called *social learning* as opposed to *individual learning,* takes the form of vertical (parents to children), horizontal (peer to peer), and oblique (non-parental elder to younger) transfer of information. The parallel between cultural and biological evolution goes back to William James (1880) and Julian Huxley (1955). The idea of treating culture as a form of epigenetic transmission was pioneered by Cavalli-Sforza and Feldman (1973), Karl Popper (1979), and Richard Dawkins, who coined the term "meme" in *The Selfish Gene* (1976) to represent an integral unit of information that could be transmitted phenotypically. There quickly followed several major contributions to a biological approach to culture, all based on the notion that culture, like genes, could evolve through replication (intergenerational transmission), mutation, and selection (Lumsden and Wilson 1981; Cavalli-Sforza and Feldman 1982; Boyd and Richerson 1985).

Richard Dawkins added a second fundamental mechanism of epigenetic information transmission in *The Extended Phenotype* (1982), noting that organisms can directly transmit environmental artifacts to the next generation, in the form of such constructs as beaver dams, bee hives, and even social structures (e.g., mating and hunting practices). Creating a fitness-relevant aspect of an environment and stably transmitting this environment across generations, known as niche construction, is a widespread form of epigenetic transmission (Odling-Smee *et al.* 2003). Moreover, niche construction gives rise to what might be called a gene-environment coevolutionary process, since a genetically induced environmental regularity becomes the basis for genetic selection, and genetic mutations that give rise to mutant niches will tend to survive if they are fitness enhancing for their constructors.

In our gene-culture coevolution model of group-structured populations, the process of differential replication affects the frequency of both individual traits, generosity toward fellow group members, say, and group traits, a system of consensus decision making or property rights. Though inspired by biological approaches, especially those of Cavalli-Sforza and Feldman (1981), Boyd and Richerson (1985), and Durham (1991), like these authors, we do not privilege biological explanation. Our approach may be summarized as follows.

First, while genetic transmission of information plays a central role in our account, the genetics of non-pathological social behavior is for the most part unknown. Knowledge of the genetic basis of the human cognitive and linguistic capacities that make cooperation on a human scale possible has expanded greatly in recent years, but virtually nothing is known about genes that may be expressed in cooperative behavior, should these exist. No "gene for cooperation" has been discovered. Nor is it likely that one will ever be found, for the idea of a one-to-one mapping between genes and behavior is unlikely given what is now known about gene expression, and is implausible in light of the complexity and cultural variation of cooperative behaviors. Thus, when we introduce genetic transmission in our models, our reasoning operates at the phenotypic level.

This phenotype-based approach is a standard tool for the study of the evolution of social behavior in humans and other animals, and has a cogent justification as a device for abstracting from inconsequential complications surrounding the mechanics of genetic inheritance (Eshel and Feldman 1984; Grafen 1991; Hammerstein 1996; Eshel *et al.* 1998; Frank 1995). Moreover, because it uses observable phenotypes rather than unknown genotypes and developmental processes as the basis for analysis, the approach is readily applied to the kinds of empirical questions we address here.

Second, as is conventional in all models of selection, relative payoffs, whether in terms of fitness, material reward, social standing, or some other metric, influence the evolution of the population shares of various behavioral types, with higher payoff behaviors tending to increase their frequency in a population. The resulting so-called *payoff monotonic dynamic* is often implemented using "as if" optimization algorithms, though in doing this we do not attribute conscious optimization to individuals. Nor do we conclude that the resulting outcomes are in any sense optimal. In general, they are not. The aggregation of individually optimal choices is universally suboptimal, except under highly unrealistic conditions.

Individuals with higher payoffs may produce more copies of their behaviors in subsequent periods either through the contribution of their greater resources to differential reproductive success or because individuals disproportionately adopt the behaviors of the more successful members of their group. The latter may occur voluntarily, as when youngsters copy stars, or coercively, as when dominant ethnic groups, classes, or nations impose their cultures on subjugated peoples. Of course, cultural transmission may also favor lower payoff behaviors (think of smoking or fast food).

Third, because positive feedbacks are common in the processes of behavioral and institutional change we study, otherwise identical populations may exhibit quite different trajectories, reflecting the multiplicity of equilibria that is typical of models with positive feedbacks. The outcome that occurs need not be that with the higher average payoff. The process of selection among equilibria may be on such a long time scale that two populations described by exactly the same model may exhibit dramatically different distributions of behaviors for thousands of generations. The process of determining which of many possible equilibria will occur, termed *equilibrium selection*, thus assumes major importance.

Fourth, the emergence, proliferation, and biological or cultural extinction of collections of individuals such as foraging bands, ethno-linguistic units, and nations, and the consequent evolutionary success and failure of distinct group-level institutions such as systems of property rights, marital practices, and socialization of the young, is an essential, sometimes the preeminent, influence on human evolutionary processes. The maintenance of group boundaries (through hostility toward "outsiders," for example) and lethal conflict among groups are essential aspects of this process. Within-group nonrandom pairing of individuals for mating, learning, and other activities also plays an important part.

Fifth, chance, in the form of mutation, recombination, developmental accidents, behavioral experimentation, deliberate deviance from social rules, perturbation of the structure of social interactions and its payoffs and other stochastic influences, plays an important role in human evolution.

Finally, an explanation of the evolution of human cooperation must hinge on the empirical evidence. The question is not "Which model works?" They all work, if mathematical coherence is the bar. The question we are asking is about something that actually happened in the human past. Thus we measure the empirical plausibility of alternative explanations against the conditions under which early humans lived during the Pleistocene, roughly 1.6 million years before the present, until the advent of agriculture beginning about 12,000 years ago, and especially the last 100 or so millennia of this period. Here is Christopher Boehm's (2007) summary, based on the common characteristics of the 154 foraging societies (about half of those in the ethnographic record) thought to approximate ancestral "highly mobile ... storage-free economic systems":

> These highly cooperative nomadic multi-family bands typically contain some unrelated families, and band size, while seasonably variable, seems to be around 20–30 individuals with families often moving from one band to another. Band social life is politically egalitarian in that there is always a low tolerance by a group's mature males for one of their number dominating, bossing, or denigrating the others ... economic life also tends to be quite egalitarian because of nomadism and a strong sharing ethic which dampens selfish and nepotistic tendencies ... regional social networks exist ... [and] socially or militarily facilitated group defense of resources is far from infrequent ... Drastic resource unpredictability, another likely factor [contributing to group conflict] could have been especially important in the changeable Pleistocene.

## Conclusion

About 55,000 years ago, a group of hunter-gatherers left Africa and began to move eastward along the shores of the Indian Ocean. They may have originated in the Upper Rift Valley in modern-day Kenya. They could have been the descendants of the cooperative early humans we described at the outset, living 30,000 years earlier at the mouth of the Klasies River far to the south. Wherever they came from, some eventually crossed hundreds of kilometers of open ocean before reaching Australia, just 15,000 years later. We do not know if they encountered or simply bypassed communities of *Homo floresiensis*, who persisted in what is now Indonesia almost to the end of the Pleistocene. As they spread northward, they also encountered the Denisovan hominins, who inhabited parts of Asia as recently as 50,000 years ago. Another branch of the African exodus crossed the Levant and somewhat later occupied Europe, then home to the soon-to-be-extinct Neanderthals. Though the possibility of multiple human origins cannot be eliminated, it is now widely thought that the descendants of this small group eventually peopled the entire world and are the ancestors of all living humans (Foley 1996; Klein 1999).

This second great exodus from Africa is remarkable for its speed and eventual spread. One cannot resist speculating about the capacities that made these particular individuals such lethal competitors for the (also large-brained, ornament-wearing and tool-making) Neanderthals or that allowed the construction of oceangoing craft. Some attractive candidates can be ruled out. The physiological innovations allowing for more effective speech, rearrangement of respiratory tract and esophagus, for example, had occurred much earlier. Likewise, the dramatic expansion of hominid brain size had occurred before two million years ago. Richard Klein (2000) suggests a "selectively advantageous mutation" that facilitated the cultural transmission of behaviors as a possible cause.

> Arguably this was the most significant mutation in the human evolutionary series for it produced an organism that could radically alter its behavior without any change in its anatomy and that could cumulate and transmit alterations at a speed that anatomical innovation could never match.
>
> (Klein 2000, 18)

But, as Klein himself points out, the only evidence for such a super-mutation are the facts it is intended to explain (Klein 2000). Whether the source was a single revolutionary innovation or, as many now think (McBrearty and Brooks 2000), the result of a long process of incremental changes, the linguistic capacities and the cultural transmission of norms of social conduct that supported cooperation were a necessary part of the human repertoire that made the peopling of the world possible. These same capabilities must be part of any account of the remarkable success of humans as a species then and since.

Humans became a cooperative species because our distinctive livelihoods made cooperation within a group highly beneficial to its members and, exceptionally among animals, we developed the cognitive, linguistic, and other capacities to structure our social interactions in ways that allowed altruistic cooperators to proliferate.

Human reliance on the meat of large hunted animals and other high-quality, large package-size, and hence high-variance foods meant that our livelihoods were risky, skill-intensive, and characterized by increasing returns to scale. Deploying skills that required years to acquire favored the evolution of large brains, patience, and long lives (Kaplan et al. 2000; Kaplan and Robson 2003). Organizing and sharing the returns of successful hunting additionally favored groups that developed practices of sharing information, food, and other valued resources (Boehm 2000). Moreover, the long period of dependency of human offspring on adults, in part the result of the prolonged learning curve associated with hunting and gathering, meant that there were substantial benefits to cooperative child-rearing practices extending beyond the immediate family. Prolonged juvenile dependency also generated a net food deficit for families with adolescent children, increasing the benefits of food sharing among unrelated individuals and other forms of social insurance (Kaplan and Gurven 2005). Our experimental evidence shows that among today's small-scale societies, those that are especially reliant on big game, like the Lamalera whale hunters that we studied in Indonesia, and those for whom livelihoods require either joint efforts in acquisition or sharing in distribution, are especially likely to exhibit the social preferences that underpin altruistic cooperation.

One of the reasons for the connection between the potential benefits of cooperation and the prevalence of cooperative behaviors that we discovered in our models and simulations is that where the benefits associated with cooperation relative to the costs are substantial, it is more likely that the evolutionary processes of gene-culture coevolution will support populations with large numbers of cooperators, whether altruistic or mutualistic. A high ratio of benefits to costs makes cooperation an evolutionarily likely outcome. In virtually any plausible evolutionary dynamic in which stochastic shocks to payoffs and behaviors play an important role, the likelihood that a population will develop and maintain cooperative practices varies positively with the net benefits of cooperation.

But the fact that cooperation was group-beneficial in the environments of early humans does not explain why it evolved, for individuals bear the costs of their cooperative behaviors, while it is often others who enjoy the benefits. Thus, the distinctive human livelihood and associated cognitive capacities and longevity are necessary but not sufficient to explain the extent and nature of human cooperation. While the benefits of cooperation accruing to the individual cooperator may sometimes offset the costs, this is not likely to have been the case in many situations in which cooperation was essential to our ancestors, including defense, predation, and surmounting environmental crises. In these situations involving large numbers of individuals facing their possible demise, people with self-regarding preferences would not cooperate, regardless of their beliefs about what others would do. As a result, for cooperation to be sustained, social preferences would have to motivate at least some of those involved.

The distinctive human capacity for institution building and cultural transmission of learned behavior allowed social preferences to proliferate. Our ancestors used their capacities to learn from one another and to transmit information to create distinctive social environments. The resulting institutional and cultural niches reduced the costs borne by altruistic cooperators and raised the costs of free riding. Among these socially constructed environments, three were particularly important: group-structured populations with frequent and lethal intergroup competition, within-group leveling practices such as sharing food and information, and developmental institutions that internalized socially beneficial preferences.

These culturally transmitted institutional environments created a social and biological niche favorable to the evolution of the social preferences on which altruistic cooperation is based. We can only speculate, of course, about the initial appearance and proliferation of these preferences. But their emergence was highly likely for two reasons. The first is that the preferences that constitute strong reciprocity and some other social preferences could appear *de novo* as the result of only a small behavioral modification of either kin-based altruism or reciprocal altruism. In the case of kin-based altruism, those behaving altruistically toward kin may have simply ceased discriminating against the non-kin members of their groups. Likewise, a reciprocal altruist could become a strong reciprocator by simply deleting the proviso that one should condition one's behavior on expectations of future reciprocation.

The second reason why the emergence of social preferences among early humans would be highly likely is the vast number of foraging bands during the Late Pleistocene and earlier. Even if strong reciprocity initially emerged in a very small fraction of the human population, it is highly likely that over tens of thousands of generations, and something like 150,000 foraging bands, it would have occurred that the strong reciprocators or other altruistic cooperators were prevalent in one or more such groups at some point. These bands would have done very well in competition with other bands.

We have sought to explain how humans came to develop these exceptional social preferences and the cooperative social practices that supported them, taking the distinctive nature of human ecology, diet, and life course as preexisting. This analytical simplification is almost surely historically inaccurate. The distinctive nature of human livelihoods, the importance of hunted and extracted as opposed to collected foods, apparently does not pre-date and is not the cause of the emergence of cooperation. Rather, it appears that the two developed in tandem.

Though we have not addressed this question, we think it likely that the models presented here, suitably amended, would illuminate the coevolution of human cooperation along with our distinctive diets, life histories, and livelihoods. The presence on the African savannah of large mammals vulnerable to attack by cognitively advanced predators must have given substantial advantages to the members of groups that developed means of coordinating the hunt and sharing its sporadically acquired prey. Correspondingly, groups that had learned how to cooperate in these ways would have benefited from preferentially targeting large animals, as opposed to food acquired in smaller packages, and thereby enlarging the place of hunted meat in their diet. Winterhalder and Smith (1992) write:

> only with the evolution of reciprocity or exchange-based food transfers did it become economical for individual hunters to target large game. The effective value of a large mammal to a lone forager ... probably was not great enough to justify the cost of attempting to pursue and capture it ... However, once effective systems of reciprocity or exchange augment the effective value of very large packages to the hunter, such prey items would be more likely to enter the optimal diet.
>
> (P. 60)

We think it likely that the distinctive aspects of the human livelihood thus coevolved with the distinctive aspects of our social behavior, most notably cooperation.

Two approaches inspired by standard biological models have constituted the workhorses of our explanation, multi-level selection and gene-culture coevolution. Could it be that altruistic cooperation became common among humans in the absence of these two processes? We think it empirically unlikely. The reason is that the kin-based and reciprocal altruism models, operating alone or in tandem, are peculiarly ill-suited to explain the distinctive aspects of human cooperation.

By contrast, explanations of the emergence and proliferation of cooperative behaviors based on gene-culture coevolution and multi-level selection are quite plausible. First, the models and simulations of our evolutionary past provide strong evidence that, in the relevant evolutionary environments, selective pressures based on the positive assortment of behaviors arising from the group-structured nature of human populations could have been a significant influence on human evolution. Second, we have also demonstrated the important contribution to the evolution of social preferences that could have been accomplished by the cultural transmission of empirically well-documented behaviors such as the internalization of norms, within-group leveling, and between-group hostility. Third, the nature of preferences revealed in behavioral experiments and in other observations of human behavior is consistent with the view that genuine altruism, a willingness to sacrifice one's own interest to help others, including those who are not family members, and not simply in return for anticipated reciprocation in the future, provides the proximate explanation of much of human cooperation. These ethical and other-regarding group-beneficial social preferences are the most likely psychological consequence of the gene-culture coevolutionary and multi-level selection processes we have described.

# References

Andreoni, James, Brian Erand, and Jonathan Feinstein. 1998. "Tax Compliance." *Journal of Economic Literature* 36 (2): 818–860.

Aristotle. 2002 [350 BC]. *Nicomachean Ethics*. Newburyport, MA: Focus Publishing.

Bewley, Truman F. 2000. *Why Wages Don't Fall during a Recession*. Cambridge: Cambridge University Press.

Blinder, Alan S. and Don H. Choi. 2000. "A Shred of Evidence on Theories of Wage Stickiness." *Quarterly Journal of Economics* 105 (4): 1003–1015.

Boehm, Christopher J. 2000. *Hierarchy in the Forest: The Evolution of Egalitarian Behavior*. Cambridge, MA: Harvard University Press.

Boehm, Christopher J. 2007. "Conscience Origins, Sanctioning Selection, and the Evolution of Altruism in *Homo Sapiens*." Unpublished ms, Department of Anthropology, University of Southern California.

Boehm, Christopher J. 2011. *Moral Origins: Social Selection and the Evolution of Virtue, Altruism, and Shame*. New York: Basic Books.

Bonner, John T. 1984. *The Evolution of Culture in Animals*. Princeton, NJ: Princeton University Press.

Boyd, Robert and Peter J. Richerson. 1985. *Culture and the Evolutionary Process*. Chicago: University of Chicago Press.

Brennan, Geoffrey and Philip Pettit. 2004. *The Economy of Esteem: An Essay on Civil and Political Society*. New York: Oxford University Press.

Cavalli-Sforza, Luigi Luca and Marcus W. Feldman. 1973. "Cultural versus Biological Inheritance: Phenotype Transmission from Parents to Children." *American Journal of Human Genetics* 25: 618–637.

Cavalli-Sforza, Luigi Luca and Marcus W. Feldman. 1981. *Cultural Transmission and Evolution*. Princeton, NJ: Princeton University Press.

Cavalli-Sforza, Luigi Luca and Marcus W. Feldman. 1982. "Theory and Observation in Cultural Transmission." *Science* 218: 19–27.

Clark, Kenneth and Martin Sefton. 2001. "The Sequential Prisoner's Dilemma: Evidence on Reciprocation." *Economic Journal* 111 (468): 51–68.

Cooley, Charles Horton. 1902. *Human Nature and the Social Order*. New York: Charles Scribner's Sons.

Dawkins, Richard. 1976. *The Selfish Gene*. Oxford: Oxford University Press.

Dawkins, Richard. 1982. *The Extended Phenotype: The Gene as the Unit of Selection*. Oxford: Freeman.

de Waal, Frans. 1997. *Good Natured: The Origins of Right and Wrong in Humans and Other Animals*. Cambridge, MA: Harvard University Press.

Durham, William H. 1991. *Coevolution: Genes, Culture, and Human Diversity*. Stanford, CA: Stanford University Press.

Edgeworth, Francis Ysidro. 1881. *Mathematical Psychics: An Essay on the Application of Mathematics to the Moral Sciences*. London: Kegan Paul.

Eshel, Ilan and Marcus W. Feldman. 1984. "Initial Increase of New Mutants and Some Continuity Properties of ESS in Two Locus Systems." *American Naturalist* 124: 631–640.

Eshel, Ilan, Marcus W. Feldman, and Aviv Bergman. 1998. "Long-Term Evolution, Short-Term Evolution, and Population Genetic Theory." *Journal of Theoretical Biology* 191: 391–396.

Fehr, Ernst and Simon Gächter. 2000. "Cooperation and Punishment." *American Economic Review* 90 (4): 980–994.

Field, Alexander J. 2004. *Altruistically Inclined? The Behavioral Sciences, Evolutionary Theory, and the Origins of Reciprocity*. Ann Arbor, MI: University of Michigan Press.

Foley, Robert A. 1996. "An Evolutionary and Chronological Framework for Human Social Behavior." *Proceedings of the British Academy* 88: 95–117.

Fong, Christina M. 2001. "Social Preferences, Self-Interest, and the Demand for Redistribution." *Journal of Public Economics* 82 (2): 225–246.

Fong, Christina M., Samuel Bowles, and Herbert Gintis. 2005. "Reciprocity and the Welfare State." In *Moral Sentiments and Material Interests: On the Foundations of Cooperation in Economic Life*, edited by Herbert Gintis, Samuel Bowles, Robert Boyd, and Ernst Fehr, 277–302. Cambridge, MA: MIT Press.

Frank, Steven A. 1995. "Mutual Policing and Repression of Competition in the Evolution of Cooperative Groups." *Nature* 377: 520–522.

Gilens, Martin. 1999. *Why Americans Hate Welfare*. Chicago: University of Chicago Press.

Grafen, Alan. 1991. "Modeling in Behavioral Ecology." In *Behavioral Ecology: An Evolutionary Approach*, edited by John R. Krebs and Nicholas B. Davies, 5–31. Oxford: Blackwell Scientific Publications.

Hagoromo Society. 1973. *Born to Die: The Cherry Blossom Squadrons*. Los Angeles: Ohara.
Hammerstein, Peter. 1996. "Darwinian Adaptation, Population Genetics and the Streetcar Theory of Evolution." *Journal of Mathematical Biology* 34: 511–532.
Hansen, Daniel G. 1997. "Individual Responses to a Group Incentive." *Industrial and Labor Relations Review* 51 (1): 37–49.
Hardin, Garrett. 1968. "The Tragedy of the Commons." *Science* 162: 1243–1248.
Hayashi, N., Elinor Ostrom, James M. Walker, and Toshio Yamagishi. 1999. "Reciprocity, Trust, and the Sense of Control: A Cross-Societal Study." *Rationality and Society* 11: 27–46.
Henrich, Joseph and Richard McElreath. 2003. "The Evolution of Cultural Evolution." *Evolutionary Anthropology* 12 (3): 123–135.
Herrmann, Benedikt, Christian Thöni, and Simon Gächter. 2008. "Anti-Social Punishment across Societies." *Science* 319: 1362–1367.
Hobsbawm, Eric. 1983. "Mass-Producing Traditions: Europe, 1870–1914." In *The Invention of Tradition*, edited by Eric Hobsbawm and Terence Ranger, 263–307. Cambridge: Cambridge University Press.
Hrdy, Sarah Blaffer. 2000. *Mother Nature: Maternal Instincts and How They Shape the Human Species*. New York: Ballantine.
Hrdy, Sarah Blaffer. 2009. *Mothers and Others: The Evolutionary Origins of Mutual Understanding*. New York: Belknap.
Huxley, Julian S. 1955. "Evolution, Cultural and Biological." *Yearbook of Anthropology*, 2–25.
Jablonka, Eva and Marion J. Lamb. 1995. *Epigenetic Inheritance and Evolution: The Lamarckian Case*. Oxford: Oxford University Press.
James, William. 1880. "Great Men, Great Thoughts, and the Environment." *Atlantic Monthly* 46: 441–459.
Kaplan, Hillard and Michael Gurven. 2005. "The Natural History of Human Food Sharing and Cooperation: A Review and a New Multi-Individual Approach to the Negotiation of Norms." In *Moral Sentiments and Material Interests*, edited by Herbert Gintis, Samuel Bowles, Robert Boyd, and Ernst Fehr, 75–114. Cambridge, MA: MIT Press.
Kaplan, Hillard and Arthur Robson. 2003. "The Evolution of Human Longevity and Intelligence in Hunter-Gatherer Economies." *American Economic Review* 93: 150–169.
Kaplan, Hillard, Kim Hill, Jane Lancaster, and Ana Magdalena Hurtado. 2000. "A Theory of Human Life History Evolution: Diet, Intelligence, and Longevity." *Evolutionary Anthropology* 9: 156–185.
Kappeler, P. K. and Carel P. van Schaik. 2006. *Cooperation in Primates and Humans*. Berlin: Springer.
Kiyonari, Toko, Shigehito Tanida, and Toshio Yamagishi. 2000. "Social Exchange and Reciprocity: Confusion or a Heuristic?" *Evolution and Human Behavior* 21: 411–427.
Klein, Richard G. 1999. *The Human Career: Human Biological and Cultural Origins*. Chicago: University of Chicago Press.
Klein, Richard G. 2000. "Archaeology and the Evolution of Human Behavior." *Evolutionary Anthropology* 9: 17–36.
Knez, Marc and Duncan Simester. 2001. "Firm-Wide Incentives and Mutual Monitoring at Continental Airlines." *Journal of Labor Economics* 19 (4): 743–772.
Kropotkin, Pyotr. 1989 [1903]. *Mutual Aid: A Factor in Evolution*. New York: Black Rose Books.

List, John A. 2006. "Friend or Foe? A Natural Experiment of the Prisoner's Dilemma." *Review of Economics and Statistics* 88 (3): 463–471.

Lorenz, Konrad. 1963. *On Aggression*. New York: Harcourt, Brace & World.

Lumsden, C. J. and Edward O. Wilson. 1981. *Genes, Mind, and Culture: The Coevolutionary Process*. Cambridge, MA: Harvard University Press.

McBrearty, Sally and Alison Brooks. 2000. "The Revolution that Wasn't: A New Interpretation of the Origin of Modern Human Behavior." *Journal of Human Evolution* 39: 453–563.

McCabe, Kevin, Vernon L. Smith, and M. LePore. 2000. "Intentionality Detection and Mindreading: Why Does Game Form Matter?" *Proceedings of the National Academy of Sciences* 97: 4404–4409.

Milo, R. 1998. "Evidence for Hominid Predation at Klasies River Mouth, South Africa and Its Implications for the Behaviour of Modern Humans." *Journal of Archaeological Science* 25: 99–133.

Moore, Jr., Barrington. 1978. *Injustice: The Social Bases of Obedience and Revolt*. White Plains: M. E. Sharpe.

Morris, M. W., W. M. Sim, and V. Girotto. 1998. "Distinguishing Sources of Cooperation in the One-Round Prisoner's Dilemma: Evidence for Cooperative Decisions Based on the Illusion of Control." *Journal of Experimental Social Psychology* 34: 464–512.

Netting, Robert. 1989. *Balancing on an Alp: Ecological Change and Continuity in a Swiss Mountain Community*. Cambridge: Cambridge University Press.

Oberholzer-Gee, Felix, Joel Waldfolgel, and Matthew W. White. 2010. "Friend or Foe? Cooperation and Learning in High-Stakes Games." *Review of Economics and Statistics* 92 (1): 179–187.

Odling-Smee, F. John, Kevin N. Laland, and Marcus W. Feldman. 2003. *Niche Construction: The Neglected Process in Evolution*. Princeton, NJ: Princeton University Press.

Olson, Mancur. 1965. *The Logic of Collective Action: Public Goods and the Theory of Groups*. Cambridge, MA: Harvard University Press.

Ostrom, Elinor. 1990. *Governing the Commons: The Evolution of Institutions for Collective Action*. Cambridge: Cambridge University Press.

Popper, Karl. 1979. *Objective Knowledge: An Evolutionary Approach*. Oxford: Clarendon Press.

Richerson, Peter J. and Robert Boyd. 1998. "The Evolution of Ultrasociality." In *Indoctrinability, Ideology and Warfare*, edited by I. Eibl-Eibesfeldt and F. K. Salter, 71–96. New York: Berghahn Books.

Richerson, Peter J. and Robert Boyd. 2004. *Not by Genes Alone*. Chicago: University of Chicago Press.

Ridley, Matt. 1998. *The Origins of Virtue: Human Instincts and the Evolution of Cooperation*. New York: Penguin.

Roughgarden, Joan. 2009. *The Genial Gene: Deconstructing Darwinian Selfishness*. Berkeley, CA: University of California Press.

Sally, David. 1995. "Conversation and Cooperation in Social Dilemmas." *Rationality and Society* 7 (1): 58–92.

Savage, Leonard J. 1954. *The Foundations of Statistics*. New York: John Wiley & Sons.

Singer, R. and J. J. Wymer. 1982. *The Middle Stone Age at Klasies River Mouth in South Africa*. Chicago: University of Chicago Press.

Sober, Elliot and David Sloan Wilson. 1998. *Unto Others: The Evolution and Psychology of Unselfish Behavior*. Cambridge, MA: Harvard University Press.
Stern, Jessica. 2003. *Terror in the Name of God*. New York: HarperCollins.
Veblen, Thorstein. 1899. *The Theory of the Leisure Class*. New York: Macmillan.
Watabe, M., S. Terai, N. Hayashi, and Toshio Yamagishi. 1996. "Cooperation in the One-Shot Prisoner's Dilemma based on Expectations of Reciprocity." *Japanese Journal of Experimental Social Psychology* 36: 183–196.
Winterhalder, Bruce and Eric Alden Smith. 1992. *Evolutionary Ecology and Human Behavior*. New York: Aldine de Gruyter.
Wood, Elisabeth Jean. 2003. *Insurgent Collective Action and Civil War in El Salvador*. Cambridge: Cambridge University Press.
Wright, Robert. 1995. *The Moral Animal*. New York: Vintage.

## 2 The theory of social cooperation historically and robustly contemplated

*Peter J. Boettke and Daniel J. Smith*

### Introduction

At the dawn of political philosophy, its goal was to support the guided perfection of human nature through religious piety, enlightenment, or heavy-handed repression (Hobbes [1651] 1962; Passmore [1970] 2000, 320; van de Haar 2009, 8). Plato, for instance, wrote on the necessity of granting political power to those graced with philosophic intelligence in order that they may rule over the "lesser natures" as philosopher kings (1985, 165). As Bernard Mandeville summarized of this historical project of political philosophy:

> The Chief Thing, therefore, which Lawmakers and other wise Men, that have labored for the Establishment of Society, have endeavor'd, has been to make the People they were to govern, believe that it was more beneficial for every Body to conquer than indulge his Appetites, and much better to mind the Publick than what seem'd his private interest.
> 
> ([1791] 1988, 42)

Rather than design institutions for man as he was, the project of political philosophy was to instigate a transformation of man through religious or moral appeal, or to force it through legal decree backed by force. Enlightened religious, moral, and legal authorities were necessary to carry forth this transformation, and thus the project of political philosophy became both to train enlightened leaders as well as to design political systems conducive to the top-down, imposed transcendence of human passions (Hirschman 1977, 16; Passmore [1970] 2000, 4). The tendency to barter and exchange was seen as just another demoralizing tendency; a baser component of human nature that was in need of divine perfection or heavy-handed repression (Levine 2011, 55).

The outcome of this project, rather than actually developing enlightened leaders, tended only to enshroud fallible leaders with the false infallibility of religious and moral authority. The realist wave that swept political philosophy beginning in the fifteenth century sought instead to take man as he was, not as he was aspired to be. Thus, the project of political philosophy shifted to that of discovering the nature of man. Institutions could then be designed that could channel man's passions into socially productive, or at least not socially destructive, outcomes. The assumption of a perfectible man was gradually dropped in favor of a more realistic view of human nature (Hirschman 1977, 12; Passmore [1970] 2000). Adam Smith, for instance, at the later end of this period, grounded his moral philosophy in the empirical observation of man as he was, not as he should be (Forman-Barzilai 2011, 58).

This is not to say that the project of self-betterment through education, worldly experience, and study was dropped (Passmore [1970] 2000, 512). In fact, it remained – and remains – important part of political philosophy. The realist movement should be seen as an early endeavor toward a robust political economy (van de Haar 2009, 8–9). Robust political economy seeks to design institutions robust to deviations away from omnisciently and behaviorally perfect humans (Boettke and Leeson 2004; Leeson and Subrick 2006; Pennington 2011). As Hayek interpreted Adam Smith's project in terms of robust political economy,

> the main point about which there can be little doubt is that Smith's chief concern was not so much with what man might occasionally achieve when he was at his best but that he should have as little opportunity as possible to do harm when he was at his worst. It would scarcely be too much to claim that the main merit of the individualism which he and his contemporaries advocated is that it is a system under which bad men can do least harm. It is a social system which does not depend for its functioning on our finding good men for running it, or on all men becoming better than they now are, but which makes use of men in all their given variety and complexity, sometimes good and sometimes bad, sometimes intelligent and more often stupid.
> (1948, 11)

Rather than attempting to suppress human nature, by positing and attempting to encourage enlightened leadership, the role of political philosophy became to discover institutions that would channel human passions to the benefit of society. The new role of that state, rather than repressing human nature, would be to harness it, taking on the role of the civilizing agent (Hirschman 1977, 16). This transition was led by thinkers such as Machiavelli ([1532] 1995), Montaigne ([1580] 2003), Hobbes ([1651] 1962), Bacon (2008), Rousseau ([1762] 1978), and Descartes (2012), and later picked up by the Scottish Enlightenment thinkers, such as Hume, who stressed that "[s]overeigns must take mankind as they find them" ([1742] 1987, 260).[1] Mercantilism, which held that the self-interest of individuals was necessarily out of alignment with the public interest, requiring corrective government control, can be seen as a project that emerged out of this development (Robertson ([1933] 1973, 66); as can the contractarianism starting with Hobbes ([1651] 1962).

Political philosophy was further revolutionized over this period by the development of the defenses of commerce based on the grounds of economic efficiency, as well as on moral and religious grounds, such as natural rights. Not only was a commercial society robust to deviations away from idealized man; it was also economically efficient and not immoral. There were historical roots for this move in the scholastic literature. Thomas Aquinas can be seen as one of the first religious defenders of capitalism, a tradition that was carried on by the Late Scholastics of the fifteenth and sixteenth centuries (Boettke 2012, xvi; Nelson 2001, ch. 10). John Locke ([1690] 1980) advanced some of the first defenses of commercial exchange based on economic efficiency and also provided a natural-rights defense for the establishment of property rights. Smith ([1776] 1976), Maitland ([1804] 1967), and Hume ([1739] 1978) all played an important role in defending free markets based upon the economic gains achievable from the division of labor and economies of scale.

Yet another defense of a commercial society emerged during this period. This was the recognition in political philosophy that commerce *itself* played a *civilizing* role in society. This new paradigm was carried forward as a major tenet of the political philosophies written by the Scottish Enlightenment thinkers. They witnessed that market institutions, with no heavy-handed molding or transformation of human nature, aligned private interest with social interest. In order to benefit from the gains from the wider prosperity enabled through the division of labor, men needed to cooperate, and the establishments of property, promise-keeping, and justice facilitated such cooperation (Hume [1739] 1978, Book III). Adam Smith's ([1759] 1976, [1776] 1976) "invisible hand" can be seen as the most famous articulation of this new perception of the coordinating benefits of such social institutions. Rather than attempting to perfect man, Smith argued that the market institutional environment would best harness man's nature to realize social order. Even where reason failed, man's passions could entice him to participate in socializing institutions. While John Calvin, Martin Luther, and Thomas Aquinas made some of the first defenses of a commercial society based upon moral justifications, the Scottish Enlightenment thinkers advanced the claim that not only could commerce be moral, but also that it was *moralizing* (See: Tawney 1926 [1954]; Stark 2005; Chafuen 2003; Rothbard 1995; Green 1959; Sirico 2011; Weber 1930 [1956].

This thesis, while being separately recognized by several Scottish Enlightenment thinkers, has been synthesized as the doux-commerce thesis. Originating from the word *douceur*, which Hirschman (1977, 59) translates as conveying calmness and gentleness (being the antonym of violence), this term signified the observation that peace and cordiality emerged precisely where there was commerce, and precisely in order to conduct commerce. While the moralizing aspects of capitalism were widely recognized as one of the major defenses of a commercial society at the time of its development, and deeply connected to the economic efficiency arguments for free markets being advanced at that time, they have been gradually dropped by economists in favor of an exclusive focus on the technical efficiency arguments for a commercial society (Hirschman 1986, 107). In an attempt to strengthen the economic efficiency arguments of a commercial society by focusing exclusively on advancing the technical arguments of efficiency, economists have lost their appreciation of both the civilizing role of commerce and its grounding in the project of robust political economy; thus they have lost much of the "moral high ground in public debate" (Sirico 2011, 3; Brooks 2010). We argue that this neglect – at least partially – explains the failure of the profession to convey even the most basic defenses of a commercial society to the general public, despite conclusive efficiency arguments (Epstein 2008; Boettke *et al.* 2011).

In what follows we seek to detail the acceptance, loss, and the dawning rediscovery of the doux-commerce thesis in political economy. The second section provides a history of the development of the doux-commerce thesis by the Enlightenment thinkers. The third section provides a history of the lost appreciation – or even denial – of the doux-commerce thesis in mainstream political economy in the twentieth century. The fourth section argues that there has been a growing rediscovery of this important aspect of a commercial society. This rediscovery is seen as being vital to a comprehensive understanding and articulation of a commercial society. The final section concludes.

## The Scottish Enlightenment

In the self-interest of engaging in trade with prospective trading partners, economic actors naturally evolve moral codes, manners, customs, and cordiality. Exchange and the division of labor not only encourage wealth production, they also encourage cooperation, as exchange creates mutually beneficial trades that foster cordial and mutually beneficial relationships in society. The incentives to cheat while conducting exchange are countered by the loss of future profits that will dissipate with a tarnished reputation.

Insights of this tendency began to be recognized where free markets started developing in the Industrial Revolution during what became known as the Scottish Enlightenment.[2] The concept became widely recognized by political philosophers and early political economists. Voltaire observed,

> Go into the Exchange in London, that place more venerable than many a court, and you will see representatives of all the nations assembled there for the profit of mankind. There the Jew, the Mahometan, and the

Christian deal with one another as if they were of the same religion, and reserve the name of infidel for those who go bankrupt. There the Presbyterian trusts the Anabaptist, and the Church of England man accepts the promise of the Quaker. On leaving these peaceable and free assemblies, some go to the synagogue, others in search of a drink; this man is on the way to be baptized in a great tub in the name of the Father, by the Son, to the Holy Ghost; that man is having the foreskin of his son cut off, and a Hebraic formula mumbled over the child that he himself can make nothing of; these others are going to their church to await the inspiration of God with their hats on; and all are satisfied.

([1733] 2003, 26)

As Smith lectured, "[w]henever commerce is introduced into any country, probity and punctuality always accompany it ... Of all the nations in Europe, the Dutch, the most commercial, are the most faithful to their word" ([1762] 1982, 538). This is not due to inherent differences of the Dutch, but because "[a] dealer is afraid of losing his character, and is scrupulous in observing every engagement. When a person makes perhaps twenty contracts in a day, he cannot gain so much by endeavouring to impose on his neighbours, as the very appearance of a cheat would make him lose" (538). Smith goes on, "[w]hen the greater part of people are merchants they always bring probity and punctuality into fashion, and these therefore, are the principal virtues of a commercial nation" (539). Smith argued that "commerce and manufactures gradually introduced order and good government, and with them, the liberty and security of individuals, among the inhabitants of the country, who had before lived almost in a continual state of war with their neighbours, and of servile dependency upon their superiors. This, though it has been the least observed, is by far the most important of all their effects" ([1776] 1976, 412).

David Hume argued that it was precisely because of the gains available from exchange that we develop property rights, just like we developed language, in order to promote social cooperation:

[n]o one can doubt, that the convention for the distinction of property, and for the stability of possession, is of all circumstances the most necessary to the establishment of human society, and that after the agreement for the fixing and observing of this rule, there remains little or nothing to be done towards settling a perfect harmony and concord.

([1739] 1978, 491)

Not only did the Scottish Enlightenment thinkers observe the cordiality and peace promoted by commerce among individuals; they also witnessed it extended to nations. Hume wrote, "nothing is more favourable to the rise of politeness and learning, than a number of neighbouring and independent states, connected together by commerce and policy" ([1742] 1987, 119).

Montesquieu observed, "[c]ommerce cures destructive prejudices, and it is an almost general rule that everywhere there are gentle mores, there is commerce and that everywhere there is commerce, there are gentle mores" ([1748] 2009, 338). Montesquieu goes on to argue that, as a result of the interaction of different mores in the global market place, mores are compared to each other and refined and the more barbaric mores are softened or dropped. Montesquieu writes, "The natural effect of commerce is to lead to peace," by encouraging justice and discouraging banditry (338).

Condorcet similarly argued that "[m]anners have become more gentle ... through the influence of the spirit of commerce and industry, those enemies of the violence and turmoil which cause wealth to flee" (1795, 238, as quoted in Hirschman 1982, 1465). This is perhaps best summed up by Samuel Ricard:

> [c]ommerce attaches [men] one to another through mutual utility. Through commerce the moral and physical passions are superseded by interest ... Commerce has a special character which distinguishes it from all other professions. It affects the feelings of men so strongly that it makes him who was proud and haughty suddenly turn supple, bending and serviceable. Through commerce, man learns to deliberate, to be honest, to acquire manners, to be prudent and reserved in both talk and action. Sensing the necessity to be wise and honest in order to succeed, he flees vice, or at least his demeanor exhibits decency and seriousness so as not to arouse any adverse judgment on the part of present and future acquaintances; he would not dare make a spectacle of himself for fear of damaging his credit standing which it might otherwise have to deplore.
> (1781, 463, as quoted in Hirschman 1982, 1465)

Such recognition of the civilizing role of commerce was prominent in the influential writings of America's Founding Fathers as well. They not only noted the civilizing role of commerce, but remarked on how government can impinge upon civil society. As Thomas Paine wrote,

> [t]he landholder, the farmer, the manufacturer, the merchant, the tradesman, and every occupation, prospers by the aid which each receives from the other, and from the whole. Common interest regulates their concerns, and forms their law; and the laws which common usage ordains, have a greater influence than the laws of government. In fine, society performs for itself almost everything which is ascribed to government.
> ([1791] 2013, 357)

The doux-commerce thesis can, and should, be seen as a distinct contribution to political economy. It was advanced concomitantly with the economic efficiency arguments for capitalism, as an outgrowth of early attempts to establish a robust political economy. To the Scottish Enlightenment thinkers, these arguments were inherently linked. Not only did capitalism produce economic efficiency; it also channeled man's self-interest towards peaceful and cooperative relations that would in turn strengthen the bonds and underpinnings of a capitalist society, which would, in turn, enhance the productive capabilities of a commercial society.

## Lost appreciation in pursuit of ruthless efficiency

Despite the wide-scale recognition of the powerful civilizing role of commerce upon civil society, the doux-commerce thesis gradually fell out of favor among political economists. This was not due to an explicit rejection of the thesis by economists, but more to scholarly neglect. Economists gradually turned to increasingly refined technical models of efficiency and optimality, neglecting those aspects of the Scottish Enlightenment that were mathematically intractable, the comparative institutional analysis of robust political economy and the doux-commerce thesis (Boettke 2010; Boettke, Fink, and Smith 2012; Boettke, Leeson, and Smith 2008; Buchanan 1964, 214; Cornuelle 1991; Hirschman 1986, 122; Kreps 1997). In the late nineteenth and into the twentieth century, the "invisible hand" argument came to be exclusively associated with the pursuit of ruthless efficiency and the obtainment of optimality conditions.

As these foundational principles of capitalism were dropped by economists in favor of the sterility of mathematical expositions and ruthless efficiency, economists became increasingly vulnerable to the attacks of political philosophy.[3] This is not to say that critiques did not appear prior to this point. On the contrary, many important critiques were levied against capitalism by thinkers such as Jean-Jacques Rousseau ([1762] 1978; [1750] 1964) and Karl Marx (1978) prior to this period. For Rousseau, the industrial organization of commerce led to inequality that would undermine the social relations necessary for civil society. For Marx, not only did the use of money atrophy social relations; the concentration of capital in the bourgeois class and the continual exploitation and alienation of the proletariat would inevitably lead to class warfare and a proletarian revolution (Roberts 1990, ch. 1). Rather, the diversion of scholarly attention toward increasingly refined technical expositions led to a lost appreciation for the project of robust political economy and the doux-commerce thesis, and thus created the vacuum for modern political theorizers to build on the market critiques of Marx and Rousseau.

These modern critiques latched onto the arguments that rather than commerce playing a civilizing role in society, commerce would bring about social discord, unrest, and dissolution of civil society. The loss of civil society, in turn, would threaten the very foundations of a capitalist society, necessitating government correction. Hirschman (1986, 110; 1982, 1466), summarizing this view as the "self-destruction thesis," explains: "capitalist society, far from fostering douceur and other fine attitudes, exhibits a pronounced proclivity to undermining the moral foundations on which any society, including its own, must rest."

Modern egalitarian ethicists have built upon similar themes. John Rawls (1971), Ronald Dworkin (2002), Charles Taylor (1985), and Iris Young (2002) can all be seen as outgrowths of the self-destruction thesis, arguing that material and structural inequality would lead to social dissolution and unrest. In order to preserve civil society, more communitarian or dialogical methods of decision making, rather than crude exchange relations, were thought to be necessary.

Fred Hirsch (2005) argues that in chasing after dollars in the "rat race" in order to obtain goods we desire due to the bombardment of advertising, economic actors give up the leisure necessary for the formation of civil relations.[4] This decline in leisure time, Hirsch (77) argues, leads to "a decline in sociability and, specifically, friendliness," in turn leading to decreased social contact and mutual concern, and a dearth of Good Samaritans. In addition, the social and geographic mobility inherent in capitalism would lead to underinvestment in sociability, and thus a decline in civil society. This occurs, Hirsch argues, because the returns on being social are lower if there is a probability that any given sociability may not be reciprocated due to someone moving on the social ladder or geographically. "The weakening of traditional social values," Hirsch argues, "has made predominantly capitalist economies more difficult to manage" (117).

Similarly, Daniel Bell argues that capitalism itself unravels "the threads which once held the culture and the economy together." According to Bell, the capitalist unraveling of the social fabric would eventually result in the loss of civil society's protection "from the hedonism which has become the prevailing value in our society" (1976, xi). Even Joseph Schumpeter (2008, 61) in asking, "[c]an capitalism survive?" answered, "[n]o. I don't think it can," arguing that the very success of capitalism, by contributing to the degradation of the family (157), leads to the atrophy of the institutions that support it (61). In fact, many notable free market scholars in the twentieth century, such as Frank Knight, held that pure capitalism would lead to the dissolution of morals and civil society (Burgin 2012, 113).

More modern-day proponents of the self-destruction thesis include Michael Sandel (2012), who argues that extending market relations can corrupt attitudes and norms. Robert Skidelsky and Edward Skidelsky (2012), similarly, argue that capitalism has led market participants away from the good life, in particular emphasizing how advertising leads to a drive to acquire more goods, and thus a reduction in leisure time.

The shortcomings of the mechanical depiction of the market society as an efficiency-directed system, based on self-interest and optimality, have become more apparent in recent years, especially since strictly technical models failed to predict or provide a consensus explanation for the 2008 financial crisis. The focus on the civilizing nature of commerce largely faded from the analytical view, creating the philosophical vacuum for market critiques to emerge due to the loss of the appreciation and defense of the doux-commerce thesis.[5] In fact, it is impossible to derive the doux-commerce thesis from the standard model of economists, because transactional mechanisms such as negotiation, mutual adjustment, and bargaining are beyond the scope of the perfect competition model (Hirschman 1986, 123). It has been only in recent years that economists have begun to undertake a more thorough reading of Adam Smith and to reconstruct the doux-commerce thesis. The civilizing function of commerce and the ability of the market system to produce social cooperation, especially among distant and different anonymous actors, were critical parts of Smith's argument for the benefits of the commercial society. This lost appreciation for the role of commerce in promoting social cooperation and civil society was due to be rediscovered (Cornuelle 1991).

## Re-enlightenment?

The financial turmoil of 2008, widely, if falsely, blamed on the greed of capitalist actors, has been accompanied by a period of political pessimism for classical liberal scholars (Allison 2012; Boettke *et al.* 2011). Defenders of the commercial society are thus beginning to realize the importance of not just a moral defense of capitalism, which has often been neglected in technical economic efficiency arguments, but also a recognition of the moralizing features of capitalism embedded in the project of robust political economy (Allison 2012; Brooks 2010; Pennington 2011). Attention is returning to the Scottish Enlightenment thinkers and those dissident scholars who have been advancing the defense of a market society not just on efficiency grounds, but also on the grounds of robust political economy and civil society.

While Mises ([1949] 2007, ch. 8) and Hayek ([1944] 2007, ch. 15, 1988) both recognized the importance of the doux-commerce thesis and its role in history, their particular contributions, while well articulated, were never widely recognized by the economics profession. Hayek, while acknowledging that competition is necessary to drive discovery and economic efficiency, argued that rules, values, and accepted practices evolve to allow the competitive process to operate beneficially (1988, 19). Mises argued that it is the efficiency achievable through commercial relations, that is, the division of labor, that makes society itself possible ([1949] 2007, 144).

Advancing this recognition by Mises and Hayek, new articulations of the doux-commerce thesis and empirical validations have been emerging in a rediscovery – so to speak – of the recognition of the civilizing role of commerce.

For example, Robert Sirico argues that commerce "serves as a moral tutor for entrepreneurs," because markets require a "moral context in which to exist and function smoothly" (2011, 11). Consumers drive the market and, through their purchasing or abstaining from purchasing, force businesses to continually maintain a reputation for honesty, quality, and customer service. Any business that neglects these considerations will soon be voted out of the marketplace. Appiah (2006) argues that exposure to capitalism through commercial exchanges aids mutual understanding and cosmopolitanism between diverse groups. While qualifying her statement with the fact that many practices and social experiences affect the conditions for the emergence of cosmopolitanism, Jacob (2006) argues that the rise of cosmopolitanism in early modern Europe was assisted by the intermixing of culture, religion, and ideas, often as the result of mercantile or scientific activity.

Empirically, Henrich *et al.* (2004, 2005) find that small-scale societies that have had more exposure to Western-style capitalism, and thus exchange, exhibit less narrowly selfish behavior and more cooperative behavior than those that have had less exposure to Western exchange. McCloskey (2006, 2010), Ridley (1996, 2010) and Seabright (2004) all explore the concomitant evolution of capitalism and virtue throughout history. McCloskey (2010) argues that the dramatic increase in economic growth witnessed since the Industrial Revolution can be traced back to the change in rhetoric surrounding the merchant community; it was precisely the recognition of the positive role of merchants and markets that fostered the environment conducive to their operation. Axelrod (1984) and Bicchieri (2006) both delve into the emergence of cooperative norms and their particulars.

Not only has modern research been rediscovering that commercial relations strengthen civil society, it has also been rediscovering the observation that increased dependence on and interference from government can also have an adverse impact on civil society. For instance, Brown argues that as "community relations become more legalistic, the social distance among us lengthens even further" (1995). Even government interventions intended to help people can lead to decline in the prevalence and influence of traditional civil society roles previously filled by churches, charities, and fraternal societies (Beito 2000). The ironic paradox is that the more the government intervenes in the economy, and civil society atrophies, the easier it is to argue for further state intervention (Taylor 1987, 168). Instead of commerce diminishing the underpinning virtues necessary for civil society, a commercial society free of excessive government intrusion may in fact promote the very virtues that promote social cooperation in the first place (Williamson 2010).

Richard Cornuelle recognized this, and realized that the bonds of civil society that emerged in a capitalist society would need to be recognized and renewed after being weakened by government intrusion for over a century (Cornuelle 1965, 1991; L. Ealy (2011). The neglect of civil society in technical models led to doubt about its capabilities and neglect when it came to public policy. A rediscovering of the role of civil society thus becomes crucial "for the long-term well-being of civilization" (S. Ealy 2011, 45).

Incorporating civil society under the purview of economics has proven difficult for most economists (Garnett 2011). Traceable back to the perceived "Adam Smith Problem," most economists can't square Smith's *Theory of Moral Sentiments*, with its emphasis on moral sympathy, with the self-interest-driven *Wealth of Nations* (Boettke 2012, 6; Paganelli 2008; Smith 1998). Unable to reconcile these two views, the economics profession often embraced scholarship advancing the second project while neglecting the first.

However, this distinction between the two irreconcilable sides of Adam Smith was a false dichotomy. The market economy, driven by the division of labor, operates in the realm of strangers and anonymity – a realm that our moral sympathy cannot be *assumed* to extend to in a project grounded in robust political economy (Bruni 2012, 124; Forman-Barzilai 2011). To operate in the extended order, rules of just conduct – related to property rights and the rule of law – which allow individuals to pursue their own ends rather than submit their efforts to ends forcefully chosen by others, is necessary to imbue competition and discovery, and call into use widely dispersed information (Boettke 2012, 17; Hayek 1945, 1988, 18).

While some philosophers decry the thin moral framework of markets – consent and contract – it is precisely the thinness of the market system that allows widely disparate groups to voluntarily subscribe to it. A thicker moral system would not be encompassing enough to provide for the vast divergence in culture, moral philosophy, and religion that is an empirical fact of the world (Pennington 2011, ch. 3–4). The thin moral framework of markets provides the framework for even individuals holding dichotomous moral philosophies to engage in mutually beneficial exchange (Bruni 2012, 62). This in turn creates the shared social space for the observation and exchange of culture, moral philosophy, and religion, and opens the door to the formation of more intimate relations; relations that would never have the opportunity to emerge through the imposition of a conquering thicker moral framework (Forman-Barzilai 2011, 126, 179, 188–192; Storr 2008). The thin moral framework of markets fosters impartiality and an ethic of tolerance, disciplined by the pursuit of profit and the avoidance of loss, in precisely those areas where animosities in culture, morals, and religion are likely to be greatest (Forman-Barzilai 2011, 216). In addition, reliance on the extended order means less material strain is placed on intimate order relations, allowing for more authentic and voluntary relations at the intimate level (Bruni 2012, 109–110).

Thus, any attempt to transfer the rules of the intimate order, the realm within which our moral sympathy does extend, to the extended order, the realm beyond which the limits of our moral sympathy cannot be assumed to extend in a world of diverse agents, will sacrifice the gains from social cooperation under the division of labor. Isolationism, imperialism, and even cronyism and political nepotism can all be seen as attempts to operate in the extended order with the rules of the intimate order.

By understanding this perspective – that there is no Adam Smith problem – economists can realize the importance of the doux-commerce thesis. Economists are not strictly positing a world with strictly self-interested actors and no moral sympathy. In fact, we witness far more human cooperation than these sterile models can predict (Powell and Wilson 2008; Smith 1998). But we are also not positing a world where all human interactions can, or should, be assumed to be conducted via the moral sympathy of the exclusionary intimate order. Rather, a cosmopolitan society requires rules for the realm in which our moral sympathy extends, and rules for the realm beyond which our moral sympathy does not extend.[6] The Scottish Enlightenment thinkers realized that private property and the rule of law would engender social cooperation in the extended order, as the pursuit of profit and the avoidance of loss would encourage reputation, reciprocity, and civility.

Rather than attempting to religiously or legislatively extend – *impose* – our moral sympathy on others (a project that failed abysmally), the Scottish Enlightenment thinkers discovered a method more conducive to human nature for fostering social cooperation: market institutions that would harness our own self-interest towards socially productive ends. In a sense, market institutions could shore up many deficiencies in our moral sympathy when it comes to the extended order, fostering social cooperation under the division of labor in a world of strangers, allowing civil society to flourish. Thus, it is not Smith's moral system that has the proclivities to reach beyond one's own group, but Smith's economic system (Forman-Barzilai 2011, 182). Without the intergroup proclivities of commerce, communitarians find themselves advocating for an exclusionary ethic that only engenders suspicion and hostility (Bruni 2012, 48–49; Forman-Barzilai 2011, 194).

Furthermore, charity administered through a market context, rather than through a coerced regime, allows the emergence of civil society in charitable contexts. Rather than a uniform state-administered social safety net, charity becomes more localized and thus more capable of addressing the underlying causes of poverty rather than alleviating the physical symptoms through anonymous programs (Forman-Barzilai 2011, 155). Coerced charity eradicates both the intent of the giver, and thus the formation of sympathy, and the dignity of the receiver (Bruni 2012, 107–110; Grosby 2009, 2010; Olasky 1992; Salamon 2003). Whereas Marx and Rousseau would prevent disparities in wealth to address social maladies, this comes at the cost of capping prosperity across the board.

While there is much research left to do in order to fully understand the many manifestations and implications of the doux-commerce thesis of the

Scottish Enlightenment, hope can be seen in the growing body of research advancing our understanding of civil society and the doux-commerce thesis. It is research along these lines that is leading to the rediscovery of the doux-commerce thesis and bringing the profession to the realization that the doux-commerce thesis should be reincorporated into the corpus of economic research and firmly embedded in the project of robust political economy. In the end, our technical models, no matter how well calibrated, will fall short of convincing the general public about the social benefits of a free commercial society if they do not recognize the moralizing aspects of commercial relations.

## Conclusion

While the doux-commerce thesis was initially an important development in the recognition of the benefits of a commercial society, the acknowledged moralizing aspects of capitalism fell out of favor while the economic profession focused exclusively on technical efficiency. More recently, there has been resurgence of scholarship bringing back this important consideration of political economy. If the economics profession is to advance as a science that has practical relevance, it lies not in increasingly sophisticated articulations of efficiency arguments but in the recognition of the benefits of a commercial society, including the moralizing features of commerce.

Future scholarship exploring the relationship between commerce and civil society is necessary to fully articulate and reincorporate the doux-commerce thesis into political economy. Both theoretical and empirical work needs to be pursued to show the limits of technical articulations in capturing the civilizing effects of commerce and the benefits of expanding this model to bring this important phenomenon into the scholarly purview of economists.

## Acknowledgments

The authors would like to thank Lenore Ealy, Robert Garnett, and Paul Lewis for helpful comments. We thank Robin P. K. Aguiar-Hicks and Liya Palagashvili for valuable research assistance.

## Notes

1 See also Levine (2011, 68) and Robertson ([1933] 1973, 58). Though related, the dropping of the assumption that the self-interest of rulers would naturally align with the interest of the general public would wait until the advent of public-choice economics for more explicit formalization (Buchanan [1979] 1999; Mueller 1976), and the more explicit adoption of methodological individualism would wait until Schumpeter (1909), Hayek ([1952] 1979), and Weber (1949, [1956] 1978).

2 While David Hume, Adam Smith, and Adam Ferguson are widely recognized to be part of the Scottish Enlightenment, James Steuart (1767), John Millar ([1771] 2006), and James Maitland ([1804] 1967) are also part of this tradition.
3 The pursuit of ruthless efficiency in formal models also made economists susceptible to market socialism and market failure critiques (Pennington 2011, ch. 2).
4 Thorstein Veblen ([1899] 2009) also made similar arguments. More recently, Skidelsky and Skidelsky (2012) echo these criticisms.
5 This is not to say that these ideas were not developed or spread, but that they largely fell out of fashion among academic economists.
6 This is not to say that these separate realms are necessarily fixed. Each individual has the unique ability to decide the limits of their own moral sympathy. The project of Smith and Hume was to recognize this and realize a set of institutions for the extended order that would lead to social cooperation and prosperity. Over time, the realms of moral sympathy can, and have, expanded and shrunk. For example, the increase in economic prosperity since the Industrial Revolution has arguably decommodified the family as decisions such as marriage and childbearing are increasingly made based upon moral sympathy considerations rather than economic considerations.

## References

Allison, John. 2012. *The Financial Crisis and the Free Market Cure*. New York: McGraw-Hill.
Appiah, Kwame Anthony. 2006. *Cosmopolitanism: Ethics in A World of Strangers*. New York: W. W. Norton.
Axelrod, Robert. 1984. *The Evolution of Cooperation*. Cambridge, MA: Basic Books.
Bacon, Francis. 2008. *Francis Bacon: The Major Works*. Edited by Brian Vickers. New York: Oxford University Press.
Beito, David. 2000. *From Mutual Aid to Welfare State: Fraternal Societies and Social Services, 1890–1967*. Chapel Hill: The University of North Carolina Press.
Bell, Daniel. 1976. *The Cultural Contradictions of Capitalism*. New York: Basic Books.
Bicchieri, Cristina. 2006. *The Grammar of Society: The Nature and Dynamics of Social Norms*. New York: Cambridge University Press.
Boettke, Peter J. 2010. "Twentieth-Century Economic Methodology." In *21st Century Economics: A Reference Handbook*, edited by Rhona C. Free, 33–44. Thousand Oaks, CA: Sage.
Boettke, Peter J. 2012. *Living Economics: Yesterday, Today and Tomorrow*. Oakland, CA: The Independent Institute.
Boettke, Peter J. and Peter T. Leeson. 2004. "Liberalism, Socialism, and Robust Political Economy." *Journal of Markets and Morality* 7 (1): 99–111.
Boettke, Peter J., Alexander Fink, and Daniel J. Smith. 2012. "The Impact of Nobel Prize Winners in Economics." *American Journal of Economics and Sociology* 71 (5): 1219–1249.
Boettke, Peter J., Peter T. Leeson, and Daniel J. Smith. 2008. "The Evolution of Economics: Where We Are, and How We Got Here." *Long Term View Journal* 7 (1): 12–22.
Boettke, Peter J., Daniel J. Smith, and Nicholas A. Snow. 2011. "Been There Done That: The Political Economy of Déjà Vu, 1950 and 2010." In *The Global Financial*

Crisis: What Have We Learnt?, edited by Steven Kates. Northampton, MA: Edward Elgar.
Brooks, Arthur C. 2010. *The Battle: How the Fight Between Free Enterprise and Big Government Will Shape America's Future*. New York: Basic Books.
Brown, David W. 1995. *When Strangers Cooperate: Using Social Conventions to Govern Ourselves*. New York: The Free Press.
Bruni, Luigino. 2012. *The Genesis and Ethos of the Market*. New York: Palgrave Macmillan.
Buchanan, James M. 1964. "What Should Economists Do?" *Southern Economic Journal* 30 (1): 213–222.
Buchanan, James M. [1979] 1999. "Politics without Romance: A Sketch of Positive Public Choice Theory and Its Normative Implications." *The Logical Foundations of Constitutional Liberty*. Indianapolis, Liberty Fund.
Burgin, Angus. 2012. *The Great Persuasion: Reinventing Free Markets since the Great Depression*. Cambridge, MA: Harvard University Press.
Chafuen, Alejandro A. 2003. *Faith and Liberty: The Economic Thought of the Late Scholastics*. Lanham, MD: Lexington Books.
Cornuelle, Richard. 1965. *Reclaiming the American Dream*. New York: Random House.
Cornuelle, Richard. 1991. "New Work for Invisible Hands." *The Times Literary Supplement*, April 5.
Descartes, René. 2012. *Selections from the Principles of Philosophy*. Calgary and Alberta, Canada: Theophania Publishing.
Dworkin, Ronald. 2002. *Sovereign Virtue: The Theory and Practice of Equality*. Cambridge, MA: Harvard University Press.
Ealy, Lenore T. 2011. "Richard C. Cornuelle and the Revolution of Social Responsibility." *Society* 48 (6): 510–516.
Ealy, Steven D. 2011. "Civil Society and Philanthropy." *Conversations on Philanthropy* VIII: 39–46.
Epstein, Richard A. 2008. *Free Markets Under Siege*. Stanford, CA: Stanford University Press.
Forman-Barzilai, Fonna. 2011. *Adam Smith and the Circles of Sympathy*. New York: Cambridge University Press.
Garnett, Robert. 2011. "Cultivating *Conversations*." *Conversations on Philanthropy* VIII: 1–6.
Green, Robert W., ed. 1959. *Protestantism and Capitalism: The Weber Thesis and Its Critics*. Lexington, MA: D. C. Heath.
Grosby, Steven. 2009. "Philanthropy and Human Action." *Conversations on Philanthropy* VI: 1–14.
Grosby, Steven. 2010. "The Myth of the Man-Loving Prometheus: Reflections on Philanthropy, Forethought, and Religion." *Conversations on Philanthropy* VII: 11–24.
Hayek, F. A. [1944] 2007. *The Road to Serfdom*. Edited by Bruce Caldwell. Indianapolis, IN: Liberty Fund.
Hayek, F. A. 1945. "The Use of Knowledge in Society." *American Economic Review* 35 (4): 519–530.
Hayek, F. A. 1948. "Individualism: True and False." In *Individualism and Economic Order*. Chicago: University of Chicago Press.
Hayek, F. A. 1952. *The Counter Revolution of Science: Studies on the Abuse of Reason*. Indianapolis, IN: Liberty Fund.

Hayek, F. A. 1988. *The Fatal Conceit*. Chicago: The University of Chicago Press.
Henrich, Joseph, Robert Boyd, Samuel Bowles, Colin Camerer, Ernst Fehr, and Herbert Gintis. 2004. *Foundations of Human Sociality: Economic Experiments and Ethnographic Evidence from Fifteen Small-Scale Societies*. Oxford: Oxford University Press.
Henrich, Joseph, Robert Boyd, Samuel Bowles, Colin Camerer, Ernst Fehr, and Herbert Gintis. 2005. "'Economic Man' in Cross-Cultural Perspective: Behavioral Experiments in 15 Small-Scale Societies." *Behavioral and Brain Sciences* 28 (6): 795–855.
Hirsch, Fred. 2005. *Social Limits to Growth*. Cambridge, MA: Harvard University Press.
Hirschman, Albert. 1977. *The Passions and the Interests: Political Arguments for Capitalism before Its Triumph*. Princeton, NJ: Princeton University Press.
Hirschman, Albert. 1982. "Rival Interpretations of Market Society: Civilizing, Destructive, or Feeble?" *Journal of Economic Literature* 20 (4): 1463–1484.
Hirschman, Albert. 1986. *Rival Views of Market Society and Other Recent Essays*. New York: Viking Penguin.
Hobbes, Thomas. [1651] 1962. *Leviathan*. Edited by Michael Oakshott. New York: Simon & Schuster.
Hume, David. [1739] 1978. *A Treatise of Human Nature*. 2nd edn. Edited by L. A. Selby-Bigge and P. H. Nidditch. New York: Oxford University Press.
Hume, David. [1742] 1987. *Essays: Moral, Political, and Literary*. Edited by Eugene F. Miller. Indianapolis, IN: Liberty Fund.
Jacob, Margaret. 2006. *Strangers Nowhere in the World: The Rise of Cosmopolitanism in Early Modern Europe*. Philadelphia, PA: University of Pennsylvania Press.
Kreps, David. 1997. "Economics: The Current Position." *Daedalus* 126 (1): 59–85.
Leeson, Peter T. and J. Robert Subrick. 2006. "Robust Political Economy." *Review of Austrian Economics* 19 (2): 107–111.
Levine, Alan. 2011. "The Idea of Commerce in Enlightenment Political Thought." In *Rediscovering Political Economy*, edited by Joseph Postell and Bradley C. S. Watson, 53–82. Lanham, MD: Lexington Books.
Locke, John. [1690] 1980. *Second Treatise of Government*. Edited by C. B. Macpherson. Indianapolis, IN: Hackett.
McCloskey, Deirdre. 2006. *The Bourgeois Virtues: Ethics for an Age of Commerce*. Chicago: University of Chicago Press.
McCloskey, Deirdre. 2010. *Bourgeois Dignity: Why Economics Can't Explain the Modern World*. Chicago: University of Chicago Press.
Machiavelli, Niccolo. [1532] 1995. *The Prince*. Edited by David Wootton. Indianapolis, IN: Hackett.
Maitland, James. [1804] 1967. *Inquiry into the Nature and Origin of Public Wealth*. New York: Augustus M. Kelley.
Mandeville, Bernard. [1791] 1988. *The Fable of the Bees: Or Private Vices, Publick Benefits*. Indianapolis, IN: Liberty Fund.
Marx, Karl. 1978. *The Marx-Engels Reader*. 2nd edn. Edited by Robert C. Tucker. New York: W. W. Norton.
Millar, John. [1771] 2006. *The Origin of the Distinction of Ranks; or, An Inquiry into the Circumstances which give rise to Influence and Authority in the Different Members of Society*. Edited by Aaron Garrett. Indianapolis, IN: Liberty Fund.
Mises, Ludwig von. [1949] 2007. *Human Action: A Treatise on Economics*. Indianapolis, IN: Liberty Fund.

Montaigne, Michel De. [1580] 2003. *The Complete Essays*. New York: Penguin.
Montesquieu, Charles Louis de Secondat, Baron de. [1748] 2009. *The Spirit of the Laws* Edited by Anne M. Cohler, Basia C. Miller, and Harold S. Stone. New York: Cambridge University Press.
Mueller, Dennis. 1976. "Public Choice: A Survey." *Journal of Economic Literature* 14 (2): 369–433.
Nelson, Robert H. 2001. *Economics as Religion from Samuelson to Chicago and Beyond*. University Park: The Pennsylvania State University.
Olasky, Marvin. 1992. *The Tragedy of American Compassion*. Wheaton, IL: Crossway Books.
Paganelli, Maria Pia. 2008. "The Adam Smith Problem in Reverse: Self-Interest in *The Wealth of Nations* and *The Theory of Moral Sentiments*." *History of Political Economy* 40 (2): 365–382.
Paine, Thomas. [1791] 2013. *Thomas Paine – Collected Writings*. CreateSpace Independent Publishing Platform.
Passmore, John. [1970] 2000. *The Perfectibility of Man*. 3rd edn. Indianapolis, IN: Liberty Fund.
Pennington, Mark. 2011. *Robust Political Economy: Classical Liberalism and the Future of Public Policy*. Northampton, MA: Edward Elgar.
Plato. 1985. *The Republic*. Translated by Richard W. Sterling and William C. Scott. New York: W.W. Norton.
Powell, Benjamin and Bart J. Wilson. 2008. "An Experimental Investigation of Hobbesian Jungles." *Journal of Economic Behavior & Organization* 66 (3–4): 669–686.
Rawls, John. 1971. *A Theory of Justice*. Cambridge, MA: The Belknap Press of Harvard University Press.
Ridley, Matt. 1996. *The Origins of Virtue: Human Instincts and the Evolution of Cooperation*. New York: Penguin.
Ridley, Matt. 2010. *The Rational Optimist: How Prosperity Evolves*. New York: HarperCollins.
Roberts, Paul Craig. 1990. *Alienation and the Soviet Economy: The Collapse of the Socialist Era*. New York: Homes & Meier.
Robertson, H. M. [1933] 1973. *Aspects of the Rise of Economic Individualism: A Criticism of Max Weber and His School*. Clifton, NJ: Augustus M. Kelley.
Rothbard, Murray. 1995. *Economic Thought before Adam Smith: An Austrian Perspective on the History of Economic Thought*, vol. I. Brookfield, VT: Edward Elgar.
Rousseau, Jean-Jacques. [1762] 1978. *On the Social Contract with Geneva Manuscript and Political Economy*. Edited by Roger D. Masters. Translated by Judith R. Masters. Boston, MA: Bedford/St. Martin's.
Rousseau, Jean-Jacques. [1750] 1964. *The First and Second Discourses*. Edited by Roger D. Masters. Translated by Judith R. Masters. Boston, MA: Bedford/St. Martin's.
Salamon, Julie. 2003. *Rambam's Ladder: A Meditation on Generosity and Why It Is Necessary to Give*. New York: Workman.
Sandel, Michael J. 2012. *What Money Can't Buy: The Moral Limits of Markets*. New York: Farrar, Straus and Giroux.
Schumpeter, Joseph. 1909. "On the Concept of Social Value." *The Quarterly Journal of Economics* 23 (2): 213–232.

Schumpeter, Joseph. 2008. *Capitalism, Socialism and Democracy*. New York: HarperCollins.
Seabright, Paul. 2004. *The Company of Strangers: A Natural History of Economic Life*. Princeton, NJ: Princeton University Press.
Sirico, Robert. 2011. "The Moral Basis for Economic Liberty." In *Rediscovering Political Economy*, edited by Joseph Postell and Bradley C. S. Watson. Lanham, MD: Lexington Books.
Skidelsky, Robert and Edward Skidelsky. 2012. *How Much is Enough? Money and the Good Life*. New York: Other Press.
Smith, Adam. [1759] 1976. *The Theory of Moral Sentiments*. Edited by D. D. Raphael and A. L. Macfie. Indianapolis, IN: Liberty Fund.
Smith, Adam. [1762] 1982. *Lectures on Justice*. Edited by R. L. Meek, D. D. Raphael, and P. G. Stein. Indianapolis, IN: Liberty Fund.
Smith, Adam. [1776] 1976. *An Inquiry into the Nature and Causes of the Wealth of Nations*. Edited by R. H. Campbell and A. S. Skinner. Indianapolis, IN: Liberty Fund.
Smith, Vernon. 1998. "The Two Faces of Adam Smith." *Southern Economic Journal* 65 (1): 2–19.
Stark, Rodney. 2005. *The Victory of Reason: How Christianity Led to Freedom, Capitalism, and Western Success*. New York: Random House.
Storr, Virgil. 2008. "The Market as a Social Space: On the Meaningful Extra-Economic Conversations That Can Occur in Markets." *Review of Austrian Economics* 21 (2&3): 135–150.
Steuart, James. 1767. *Inquiry into the Principles of Political Economy*. Dublin: Skinner-Row and Caple-Street.
Tawney, R. H. [1926] 1954. *Religion and the Rise of Capitalism*. New York: The New American Library.
Taylor, Charles. 1985. *Philosophy and the Human Sciences*. New York: Cambridge University Press.
Taylor, Michael. 1987. *The Possibility of Cooperation*. New York: Cambridge University Press.
van de Haar, Edwin. 2009. *Classical Liberalism and International Relations Theory: Hume, Smith, Mises, and Hayek*. New York: Palgrave Macmillan.
Veblen, Thorstein. [1899] 2009. *Theory of the Leisure Class*. New York: Oxford University Press.
Voltaire, Francois-Marie Arouet. [1733] 2003. *Philosophical Letters*. Mineola, NY: Dover Publications.
Weber, Max. [1930] 1956. *The Protestant Ethic and the Spirit of Capitalism*. Translated by Talcott Parsons. New York: Charles Scribner's Sons.
Weber, Max. 1949. *The Methodology of the Social Sciences*. Edited and translated by Edward A. Shils and Henry A. Finch. Glencoe, IL: The Free Press.
Weber, Max. [1956] 1978. *Economy and Society*. Berkeley and Los Angeles, CA: University of California Press.
Williamson, Claudia. 2010. "Civilizing Society." *Journal of Private Enterprise* 27 (1): 99–120.
Young, Iris. 2002. *Inclusion and Democracy*. New York: Oxford University Press.

# 3 Commerce and beneficence
## Adam Smith's unfinished project

*Robert F. Garnett, Jr.*

**Introduction**

Adam Smith says the modern individual "stands at all times in need of the cooperation and assistance of great multitudes" ([1776] 1981, 26). In this evocative phrase, Smith poses a defining problem of modern political economy, namely: how and from whom individuals might obtain the extensive cooperation and assistance they require. Or, conversely, how might the common individual be "induced, by his own choice and from the motives which [determine] his ordinary conduct, to contribute as much as possible to the need of all others" (Hayek [1945] 1948, 12–13)?

For Friedrich Hayek and many classical liberal economists, the singular answer to these questions – the Smithian answer, in their view – is commercial specialization and trade (Hayek [1976] 1978; Friedman 1962; Coase 1976; Heyne [1982] 2008; Boettke 2012). The butcher, baker, and brewer might provide us with our dinner "from their benevolence only" if they happened to be our sons or brothers but we cannot expect such generosity from strangers (Smith [1776] 1981, 26). "The great advantage of the market," Ronald Coase (1976, 544) explains, "is that it is able to use the strength of self-interest to offset the weakness and partiality of benevolence, so that those who are unknown, unattractive, or unimportant will have their wants served."

This familiar apologia for commerce is based on an epistemic-cum-ethical division of social relations into two distinct spheres:

| *Intimate order* | *Extended order* |
|---|---|
| known persons | unknown persons |
| community | commerce |
| taxis | cosmos |
| benevolence | self-interest |
| solidarity | competition |
| concrete needs | abstract rules |
| personal | impersonal |

Effective aid to strangers is assumed to require on-the-ground knowledge that is difficult if not impossible to attain, whereas market processes enable individuals to overcome their ignorance of others' needs by leveraging the social knowledge embedded in price and profit signals, hence to be "led by the invisible hand of the market to bring the succor of modern conveniences to the poorest homes [they do] not even know" (Hayek [1976] 1978, 145). Hayek advises persons committed to finding "a proper cure for misfortunes about which we are understandably concerned" (1988, 13) to "[withhold] from the known needy neighbors what they might require in order to serve the unknown needs of thousands of others" (1978, 268) since the latter "[confers] benefits beyond the range of our concrete knowledge" and provides "a greater benefit to the community than most direct 'altruistic' action" (1988, 81 and 19).

Hayek, Coase, Boettke, and others ascribe this "two worlds" ontology to Smith himself. They interpret his *Wealth of Nations* (*WN*) as a discourse on impersonal commercial cooperation and *The Theory of Moral Sentiments* (*TMS*) as a treatise on cooperation within families and other face-to-face communities where "members know one another well" and can "reasonably be expected to take [others'] specific interests and values into account" (Heyne [1993] 2008, 6). Jacob Viner (1972, 82), in his venerable synopsis of *WN*, affirms this dichotomous view of Smith's moral philosophy: "In his economic analysis, Smith operates from the categorical premise that economic relations between men are in effect fundamentally impersonal, anonymous, infinitely 'distant,' so that the sentiments, with one exception of 'justice,' remain dormant."

My goal in this essay is to build a prima facie case for recasting Smith as a thoroughgoing critic of the "two worlds" vision of commercial society. Smith himself provides no integrated *TMS*-and-*WN* theory of commercial society; he "forces the reader to do the labor of unification" (Griswold 1999, 30). Yet by taking seriously the standpoint of contemporary interpreters who regard *TMS* as the philosophical center of Smith's thought (Macfie 1967, 75–76) and Smith's own view of *TMS* as a "much superior work to [the] *Wealth of Nations*" (Klein 2012, 243, citing Romily 1840, 404), we can see in his two great works an appreciation of commercial and noncommercial (sympathy-seeking) exchange as engines of human flourishing, and a nascent view of commercial society itself as an institutionally heterogeneous web of "voluntary collaboration" (Hayek [1945] 1948, 23).

## Commerce and *beneficence*?

The virtue of beneficence plays a crucial role in Smith's theory of noncommercial cooperation. Smith defines beneficence as a virtue that "prompts us to promote [the] happiness of others" ([1790] 1984, 262) by providing care and attention in excess of that required by ordinary prudence or justice. Yet beneficence is not selfless altruism. Like all virtues, it entails a judicious balance between care of self and care for others (304). Smith also (106) associates beneficence with the performance of meritorious "good offices," in contrast to benevolence, which requires only "good intentions" (Hanley 2009, 183). Further, Smithian beneficence is not condescending but is "marked by the benefactor's commitment to the moral equality and dignity he shares with other human beings" (Hanley 2009, 204 and 208). In all, Smith assigns two related but distinct meanings to beneficence: as a form of human action and as a virtue possessed by human actors. Beneficence is the performance of good offices that achieve praiseworthy results (a desired "end") and the acquired habit (a "means") of performing such actions.

Smith ascribes multiple motives to beneficent action, including fulfillment of social norms and identities, perceived influence over others' well-being, reciprocal gratitude, and in all cases a desire for the eudaimonic happiness of being "beloved and [knowing] that we deserve to be beloved" ([1790] 1984, 113). The richness of his analysis (especially in *TMS* Book VI) opens the door to understanding the diverse moral attachments that arise among non-kin and the emergent nature of the order in which individuals are recommended to our care and attention (Lewis 2011).

To begin to see how beneficence and commerce might be theorized as complementary forms of social cooperation, consider these working definitions:

- *Social cooperation* refers to value-generating (mutually beneficial, positive-sum) transactions that increase the wealth or well-being of a human community.
- *Commerce* refers to acts of social cooperation that meet but do not exceed the requirements of justice and ordinary prudence – acts performed "as among different merchants, from a sense of [their] utility, without any mutual love or affection ... a mercenary exchange of good offices according to an agreed valuation" (Smith [1790] 1984, 86).
- *Beneficence* refers to acts of social cooperation whose generosity exceeds what justice and ordinary prudence would require, wherein cooperation and assistance are "reciprocally afforded from love, from gratitude, from friendship, and esteem" (Smith [1790] 1984, 85).

Note that beneficence is defined not as pure love but as value creation by noncommercial means. And though conceptually distinct, beneficence and commerce are not assumed to exist as pure types. Just as multiple virtues are generally present in every form of human action (McCloskey 2006, 352–360), commerce and beneficence are assumed to be present in most forms of social cooperation.

Generations of economists, philosophers, and social theorists have recognized the important role of noncommercial benefaction in the social provisioning process (Boulding [1965] 1974). Champions of noncommercial value creation today speak in terms of philanthropy (Arrillaga-

Andreessen 2011; Bishop and Green 2010) and social entrepreneurship (Bornstein 2007), broadly defined as "giving anything – time, money, experience, skills, or networks – in any amount to create a better world" (Arrillaga-Andreessen 2011, 1). Analogous notions can be found across the sciences and humanities, where noncommercial goods have been analyzed as *public goods* (Samuelson 1954; Buchanan 1968), *commons* (Ostrom 1990; Lohmann 1992), *gift* (Godbout 1998; Vandevelde 2000), *care* (Held 2005; Nelson and England 2002; van Staveren 2005), *interpersonal relations* (Gui and Sugden 2005), *peer-to-peer collaboration* (Benkler 2006; Lessig 2008), *reciprocity* (Bruni 2008; Kolm 2008; Gintis *et al.* 2005; Bowles and Gintis 2011), and *social capital* (Chamlee-Wright 2010; Lewis and Chamlee-Wright 2008). Also noteworthy are the pioneering works of Kenneth Boulding and Richard Cornuelle, which illuminated the noncommercial dimensions of civil society through their coinage of the terms *integrative sector* (Boulding 1968) and *independent sector* (Cornuelle [1965] 1993).

---

*Volunteer labor*

- Thousands of ongoing projects such as adult language education or Habitat for Humanity

*Mutual aid*

- Favors given and received by neighbors or by members of organizations and groups
- Favors done for strangers qua serial reciprocity such as "pay it forward" or disaster relief

*Constitutional citizenship: renegotiating social rules and norms* (Buchanan 1991)

- ONE: international campaign to increase awareness of extreme poverty and preventable disease, particularly in Africa
- Alice Seeley Harris: English missionary whose arresting photographs of Belgian torture of Congolese slaves in 1905 hastened the ouster of King Leopold II (Grant 2001)

*Valuable intangibles given to others, near and far*

- Regard (Offer 1997)
- Dignity (McCloskey 2010)

*Professionalism: going above and beyond for clients and colleagues*

- Heroic cases such as transnational collaboration among eleven research labs in 2003, leading to the rapid isolation of the SARS virus (Fulton and Blau 2005)

---

*Figure 3.1* Contemporary examples of noncommercial value creation (including commercial/noncommercial hybrids)

- The quiet heroism of nurses, doctors, teachers, therapists, child- and elder-care providers who treat their clients (and client's family members) with the same loving care and attention they give to their own loved ones

*Social enterprises*

- B-corps and other stakeholder-centered business models
- Worker-owned firms and coops

*Micro-philanthropy*

- Philanthropic marketplaces, accessible to individuals of all means, ages, and locations via forums like Kiva or DonorsChoose, where rival projects compete for donors' support, mission-specific platforms like stoptb.org, and crowd-funding sites like Kickstarter

*Digital collaboration*

- Knowledge provided by open-source software authors, bloggers, Wikipedia contributors, product reviewers, crowdsourcing responders, and YouTube do-it-yourselfers
- Computational resources pooled via distributed computing projects such as SETI@home

*Figure 3.1 (cont.)*

How does Adam Smith's work contribute to these conversations? Smith famously describes beneficence as "less essential to the existence of society than justice," "the ornament which embellishes, not the foundation which supports the building" ([1790] 1984, 86). Two paragraphs earlier, however, Smith casts the justice/beneficence relationship in a very different light, juxtaposing two kinds of society: (1) a "mercenary society," propelled by justice and prudence only, with "no mutual love and affection" among the different members, yielding a society that is "less happy and agreeable" but "will not necessarily be dissolved"; and (2) a "flourishing and happy society," "[w]here the necessary assistance is reciprocally afforded from love, from gratitude, from friendship, and esteem" (85).

Smith posits here a spectrum of societies, from "prudence and justice only" to "beneficence only." His focus is not on the polar extremes but on the golden mean – commerce and beneficence not as alternatives but as complements. Parallel to his discussion of ordinary and superior prudence ([1790] 1984, 216), Smith's point is that beneficence is an essential element in more civilized forms of commercial society. Indeed, he makes beneficence the line of demarcation separating "flourishing and happy" commercial societies from those that merely "subsist" based on the "mercenary exchange of good offices" (85–86). Justice is a necessary condition for any society; but once a society crosses this subsistence threshold, people generally seek and achieve higher levels of flourishing and happiness.

The complex fusion of mercenary and beneficent modes of cooperation – the motivational and institutional pluralism – implicit in Smith's vision of the flourishing and happy society is supported by two other pillars of his theory. One is his definition of commercial society as a society in which "every man ... lives by exchanging" ([1776] 1981, 37) and the related claim that our human propensity to "truck, barter, and exchange" derives from our "faculties of reason and speech" (25). Across *TMS* and *WN*, Smith develops a rich, multifaceted analysis of exchange, including sympathetic exchange, as a social process that emerges from and also cultivates our human capacity to "treat strangers as though they were honorary relatives or friends" (Seabright 2004, 34).

A second pillar is Smith's notion of a "common centre of mutual good offices" ([1790] 1984, 85), a banking metaphor he employs in *TMS* and *WN* to describe the fruits of complex collaboration. In his *WN* account of the common stock of mutual assistance generated by networks of specialization and trade, Smith writes:

> As it is by treaty, by barter, and by purchase, that we obtain from one another the greater part of those mutual good offices which we stand in need of, so it is this same trucking disposition which originally gives occasion to the division of labour ... The most dissimilar geniuses are of use to one another; the different produces of their respective talents, by the general disposition to truck, barter, and exchange, being brought, as it were, into a common stock, where every man may purchase whatever part of the produce of other men's talents he has occasion for.
>
> ([1776] 1981, 27, 30)

Similarly, in *TMS* he describes the societal fund of mutual aid afforded from love, gratitude, friendship, and esteem as a "common centre of mutual good offices" ([1790] 1984, 85). These parallel statements, designating "mutual good offices" as Smith's general concept of value or wealth, provide an analytic bridge linking his discussions of commercial and noncommercial exchange and highlighting a common premise of *TMS* and *WN*, that without "the power or disposition to barter and exchange" (broadly understood), the diverse goals, ideas, and labors of individuals "cannot be brought into a common stock, and do not in the least contribute to the better accommodation and conveniency of the species" ([1776] 1981, 30).

On this interpretation, Smith provides the conceptual architecture for a "humanomic" reconstruction of political economy (McCloskey 2011) in which the extended order of human cooperation is inextricably commercial and noncommercial. Commercial society is one world, one great web of benefaction ("one common centre of mutual good offices"), generated by one integrative complex of commercial and noncommercial exchange.

## Social cooperation in *TMS*

The object of Smith's *TMS* is extensive noncommercial cooperation generated though sympathy-based exchange and the ongoing (re)formation of social rules. As in *WN*, Smith's analysis is framed by the general problem of all-around interdependence, the fact that "[a]ll the members of human society stand in need of each others assistance" ([1790] 1984, 85), with the added stipulation that humans face a fundamental knowledge problem in their efforts to understand and assist one another. Our senses cannot "carry us beyond our own person," Smith argues; hence "we have no immediate experience of what other men feel" (9).

The key to overcoming our epistemic isolation and the conceptual cornerstone of Smith's moral theory is sympathy. Smith defines sympathy not as pity or sorrow but "fellow-feeling with any passion whatever" ([1790] 1984, 10). It is, above all, *fellow*-feeling, a sense of identification and equality (my fellow, my equal) with others. Smith stresses that sympathy is not merely a passive feeling or imitative reflex. To sympathize is to render an affirmative judgment on the propriety or the merits of the motives and conduct we observe in others and in ourselves. To render these various judgments, we must perform an "imaginary change of situation," to imagine "what we ourselves should feel in the like situation" (21 and 9).

Smith insists that the capacity for sympathy is not confined to "the virtuous and humane" but is present and ripe for cultivation in all human beings ([1790] 1984, 9). He likewise assumes that all persons are capable of obtaining the sympathy or approbation they desire from others. Acquiring sympathy is not automatic either. Since sympathy requires another person's positive judgment of our case, and since our individual lifeworlds are idiosyncratic and private, sympathy must be negotiated. We must persuade others that our case warrants their sympathy.

Sympathetic exchange between actor (demander) and spectator (supplier) is thus a process of persuasion and compromise. If the demander is unable to obtain the sympathy she seeks, she can modify the terms of her proposal until she and the spectator strike a mutually agreeable "concord" ([1790] 1984, 22). This exchange process generates knowledge and value ("mutual good offices") for both parties. Just as the spectator must exercise his sympathetic imagination in order judge the actor's case, the actor too must try to imagine how her situation will appear to the spectator (21–22). In so doing, both parties gain valuable knowledge of self and others and enhanced capacities for obtaining and providing sympathy in other situations.

Smith's discussion of bilateral exchange between actor and spectator sets the stage for the main event in *TMS*: the shift from this person-to-person mode of sympathetic exchange to an impersonal mode in which the spectator is no longer a 'partial' spectator but a neutral, well-informed third party, an "impartial spectator" ([1790] 1984, 24). The impartial spectator serves as a social mirror to the actor. In response to the actor's tacit bids for sympathy, the impartial spectator issues positive and negative feedback in accord with evolved social rules and norms, enabling the actor to "[view] himself in the light in which he is conscious that others will view him" and encouraging him to "humble the arrogance of his self-love, and bring it down to something which other men can go along with" ([1790] 1984, 83).

In short, *pace* Otteson (2002), we find a deep congruence between the impartial spectator of *TMS* and the commercial market of *WN* as engines of social learning. The impartial spectator plays a coordinating role, nudging each individual toward mutually beneficial compromises between their interests and the interests of others ([1790] 1984, 134). General rules and norms of propriety and merit tell actors which motives and forms of conduct are valued and how much. The impartial spectator communicates these socio-cultural "price structures," telling individuals how the world at large is likely to judge them. In this way, Smith's *TMS* shows how evolved rules and norms serve as knowledge surrogates in a manner analogous to market prices, providing valuable feedback that enables us to cooperate more effectively with others, even without detailed knowledge of others' needs and difficulties.

Like market prices, social rules and norms are subject to ceaseless pressures for change. As Otteson explains (2002, 101–133), Smith conceives the relationship between actors and impartial spectators as a two-way conversation. Working from the premise that each individual is free to judge the prevailing rules of his or her society, Smith argues that "general rules of morality … are ultimately founded upon experience of what, in particular instances, our moral faculties, our natural sense of merit and propriety, approve, or disapprove of" ([1790] 1984, 159). Based on our "continual observations upon the conduct of others," we "form to ourselves certain general rules concerning what is fit and proper either to be done or to be avoided" (159). Social rules emerge and evolve from these case-by-case assessments, becoming operative "standards of judgment" (160). Implicit in Smith's theory is the important role of constitutional entrepreneurs who perceive gaps or inconsistencies in the prevailing value structure and respond by introducing new or revised rules, fueling competition over social rules and thus providing a civilizing check on inhumane customs and traditions.

## Beneficence unbound

A key premise of the Hayek–Coase interpretation of *TMS* and *WN* is that Smith embraced the Stoic view of the human condition according to which "human affection and care are ordered spatially around the self in a concentric pattern" (Forman-Barzilai 2011, 8). Smith seems to affirm this view in the memorable opening paragraph of *TMS* VI ([1790] 1984, 219):

> Every man, as the Stoics used to say, is first and principally recommended to his own care ... After himself, the members of his own family, those who usually live in the same house with him, his parents, his children, his brothers and sisters, are naturally the objects of his warmest affections. They are naturally and usually the persons upon whose happiness or misery his conduct must have the greatest influence. He is more habituated to sympathize with them. He knows better how everything is likely to affect them, and his sympathy with them is more precise and determinate, than it can be with the greater part of other people.

Yet after granting this stylized fact as a starting point for his Book VI discussion of the virtues, Smith proceeds to undercut and deviate from the Stoic anthropology in numerous ways, particularly in his discussion of beneficence. Smith's appropriation of the Stoic concentric circles premise is thus undoubtedly, as Forman-Barzilai (2011, 8) argues, "conflicted and incomplete."

The crucial question becomes: What is the spatial/ethical range of Smithian sympathy? Does it extend beyond the intimate order? Can it enable ordinary persons to render effective help to distant others? Smith addresses these issues in his well-known "Empire of China" parable. The story unfolds in three parts. Smith initially frames the issue as follows:

> Let us suppose that the great empire of China, with all its myriads of inhabitants, was suddenly swallowed up by an earthquake, and let us consider how a man of humanity in Europe, who had no sort of connexion with that part of the world, would be affected upon receiving intelligence of this dreadful calamity.
>
> ([1790] 1984, 136)

Smith asserts that in the absence of any "connection with that part of the world," the man of humanity would feel only fleeting sympathy for the disaster victims:

> [W]hen all [his] humane sentiments had been once fairly expressed, he would pursue his business or his pleasure, take his repose or his diversion, with the same ease and tranquility, as if no such accident had happened. The most frivolous disaster which could befal [sic] himself would occasion a more real disturbance. If he was to lose his little finger tomorrow, he would not sleep tonight; but, *provided he never saw them*, he will snore with the most profound security over the

ruin of a hundred millions of his brethren, and the destruction of that immense multitude seems plainly an object less interesting to him, than this paltry misfortune of his own.

(Ibid., 136–137, emphasis added)

Some commentators, presupposing the "concentric circles" view of Smith's moral theory, reduce the entirety of Smith's argument to this initial stage (Singer 2009, 50). But the parable's main lessons only emerge after Smith asks a second question: "To prevent, therefore, this paltry misfortune to himself, would a man of humanity be willing to sacrifice the lives of a hundred millions of his brethren, provided he had never seen them?" Smith answers "no," but then poses his ultimate question:

> [W]hat makes this difference? When our passive feelings are almost always so sordid and so selfish, how comes it that our active principles should often be so generous and so noble? When we are always so much more deeply affected by whatever concerns ourselves, than by whatever concerns other men; what is it which prompts the generous, upon all occasions, and the mean upon many, to sacrifice their own interests to the greater interests of others?

It is not "that feeble spark of benevolence which Nature has lighted up in the human heart," Smith argues. Rather, it is the voice and authority of the impartial spectator.

> It is reason, principle, conscience, the inhabitant of the breast, the man within, the great judge and arbiter of our conduct … he who, whenever we are about to act so as to affect the happiness of others, calls to us, with a voice capable of astonishing the most presumptuous of our passions, that we are but one of the multitude, in no respect better than any other in it; and that when we prefer ourselves so shamefully and so blindly to others, we become the proper objects of resentment, abhorrence, and execration … It is he who shows us the propriety of generosity and the deformity of injustice; the propriety of resigning the greatest interests of our own, for the yet greater interests of others, and the deformity of doing the smallest injury to another, in order to obtain the greatest benefit to ourselves.

Resisting once more the spurious equation of conscience with benevolence, Smith concludes:

> [U]pon many occasions … [what] prompts us to the practice of those divine virtues is not the love of our neighbor, it is not the love of mankind … It is a stronger love, a more powerful affection, which generally takes place upon such occasions; the love of what is honourable

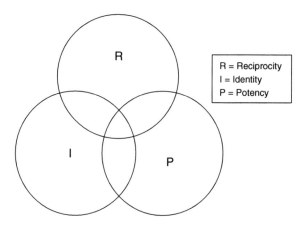

*Figure 3.2* Engines of extended sympathy

and noble, of the grandeur, and dignity, and superiority of our own characters.

([1790] 1984, 137)

This parable captures, in microcosm, the logic of Smith's theory of sympathy, virtue, and care. All four cardinal virtues (prudence, beneficence, justice, and self-command) are in play; and Smith affirms his general premise that all persons, not just "men of extraordinary magnanimity and virtue," possess the full suite of virtues ([1790] 1984, 138). The central lesson, however, is that the actor's sense of duty – inspired by "the propriety of generosity" (beneficence) and "the deformity of injustice" (justice) and rendered active by his self-command – is triggered by the man's awareness of his influence over the welfare of the distant Chinese. Initially he was powerless to prevent or ameliorate their suffering. But once in a position "to affect the happiness of others," his conscience and dignity compel him to sacrifice his little finger (137–138). A secondary lesson lies in Smith's claim that the man's sacrifice is motivated more by the "superiority of his own character" than by any real empathy or concern. The ethical shallowness of the actor's response reflects the premises of Smith's parable, namely: (1) "he never saw them" and (2) he had "no connection to that part of world," hence no reservoir of gratitude or fellow-feeling for the imperiled strangers; hence (3) the man's *only* connection to them is his supposed ability to prevent the disaster by sacrificing his finger.

Together, the Empire of China story and Smith's discussion of the virtues in *TMS* VI provide the elements for a robust theory of "extended sympathy" beyond the intimate order. As described in Figure 3.2, Smith posits three overlapping sets of circumstances that singly or in combination activate a person's conscience or sense of duty, signaling a change of circumstances and urging the individual to reassess and possibly reallocate their "limited powers of beneficence."

## Potency

In contrast to the ethical atomism of the neoclassical "perfect competition" model that many undergraduate textbooks identify as Smith's invisible hand theory (Milgate 2009), Smith assumes that actors are conscious of their influence – their causal potency – over others' well-being within certain domains. He further assumes that our beneficent inclinations are generally "stronger or weaker in proportion as our beneficence is more or less necessary, or can be more or less useful" ([1790] 1984, 218). Hence, other factors being equal, we are inclined to give more in situations where we discover ways to make a positive difference in the lives of others.

## Reciprocity

Smith highlights our ingrained human propensity to extend beneficence to persons "whose beneficence we have ourselves already experienced" and the multiple ways in which this reciprocating impulse is reinforced by the intrinsic rewards of conscience ("the sympathetic gratitude of the impartial spectator") and the extrinsic recompense of others.

> No benevolent man ever lost altogether the fruits of his benevolence. If he does not always gather them from the persons from whom he ought to have gathered them, he seldom fails to gather them, and with a tenfold increase, from other people.
> ([1790] 1984, 225)

Smith's notion of reciprocity also encompasses a broader logic of tit-for-tat retaliation:

> As every man doth, so shall it be done to him, and retaliation seems to be the great law which is dictated to us by Nature. Beneficence and generosity we think due to the generous and beneficent. Those whose hearts never open to the feelings of humanity, should, we think, be shut out, in the same manner, from the affections of all their fellow-creatures, and be allowed to live in the midst of society, as in a great desert where there is nobody to care for them, or to inquire after them.
> ([1790] 1984, 82)

## Identity

Smith designates two categories of person recommended to our beneficence by a sympathy-based identification or fellow-feeling. One is persons "distinguished by their extraordinary situation; the greatly fortunate and the greatly unfortunate, the rich and the powerful, the poor and the wretched" ([1790] 1984, 225). The other is defined broadly as persons "who most resemble ourselves" ([1762–3] 1982, 184), with whom we share a common identity as members of particular groups. Smith cites "colleagues in the office," "partners in trade," "neighbours," and persons "to whom we attach ourselves [as] the natural and proper objects of esteem and approbation" ([1790] 1984, 224–225). However, the general category of persons "who most resemble ourselves" would also include persons recommended to us by shared bonds of culture, ethnicity, race, nationality, ideology, gender, class, or other forms of affinity through which we come to regard fellow members as part of "us." Smith assumes that our shared sense of community or belonging will inspire added degrees of sympathy for these persons. The shared identity and added sympathy serve as a knowledge surrogate, a means of imagining the lives of our fellows. In this sense "[a] common identity can substitute for face-to-face relations" (Offer 1997, 468).

## Competing claims on our limited beneficence

Smith acknowledges the endless ethical dilemmas inherent in these multiple objects of sympathy and beneficence, but claims "[w]e shall stand in need of no casuistic rules to direct our conduct" as we negotiate these competing claims. When such conflicts arise, individuals are capable of resolving them by exercising their own ethical judgment:

> When those different beneficent affections happen to draw different ways, to determine by any precise rules in what cases we ought to comply with the one, and in what with the other, is, perhaps, altogether impossible ... [and] must be left altogether to the decision of the man within the breast, the supposed impartial spectator, the great judge and arbiter of our conduct. If we place ourselves completely in his situation, if we really view ourselves with his eyes, and as he views us, and listen with diligent and reverential attention to what he suggests to us, his voice will never deceive us.
> 
> ([1790] 1984, 227)

## Eccentric, not concentric

Smith upholds the Burkean view that our active duties must not exceed "our very limited powers of beneficence" (Smith [1790] 1984, 218). Yet by emphasizing the multiple avenues by which persons about whom we know relatively little are "called ... to our benevolent attention and good offices" (225), he casts ethical proximity as an emergent property of human interaction, a result whose characteristics cannot be deduced from properties of its constituent elements (Lewis 2011). Borrowing James Buchanan's powerful phrase, Smith suggests that the order in which individuals are "recommended to our beneficence" is not a predetermined order based on blood ties or geographic proximity but "an order defined in the process of its emergence" (Buchanan 1982), shaped by the shifting interests, associations, and judgments that constitute our "natural affections" and moral imaginations.

Smith's analysis thus conforms less to a "concentric circles" view of sympathy and beneficence and more to an image of what William Connolly (2002) calls "eccentric" connections: "'cross-cutting allegiances' that 'exceed,' 'complicate' and often 'compromise' the concentric connections of place that governed in the ages when people lived slow, local lives" (Forman-Barzilai 2011, 5–6). By describing Smith as an "eccentric circles" theorist, I do not mean to suggest that he sees ethical geographies as random or ever-more-cosmopolitan. Clearly, Smith believes that important differences generally exist between the types and intensities of care people are willing and able to provide for distant and intimate others. What Smith invites is a more fine-grained, social-scientific analysis of "distance" and "proximity," to examine the variable forms of cooperation and assistance that emerge from connections animated by reciprocity, identity, or causal potency ("when the happiness or misery of others depends in any respect upon our conduct" [Smith (1790) 1984, 137–138]).

## The strength of weak duties

Smith never lost sight of our "very limited powers of beneficence" ([1790] 1984, 218) or the destructive potential of the factional dynamics engendered by the human thirst for sympathy (Levy and Peart 2009a, 2009b). Persons in the heat of coalitional battle lose touch with their better judgment as factions become echo chambers, cut off from the critical give-and-take of competing perspectives and depriving actors of impartial feedback on the (im)propriety or (in)justice of their thoughts and actions. Smith also emphasizes our human propensity to lionize superiors and denigrate those of inferior rank (Hanley 2009, 50), and the myriad forms of parochialism that incline us to give preferential regard to certain types of persons over others. For example, he would be unsurprised by critics of contemporary philanthropy who claim that certain groups or problems (e.g., those with identifiable victims) tend to receive disparate shares of public attention and help while others remain faceless statistical abstractions (Atkins and Aguilar 2012).

At the same time, Smith would reject the Hayek–Boettke premise that commercial cooperation alone provides an institutional structure capable

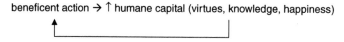

Figure 3.3 The virtuous cycle of beneficent action

of channeling the limited knowledge and coalitional tendencies of human actors into effective social cooperation (Boettke 2012). In fact, Smith posits a host of noncommercial motives and feedback loops that serve to inspire and guide beneficent action, and which foster growth in individuals' beneficent desires and capacities over time.

The most powerful source of corrective feedback to beneficent actors is the ongoing competition for their limited supplies of attention, care, time, money, and other resources. As new knowledge and circumstances create new overlaps and conflicts among each person's "eccentric circles of sympathy," individuals assess the opportunity costs of their current commitments and allocate greater care and attention to persons or projects where they feel the greatest senses of duty, joy, commitment, or efficacy. As Chamlee-Wright (2010) argues, corrective feedback need not take the form of calculable prices in order to spur entrepreneurial discovery and cooperative adjustment.

Beneficent action is also a positive-sum process, generating extrinsic rewards and profitable returns from one's impartial spectator (the "consciousness of deserved reward" [(1790) 1984, 86]). This "wealth," in turn, sets in motion a humanomic growth process, a virtuous cycle in which beneficent action fuels the extension and refinement of our humane capabilities and vice versa, as described in Figure 3.3.

The first phase of this cycle – beneficent action increasing individuals' stocks of virtue, knowledge, and happiness – is corroborated by experimental evidence from positive psychologists Martin Seligman and Jonathan Haidt, who find significant differences in the level and quality of eudaimonic happiness obtained by individuals who engaged in philanthropic activities vs. activities classified as "fun" (Seligman 2002, 9; Haidt 2006, 97–98, 173–174). Such actions expand givers' "humane capital" along several dimensions, including increases in their local and tacit knowledge of where and how their beneficent resources might be most effectively invested and the cultivation of what Amy Kass calls the *philanthropos tropos*: a disposition to promote the happiness and well-being of others (Kass 2005, 20). The humane capital of recipients is similarly augmented: enriched by gifts received, inspired by gratitude, and better informed about how to deploy their own resources to promote the happiness of others. In the second phase of the cycle, donors' and recipients' higher levels of humane capital expand their potential for sustained giving and civic engagement (Gable and Haidt 2005). As Seligman reports:

In the laboratory, children and adults who are happy display more
empathy and are willing to donate more money to others in need.
When we are happy, we are less self-focused, we like others more, and
we want to share our good fortune even with strangers. When we are
down, though, we become distrustful, turn inward, and focus defensively on our own needs.

(2002, 43; see also Haidt 2006, 173–174)

This simple circuit helps us to envision how noncommercial action and interaction can become a generative process of discovery and human betterment. It suggests that "our powers of beneficence" as individuals and communities, though always limited, are not a fixed pie. Note that beneficence figures prominently in both parts of the noncommercial growth loop, affirming Smith's dual definition of beneficence as (1) good deeds that achieve praiseworthy results and (2) the learned habit (virtue) of performing such deeds.

The larger point of the foregoing argument is that Adam Smith's moral philosophy celebrates what Mark Granovetter (1973) might call the strength of weak duties: the humanomic quest for meaning, happiness, love, gratitude, admiration, autonomy, and growth that inspires all manner of creative, committed efforts to serve others (Cornuelle [1965] 1993; McCloskey 2006). From a classical liberal point of view, the very weakness of beneficence as an informal duty which "cannot, among equals, be extorted by force" (Smith [1790] 1984, 78, 80) and whose reach is constrained by individuals' limited concerns, knowledge, and imagination can also be seen as its unique and enduring strength, as a wellspring of private initiative and collaboration.

Adam Smith was not altogether sanguine about sympathy-based cooperation. He readily acknowledged that the "strength" of weak duties may be good or bad – productive or corrosive of social order – depending on the rules and norms taken up by culturally imbued agents. For Smith this is not a damning indictment, however, since social interdependence in his view always cuts both ways, as "[a]ll the members of human society stand in need of each other's assistance, and are likewise exposed to mutual injuries" ([1790] 1984, 85). He remained to the end a sober optimist about commerce, despite growing concerns about the corruptibility of commercial actors. He strikes a similarly hopeful balance of realism and idealism in *TMS*, never losing sight of the humbler and nobler aspects of the human condition and leaving us finally with a vision of the liberal-commercial prospect that offers a glass half full.

## A new Smithian economics

Much as Boulding (1969), Sen (1977), Brown (1994), Young (1997), Griswold (1999), Otteson (2002), Montes (2004), Evensky (2005), McCloskey (2006),

Hanley (2009), Forman-Barzilai (2011), Klein (2012), and others have recast the once axiomatic view of Smith's economics as "a stupendous palace erected upon the granite of self-interest" (Stigler 1971, 265), the "commerce and justice only" view of the institutional infrastructure of commercial society stands in need of substantive revision, on the strength of Smith's own arguments suggesting that a "commerce and justice plus beneficence" society would be happier, more robust, and more conducive to human flourishing.

Adam Smith could not begin to fathom the transglobal torrents of words, images, commodities, and sympathies through which social cooperation occurs today. Yet I suspect he would feel at home with a description of twenty-first-century commercial society as a "networked society ... of individuals connected with each other in a mesh of loosely knit, overlapping, flat connections" (Benkler 2006, 376), wherein individuals are "induced ... to contribute as much as possible to the need of all others" (Hayek [1945] 1948, 12–13) via a broad spectrum of beneficence-infused processes of "loving, befriending, helping, sharing, and otherwise intertwining our lives with others" (Haidt 2006, 134), including but not limited to market competition.

The old interpretation of Smithian economics is characteristically monist:

- the individual: one human nature (narrow self-interest)
- the economy: one cooperative institution (markets; specialization and trade)
- Adam Smith: one ideological position (Chicago School free-market economics).

The new Smithian economics, visibly emergent since 1990 and more faithful to the letter and spirit of Smith's writings, is philosophically pluralist:

- the individual: multiple motives; variable mixtures of self- and other-regarding behavior
- the economy: complex web of commercial and noncommercial cooperation
- Adam Smith: an ideologically diverse conversation in which "more liberal elements of the left and right sides of the old political spectrum" can "work together to articulate a new vision of the free society" (Lavoie 1994, 283).

For twenty-first-century economists, Smith's most valuable gift and challenge may be his provocative effort to rethink the Stoic concept of *oikeiōsis*, commonly translated as the act or process of "appropriation or ownership, of making something one's own ... [or] of something coming to belong to oneself" (Montes 2004, 89). In light of the preceding discussion, *oikeiōsis* seems an apt description of Smith's object of analysis in *TMS* and *WN*: the processes and results of exchange whereby individuals learn to "treat strangers as though they were honorary relatives or friends" (Seabright 2004, 34). Hayek famously celebrates commerce as *oikeiōsis*, the catallactic communalism in which "to exchange" means "to receive into the community" and "to turn from enemy into friend" (Hayek 1988, 112). Yet Hayek fails to recognize the *oikeiōsis* of sympathy and beneficence: individuals attending to the "humbler department" of taking care of their own (Smith [1790] 1984, 237), apportioning their good offices to persons and projects they have adopted as "their own," on whose behalf they are willing to assume some measure of responsibility. An economics (*oikonomos*) that encompasses both forms of *oikeiōsis*, the commercial and the beneficent, might finally become a science of exchange that is properly Smithian.

## Acknowledgments

Preliminary versions of this paper were presented at St. Lawrence University, King's College London, and Texas Christian University. I am grateful to Lenore Ealy, Paul Lewis, Ted Burczak, Steve Horwitz, Emily Chamlee-Wright, Charles Hamilton, Dave Elder-Vass, Darren Middleton, and my TCU History of Economic Thought students for their thoughtful engagement and generous encouragement of my ideas.

## References

Arrillaga-Andreessen, Laura. 2011. *Giving 2.0: Transform Your Giving and Our World*. San Francisco: Jossey-Bass.

Atkins, Avis and Orson Aguilar. 2012. *A Promise to Diverse Communities: Summary of the Foundation Coalition's Efforts*. San Francisco: The Greenlining Institute.

Benkler, Yochai. 2006. *The Wealth of Networks: How Social Production Transforms Markets and Freedom*. New Haven: Yale University Press.

Bishop, Matthew and Michael Green. 2010. *Philanthrocapitalism: How the Rich Can Save the World*. New York: Bloomsbury.

Boettke, Peter J. 2012. *Living Economics: Yesterday, Today, and Tomorrow*. Oakland, CA: The Independent Institute.

Bornstein, David. 2007. *How to Change the World: Social Entrepreneurs and the Power of New Ideas*. Oxford: Oxford University Press.

Boulding, Kenneth E. [1965] 1974. "The Difficult Art of Doing Good." In *Collected Papers of Kenneth Boulding*, vol. IV, edited by Larry D. Singell, 247–261. Boulder, CO: Colorado Associated University Press.

Boulding, Kenneth E. 1968. *Beyond Economics: Essays on Society, Religion, and Ethics*. Ann Arbor, MI: University of Michigan Press.

Boulding, Kenneth E. 1969. "Economics as a Moral Science." *American Economic Review* 59 (1): 1–12.

Bowles, Samuel and Herbert Gintis. 2011. *A Cooperative Species: Human Reciprocity and its Evolution*. Princeton, NJ: Princeton University Press.

Brown, Vivienne. 1994. *Adam Smith's Discourse: Canonicity, Commerce, and Conscience.* London: Routledge.

Bruni, Luigino. 2008. *Reciprocity, Altruism, and the Civil Society: In Praise of Heterogeneity.* London: Routledge.

Buchanan, James M. [1968] 1999. *The Demand and Supply of Public Goods.* Indianapolis, IN: Liberty Fund.

Buchanan, James M. 1982. "Order Defined in the Process of Its Emergence." *Literature of Liberty* 5 (4): 5.

Buchanan, James M. 1991. *The Economics and Ethics of Constitutional Order.* Ann Arbor, MI: University of Michigan Press.

Chamlee-Wright, Emily. 2010. *The Cultural and Political Economy of Recovery: Social Learning in a Post-Disaster Environment.* New York: Routledge.

Coase, Ronald. 1976. "Adam Smith's View of Man." *Journal of Law and Economics* 19 (3): 529–546.

Connolly, William E. 2002. "Eccentric Flows and Cosmopolitan Culture." In *Neuropolitics: Thinking, Culture, Speed*, edited by William E. Connolly, 177–201. Minneapolis, MN: University of Minnesota Press.

Cornuelle, Richard C. [1965] 1993. *Reclaiming the American Dream: The Role of Private Individuals and Voluntary Associations.* New Brunswick, NJ: Transaction Publishers.

Evensky, Jerry. 2005. *Adam Smith's Moral Philosophy: A Historical and Contemporary Perspective on Markets, Law, Ethics, and Culture.* Cambridge: Cambridge University Press.

Forman-Barzilai, Fonna. 2011. *Adam Smith and the Circles of Sympathy: Cosmopolitanism and Moral Theory.* Cambridge: Cambridge University Press.

Friedman, Milton. 1962. *Capitalism and Freedom.* Chicago: University of Chicago Press.

Fulton, Katherine and Andrew Blau. 2005. *Looking Out for the Future: An Orientation for Twenty-First Century Philanthropists.* Cambridge, MA: The Monitor Group.

Gable, Shelly L. and Jonathan Haidt. 2005. "What (and Why) is Positive Psychology?" *Review of General Psychology* 9 (2): 103–110.

Gintis, Herbert, Samuel Bowles, Robert T. Boyd, and Ernst Fehr. 2005. *Moral Sentiments and Material Interests: The Foundations of Cooperation in Economic Life.* Cambridge, MA: MIT Press.

Godbout, Jacques T., with Alain Caillé. 1998. *The World of the Gift.* Translated by Donald Winkler. Montreal: McGill-Queen's University Press.

Granovetter, Mark. 1973. "The Strength of Weak Ties." *American Journal of Sociology* 78 (6): 1360–1380.

Grant, Kevin. 2001. "Christian Critics of Empire: Missionaries, Lantern Lectures, and the Congo Reform Campaign in Britain." *Journal of Imperial and Commonwealth History* 29 (2): 27–58.

Griswold, Charles L., Jr. 1999. *Adam Smith and the Virtues of Enlightenment.* Cambridge: Cambridge University Press.

Gui, Benedetto and Robert Sugden. 2005. *Economics and Social Interaction: Accounting for Interpersonal Relations.* Cambridge: Cambridge University Press.

Haidt, Jonathan. 2006. *The Happiness Hypothesis: Finding Modern Truth in Ancient Wisdom.* New York: Basic Books.

Hanley, Ryan P. 2009. *Adam Smith and the Character of Virtue.* Cambridge: Cambridge University Press.

Hayek, Friedrich A. [1945] 1948. "The Use of Knowledge in Society." In *Individualism and Economic Order*, 77–91. Chicago: University of Chicago Press.

Hayek, Friedrich A. [1976] 1978. "Adam Smith (1723–1790): His Message in Today's Language." In *New Studies in Philosophy, Politics, Economics and the History of Ideas*, 116–122. Chicago: University of Chicago Press.

Hayek, Friedrich A. 1978. *New Studies in Philosophy, Politics, Economics and the History of Ideas*. Chicago: University of Chicago Press.

Hayek, Friedrich A. 1988. *The Fatal Conceit: The Errors of Socialism*. Edited by William W. Bartley. Chicago: University of Chicago Press.

Held, Virginia. 2005. *The Ethics of Care*. Oxford: Oxford University Press.

Heyne, Paul. [1982] 2008. "What is the Responsibility of Business under Democratic Capitalism?" In *"Are Economists Basically Immoral?" and Other Essays on Economics, Ethics, and Religion by Paul Heyne*, edited by Geoffrey Brennan and Anthony Waterman, 391–408. Indianapolis, IN: Liberty Fund.

Heyne, Paul. [1993] 2008. "Are Economists Basically Immoral?" In *"Are Economists Basically Immoral?" and Other Essays on Economics, Ethics, and Religion by Paul Heyne*, edited by Geoffrey Brennan and Anthony Waterman, 1–9. Indianapolis, IN: Liberty Fund.

Kass, Amy A. 2005. "Comment on Gunderman." *Conversations on Philanthropy* II: 19–24.

Klein, Daniel B. 2012. *Knowledge and Coordination: A Liberal Interpretation*. New York: Oxford University Press.

Kolm, Serge-Christophe. 2008. *Reciprocity: An Economics of Social Relations*. Cambridge: Cambridge University Press.

Lavoie, Donald C. 1994. "A Political Philosophy for the Market Process." In *The Market Process: Essays in Contemporary Austrian Economics*, edited by Peter J. Boettke and David L. Prychitko, 274–86. Brookfield, VT: Edward Elgar.

Lessig, Lawrence. 2008. *Remix: Making Art and Commerce Thrive in the Hybrid Economy*. New York: Penguin.

Levy, David M. and Sandra J. Peart. 2009a. "Sympathy, Evolution, and *The Economist*." *Journal of Economic Behavior and Organization* 71 (1): 29–36.

Levy, David M. and Sandra J. Peart. 2009b. "Adam Smith and the Place of Faction." In *Elgar Companion to Adam Smith*, edited by Jeffrey T. Young, 335–45. Cheltenham, UK: Edward Elgar.

Lewis, Paul. 2011. "Varieties of Emergence: Mind, Markets, and Novelty." *Studies in Emergent Order* 4: 170–92.

Lewis, Paul and Emily Chamlee-Wright. 2008. "Social Embeddedness, Social Capital, and the Market Process: An Introduction to the Special Issue on Austrian Economics, Economic Sociology, and Social Capital." *Review of Austrian Economics* 21 (2 and 3): 107–18.

Lohmann, Roger A. 1992. *The Commons: New Perspectives on Nonprofit Organizations and Voluntary Action*. San Francisco: Jossey-Bass.

McCloskey, Deirdre N. 2006. *The Bourgeois Virtues: Ethics for an Age of Commerce*. Chicago: University of Chicago Press.

McCloskey, Deirdre N. 2010. *Bourgeois Dignity: Why Economics Can't Explain the Modern World*. Chicago: University of Chicago Press.

McCloskey, Deirdre N. 2011. "Ethics, Friedman, Buchanan, and the Good Old Chicago School: Getting (Back) to Humanomics." Paper presented at the 12th annual Summer Institute for the History of Economic Thought, University of Richmond, June 24–27.

Macfie, Alec L. 1967. *The Individual in Society: Papers on Adam Smith*. London: Allen & Unwin.

Milgate, Murray. 2009. "The Economic Machine and the Invisible Hand." In *After Adam Smith: A Century of Transformation in Politics and Political Economy*, edited by Murray Milgate and Shannon C. Stimson, 77–96. Princeton, NJ: Princeton University Press.

Montes, Leonidas. 2004. *Adam Smith in Context: A Critical Reassessment of Some Central Components of His Thought*. New York: Palgrave Macmillan.

Nelson, Julie and Paula England. 2002. "Feminist Philosophies of Love and Work." *Hypatia* 17 (2): 1–18.

Offer, Avner. 1997. "Between the Gift and the Market: The Economy of Regard." *Economic History Review* 50 (3): 450–476.

Ostrom, Elinor. 1990. *Governing the Commons: The Evolution of Institutions for Collective Action*. Cambridge: Cambridge University Press.

Otteson, James R. 2002. *Adam Smith's Marketplace of Life*. Cambridge: Cambridge University Press.

Romily, Samuel. 1840. *Memoirs of the Life of Sir Samuel Romily, with a Selection from His Correspondence*, vol. I. London: John Murray.

Samuelson, Paul A. 1954. "The Pure Theory of Public Expenditure." *Review of Economics and Statistics* 36 (4): 387–389.

Seabright, Paul. 2004. *The Company of Strangers: A Natural History of Economic Life*. Princeton, NJ: Princeton University Press.

Seligman, Martin E. P. 2002. *Authentic Happiness*. New York: Free Press.

Sen, Amartya K. 1977. "Rational Fools: A Critique of the Behavioral Foundations of Economic Theory." *Philosophy and Public Affairs* 6 (4): 317–344.

Singer, Peter. 2009. *The Life You Can Save*. New York: Random House.

Smith, Adam. [1762–3] 1982. *Lectures on Jurisprudence*. Glasgow edition. Edited by Ronald L. Meek, David D. Raphael and Peter G. Stein. Indianapolis, IN: Liberty Fund.

Smith, Adam. [1776] 1981. *An Inquiry into the Nature and Causes of the Wealth of Nations*. Glasgow edition, vols. 1 and 2. Edited by Roy H. Campbell and Andrew S. Skinner with assistance from W. B. Todd. Indianapolis, IN: Liberty Fund.

Smith, Adam. [1790] 1984. *The Theory of Moral Sentiments*. Glasgow edition. Edited by David D. Raphael and Alec L. Macfie. Indianapolis, IN: Liberty Fund.

Stigler, George J. 1971. "Smith's Travels on the Ship of State." *History of Political Economy* 3 (2): 265–277.

van Staveren, Irene. 2005. "Modelling Care." *Review of Social Economy* 63 (4): 567–86.

Vandevelde, Antoon, ed. 2000. *Gifts and Interests*. Leuven, Belgium: Peeters.

Viner, Jacob. 1972. *The Role of Providence in the Social Order: An Essay in Intellectual History*. Philadelphia: American Philosophical Society.

Young, Jeffrey T. 1997. *Economics as a Moral Science: The Political Economy of Adam Smith*. Cheltenham, UK: Edward Elgar.

# 4 Comment: Entering the "great school of self-command"
## The moralizing influence of markets, language, and imagination

*Sandra J. Peart*

> How selfish soever man may be supposed, there are evidently some principles in his nature, which interest him in the fortune of others, and render their happiness necessary to him, though he derives nothing from it except the pleasure of seeing it.
> (Adam Smith, *The Theory of Moral Sentiments* (1759))

Economists for centuries have struggled to understand the self–other relationship and its implications for economic life. For economists in the classical tradition of Adam Smith, this was a central question regarding the wealth and flourishing of nations. Later, as this volume demonstrates, the relationship of the self to others was forgotten as economics became associated almost exclusively with the pursuit of what Peter Boettke and Daniel Smith describe as "ruthless efficiency."

In the wake of the 2008 financial crisis and a growing body of experimental and empirical evidence showing the predictive shortcomings of narrow self-interest models, a more capacious economics has recently reemerged. Reimagining the economic problem to include what Samuel Bowles and Herbert Gintis refer to as "the evolution of human cooperation," growing numbers of economists are investigating the relationship between self-regarding and other-regarding preferences. The essays by Bowles and Gintis, Boettke and Smith, and Robert Garnett are part of this reimagining and remind us that an economics in which actors are assumed to be entirely self-regarding is at odds with evidence about how people actually behave.

This reimagining has employed insights from Smith's *Theory of Moral Sentiments* to examine experimental regularities such as cooperation and sharing (Ashraf *et al.* 2005). At the heart of this shift in analytic focus and perspective is an emerging consensus that economic actors are not simply selfish or even self-interested but frequently sacrifice their own material or physical well-being to help others, even in cases where, as Smith put it, they "derive nothing" from doing so: no promise of future reciprocity, no reputational gain, nothing but the pure joy associated with a praiseworthy act. For Smith, one becomes generous and virtuous through the pursuit of approbation from actual and imaginary spectators, the "great school of self-command."

Taken together, these three essays defend the Smithian claim that economic activity is a means by which people acquire a sense of ethics, reciprocity, fairness, trust, generosity, and virtue. The authors remind us, first, that economists did not always view efficiency as the chief normative desideratum or economic actors as primarily selfish or entirely unconnected to fellow beings. Instead, as Garnett and Boettke/Smith argue, the standard account of economics, which focuses on the *Wealth of Nations* exclusively and treats the subject matter of *The Theory of Moral Sentiments* as external to economics, is simply wrong-headed, notwithstanding its endorsement by eminent scholars such as Jacob Viner (1927). This narrow interpretation of Smith's economics, which coincides with twentieth-century attempts to develop an economics of the disembedded self, of isolated economic actors unconnected to others by bonds of friendship, language, ethics, or reciprocity, lent itself well to the pursuit of economic efficiency. It did not fare well, however, in predicting human behavior or explaining the emergence of economic cooperation; nor did it leave any room to explain how and why actors enter into the "school of self-command," of language, reciprocity, trust, forgiveness, or self-sacrifice.

The gap between predicted and actual behavior has been a source of discomfort at various points in the history of economics. In 1870, William Stanley Jevons wrote about a "being of perfect good sense and foresight," whose actions, he acknowledged, were surely at odds with his predictions (72; see also Peart 1996). Indeed, economists late in the nineteenth and early in the twentieth century posited that individuals were hopelessly irrational when it came to decisions about how much to save and when and whom to marry. The question for early neoclassical economists such as Jevons, Alfred Marshall, Irving Fisher and A. C. Pigou was whether or not economic theory was sufficiently close to life on the ground to serve as an approximation for predicting behavior, and, more importantly, how best to "fix" myopic and ignorant economic people (Peart 2000). In this line of thought, the role of the economist was to serve the goal of economic efficiency by teaching actors how best to behave.[1]

The authors of these essays, like Smith himself, place faith in people themselves to learn, adapt, and become moral by acting in the context of institutions that are largely outside the scope of human design – first and foremost the market. In addressing the moralizing influence of commerce, these essays address at least partially the question for which neoclassical economists of the early twentieth century had no answer, namely: why do humans cooperate? The answer, evident in all three chapters, is that economic interactions have a schooling effect, helping to correct myopia and generate welfare-enhancing cooperation.

Smith recognized that the first and most steadfast myopia is that which places the human self at the center of the universe. We overcome this illusion, he argues, through a process of social exchange that cultivates our ethical imagination. As we exchange ideas, images, and sentiments with persons within and beyond our intimate circles, we develop our linguistic capacity and our habits of self-command. We learn to take account of others as we act and to act in such a way as to earn, at least on balance, the approval of others. This socializing commerce tempers our concern for the self.

Bowles and Gintis are also centrally concerned with self–other relationships as determinants of action. In their view, predictions by economists based on purely self-interested behavior often fall far from the mark as they fail to recognize the power of "social preferences" or pro-social motivations such as fairness, equity, concern for the well-being of others, or desire to uphold ethical norms. Bowles and Gintis take an instrumental view of cooperation, that humans cooperate because it is in our interests to do so, and argue that we acquired an evolved capacity to cooperate because our unique cognitive and linguistic skills enabled us "to structure our social interactions in ways that allowed altruistic cooperators to proliferate."[2] As a result of their instrumental approach and their interest in the evolution of human cooperation, Bowles and Gintis put the prisoner's dilemma and the concept of "strong reciprocity" at the center of their analysis.

Boettke and Smith write about the "doux-commerce thesis," which was developed to explain the "civilizing function" of commerce whereby "the market system" produces "social cooperation, especially among distant and different anonymous actors." Garnett, in contrast, argues that Smith's vision of social cooperation is much broader than "commerce" per se. He reads *TMS* and *WN* as an integrated theory of human collaboration in which wealth and human flourishing are generated by commercial and noncommercial (sympathy-seeking) exchange.

All three essays thus emphasize the importance of exchange in the development of cooperative behavior. As exchange multiplies and evolves over time, so too do institutions that corral our selfish and less cooperative impulses. Yet they disagree about the meaning of "social cooperation" and the types of institutions that induce it. Boettke and Smith defend a Hayekian view, according to which social cooperation is synonymous with the extended order of commercial specialization and trade, whereas Bowles, Gintis, and Garnett define cooperation as any form of mutually beneficial activity, commercial or noncommercial.

The role of language looms large but remains mostly implicit in each essay and is one area that warrants further attention. For it is through language that reciprocity and civility are cultivated. Through language, people learn to understand and persuade others, and to understand how others perceive them. They exchange ideas and emotions with others. Language is the basis for imaginative exchange, for placing oneself in another's shoes, for giving and receiving approval or approbation.

Language is necessary to the exchange of approbation just as it is necessary for the barter and exchange of the commercial market.

It is important to note, as does Garnett, that for Smith, and the economists who follow in his tradition, exchange occurs in two related but incommensurable dimensions: in material goods and in approval. Language is essential to both: to convey what belongs to whom and the advantages of giving "that which I want" in exchange for "this which you want" in material trades; and to convey what action is proper and how much self-command is necessary for trades in approbation. The virtuous society is one in which self-command is exercised and developed in both spheres.

As is well known, Smith distinguished between praise and praiseworthiness in *The Theory of Moral Sentiments*, and held that we are all subject to the desire to be praiseworthy. While we do not come into the world knowing how to obtain the approbation of others, we observe people's reactions to our acts and the actions of others and come to understand what constitutes appropriate and virtuous conduct by observing what is generally approved. We come to moderate our actions in order to obtain general approval. We come to understand that we are not the center of the universe and to regulate our behavior accordingly (Smith [1759] 1976, 145). As Smith tells us, "ignorant and groundless praise can give no solid joy" but we are pleased "with having done what is praise-worthy. We are pleased to think that we have rendered ourselves the natural objects of approbation" even if no explicit approbation is voiced (Smith 1759)!

Our authors help us recognize that exchange induces moderation and even what we would today describe as tolerance. Exchange provides the training ground for trustworthiness (independently of reputational effects), forgiveness, and civility. Trade of course also generates significant material benefits. As noted, Smith famously held that without discussion there is no trade. Without the ability to converse and persuade, creatures like greyhounds and mastiffs are unable to obtain the material benefits of specialization, trade, and cooperation that flow from reason and speech (Smith [1776] 1976, 30). On this view, in addition to the enormously important moral improvement associated with language, discussion is also the key means by which wealth is produced and increased over time. In today's vernacular, it is via discussion – exchange or commerce, broadly defined – that we are best able to cooperate, to decide who should do what for whom.

These essays fill an increasingly apparent gap in our understanding of the relationship between Smith's teaching on economic development as outlined in *The Wealth of Nations* and his teaching in moral philosophy in *The Theory of Moral Sentiments*. More than this, they shed light on the evolution of institutions that support cooperation, rules that harness our self-interested actions in order better to enable our sympathetic natures to flourish. While one is left wondering about whether and how best to distinguish between "commercial life" and the messy forms of crony capitalism that are flourishing currently, that is surely a subject for another collection and should by no means diminish the significance of the contribution here.

## Notes

1 See Peart 2000 for a detailed examination of policy prescriptions designed to "correct" the myopia and other "irrationalities" discussed by Jevons and other early neoclassical economists.
2 Smith wrote a great deal about what happens when the desire for approval is warped by the desire for within-group (factional) approval; so, for Smith, there can be *too much* cooperation, as when sub-groups cooperate within a prisoner's dilemma setting (Levy and Peart 2009). While Bowles and Gintis examine how rules evolve to serve groups, theirs is a more positive story than Smith's.

## References

Ashraf, Nava, Colin F. Camerer, and George Loewenstein. 2005. "Adam Smith, Behavioral Economist." *The Journal of Economic Perspectives* 19 (3): 131–145.

Jevons, William Stanley. [1870] 1911. *Theory of Political Economy*. London: Macmillan.

Levy, David M. and Sandra J. Peart. 2009. "The Place of Factions." In *Elgar Companion to Adam Smith*, edited by Jeffrey Young, 235–246. Northampton, MA: Edward Elgar.

Peart, Sandra J. 1996. *The Economics of William Stanley Jevons*. London: Routledge.

Peart, Sandra J. 2000. "Irrationality and Intertemporal Choice in Early Neoclassical Analysis." *Canadian Journal of Economics* 33: 175–188.

Smith, Adam. [1759] 1976. *The Theory of Moral Sentiments*. Edited by D. D. Raphael and A. L. Macfie. Oxford: Clarendon Press.

Smith, Adam. [1776] 1976. *An Inquiry into the Nature and Causes of the Wealth of Nations*. Edited by W. B. Todd. Oxford: Clarendon Press.

Viner, Jacob. 1927. "Adam Smith and Laissez Faire." *Journal of Political Economy* 35 (2): 198–232.

# Part II
# Identity and association

# 5 Commerce, reciprocity, and civil virtues

## The contribution of the Civil Economy

*Luigino Bruni*

> Studying the broad currents of European philosophical thought regarding the definition of what it means to be human, one reaches an unexpected conclusion: the social aspect, the element of life in community, is not generally considered necessary for humankind. However, this thesis is never presented as such; it is rather a presupposition that is never formulated.
>
> (Todorov 1998, 15)

## Introduction

The ethical foundations of both market economy and economics are under attack. Recent economic, environmental and financial crises have exacerbated an old criticism of classical economic science, namely the incompatibility between the axioms and anthropological assumptions of economics and a moral vision of a society based on virtues. The market, says the accusation, depends on instrumental motivations. Market interactions therefore fail to express virtue and intrinsic motivation; economics normalizes instrumental motivations, not only in markets but also in social life more generally; therefore economics is complicit in an assault on virtue. These ideas have been developed in a rarefied discourse of academic moral philosophy (see McIntyre 1981; Anderson 1993; Sandel 2009), but they are also echoed in attitudes of anti-capitalism and anti-globalization and in popular criticisms of economics. One outcome of this criticism is to draw sharp contrasts between communitarian values (e.g., friendship, solidarity, and altruism) and market ones (e.g., self-interest, anonymity, and exchange).

In this chapter, I argue that the tradition of Civil Economy transcends the opposition between economics and moral values, or between community and market.[1] The paper begins with a short reflection on the roots of the market/gift and economy/society dichotomies. I then analyze Adam Smith's approach to the issue of market/community to set the stage for my presentation of an alternative perspective, here termed Civil Economy. Finally, I focus on the vision of the commerce/community nexus in the

Civil Economy approach. As we shall see, the Civil Economy framework adopts a less dualistic approach to the relationship between commerce and community than does standard economics, portraying those two aspects of social life as being integrated by a common reliance on the role of reciprocity in human interaction.

## At the root of the market/gift, commerce/community dualities

In the course of their historical development, capitalistic market economies have brought about a change in the nature of human relations. The market has truly become a culture in its own right, an *ethos*. More than ethics as we intend this expression today, an *ethos* is a custom or a lifestyle that surrounds and informs all dimensions of common life (Bruni 2012a). The market society gives birth to and fosters its own sense of being human, in particular, the promise of interpersonal relationships without the "wound," that is without the vulnerability associated with any genuine communitarian life (Bruni 2012b). The attempt to escape the vulnerability of social life has tended to produce a sharp dichotomy between contract and gift, economy and community. "Business is business" *and* "gift is gift" – with little opportunity for overlap.

The word community comes from the Latin *communitas*. *Communitas* in turn is the compound *cum–munus*, an old complex expression that reflects the ambivalence of the Latin word *munus*, which denotes simultaneously a gift and an obligation. A similar ambivalence can be seen in the Old English *gift*, which translates as *poison* in German (Esposito 2009). Smithian political economy tried to resolve this tension between gift and obligation by theorizing a market economy that was anchored on exchange, free from the social bonds and obligations of community.

As we shall see below, another tradition of economic thought was developing in parallel to Scottish political economy on the basis of a more integrated vision of the nexus between community and market, gift and contract. This other tradition, basically Italian and southern European, was called *Economia Civile*. In order to contrast these traditions, we must set out the key features of the Scottish approach.

Imagining, thinking, and then theorizing a distinct economic sphere governed by essentially different principles from the social sphere is a typical element of modernity. In fact, it was only in the eighteenth century that the economic sphere began to be conceived and presented as the ideal place for instrumental, self-interested and calculable relations, and that the market began to be portrayed as the essentially self-regulating interweaving of these relationships. In Anglo-Saxon culture, and in Scotland in particular, modern economic thought, and with it economic science, emerged from Protestant Reformation humanism – it can be useful to keep in mind that Smith was living in a Protestant culture, and that his lectures on moral philosophy were attended mainly by future leaders of the Calvinist Church of Scotland.

The Reformation originated, as is well known, mainly as a reaction to the "commercialization" or commodification of grace, of the *charis*, namely the gratuitousness of salvation. The Roman Church in particular, just before the *Rinascimento*, had mixed up market and gift, religion and money, and Martin Luther and the Protestant reformers strongly reacted against this quantification of spirituality and reduction of the gifts of God to something measurable and exchangeable for mundane coinage. In the Lutheran ecclesiology the "city of God" and the "city of men" are distinct, being sharply separated and governed by different laws. Protestant culture later developed a social theory characterized by sharply distinct domains of social life: (1) the market, governed by quantity and prices, and (2) the non-market domain (family, churches, etc.), governed by the sole law of charity and gift.[2] Because every individual was believed to have direct access to God, there was no need, according to Protestant humanism, for any mediation on the part of the church hierarchy or of the community. It is not by chance, then, that modern political economy was born in this Protestant milieu, characterized by individuals-without-community, perhaps in part as a reaction to the *ancien regime* characterized by the community-without-individuals (Bruni 2012a).

The emergence of modern economic science is thus closely linked to the emergence of two anthropological and cultural elements. The first is the affirmation of the category of individuality as a separate category, in some ways opposed to the community. Individuality enhanced the value of one's rights and especially one's freedom.[3] The second element is the affirmation of equality. The French anthropologist Louis Dumont (1980) expressed the idea of this transition in the very title of his books when he contrasted the *homo aequalis* of modern societies to the *homo hierarchicus* of pre-modern feudal culture (or non-Western cultures, such as the Indian caste system). Within this modern cultural process, the market thus became a privileged mechanism that could incorporate two of the founding principles of modernity: the freedom of individuals and the equality between them. The power of these ideas inclined some to take them to their extreme consequences.

The "invention" of the market economy in fact started a slow but inexorable process of undermining rigid vertical social structures and progressively overturning feudal society. Adam Smith, following in the footsteps of Thomas Hobbes, David Hume and the entire movement of the Scottish Enlightenment, most eloquently expressed the cultural and anthropological innovation of the market economy with respect to past societies. When we enter the market we no longer depend hierarchically on others – the beggar on the rich, or the farmer on the landlord – and in the interaction of the market we meet on equal footing, where, thanks to the contract, we are freed from dependence on the benevolence of others. The market is the higher expression of a civil society; economic development is also an indication of social development, and economic freedom is a precondition for all other freedoms. In particular, the extension of markets and their logic is considered by the liberal tradition to be the *conditio sine qua non* for genuine social cohesion; the market frees us from vertical and asymmetric relations and from those that are not chosen, and it creates the conditions for a horizontal sociality between subjects who tend to be free and equal.

Within this tradition, then, the market or the economic sector is seen as being in structural (or ontological) harmony with civil society, but – this is a key point – in opposition to community and its values (fraternity, identity, tradition, etc.). This friendship (market economy and civil society) and this opposition (market/civil society and community) are central in the Scottish Enlightenment, particularly in the work of Smith.

## Adam Smith's market relationality

Adam Smith, in particular the Smith of *The Wealth of Nations*, remains today an important interpretive key for understanding the humanism that lies behind the confidence in the expansion of markets and globalization. Smith wanted to emphasize independence from the "benevolence of our fellow citizens" as a positive virtue related to the new form of sociality introduced by the market. Market relationships allow us to satisfy our needs without having to depend on others' love. When we all depend impersonally and anonymously on the "invisible hand" of the market, we do not need to depend personally on anyone else, nor do we have to encounter anyone personally (and potentially painfully). In depending on many, we depend on no one with a name:

> Each tradesman or artificer derives his subsistence from the employment, not of one, but of a hundred or a thousand different customers. Though in some measure obliged to them all, therefore, he is not absolutely dependent upon any one of them.
> (Smith [1776] 1981, III.iv.12)

We depend anonymously, and without the risk of personal injury, on the market. This is why, for Smith, the market economy is an immediately civilizing mechanism: it is civil society; it is civilization, though a civilization based on *immunitas*. In this respect, a famous passage from his discussion "Of Police" in *Lectures on Jurisprudence* is emblematic:

> Whenever commerce is introduced into any country, probity and punctuality always accompany it. These virtues in a rude and barbarous country are almost unknown. Of all the nations in Europe, the Dutch, the most commercial, are the most faithfull to their word. The English are more so than the Scotch, but much inferiour to the Dutch.
> ([1763] 1896, 253)

To do justice to the complexity of Smith's thought, we should immediately add that the social and cultural target he has in mind is a social relationship typical of asymmetric and unequal pre-modern societies. In such societies the benevolence of some (the powerful and affluent) towards others (the poor and beggars) actually conceals what G. W. F. Hegel would call a 'master–slave' power relationship, an asymmetric social relationship that is a direct cultural consequence of a certain understanding of the Absolute. The ethical justification of Smith's humanism of independence is grounded on his observation that "Nobody but a beggar chuses to depend chiefly upon the benevolence of his fellow-citizens" (Smith [1776] 1981, I.ii.2). Rather than the gift as an expression of gratuitousness and mutual freedom, the benevolence that Smith has in mind more closely resembles the *munus* about which Marcel Mauss ([1925] 1990) wrote (that is, a gift that expresses and reinforces an asymmetry of power and of status in social relationships, which in turn obligates the recipient to return the gift). Smith's *communitas* is this reciprocal *munus*.

The "other" that Smith has in mind when he imagines life in pre-modern societies is not one that blesses me and makes me happy; rather, in continuity with Hobbes, he is referring to one that is above or below me, not beside me as an equal. In other words, for Smith, the direct and personal relationship with the other in the public sphere is synonymous with the mutual (and potentially burdensome) social obligations of the feudal world; as such, it must be overcome by a new anonymous and mediated sociality, which for Smith is more civil because it is free from dependence on the benevolence and gift–*munus* of others. The humanistic inspiration of Smith – or of the civil economists Antonio Genovesi or Pietro Verri – cannot be understood unless one understands his enthusiasm for the market together with an indignation for the suffering and humiliation inflicted by a few feudal masters on the many servants in pre-modern *communitas*.

For these reasons, there is in Smith not only the recognition that friendship is not sufficient to live in society at large – "In civilized society he stands at all times in need of the cooperation and assistance of great multitudes, while his whole life is scarce sufficient to gain the friendship of a few persons" ([1776] 1981, I.ii.2) – but we also find the argument that, were we ever to have sufficient friends to obtain the things we need (as can happen in small village communities), the broad commercial society nevertheless still allows a more civil relationality, a new form of *philia*, which is morally higher because it is freely chosen.[4]

In summary, Smith takes recourse in the mediation of the market (and in a certain sense he invents it, at least theoretically), because the alternative form of asymmetric and vertical relations are redolent of an uncivilized, feudal world. In the feudal world, the other may harm me because he or she is a powerful person or a master who rules me, one who does not contend with me on equal terms. The market avoids this unmediated, uncivilized relationship and constructs a mediated, more civilized one that is more humane: when the beggar enters the butcher shop with money in hand, when, that is, he or she can effect an equal exchange with the seller, that relationship – precisely because it is mediated by the market – is for Smith more humane with respect to the dependent relationships than a world without markets. Of course, Smith does not deny (and affirms in his *Theory of Moral Sentiments*, [1759], 1984) that in private life there may be an unmediated face-to-face relationality, but precisely and only in the private sphere, among one's family and close circle of friends. In civil society, including the market (for Smith, the market is civil society only from this standpoint), it is good to meet others anonymously because the other with a face is not necessarily a "brother" who is like me, but may be a superior (or an inferior).

There is also a second aspect to Smith's methodological foundation for political economy. In *The Theory of Moral Sentiments* Smith reminds us that "[b]eneficence, therefore, is less essential to the existence of society than justice. Society may subsist, though not in the most comfortable state, without beneficence; but the prevalence of injustice must utterly destroy it" ([1759] 1984 II.ii.3.5). On this basis, Smith states that:

> Society may subsist among different men, as among different merchants, from a sense of its utility, *without any mutual love or affection*.
> (II.ii.3.4; italics mine)

This is an important argument that is finding increasing consensus in a global society, and one that apparently evokes wide agreement. In reality, it conceals a snare, represented by the idea that civil society can function and develop without gratuitousness (which can be viewed as a synonym of beneficence, or charity), or that a contract can take the place of a gift. It is said that the gifts of oneself and of friendship are important in the private sphere, but in the market and in civil society we can easily do without them; rather, as we have seen, Smith makes an even stronger argument in that we do well to do without them, precisely because of their potential burden of pain and injury.

The growth of loneliness and misery in our affluent economies seems to invite us to reconsider: a society free from gratuitousness turns out not to be a habitable place, much less a place of joy or human flourishing. This is especially true in post-modern societies, where the boundary between "private" and "public" is disappearing in the market, because, on the one hand, for many jobs the time of work and the time of non-work are deeply intertwined, and, on the other, the logic of prices and incentives is spreading in almost all areas of social life (health, school, even family). Therefore, in our societies, if we do not live in gratuitousness in public (work, politics, associations, and so forth), neither will we live it in private.

Nothing like Smith's idea is currently posited explicitly within the core of economic science. Smith's economic theory is not taught in most universities (except for a few references to the "invisible hand"), but the idea of economic exchange as mutual indifference and of the market as the place of virtuous, anonymous, and impersonal relationships still sustains the entire system of contemporary economics that, from this point of view, is heir to Adam Smith.

## The tradition of Civil Economy

The "classic" tradition of sociality, the so-called Aristotelian-Thomistic approach, found a significant expression in social issues within the Italian tradition of Civil Economy (Bruni and Zamagni 2007). This tradition represents an important attempt to keep alive within modernity the tradition of civil life based on *philia* and a more integrated vision of the nexus between commerce and community.

To learn more about this tradition, we shall first of all examine the works of Antonio Genovesi, a Neapolitan philosopher and economist, who lived around the same time as Smith. In many key aspects of their thought, Genovesi and Smith are surprisingly similar, but there are important differences.[5]

The Civil Economy tradition of the eighteenth century may be seen as the modern expression of the civil tradition that originated in Aristotelian Greece and was rediscovered in the Middle Ages. Like the first civil humanists, Genovesi sees civil life as the place where happiness may be fully realized thanks to good and just laws, to trading, and to the civil bodies where men are free to practice their natural sociability: "Even if companionship can bring evils, on the other hand it also assures life and its goods; it is the source of the greatest pleasures, unknown to the men of nature" ([1766] 1973, 37). And like the civil humanists and the Franciscans, Genovesi also thinks the market is a matter of *philia*.

On the natural (and non-artificial) character of sociality and on its essential role for a fully humane and happy life, Genovesi is also aligned with the ancient Aristotelian-Thomistic tradition:

> Every person has a natural and inherent obligation to study how to procure her happiness; but the political body is made of persons; therefore, the entire political body and each of its members has an obligation to do what is on their part, i.e. all that they know and can for the sake of common prosperity, as long as that which is done does not offend the rights of the other civil bodies. From the civil body, this obligation returns with beautiful and divine ties to each family and each person for the common pacts of society. Each family and each person is therefore under the obligation to procure, for what she knows and can do, common happiness, due to two obligations, one of which is within nature, and the other is among the first pacts that subsequently continue with posterity ... for the sake of living in a

community. A third obligation may be added, that of one's own utility. What Shaftesbury proclaimed (*Inquiry of Virtue and Merit*) will be eternally true, that true utility is the daughter of virtue for it is eternally true that the great depth of every man is the love for those with whom he lives. This love is indeed the daughter of virtue.

([1765–67] 2005, 29)

Only a few decades earlier, the Neapolitan Paolo Mattia Doria argued in the introduction to his *Della Vita Civile*:

To this rather impossible goal of men to possess all the virtues and to the property for which they each possess only a few, the invention of civil life aspires to offer a solution ... which reveals the true essence of civil life as a mutual help of virtues, and of natural faculties, that men lend to each other in the attempt to attain human happiness.

(1710, 1)

However, at the heart of the view of life in common held by the authors of the Neapolitan School of Civil Economy (not only Genovesi) is the idea that "mere" sociability, man's character as a "political animal," cannot suffice to distinguish the human from other animals. The kind of sociality that is typical of human beings is a *qualified* type of sociality – which we must call reciprocity, friendship, mutual assistance, or fraternity, all basically synonyms in the vocabulary of Genovesi and of the other authors belonging to this tradition:

Man is a naturally sociable animal: goes the common saying. But not every man will believe there is no other animal on earth that is not sociable. ... In what way then is man more sociable than the others? ... [in] the reciprocal right to be assisted and consequently his reciprocal obligation to assist us in our needs.

([1765–67] 2005, 283)

This passage contains something that we do not find in Aristotle or in Smith: for Genovesi, *reciprocity* (not only a general *relationality*, nor simple sociability) is the typical element of human sociality. For Smith, by contrast, what constitutes the typical character of human sociality is the "propensity in human nature ... to truck, barter, and exchange one thing for another" ([1776] 1981, 25), founded, as we have seen, on the power of persuasion.

Genovesi portrays market relationships as relations of mutual assistance, hence neither impersonal nor anonymous. In fact, the market itself is conceived as an expression of the general law of society, that is, reciprocity. This is both clear, and important, especially in his analysis of trust, or "public faith," which lies at the heart of his *Lezioni di economia civile*.

As for the Franciscans in the fourteenth and fifteenth centuries, for the civil humanists the market is a matter of *fides*, trust. One of the key elements in Genovesi's theory of Civil Economy is "public faith," something he considers as the true precondition for economic development: "confidence is the soul of commerce, and without confidence all the component parts of this mighty structure would crumble under it" (Filangieri [1780] 1806, II, 145). In his thought there is a substantial difference between *private* and *public* trust: while the first can be assimilated to reputation, that is, a private good that can be "spent" on the market, the latter is not the sum of private "reputations"; rather, it entails genuine love for the Common Good (as intended in the classical philosophical tradition, i.e., Aristotle or Aquinas). This concept is similar to what modern theorists have called "social capital," that is, the fabric of faith and civil virtues that allows human and economic development to get into motion and preserve itself over time.

According to Genovesi, the lack of "public faith" is what caused the lack of civil and economic development in the Kingdom of Naples – an argument that more than two and a half centuries later has lost none of its currency. In the Kingdom, as denounced by the tradition of Civil Economy, "private trust" (intended in particular as blood ties or bonds based on feudal pacts of vassalage), or honor, was abundant, but public and generalized trust, the kind that originates from the cultivation of civil virtues, was scanty. Some decades later, Gaetano Filangieri similarly maintained that no civil and economic development can be achieved without man having "confidence in the government, the magistrates, and his fellow citizens" ([1780] 1806, I: 10–11), who are the first and most important resources for any kind of collective and individual development.

If on one side market development brings civil and economic development, for the Neapolitan School it is even more important to stress that *cultivating* public faith is the precondition for any possible discourse concerning civil and economic development: "nothing is more necessary than public trust in a wise and easy circulation" (Genovesi [1765–67] 2005, 751). Very significant is also this footnote by Genovesi: "This word *fides* means *rope that ties and unites*. Public faith is therefore the bond of families united in companionship."

The civil economist then takes one further step. In the *Lezioni* ([1765–67] 2005, Chapter X, Book II), Genovesi explains to his students and fellow citizens that public faith is above all a matter of authentic reciprocity and not merely a matter of contracts. According to the Neapolitan economist, public faith is not the kind of capital that can be built outside the market and later be used on the market. On the contrary, the market is conceived as part of civil society, which produces what today we would call social capital and relational goods. For this reason, his discourse on public faith is directly economic:

> Where no trust exists – not in the part that constitutes the reciprocal confidence of citizens in each other, nor in the certainty of contracts, or

in the vigour of laws, or in the science and integrity of judges ... there is no certainty of contracts, no power of laws, no trust of man towards man. Because contracts are bonds and civil laws are also themselves *public pacts and contracts.*

(Ibid., 752.)

## Commerce as mutual assistance and the "spirit" of commerce: Dragonetti and Genovesi

In line with most of the European Enlightenment, the Neapolitan tradition considers economic activity to be a genuine expression of civic life. It sees commerce as a *civilizing factor*. Like the fifteenth-century Italian civic humanists, Genovesi and the Neapolitans see commercial activity as an expression of civic virtue and civic life as the place where virtues could be expressed to their fullest.

An important figure in the Civil Economy tradition is Giacinto Dragonetti (1738–1818), a student of Genovesi, who is well known for his book *A Treatise on Virtues and Rewards* ([1766] 1769), in which he emphasized the crucial role of rewarding virtues for implementing a good society.

Dragonetti considered commerce as a key opportunity for cultivating and *rewarding* civic virtues. If in the Civil Economy tradition the market is construed as a form of "mutual assistance," then commerce itself becomes a virtue, because by trading and contributing to developing the market, individuals are ultimately contributing to the common good. Moreover, starting a commercial enterprise in eighteenth-century Naples required the ability to take risks, and this entrepreneurial activity, too, could be interpreted as a token of public virtue, since the entire community benefited from its results. From a Civil Economy perspective, the market is a place where virtues can be encountered and cultivated. Both market and trade are essential to public happiness. As Dragonetti notes, "Commerce is the reciprocal communication of the produce and industry of various countries ... The citizens of earth carry on a war of industry against each other, and where that ceases, there the supports of life decay" ([1766] 1769, 113, 121).

For this reason, society ought to recognize commercial virtues and publicly reward virtuous merchants, as in ancient Rome, where the best merchants were allowed to join the equestrian order. "Commerce influences manners. Its spirit is that of frugality, moderation, prudence, tranquility, order. Whilst these subsist, riches are harmless. Commerce has everywhere propagated the study of social habits ... If these are the advantages of the commerce, *the trader should not want his reward*" (131, my italics).

Neglecting to reward commercial virtues would discourage market transactions and, therefore, diminish the market as an institution; and without markets there can be no public happiness. Dragonetti treats the subjects of war and navigation in similar terms (78 ff.). Without adequate naval protection for trade there can be no safe commerce; therefore defense should not be left to mercenary troops. Instead, the pure military virtues that keep the state safe and, hence, free and happy, should be rewarded. A similar attitude emerges at the conclusion of an unpublished letter from Dragonetti to his brother Gian Battista, in response to a question concerning the connection between the first and the second part of his book: "If I did not discuss agriculture, war, navigation and commerce, that are the ... main human virtues, what would my ... little treatise be worth?" (Dragonetti, in Bruni 2010).

Such a vision of commerce, which (as Hirschman (1977) and others have explained) was quite common in Europe at that time, implies that Dragonetti considered commerce to be part of the system for the reward of virtue. It is virtuous to satisfy other people's needs, and by facilitating mutually advantageous transactions, the market rewards virtue.

His chapter on commerce states:

> A thousand proofs convince us that man was made for society, but above all, the mutual dependence on mutual wants, that basis of all unions ... The barrenness of one place is to be supplied by the fertility of another, and industrious nations provide for the want of slothful ones. Without commerce trade is impossible. Commerce is the reciprocal communication of the produce and industry of various countries ... To make each individual participate in the benefits of nature, and to give to the political body all the strength it is capable of, ought to be the effect of commerce.
>
> ([1766] 1769, 113, 122, 123)

One possible and legitimate reading of such passages on commerce, which corresponds to a fundamental concept in the Civil Economy tradition, is that the market serves as a key mechanism for rewarding virtues.

From that perspective, markets and trade are perfectly moral or virtuous; mutual advantage, reciprocity, and morality go hand in hand. Although the Civil Economy tradition emphasizes virtue and its reward, it follows a different cultural path than the one followed by "communitarian" authors such as Anderson (1993) or McIntyre (1981). These authors see a contrast between true moral relationships and standard economic or market interactions. For Dragonetti (and Genovesi), however, the market and the virtues are fully consistent with one another (Bruni and Sugden 2013).

Only one sentence in Dragonetti's small book has achieved widespread notoriety – the one Thomas Paine cited in *Common Sense*. Paine seemed to take particular pleasure in the political aspects of the pamphlet ([1776] 1923, 30), and he quoted the following passage:

> A mode of government that contained the greatest sum of individual happiness, with the fewest wants of contribution [in terms of liberty].

> ... *The science of the politicians consists in fixing the true point of happiness and freedom.* Those men would deserve the gratitude of ages, who should discover a mode of government that contained the greatest sum of individual happiness, with the least national expense.
>
> (155; the sentence in italics is the one quoted by Paine)

Dragonetti's emphasis on civic virtues and their rewards did not generate (as often happens) an illiberal or authoritarian vision of politics and democracy. In his political project of reforming the Kingdom of Naples, virtues, public happiness, and freedom go hand in hand, a vision that may put Dragonetti alongside liberal proponents of freedom, happiness, *and* virtues, such as Paine or J. S. Mill. At the same time, Dragonetti never formulated an actual and complete theory of the relationship between virtues and rewards, nor did he ever lay out the theoretical mechanisms for rewarding virtues, a shortcoming that marks the greatest limit of his work. Nevertheless, several of his insights can be read and appreciated within the general framework of Civil Economy.

The vision of the economy as a sign of civilization, then, runs through Genovesi and all Neapolitan writings. Expressing the mainstream thought about commerce and civilization, in the first edition of the *Lezioni* Genovesi too writes that one of the fruits of commerce "is to bring the trading nations to peace ... War and commerce are as opposite as motion and quiet" ([1765–67]2005, 513). In most of his theory, commerce is considered one of the main tools in creating the civilization and wealth of a nation.

In the last years of his life, nevertheless, his attitude towards commerce became more ambivalent. His sentence in *Lezioni* on the spirit of commerce is well known: "The *spirit* of commerce is that of the conquests. Barbarous people conquer people and lands; trading people conquer riches" (522). This controversial sentence, in relation to the "spirit" of his time, is important for understanding Genovesi's critique of Montesquieu's thesis regarding "the doux commerce" in his annotations to the Neapolitan edition of the *L'Esprit des lois* (Genovesi 1777). His annotations for books XX and XXI of Montesquieu's masterpiece note that "commerce is the great source of wars" (Genovesi 1777, II: 195), which seems to contradict many other statements in the *Lezioni*, some of them quoted above. Why?

Genovesi composed the annotations to *L'Esprit des lois* toward the end of his life, in the same period during which he wrote the *Lezioni*. Since that is the case, there must be a consistency between his theory of commerce and his vision of the market based on the law of reciprocity. The same annotation that contains his statement on commerce as the "source of wars," in fact, mentions a few lines later that "If two nations trade together for reciprocal needs, these needs are in opposition to war, not the spirit of commerce" (ibid.). Reflecting on the commercial enterprises of past and present empires, Genovesi writes: "The driving principle of such enterprises is not commerce, but the consciousness of their power, greed. Commerce is a mere instrument" (198–199).

Therefore, the later Genovesi distinguishes between the commerce of nations and its *spirit* (which for him is intricately connected with military power and strategies for political conquest), and commerce among peoples, in particular domestic commerce (based on reciprocity among equals and expressions of different needs). He maintains that commerce among nations (as it was actually conducted during the mercantilist system) generally was not an expression of reciprocal advantage or assistance but unilateral exploitation. This interpretation runs through all of Chapter XVII in the first book of *Lezioni*. Looking across the development of his theory, it is possible to trace the evolution of Genovesi's evaluation of the spirit of commerce from the first draft of his treatise (*Elementi di commercio*, written in 1758) up to the second Neapolitan edition of the *Lezioni* (1769), where his negative judgment of the spirit of commerce is even tougher than in the 1765 first edition.

At the beginning of his career as an economist his evaluation was more positive, but became much more elaborated and generally critical toward the end. Particularly in his latest works, Genovesi became more aware of the darker possibilities of international trade, an aspect that became more and more significant within his notion of Civil Economy.

## Conclusion

The vast sociological tradition – from Max Weber to Ferdinand Tönnies to Georg Simmel, to say nothing of the modern philosophical tradition (Hegel would suffice) – has grasped, and in a certain manner discovered, with extreme clarity the duplicity and the ambivalence of life together, or the "unsocial sociability" of humanity (Kant). It has discovered the "not," the negative, that is hidden in the other who is like me but who is not me, a tragic negative that lurks at the heart of life together in *communitas*. But, rather than traversing that obscurity, that negative, it has sought escape routes. A major escape route was the invention of the capitalistic market. One cannot but be amazed that, while modern philosophy came to understand over the course of a few decades – from Hegel to Nietzsche – that flight from the "not" of the other led to nothingness and nihilism, modern political economy has been living in its infancy for two and a half centuries, claiming that it is possible to write a true theory of human interactions (economics is a matter of human interactions) without taking seriously the relational dimension and its ambivalence.

Apart from our age of globalization, no other age has been so convinced that it can resolve the contradiction of sociality by trusting in the alchemy of contracts and markets. The great crisis of contemporary economics is concealed in this excessively prolonged infancy, eloquently symbolized by the paradox of unhappiness. In fact, if the extension of anonymous contracts and the limits on personal encounters exceed a critical point, life in common becomes dismal. If to avoid conflict we design housing regulations, workplaces, and cities that prevent our crossing paths in the halls, stairways, common spaces, and the town square (and the decline in public spaces in our cities is worrying), then the cure becomes far worse than the disease. This is also one of the messages of the crisis of our age.

In the period in which we – Europeans in particular – are living, the message of Civil Economy can be useful. Antonio Genovesi's and Giacinto Dragonetti's vision of economy based on a more socialized idea of the person was critical of the mercantilist idea of commerce as a zero-sum game. If nations and people *trade together for reciprocal needs*, the fulfillment of these needs is in opposition to war, because commerce in the right spirit expresses the principles of reciprocity and mutual assistance that are, in the Civil Economy tradition, the golden rule of *both* market and community.

## Notes

1 In Bruni and Sugden (2013), we argue that the opposition market/virtues does work in general (not only in the Civil Economy tradition but also in classical political economy, if "properly" understood.
2 From this point of view, it is important to recall that Luther was originally an Augustinian monk, and in the Augustinian theology, this Manichean dichotomy was central and very influential in the early Middle Ages, at least up to the new movements of Franciscans and Dominicans and the theologies of Bonaventura, Duns Scotus, Occam, and, of course, Aquinas. Later medieval theology paid significant attention to the social and political dimensions of the Christian faith, and was characterized by a less accentuated separation between the "city of God" and the "city of men."
3 I use the term "individual" in a technical sense, which is distinct from the category of "person." According to the Scholastic tradition, from St. Thomas to Jacques Maritain, a person is a being-in-relation that exists only in relationship with others; an individual, however, subsists in and of him- or herself and is characterized by self-sufficiency and indivisibility (*in-dividuum*). The anthropological idea that post-Smithean political economy took is that of the individual, certainly not that of the person; I say 'post-Smithean' because Smith's anthropological discourse is more complex (see Bruni and Sugden 2008).
4 Allan Silver writes: "According to Smith, the replacement of *necessitudo* with commercial society brings with it a morally superior form of friendship – voluntary, based on natural sympathy, unconstrained by necessity" (1990, 1481). On this basis, the conditions can be created for the emergence of civil society free from the categories of indifference or foreignness: the other is neither my enemy nor my ally, he or she is simply indifferent to me: the "stranger is not a friend from whom we can expect any special favor and sympathy. But at the same time, he is not an enemy" (ibid., 1483).
5 A few biographical notes about Antonio Genovesi. Born November 1, 1713 in Castiglione (now Castiglione del Genovesi) near Salerno, from a noble but modest family, Genovesi became involved very early in the ecclesiastical way of life, until officially becoming a priest in 1737. After living in Buccino (Salerno) for a few years, he moved to Naples in 1738. There he studied philosophy and attended the lectures of Gianbattista Vico, whose thought remained a constant source of inspiration for Genovesi (akin to Hume's inspirational influence on

Smith). In 1739 he established a private school, teaching philosophy and theology, and thus gained some experience in pedagogy. During these years, he met Celestino Galiani (the uncle of the economist Ferdinando), thanks to whom he was offered his first university teaching position and thus became professor of metaphysics in 1745. Meanwhile, in 1743, he published the first part of *Elementa Metaphysicae*, a philosophical work that was strongly disputed in the ecclesiastic sphere. In the same period he met and befriended Ludovico Antonio Muratori, another important figure of the so-called "public happiness" School. He thus became a member of the circle of Bartolomeo Intieri, an academic from Florence, whose Galilean approach was significant for Genovesi's transition from metaphysics to economics, "*Da metafisico a mercatante*" (cf. Bellamy 1987). In 1753 he published the circle's reformist manifesto: *Discorso sopra il vero fine delle lettere e delle scienze* ("Discourse on the true end of letters and sciences"). Between 1765 and 1769, his most important work was published, including *Lezioni di economia civile*, and *Della diceosina o sia della filosofia del giusto e dell'onesto* ("Della diceosina, that is the philosophy of just and honest").

# References

Anderson, Elizabeth. 1993. *Value in Ethics and Economics*. Cambridge, MA: Harvard University Press.

Aristotle. 2009. *The Nicomachean Ethics*. Translated by David Ross and edited by Lesley Brown. Oxford: Oxford World's Classics.

Bellamy, Richard. 1987. "'Da metafisico a mercatante': Antonio Genovesi and the Development of a New Language of Commerce in Eighteenth-Century Naples." In *The Languages of Political Theory in Early-Modern Europe*, edited by Anthony Pagden, 277–299. Cambridge: Cambridge University Press.

Bruni, Luigino. 2010. "Su Delle virtù e de' Premi di Giacinto Dragonetti (e una polemica di Benedetto Croce)." *Il pensiero economico italiano* 18: 33–49.

Bruni, Luigino. 2012a. *The Wound and the Blessing: Economics, Relationships, and Happiness*. Hyde Park, NY: New City Press.

Bruni, Luigino. 2012b. *The Genesis and Ethos of the Market*. London: Palgrave Macmillan.

Bruni, Luigino and Robert Sugden. 2008. "Fraternity: Why the Market Need Not Be a Morally Free Zone." *Economics and Philosophy* 24 (1): 35–64.

Bruni, Luigino and Robert Sugden. 2013. "Reclaiming Virtue Ethics for Economics." *Journal of Economic Perspectives* 27 (4): 35–64.

Bruni, Luigino and Stefano Zamagni. 2007. *Civil Economy*. Oxford: Peter Lang.

Doria, Paolo Mattia. 1710. *Della Vita Civile, s.l.* Naples.

Dragonetti, Giacinto. [1766] 1769. *A Treatise on Virtues and Rewards*. London: Johnson and Payne. First Italian edition, *Delle virtù e de' Premi*. Naples.

Dumont, Louis. 1980. *Homo Hierarchicus: The Caste System and Its Implications*. Chicago: University of Chicago Press.

Esposito, Roberto. 2009. *Communitas: The Origin and Destiny of Community*. Redwood City, CA: Stanford University Press.

Filangieri, Gaetano. [1780] 1806. *The Science of Legislation*, vols. 1 and 2. Translated by Sir Robert Clayton. Bristol: Emery and Adams.

Genovesi, Antonio. [1765–67] 2005. *Lezioni di commercio o sia di Economia civile*, Critical edition, edited by Maria Luisa Perna. Naples: Istituto Italiano per gli studi filosofici. Second Neapolitan Edition: Naples, Simone, 1769.

Genovesi, Antonio. [1766] 1973. *Della diceosina o sia della filosofia del giusto e dell'onesto*. Milan: Marzorati.

Genovesi, Antonio. 1777. *Spirito delle leggi del Signore di Montesquieu, con le note dell'Abbate Antonio Genovesi*. Tomo Secondo. Naples: Domenico Terres.

Hirschman, Albert O. 1977. *The Passions and the Interests: Political Arguments for Capitalism before Its Triumph*. Princeton, NJ: Princeton University Press.

McIntyre, Alistair. 1981. *After Virtue*. Notre Dame, IN: Notre Dame University Press.

Mauss, Marcel. [1925] 1990. *The Gift: Forms and Functions of Exchange in Archaic Societies*. London: Routledge.

Paine, Thomas. [1776] 1923. "Common Sense." In *Selections from the Works of Thomas Paine*. New York: Harcourt.

Silver, Allan. 1990. "Friendship in Commercial Society: Eighteenth-Century Social Theory and Modern Sociology." *American Journal of Sociology* 95 (6): 1474–1504.

Smith, Adam. [1759] 1976. *The Theory of Moral Sentiments*. Edited by D. D. Raphael and A. L. Macfie. Oxford: Oxford University Press.

Smith, Adam. [1763] 1896. *Lectures on Justice, Police, Revenue and Arms*, delivered to the University of Glasgow by Adam Smith. Reported by a student in 1763 and edited with an Introduction and Notes by Edwin Cannan, 1896.

Smith, Adam. [1776] 1981. *An Inquiry into the Nature and Causes of the Wealth of Nations*. Indianapolis, IN: Liberty Fund.

Sandel, Michael J. 2009. *Justice: What's the Right Thing to Do?* London: Penguin.

Todorov, Tzvetan. 1998. *La vita in comune*. Milan: Pratiche.

# 6 What does true individualism really involve?

Overcoming market–philanthropy dualism in Hayekian social theory

*Paul Lewis*

## Introduction

Philanthropy and commerce are often portrayed as motivationally and institutionally distinct forms of social cooperation. Markets are thought to involve large-scale interaction among people who know little if anything about each other, while philanthropy is said to centre on personal relationships between small groups of individuals who are well acquainted with one another's needs (Hayek 1988, 18–19). Accordingly, markets are viewed as impersonal and amoral spheres of action, in which people are treated as no more than means to one another's ends, while philanthropy is said to involve a more principled treatment of others as ends in themselves. Consequently, while behaviour in markets is usually said to be driven exclusively by self-interest, philanthropic activity is often said to be motivated by a more altruistic concern for the welfare of others. This tendency to portray markets and philanthropy as distinct, self-contained modes of cooperation is an example of dualism, "the practice of organising thought by means of all-encompassing mutually exclusive categories" (Dow 1990, 143). The works of Friedrich Hayek, and also of other thinkers such as Kenneth Boulding, are often said to exemplify such a dualistic approach (Garnett 2007, 2009).

This paper utilises recent developments in social theory and philosophy to suggest how this dualism between commerce and philanthropy might be overcome, thereby pointing the way towards a more integrated and inclusive, but still distinctly Hayekian, approach to social theory. In particular, the paper draws on recent developments in social theory and philosophy centring on the notion of 'collective intentionality' to argue that – even viewed through a Hayekian lens – market exchange and philanthropy bear greater similarities to one another than is often recognised. In particular, it will be argued that both forms of activity involve *collective* or *we*-intentions that are quite distinct from the individual intentions, whether self- or other-regarding, that dualists typically assume characterise people's behaviour in (respectively) markets and the independent sector.

On this view, voluntary market exchange can be thought of not as an exclusively self-interested affair, but rather as involving a shared commitment on the part even of anonymous individuals to engage in mutually beneficial interactions governed by norms of promise-keeping, honesty, the rule of law, and generalised reciprocity. Similarly, philanthropy can be thought of as involving people formulating collective or we-intentions that commit them to furthering a particular cause, from which they themselves benefit (either directly, from the gratitude of the recipients of their largesse, or less immediately, and with less certainty, through a reciprocal gift given at some indeterminate point in the future). In both cases, the pursuit of self-interest is tempered, albeit to different degrees, by a commitment to shared goals and common norms of conduct, within – significantly, as we shall see – a world of (radical) uncertainty.

One implication of this view, of course, is that Hayek's distinction between small-group activity and the kind of behaviour that gives rise to the extended order of the Great Society is over-drawn; both kinds of endeavour involve collective intentionality and a measure of commitment to various social norms and rules. Notwithstanding the departure this marks from the dualistic position Hayek stakes out in his explicit remarks about the limited role played by altruism in the creation of the extended order of the Great Society, the claims advanced in this paper arguably draw out, build on, and develop some underappreciated aspects of Hayek's own distinctive view of human nature. Hayek christens his account of human nature "true individualism", the better to distinguish it from the narrow view of man as an anti-social atom or desiccated calculating machine so often associated with economics:

> What, then, are the essential characteristics of true individualism? The first thing that should be said is that it is primarily a *theory* of society, an attempt to understand the forces which determine the social life of man, and only in the second instance a set of political maxims derived from this view of society. This fact should by itself be sufficient to refute the silliest of the common misunderstandings: the belief that individualism postulates (or bases its arguments on the assumption of) the existence of isolated or self-contained individuals, instead of starting from men whose whole nature and character is determined by their existence in society
> (Hayek [1945] 1948, 6)

For Hayek, people are profoundly social beings whose values, motivations, goals, and conduct are all shaped by the nexus of social context within which they live (11–13). The argument developed below is that the theory of collective intentionality can be used to flesh out this notion of true individualism so that it can encompass both commercial and philanthropic activities. In doing so, the paper aims to signpost the possibility of a broader, but still Hayekian, notion of economics as the study of human provisioning in its broadest sense, encompassing both commercial and philanthropic activity.

The structure of the paper is as follows. The following section sets out the key concept of collective intentionality and explains how it can be used to portray market transactions as endeavours in which the contracting parties commit to a joint project that will benefit them all. Next, I argue that this account of the market as involving people forming collective intentions to engage in mutually beneficial transactions is not only quite consistent with the Hayekian portrayal of the market order as a rule-governed social process but also adds to the Hayekian analysis a sense of how, through the use of collective or we-intentions, an individual can identify him- or herself with a group or society in which certain rules prevail. The notion of collective intentionality is then applied to philanthropy, in order to show that – far from being separate domains of human activity involving radically different forms of motivation – the market and philanthropic orders are both parts of civil society, with people's behaviour in both being driven by the same kind of human inclination towards mutual assistance. Finally, I summarise and draw conclusions, in particular concerning the nature of economics as a discipline.

## Collective intentionality and market transactions

Reciprocity is a human inclination towards mutual assistance and manifests itself in people's willingness to act together to secure their mutual benefit (Bruni and Sugden 2008, 46; Seabright 2004, 27, 54–58). On the view developed in this paper, reciprocity is a wellspring of human action, both in the market and also in what is variously called the voluntary, independent, or philanthropic sector. For Luigino Bruni and Robert Sugden, on whose account of reciprocity this paper relies, both market-based and other, non-market forms of human behaviour involve a human inclination or disposition towards *reciprocity* or *mutual assistance*. In contrast to the standard conception of mutually advantageous exchange, in which each party benefits from a transaction that happens – as a contingent matter – to benefit the other, but in which one person's benefiting is not part of the other's intention, the notion of assistance "implies an *intention* on the part of the person who assists to benefit the person who is assisted" (2008, 46). Bruni and Sugden elaborate as follows:

> Assistance is intentionally directed towards helping another person in her needs, towards being useful to others. If assistance is mutual, these intentions are reciprocal: each stands ready to help the other in the expectation that they stand ready to help her.

On this view, market transactions are – like philanthropy and other forms of reciprocity – instances of mutual assistance, whereby once they have decided to trade with each other, the relevant parties are committed to securing their mutual benefit. And this understanding of market transactions as mutually beneficial enters into people's understandings of the market relationships in which they participate, in a way that can be understood using the notion of collective or we-intentionality.

The philosophical literature on collective intentionality suggests that, in addition to having their own separate goals and commitments, the individual members of a group can also possess "collective" intentions that involve them making a commitment to act in concert with one another, as a group, in order to achieve some shared goal. Each member of the group that holds a collective intention conceives of him- or herself as acting *as a member of that group* and, therefore, as performing part of a *profile* of actions that, if each member does his or her part, will – it is believed – promote the group's shared objective. In other words, each individual's intention is to *join with* the others in achieving some shared goal (Gilbert 1989, 1996; Searle 1990; Bratman 1993; Bruni and Sugden 2008, 49–50).

Consider, for example, the members of an American football team that is about to try to run a pass play. In that case, the collective intention – held by the members of the team's offence – is expressed by the statement, "We are executing a pass play." Of course, each individual member of the offence will have a specific contribution to make towards achieving that goal: the offensive linemen will have their individual blocking assignments; the wide receivers will all have particular pass patterns to run; the running backs will either stay in the backfield to block blitzing linebackers or run pass patterns as so-called check-down receivers; and the quarterback will have a series of "reads" whereby he has to scan various potential receivers of the ball and decide whether or not to pass it to them, or to run with the ball himself, or to throw the ball away. The point, though, is that all of these individual intentions arise only within the context of the shared intention to run a pass play, and they cannot be expressed without that overall collective intention; the individual intentions all derive, and only gain their meaning from, the collective intention, "We are executing a pass play." When each player performs his or her designated action, he or she construes it as part of the collective intention and acts in the confidence that the other members of the group view things the same way and will therefore also perform their allotted tasks (cf. Searle 1990).

What this example suggests is that collective intentions have two key characteristics. First, the individuals who hold them believe that the intention in question is widely – though not necessarily universally – held by the other members of the group. Second, the individual believes that the intention is *mutually* or reciprocally held by members of the group, in the sense that they too believe that it is widely held by their fellow members. All the players on the offence need to be "on the same page," as the saying goes, in the sense that they all need to believe that they are executing the same pass play (rather than, say, a running play). In short, we-intentions involve a structure of mutually reinforcing, reciprocal beliefs, shared by the individual members of the relevant group, such that each believes that the others hold the same belief, and each also believes that the others think the same about their fellow members (cf. Davis 2002, 14).

When it comes to market transactions, the significance of collective intentionality is as follows. Bruni and Sugden argue that the market contracts into which people enter can be thought of as "constituting the contracting parties as a collective agent with respect to whatever joint enterprise is the subject of the contract" (2008, 51). On this view, in signing the contract, each party commits him- or herself to playing his or her part in bringing about a shared goal, namely carrying out some transaction that will be to *the joint benefit of both of the parties*. According to this perspective, when two people agree to trade with each other and sign a contract, what they are doing is effectively saying to one another, "Here is a plan for a joint enterprise from which both of us can benefit: you help me by selling me the car that I want; and I assist you by giving you the money you need in return. If we both play our parts, then both of us will be better off after the trade than before it." The point is that, if trade is indeed based on shared intentions of this kind – intentions that stipulate that, "We are involved in a mutually advantageous trade" – then each party acts with the intention of playing his or her part in a combination of actions that is intended to benefit *both of them*. The contrast with the conventional view of market exchange, according to which people trade with one another with the intention only of advancing their own narrow self-interest and not that of their trading partner, so that mutual advantage emerges only as an unintended consequence of the transaction, is stark (Bruni and Sugden 2008, 46, 50; cf. Sen 1999, 257).

For Bruni and Sugden, then, market transactions are – like philanthropy and other forms of reciprocity – instances of mutual assistance, whereby once they have decided to trade with each other the parties to a transaction are committed to securing their mutual benefit. And the fact that market transactions are mutually beneficial enters into people's own understandings of the market relationships into which they enter, so that they internalise that idea. The parties are jointly intending a combination of mutually beneficial actions and each party thinks of him- or herself as a member of a group and as performing – indeed, as we shall see, as being obliged to perform – his/her part of the set of actions agreed upon by the group in its efforts to pursue the agreed objective. It is this notion of market transactions as being based on collective or shared intentions that – according to this perspective – makes those transactions genuinely social. The relationship is social because, rather than being based on individual intentions – whether they be selfish (taking the perspective of an "I") or selfless (viewing things from the vantage point of "You") – it is couched in terms of the shared intentions of a group of people (of the "we" or "us").

It is important to note that, according to this account, the collective intentions that undergird market contracts are formed only when the contract is made; they do not exist prior to the contract and so do not provide the motivation for the contract. People are free to pursue their own interests in choosing which contracts to make, only becoming committed to a shared goal after the contract has been drawn up. In this way, the approach developed by Bruni and Sugden makes it possible to treat market relationships as genuinely social and as involving mutual assistance while retaining the view that they also involve competition based on private incentives and price signals (2008, 49, 51–52).

## A Hayekian account of the market

How does all this bear upon Hayek? Notwithstanding his explicit remarks about the shortcomings of altruism (1988, 18–19, 81), Hayek's own explanation of how the extended order of the Great Society is brought about reveals a more balanced position, in which people's pursuit of their goals is tempered by their commitment to certain abstract norms and rules (such as moral norms of promise-keeping and of truth-telling, generalised norms of reciprocity, and formal laws of property, tort and contract) (Hayek 1960, 62–63; 1976, 14, 16–17). "Man is as much a rule-following animal as a purpose-seeking one," Hayek (1973, 11) says, elaborating on that theme by quoting a passage from the philosopher R. S. Peters:

> Man is a rule-following animal. His actions are not simply directed towards ends; they also conform to social standards and conventions, and unlike a calculating machine he acts because of his knowledge of rules and objectives. For instance, we ascribe to people traits of character like honesty, punctuality, considerateness and meanness. Such terms do not, like ambition, or hunger, or social desire, *indicate the sort of goals that a man tends to pursue; rather they indicate the type of regulations that he imposes on his conduct whatever his goals may be.*
> (1973, 147–48 n. 7; emphasis added)

> The rules of morals are instrumental in the sense that they assist mainly in the achievement of other human values; however, since we only rarely can know what depends on their being followed in the particular instance, to observe them must be regarded as *a value in itself, a sort of intermediate end which we must pursue* without questioning its justification in the particular case.
> (Hayek 1960, 67; emphasis added; also see Hayek 1976, 16–17)

For Hayek, then, social rules and norms are not goals that people pursue. Rather, they are ethics, laws, and customs to which people submit in order to restrain the ardour with which they pursue their own goals.[1]

A similar perspective on Hayek's work is developed by Buchanan (2005, 72, 75–76), who describes what he terms "the communitarian elements in [Hayek's] own description of the moral order of liberal society" as involving an "ethics of mutual respect and of reciprocity in dealings [whereby] … persons behave in accordance with norms that may be externally classified as exhibiting non-exploitative, non-opportunistic and non-discriminatory treatment of others". Buchanan elaborates on his account of Hayek's approach as follows:

> Persons are treated as *persons*, as reciprocating human beings, deserving of mutual respect. This conception [like Sen's notion of commitment] finds its philosophical roots in Kant's precept that persons are to be treated as ends and never as means. But, as properly understood and as influential in Hayek's thought … [t]he Kantian precept enters the choice calculus as a moral constraint rather than as an argument in a utility function.
>
> (P. 76)

In terms redolent of Bruni and Sugden's work, Buchanan goes on to argue that at the heart of Hayek's approach is the insight that "there exist mutual gains from exchange between and among any and all potential trading partners – gains that may be realised upon guarantees that behaviour in the exchange process itself does not exhibit effort to secure differential opportunistic advantage" (2005, 75). In highlighting how on Hayek's account such guarantees are in large measure provided by people's commitment to "the norm of generalised reciprocity" whereby "persons' interaction one with another is motivated by the prospect that reciprocal interaction will generate expected gains for both parties", Buchanan helps us to see more clearly the importance of the norm of reciprocity – and, dare one say it, mutual assistance – in Hayek's scheme of thought (2005, 27, 45; also see 83, 84).[2]

People's willingness to abide by such norms and rules – and the way their commitment to them constrains the goals they are willing to pursue – can be conceptualised in terms of collective intentionality. More specifically, people's commitment to social norms can be thought of as involving shared intentions to the effect that "We believe that members of our community should do x in circumstances z" (where the phrase "do x" should be interpreted broadly as a placeholder for a variety of injunctions such as, "count as", "take to mean", "refrain from", "donate to", and so forth) (Davis 2004, 390; cf. Lawson 2003, 36–39). Such rules and norms specify what types of behaviour the members of a particular group – whether it be a small, intimate group such as a family or a larger "imagined community" such as a race or nation (Anderson 1991) – count as "correct", "honourable", "considerate", "mean", etc., and in effect constitute a set of guidelines that specifies what people have to do in order to identify themselves with the other members of the group and thereby to cultivate and to express publicly their identity as group members (Sen [1985] 2002, 215).

On this view, a person's identity is best thought of in terms of the groups with which (s)he chooses to affiliate him- or herself. More specifically, the position outlined here attempts to capture people's ability to define who they are in terms of their use of collective intentions or we-language and, in particular, by considering how the use of such language requires them to embrace the views of other group members about what counts as acceptable behaviour, etc. (Lewis 2009, 51–55). Such rules and norms have motivational force because they furnish people who wish to become, or remain, members of a particular community with reasons for acting in certain ways.

Amartya Sen, in a passage that seems to be quite compatible with those from Hayek quoted above, has described this as follows:

> One of the ways in which the sense of identity can operate is through making members of a community accept certain rules of conduct as part of obligatory behaviour towards others in a community. It is not a matter of asking each time, What do I get out of it? How are my own goals furthered in this way?, but of taking for granted the case for certain patterns of behaviour towards others.
> 
> ([1985] 2002, 216–17)

From this perspective, the motivational force of social norms derives from the fact that group members accept the authority of "us" – of "our" shared view of how "we" should behave – to determine certain features of their conduct in the domain defined by the norm.[3]

Significantly, behaviour that is driven by we-intentions is not reducible to instrumentally rational behaviour (Searle 1995, 23–25; Davis 2002, 20–22, 2004, 392–93). The reason is as follows. An individual's we-intention centres on what (s)he thinks the intentions of the other individuals in the group actually are, not what (s)he would like them to be, so that there arises the possibility of a tension between what an individual believes a group's collective intention to be and what (s)he would prefer it to be. If an individual (sincerely) expresses a we-intention in a situation where that tension has indeed arisen, then (s)he has effectively made a commitment to act in accordance with the group's collectively expressed view that a particular goal should be pursued, or that a particular type of action is required, even though that might not be what the individual would have preferred were (s)he not a member of the group in question. On this view, the shared intentions that arise when a person uses we-language involve him or her imposing upon him/herself obligations or commitments that qualify the unconstrained pursuit of his or her own goals, simply because expressing a we-intention requires the individual to conform to how other people use that same 'we.' Hence, people may share a collective goal without each of them also having it as a personal goal (Davis 2002, 21–22; 2004, 399; Anderson 2003, 191–193).

In this way, the notion of collective intentionality makes it possible to conceptualise how people can have sources of motivation above and beyond the instrumental desire to satisfy their individual preferences and pursue their individual goals. People not only have the capacity to behave in an instrumentally rational fashion, asking what they should do in order to satisfy their own individual goals; they also have the (often countervailing) ability to act in accordance with social rules, their commitment to which may involve them stepping back from their individual goals and asking what is the best strategy for us to adopt:

> Behaviour is ultimately a social matter as well [as an individual one], and thinking in terms of what "we" should do, or what should be "our" strategy, may reflect a sense of identity involving recognition of other people's goals and the mutual interdependencies involved.
> (Sen 1987, 85)

The members of a social group think of themselves as a "we", and understand one another to be jointly committed to various goals, including that of upholding shared social rules and norms. In identifying with a group, therefore, an individual understands that (s)he has accepted responsibility for doing his/her part to advance the group's goals and to uphold the rules and norms that operate within it, making a commitment that motivates his/her subsequent actions. In sincerely using the first-person plural, therefore, a person embraces the obligation in question, acknowledging – not least to him- or herself – that it applies to him/her and therefore taking it upon him- or herself to fulfil it (e.g., by adhering to some social norm or rule) (Davis 2004, 139, 143).

It is, of course, just this kind of constraint on individuals' choice of goals and conduct to which Hayek is alluding when he describes in the passages quoted above how social and moral rules constrain people's conduct. Like Sen, Hayek views social rules as imposing "side constraints" on individual behaviour that rule out of court certain goals as no longer being legitimate objects of choice. What the notion of collective intentionality adds to the Hayekian account is a sense of how, via their use of the first-person plural, people acknowledge that social norms and rules apply to themselves. A person who is sincere in using we-language to identify him- or herself with a group has embraced the rules that are observed by members of that group, acknowledging that they apply to him/her and therefore taking it upon him- or herself to observe them (Davis 2004, 138, 143–146).

It is time to bring the two parts of our argument together. Recall first of all that, according to Bruni and Sugden, market transactions can be thought of – indeed, *are* effectively thought of by participants in markets – as involving collective intentions along the line of: "We are engaged in mutually beneficial trade." We have also seen, second, that – according to scholars such as Amartya Sen and Elizabeth Anderson – the way in which social and moral rules of the kind that Hayek argued are central to the extended order of the Great Society affect people can also be conceptualised using the notion of we-intentions. We can now put these two ideas together by arguing that the kind of commercial morality – the general confidence in people's intentions to honour contracts and eschew fraud – that Hayek believes is one of the building blocks of the market order can be conceptualised using the notion of collective or we-intentionality (Bruni and Sugden 2008, 49–58; Lewis 2009, 57–60), along the following lines: "We are part of a mutually beneficial transaction that will take place in accordance both with the rule of law and with certain norms prevalent in our group or society, such as promise-keeping, honesty, fairness, etc." As Paul Zak has put it:

> [A] mutual decision to exchange requires an understanding that both parties to the transaction must be made better off if the exchange is going to occur. If one makes unreasonable demands, then exchange will fail and the gains from trade will be lost … [B]ecause uncoerced market exchange requires gains for both parties … exchange itself is necessarily other-regarding. The "win–win" aspect of exchange is known to all parties, and therefore a buying decision is contingent on understanding that the producer needs to make a fair profit to stay in business and that consumers have budget constraints and alternative suppliers. In reasonably competitive markets, sharing the gains from exchange is the norm; a variety of field and laboratory evidence reveals that excessive greed results in an absence of exchange and a subsequent loss of the gains from trade (Babcock and Loewenstein 1997; Cooter and Rubinfeld 1989). Neuroeconomics experiments show that the human brain is finely tuned to punish those who violate sharing norms. Fairness is part of human nature.
> 
> (2011, 226, 213–14)

On this view, in entering into a transaction, people are committing themselves to a venture that they intend to be mutually advantageous and to be undertaken in accordance with the intersubjectively shared social rules and norms that prevail in their community.

Behaviour that is underpinned by collective intentions of this kind can be seen to be especially important once it is recalled that formal contracts are highly likely to be incomplete, both because of the transaction costs of negotiating and drafting such contracts, and also because bounded rationality and the existence of radical uncertainty imply that it is simply impossible for people to foresee all of the contingencies that might impinge upon their transactions (especially if they are drawn out over time). The question then arises of what the parties will do if an unforeseen contingency does indeed arise. Standard economic analysis, of the kind that is based on the notion of singular or "I"-intentions, might suggest that each party would strive to turn the unforeseen event to his or her advantage, opportunistically exploiting its occurrence whenever it is in their narrow self-interest to do so. The analysis presented here, however, suggests something rather different. For if it is the case that the parties of a transaction are motivated by a shared commitment that it should be to their mutual advantage, then they are under an obligation not merely to adhere to the letter of their contract but to respond to unforeseen contingencies in ways that continue to promote the shared goal of mutual assistance, which will in turn require that they refrain from opportunistically exploiting each other even when an unforeseen event gives them a chance to do so (Bruni and Sugden 2008, 41, 53–55; cf. Hayek 1960, 66–68).

Consider, for example, two businesses: the first is a garment manufacturer; the second supplies the manufacturer with fabric. Suppose for the sake of argument that they have entered into a contract specifying that the fabric supplier will supply the garment manufacturer with a certain amount of a particular kind of fabric for a certain price. However, because of an unexpected change in the kind of garments that have to be made, the manufacturer now requires a slightly different type of fabric. The fabric supplier might exploit the situation by refusing to change the specification unless the garment manufacturer pays a considerable extra sum of money. However, such opportunism would be inconsistent with the notion that the transaction should be mutually advantageous. If the two parties understand that, by entering into the contract, they have made a joint commitment to securing their mutual benefit, then the fabric supplier will feel obliged to adhere to the spirit of that agreement by complying with the manufacturer's request without precipitously raising the price of the fabric, thereby ensuring that the transaction remains mutually advantageous. What this example, which is based on a study of the behaviour of firms in the New York City garment industry, is meant to illustrate is that if the parties of a contract view themselves as joint partners in a mutually beneficial series of actions, they will (have good reason to trust each other to) respond to unforeseen contingencies by acting in good faith, eschewing narrowly self-interested and opportunistic modes of conduct in favour of actions that are in accordance with norms of fairness and reciprocity. As one of the businessmen interviewed as part of the study put it, "Trust means that he's not going to find a way to take advantage of me. You are not selfish for your own sake. The partnership comes first" (Uzzi [1997] 2001, 213–216, 224–25; Lewis 2008, 184–190).

On this view, market transactions are instances of *mutual assistance*, whereby – once they have decided to trade with each other – the parties to a transaction are committed to securing their *mutual* benefit, subject to the intersubjectively shared rules and norms that prevail in the community from which the contracting parties are drawn. As a result, the parties in question are obliged to be "mutually responsive" to each other's needs in the sense that they must adapt their behaviour to unforeseen circumstances in order to do their best to be useful to one another and to advance towards their agreed goal (Bratman 1993). The importance of such behaviour has been underlined by Nobel Laureate Kenneth Arrow, who has commented that:

> [T]here has to be some kind of commercial morality for contracts to be executed ... a theory which depends merely on reputation is not enough because there will always be circumstances when it pays to violate the rule ... So the economic system – the self-seeking, laissez faire system – would not work without the presence of these non-laissez faire, non-self-seeking norms.
>
> (1990, 139)

(See also Arrow [1973] 1984, 150–52 and [1973] 1985, 139; Sen 1977, 332; Seabright 2004, 56–59; Buchanan 2005, 42; and Zak 2011, 6, 15.) Such behaviour, if it does indeed redound to the mutual benefit of both parties, can be thought of as being rational, not in the sense of the instrumental conception of rationality presupposed by standard rational choice theory, but rather in the sense that it involves the discipline of subjecting one's choices – not only of actions, but also of goals – to reasoned scrutiny. As Hayek put it, "Rationality ... can mean no more than some degree of coherence and consistency in a person's action, some lasting influence of knowledge or insight which, once acquired, will affect his action at a later date and in different circumstances" (Hayek 1960, 77).

It is also worth noting, with Bruni and Sugden (2008, 52), that because market interactions involve a shared commitment to mutually beneficial exchange, they may well give rise to feelings of friendliness and goodwill as the participants warm to one another's efforts at mutual assistance. In this way, the interaction that takes place in markets can become imbued with additional social and affective content, giving rise to social relations – of trust, for example, and of friendship – whose reach extends beyond the narrowly commercial confines in which they were engendered. It is not a coincidence that the original meaning of the term catallaxy was "to change from an enemy into a friend" and "to admit into the community" (Hayek 1976, 108). In this way, viewing market transactions as involving genuinely social relations of mutual assistance, based on collective intentions for mutual benefit, lends support to the view, outlined most notably by Virgil Storr (2008, 2009), that the market is an area of social life where social as well as commercial ties are formed, so that what were initially business or business-like relations spill over into broader forms of sociability.[4]

Overall, then, the account of market behaviour presented here implies the unsustainability of the binary opposition that Hayek attempts to establish between the other-regarding motives that (he believes) characterise the micro-cosmos and the narrowly self-interested behaviour (he claims) typifies the extended order. The account presented here suggests, far from being confined to the face-to-face world of small groups of known associates, the notion of mutual assistance is also an important part of (people's understanding of) the kind of interaction that takes place in markets. If it is indeed the case, as Cornuelle ([1965] 1993, 38) has argued, that the independent sector "functions at any moment when a person or group acts directly to serve others," then we can see from the account of the nature of market transactions presented above that such behaviour is not entirely absent from the market, manifesting itself in the efforts of trading partners to assist one another. It is also, as we shall see, an important element in philanthropic activity.

## The role of collective intentions in philanthropic projects

Philanthropy has been defined as "voluntary giving and association that serves to promote human flourishing" (Ealy 2005, 2). Two key features of philanthropic activity are often mentioned, both of which – I shall argue – can be encompassed by a view of philanthropy as involving donors and recipients sharing collective or we-intentions for mutual assistance. In the first place, philanthropy is said to involve behaviour that is in some sense, often left rather vague, "benevolent" or "altruistic", involving one-way transfers or gifts of money from donors to recipients (albeit ones that may be balanced by non-pecuniary benefits – such as gratitude or friendship – that accrue to the donors) (Boulding 1973, 1–3; Dobuzinskis 2009; Grosby 2008; Henderson 2009). Second, such disinterested behaviour is often said to involve the donors of largesse identifying with others and thereby forging a sense of their own identity (that is, a sense of who they, the donors, really are) (Schervish 2009).

The vantage point provided by the notion of collective intentionality suggests that philanthropy involves genuinely social relationships that see donors and recipients commit themselves to a shared goal of mutual betterment, of being useful to each another. As James Otteson has put it:

> True philanthropy is undertaken by free and accountable beings *in the service of* other free and accountable beings, and the demands it places on both parties *unite them in a joint project* of making human life better … [W]e are made better by *acting philanthropically to help others realise their own ends*.
> 
> (2009, 25; emphasis added)

Paul Schervish, a commentator on philanthropy with whose views the approach outlined here bears strong affinities, elaborates on the nature of philanthropic projects as follows:

> At its best ... philanthropy unifies individuals in caring relationships that enrich the receiver and giver alike ... [Philanthropy involves] ... a sense of 'we-ness,' as the specific mobilising impetus that spurs the caring orientation ... [T]his we-ness, 'the sense of being connected with another or categorising another as a member of one's own group,' is a central determinant of helping and results from the combination of personal beliefs and associational ties that brings the needs of others into one's purview.
> (Schervish 2009, 38, quoting Martin 1994 and Jackson et al. 1995)

In the language of collective intentionality, donors and recipients are effectively saying to one another: We are involved in a joint endeavour in which we can serve each other and from which both of us can benefit: I, the philanthropist, will help you by donating funds that will enable you to advance a project that is dear to you, and which falls within the boundary of those projects that are acceptable to me; and you will assist me by enabling me to fulfil the obligations I feel to particular groups or causes within society and to develop my ability to make a difference to the lives of others. If we both play our parts, then both of us will be better off after the project has been fulfilled than we were before it" (cf. Bruni and Sugden 2008, 57–63; Schervish 2009, 40–41).[5] Moreover, in using we-language to express their commitment to philanthropic projects, and to working with recipients – and, possibly, other donors – to bring shared projects to fruition, donors are able to express their attachment to those other groups or causes and thereby cultivate a sense of their own identity (Lewis 2009, 55–58; also see Schervish 2006, 477–478, 484–485, 2009, 39, 41–42).

By focusing on what Schervish aptly refers to as "the inherent mutuality" involved in philanthropy, the approach outlined here attempts to transcend the dualism of narrow self-interest and selfless altruism in order to portray philanthropy as "an act of mutual nourishment" whereby people "do things to help others and themselves at the same time" (2009, 41–42, 37). Such behaviour can, of course, be thought of as being animated by what Tocqueville refers to as "the principle of self-interest, properly understood" whereby "an enlightened self-love continually leads [people] to help one another and disposes them freely to give part of their time and wealth for the good of the state" (Tocqueville [1835] 1966, 526; also see Cornuelle [1965] 1993, 55–64, 1992, 6; Henderson 2009, 143; Schervish 2009, 38).

The significance of all this for our present purposes is, of course, that the accounts of market transactions and philanthropy sketched above suggest that both kinds of conduct can be thought of as manifestations of the same general disposition for human beings to engage in shared projects for mutual benefit. It is reciprocity – understood as a human inclination towards mutual assistance, or as exchange broadly defined – that is the wellspring of both kinds of action. In both cases, people form collective or we-intentions for mutual assistance and thereby commit themselves to joint ventures that each of them intends to be *mutually* advantageous. And in each case, people's commitment to that goal obliges them both to adhere to certain social rules and norms and also to respond flexibly to unforeseen contingencies in ways that are consistent with the shared intention of mutual assistance, as for example when, in the event of unanticipated and genuinely unavoidable increases in a project's costs, donors might feel under an obligation to find the extra funding required to bring the unfinished project to a successful conclusion.

Far from reducing economic life to narrowly self-interested behaviour alone, this approach therefore acknowledges an important role in commercial transactions for the very kind of other-regarding motivation that is said to characterise philanthropy. On this view, there is in fact a continuum of different types of commercial transaction, and associated motivations, ranging from spot transactions, where trades are completed almost instantaneously and the scope for trust and mutual assistance is limited, to more protracted exchanges where, because the long time lag between payment and completion allows considerable scope for unforeseen events to impinge upon the transaction, there is more scope (and need) for the kind of reciprocal adjustment to which collective intentions for mutual benefit give rise. In this way, the notion that transactions might be drawn out over (real, historical) time acts as a (metaphorical) solvent that, by breaking down the barriers that divide commercial transactions from philanthropy, allows an essential role for the kinds of motives that drive philanthropic behaviour in commercial life as well (cf. Danby 2002, 15, 28–32). In a similar vein, rather than reducing philanthropy to pure, unreciprocated altruism, the perspective outlined above acknowledges that donors may well gain any one of a variety of benefits from the gifts they make, including the satisfaction of promoting a cause that is close to their hearts, enjoyment deriving from the gratitude of those they assist, or even relief from assuaging guilt, so that – as in the case of commercial transactions – there exist a variety of different kinds of motivation in the case of philanthropy (Boulding 1973, 5; Dobuzinskis 2009; Henderson 2009).

In short, there is a continuum of different kinds of exchange – or, as Garnett (2010, 13) has put it, "multiple modes of reciprocity" – that vary both (1) according to the time lag between payment and completion of the transaction and consequent scope for mutual assistance to play a significant role, and also (2) according to the precise objects being exchanged (typically money for goods, in the case of market transactions, but also money for other less tangible gifts in the case of philanthropy). And what this suggests, of course, is that the divide between (behaviour within) the markets and (the type of conduct involved in) philanthropy is not as sharp as commentators like Hayek often seem to suggest. Far from being separate domains, governed by different kinds of motivation, the market and the philanthropic order are both parts of civil society, with people's behaviour in both involving joint commitments to mutual support and assistance: "No part of the economy [is] conceived as inherently commercial or philanthropic. The general presumption [is] that every aspect of the economy is comprised of commercial and philanthropic elements" (Garnett 2010, 16; also see Bruni and Sugden 2008, 46–48, 62–63 and Henderson 2009, 142).

## Conclusion

This account advanced above can be thought of as a response to Garnett's plea for a "spectral view of social phenomena" according to which "[n]o part of the economy would be conceived as inherently or exclusively 'commercial' or 'philanthropic'". The general presumption would be that "every aspect of the economy is [potentially] shaped and propelled by a mixture of commercial and philanthropic elements" (Garnett 2007, 27). Whereas the standard understanding of market relationships juxtaposes two binary opposites – namely, market/social and self-regarding/self-sacrificing – the approach developed here offers a way of conceptualising a relationship between two individuals *both* as a mutually beneficial exchange and *also* as a genuinely social interaction that is imbued with intrinsic value in virtue of this social content. Contrary to the dualistic view that market interactions can only be instrumental and impersonal, and that non-instrumental behaviour and concern for others arise only in the case of small groups such as the family, the view advanced here suggests that market interactions can take the form of genuinely social relationships whose participants understand themselves as engaging in a shared plan for mutual betterment, thereby providing a way of transcending the dualism between (ostensibly) other-regarding activity of the kind involved in philanthropy and narrowly self-interested market-based activity. In stark contrast to dualistic perspectives that provide conceptual space for only two (mutually exclusive) kinds of behaviour, each of which is confined to one particular domain of social life, the approach outlined above affords conceptual room for a whole range of intermediate types of behaviour that involve different degrees of (willingness to provide) mutual assistance and which arise in all parts of civil society.

If it is true that certain human capabilities – most notably the capacity for reciprocity and mutual assistance – are central both to commerce and philanthropy, then it is also the case that those capabilities are likely to give rise to behaviour that produces orderly outcomes of the kind that make society possible on a large scale only if they are channelled by certain social institutions that – in Paul Seabright's memorable phrase – "make it possible for us to deal with strangers by persuading us, in effect, to treat them as honorary friends" (2004, 4; also see 1–9, 27–28, 48–102 and Zak 2011, 14–18). While this essay has focused on the human capabilities themselves, that should not divert attention from identifying and analysing (the properties of) the requisite institutions. It is worth noting in this context that, just as there is a competitive process of selection whereby participants in markets decide with whom to make a contract, so too in the case of philanthropy must there be a process of selection whereby donors decide which potential recipients to support. Their efforts to do so will not, of course, be informed by price signals, and the outcomes of decisions cannot be summarised via profit and loss accounts, giving rise to the question of how recipients are to be chosen and projects evaluated. The key issue concerns whether there exist mechanisms in the world of philanthropy that make it possible for donors to receive signals and forms of feedback, analogous to market prices and profit and loss calculations, that can help them to husband their scarce resources and deploy them in ways that best promote their preferred causes (Boettke and Prychitko 2004; Chamlee-Wright and Myers 2008).

If it is indeed the case – as seems eminently reasonable – that the Hayekian project can be thought of as an attempt to explore the institutional foundations of the market (Vaughn 1999; Lewis 2015), then one of the aims of this essay has been to broaden the scope of that project by undermining the dualism between self- and other-regarding motives that Hayek strove to establish and thereby persuade his latter-day followers that the set of institutions to be explored in Hayekian social theory should include not only those ostensibly devoted to commercial pursuits but also – as Cornuelle ([1965] 1993) has argued – those involved in the so-called independent sector (Garnett 2009, 2010). On this view, the discipline of economics is best thought of neither as involving one particular analytical method (e.g., rational choice theory), nor as focusing only on one particular set of activities or institutions (commerce or market), but rather as an attempt to analyse (the interplay between) all those human capacities and social institutions that make it possible to meet people's needs and thereby sustain the extended order of the Great Society (Boulding 1973, 13; Lawson 2003, 141–164; Garnett 2007, 25–27).

## Acknowledgments

I am grateful to Robert Garnett, Lenore Ealy, and participants in the 2011 APEE conference in Nassau, the Bahamas, for very helpful comments on an earlier version of this essay. The usual disclaimer applies.

## Notes

1 "Civilisation largely rests on the fact that ... individuals have learnt to restrain their desires for particular objects and to submit to generally recognised rules

of just conduct" (Hayek 1979, 7; also see 1960, 62, 435–436 n. 36). On this view, the Hayekian good society is "not laissez faire without qualifying adjectives" but rather an extended "nexus of reciprocity ... generalized to include all mutual agreements up to and including the political" (Buchanan 2005, 84, 78).
2 As Buchanan puts it elsewhere, "The market, as an organisational form, will work well only if participants are presumed to be motivated by self-interest, but only within the discipline imposed by mutuality of respect for trading partners. The market order in which persons deal, one with another, strictly in terms of opportunistic self-interest would be neither efficient nor tolerably just ... The required 'laws and institutions', mentioned by Adam Smith, include not only formal rules of conduct but also the institutionalised ethics of mutual respect or reciprocity" (2005, 26).
3 See also Hayek, who writes that "it is acceptance of ... common principles that makes a collection of people a community ... A group of men normally become a society ... by obeying the same rules of conduct" (1960, 106–07). In Buchanan's words, social rules "may emerge from a process of cultural evolution, as Hayek suggests, while at the same time offering adherents a concrete means of identifying one with another and, thereby, satisfying personal desires for community membership" (1985, 79).
4 For a Hayekian account of the psychological mechanisms through which this might come about, see Lewis (2012, section 6).
5 For more on how donors can benefit from their philanthropic endeavours, see Haidt (2006, 134) and Gunderman (2007, 42).

## References

Anderson, Benedict. 1991. *Imagined Communities: Reflections on the Origin and Spread of Nationalism*. London: Verso.
Anderson, Elizabeth. 2003. "Beyond Homo Economicus: New Developments in Theories of Social Norms." *Philosophy and Public Affairs* 20: 170–200.
Arrow, Kenneth J. [1973] 1984. "Information and Economic Behaviour." In *The Collected Papers of Kenneth J. Arrow*, vol. IV: The Economics of Information. Oxford: Basil Blackwell.
Arrow, Kenneth J. [1973] 1985. "Social Responsibility and Economic Efficiency." In *The Collected Papers of Kenneth J. Arrow*, vol. VI: Applied Economics. Oxford: Basil Blackwell.
Arrow, Kenneth J. 1990. "Kenneth J. Arrow." In *Economics and Sociology*, edited by R. Swedberg. Princeton, NJ: Princeton University Press.
Babcock, Linda and George Lowenstein. 1997. "Explaining Bargaining Impasse: The Role of Self-Serving Biases." *Journal of Economic Perspectives*, 11: 109–126.
Boettke, Peter J. and David L. Prychitko. 2004. "Is an Independent Non-profit Sector Prone to Failure? Toward an Austrian Interpretation of Non-profit and Voluntary Action." *Conversations on Philanthropy*, I: 1–40.
Boulding, Kenneth E. 1973. *The Economy of Love and Fear: A Preface to Grants Economics*. Belmont, CA: Wadsworth.
Bratman, Michael. 1993. "Shared Intentions." *Ethics* 104: 97–113.
Bruni, Luigino and Robert Sugden. 2008. "Fraternity: Why the Market Need Not be a Morally Free Zone." *Economics and Philosophy* 24: 35–64.
Buchanan, James. 2005. *Why I, Too, Am Not a Conservative: The Normative Vision of Classical Liberalism*. Cheltenham: Edward Elgar.

Chamlee-Wright, Emily and Justin Myers. 2008. "Discovery and Social Learning in Non-Priced Environments: An Austrian View of Social Network Theory." *Review of Austrian Economics* 21: 151–166.

Cooter, Robert and Donald Rubinfeld. 1989. "Economic Analysis of Legal Disputes and Their Resolutions." *Journal of Economic Literature* 27: 1067–1097.

Cornuelle, Richard C. [1965] 1993. *Reclaiming the American Dream: The Role of Private Individuals and Voluntary Associations*. New Brunswick, NJ: Transaction.

Cornuelle, Richard C. 1992. "The Power and Poverty of Libertarian Thought." *Critical Review* 6: 1–10.

Danby, Colin. 2002. "The Curse of the Modern: A Post-Keynesian Critique of the Gift/Exchange Dichotomy." *Research in Economic Anthropology* 21: 13–42.

Davis, John. 2002. "Collective Intentionality and Individual Behavior." In *Intersubjectivity in Economics: Agents and Structures*, edited by Edward Fullbrook. London: Routledge.

Davis, John. 2004. "The Agency-Structure Model and the Embedded Individual in Heterodox Economics." In *Transforming Economics: Perspectives on the Critical Realist Project*, edited by Paul A. Lewis. London: Routledge.

Dobuzinskis, Laurent. 2009. "French Perspectives on the Origin and Logic of the 'Philanthropic Order': A Critical Account." *Conversations on Philanthropy* VI: 115–139.

Dow, Sheila. 1990. "Beyond Dualism." *Cambridge Journal of Economics* 14: 143–57.

Ealy, Lenore T. 2005. "The Philanthropic Enterprise: Reassessing the Means and Ends of Philanthropy." *Economic Affairs* 25: 2–4.

Garnett, Robert. 2007. "Philanthropy, Economy and Human Betterment: A Conversation with Kenneth Boulding." *Conversations on Philanthropy* IV: 13–31.

Garnett, Robert. 2009. "Philanthropy, Markets, and Commercial Society: Beyond the Hayekian Impasse." *Journal of Markets and Morality* 11: 205–219.

Garnett, Robert. 2010. "Hayek and Philanthropy: A Classical Liberal Road not (yet) Taken." In *Hayek, Mill and the Liberal Tradition*, edited by A. Farrant. London: Routledge.

Gilbert, Margaret. 1989. *On Social Facts*. London: Routledge.

Gilbert, Margaret. 1996. *Living Together: Rationality, Sociality, and Obligation*. Lanham, MD: Rowman & Littlefield.

Grosby, Steven. 2008. "Philanthropy and Human Action." *Conversations on Philanthropy* VI: 1–14.

Gunderman, Richard B. 2007. "Imagining Philanthropy." *Conversations on Philanthropy*, IV: 36–46.

Haidt, Jonathan. 2006. *The Happiness Hypothesis: Finding Modern Truth in Ancient Wisdom*. New York: Basic Books.

Hayek, F. A. [1945] 1948. "Individualism: *True and False*." In *Individualism and Economic Order*. Chicago: University of Chicago Press.

Hayek, F. A. 1960. *The Constitution of Liberty*. London: Routledge.

Hayek, F. A. 1973. *Law, Legislation, and Liberty: A New Statement of the Liberal Principles of Justice and Political Economy*, vol. I: Rules and Order. London: Routledge.

Hayek, F. A. 1976. *Law, Legislation and Liberty: A New Statement of the Liberal Principles of Justice and Political Economy*, vol. II: The Mirage of Social Justice. London: Routledge.

Hayek, F. A. 1979. *Law, Legislation and Liberty: A New Statement of the Liberal Principles of Justice and Political Economy*, vol. III: The Political Order of a Free People. London: Routledge.

Hayek, F. A. 1988. *The Fatal Conceit: The Errors of Socialism*. Edited by W.W. Bartley III. London: Routledge.
Henderson, Christine. 2009. "Comment: Traditions of Philanthropic Order." *Conversations on Philanthropy* VI: 141–145.
Jackson, Edward, Mark Bachmeier, John Wood, and Edward Craft. 1995. "Volunteering and Charitable Giving: Do Religious and Associational Ties Promote Helping Behavior?" *Nonprofit and Voluntary Sector Quarterly* 24 (1): 59–78.
Lawson, Tony. 2003. *Reclaiming Reality*. London: Routledge.
Lewis, Paul A. 2008. "Uncertainty, Power and Trust." *The Review of Austrian Economics* 21: 183–198.
Lewis, Paul A. 2009. "Commitment, Identity and Collective Intentionality: The Basis for Philanthropy." *Conversations on Philanthropy* VI: 47–64.
Lewis, Paul A. 2012. "Emergent Properties in the Work of Friedrich Hayek." *Journal of Economic Behavior and Organization* 82 (2): 368–378.
Lewis, Paul A. 2015. "Hayek's Economics: From Market Equilibrium to Social Order." Forthcoming in *The Elgar Companion to Hayekian Economics*, edited by Norman Barry and Roger Garrison. Cheltenham: Edward Elgar.
Martin, M. 1994. *Virtuous Giving: Philanthropy, Voluntary Service, and Caring*. Bloomington, IN: Indiana University Press.
Otteson, James R. 2009. "'The Gospel of Wealth' and True Philanthropy." *Conversations on Philanthropy* VI: 21–26.
Schervish, Paul. 2006. "The Moral Biography of Wealth: Philosophical Reflections on the Foundations of Philanthropy." *Nonprofit and Voluntary Sector Quarterly* 35: 477–492.
Schervish, Paul. 2009. "Beyond Self-Interest and Altruism: Care as Mutual Nourishment." *Conversations on Philanthropy* VI: 33–43.
Seabright, Paul. 2004. *The Company of Strangers: A Natural History of Economic Life*. Princeton, NJ: Princeton University Press.
Searle, John. 1990. "Collective Intentions and Actions." In *Intentions in Communication*, edited by Philip Cohen, Jerry Morgan, and Martha Pollack. Cambridge, MA: MIT Press.
Searle, John. 1995. *The Construction of Social Reality*. London: Penguin.
Sen, Amartya K. 1977. "Rational Fools." *Philosophy and Public Affairs* 6: 317–344.
Sen, Amartya K. [1985] 2002. "Goals, Commitment and Identity." In *Rationality and Freedom*. Cambridge, MA: Harvard University Press. Originally published in *Journal of Law, Economics and Organization* 1: 341–355 (1985).
Sen, Amartya K. 1987. *On Ethics and Economics*. Oxford: Basil Blackwell.
Sen, Amartya K. 1999. *Development as Freedom*. Oxford: Oxford University Press.
Storr, Virgil. 2008. "The Market as a Social Space: On the Meaningful Extra-Economic Conversations that can take place in Markets." *The Review of Austrian Economics* 21: 135–150.
Storr, Virgil. 2009. "Why the Market? Markets as Social and Moral Spaces." *Journal of Markets and Morality* 12: 277–296.
Tocqueville, Alexis de. [1835] 1966. *Democracy in America*. Translated by George Lawrence. New York: HarperCollins.
Uzzi, Brian. [1997] 2001. "Social Structure and Competition in Interfirm Networks: The Paradox of Embeddedness." In *The Sociology of Economic Life*. 2nd edn.,

edited by Mark Granovetter and Richard Swedberg. Boulder, CO: Westview Press. Originally published in *Administrative Science Quarterly* 42: 35–67.

Vaughn, Karen I. 1999. "Hayek's Implicit Economics: Rules and the Problem of Order." *Review of Austrian Economics* 11: 128–144.

Zak, Paul. 2011. "Moral Markets." *Journal of Economic Behavior and Organization* 77: 212–233.

# 7 Methodological individualism and invisible hands

Richard Cornuelle's call to understand associations

*Steven Grosby*

In his arresting article, "New Work for Invisible Hands," Richard Cornuelle (1991), student of Ludwig von Mises and the person who in 1965 brought the phrase "the independent sector" into our discourse with *Reclaiming the American Dream*, observed that the collapse of the Soviet Union confirmed "that the invisible hand of the market is a more reliable organizer of the economic life of nations than the visible hand of the state" (1991, 1). There was nothing remarkable in that observation, except that, as a student of Mises, that collapse had for decades been viewed as inevitable. What was remarkable was that Cornuelle continued by noting that, despite the theoretical sophistication of Mises and his circle that had led to that accurate prediction, there remained a "lack of a coherent, comprehensive vision of voluntary community beyond the market" (1991, 4). He rightly thought that this inability to understand properly the character of associations was a consequence of an overly "individualist emphasis, a suspicious aversion to any kind of communal activity beyond the commercial" (1991, 4). The challenge Cornuelle raised in that article was the need to understand better the character of what he called "voluntary community" – those associations about which Tocqueville had written so compellingly in *Democracy in America* ([1840] 2012), the tradition of which Cornuelle had sought to revive with the publication of *Reclaiming the American Dream*. Like Tocqueville, Cornuelle knew that associations were necessary for liberty and its preservation; but could those who had understood so well the significance of free markets both for the economic life of the nation and the liberty of the individual suspend that suspicious aversion and tackle the "unsettled questions" of the "less familiar territory" of the character of associations beyond the commercial firm?

A theory of community, whether natural (where membership is dependent upon recognition of the primacy of the primordial criteria of birth or location) or voluntary, involves numerous complications. There is the analytical tradition of the conceptual and historical dichotomy between the earlier, tradition-bound, local, face-to-face community (*Gemeinschaft*) of individuals with putatively little individuality and the modern, territorially extensive society (*Gesellschaft*) of individuals putatively exclusively pursuing their self-interest. Whether or not this still influential dichotomy, initially formulated in 1887 by Ferdinand Tönnies (2001), is theoretically antiquated and, thus, heuristically of questionable use, is one of the problems circling around the various chapters of this book. This kind of bifurcation appears to leave little place for modern associational life. The related problems of how one is to understand what Cornuelle referred to as that overly "individualist emphasis" in the analysis of human action, the very terms "individual" and "interests," and the character of spontaneous orders beyond that of the market place, for example, language groups, the "republic of science" as described by Michael Polanyi (1962, [1951] 1998), and perhaps even nations (as distinct from national states) quickly come to the fore. Once they do, that vexing theoretical postulate of human action, methodological individualism, surfaces as a problem.

Human action is the action and reaction of individuals; thus the analysis of any social relation must begin with the individual – hence the principle of methodological individualism (Schumpeter 1909; Arrow 1994; see Hodgson 2007). This does not necessarily mean, however, as a recent analyst of this long acknowledged problem rightly observed (Davis 2002), that the motivation for action is entirely a product of, and confined to, the mind of the individual. Of course, we know that the actions of individuals are often coordinated, markets being one obvious example. However, the problem before us comes into greater focus when we concern ourselves not only when individuals act in response to one another in the buying and selling of goods and services, but also when they act "in concert with" one another. How are we to understand this kind of coordination, expressed by the ubiquitous use of the pronoun "we" (Davis 2002; Shils 2006)? Can concerted action be adequately accounted for if we adopt an overly "individualist emphasis," that is, by an assumption that the orientation of the mind of the individual is solely a consequence of the individual's pursuit of only his or her advantage? Is there an ambiguity of our understanding of "advantage" or "interest" that has to be clarified if the variety of human actions (if variety there be) are to be understood? If two persons together do something, is it in some way different than if each only does it for himself or herself? Is such concerted action something analytically different from the reciprocal action typical of commercial exchanges? These are but a few of the complications facing the challenge that Cornuelle put before us, the formulation of a theory of the social processes of associational life.

The more one ponders what might be meant by the term "community," the number of complications only increases such that one begins to wonder if a comprehensive theory of the social processes of associational life is possible. Max Weber's ([1921] 1978) formulation of the ideal types of social action (instrumental rational, value rational, affectual, and traditional) and legitimate domination (rational, traditional, and charismatic) should be seen as his recognition that the categories "community" and "society," the forms of action that they imply, their formulation as a conceptual dichotomy, and their historical periodization were too simplistic to account adequately for human action; they had to be differentiated. Herman Schmalenbach ([1922] 1977) reached a similar conclusion in his differentiation of community (*Bund*) by noting that the intense and highly integrative attachments characteristic of the category "community" were to be observed not merely in the tradition-bound village as described by Tönnies, but also in, for example, the religious sect that often had no territorially (or temporally) local referent and even friendship. In fact, Adam Smith had already noted in *The Theory of Moral Sentiments* ([1759] 1982, 191–192) that the heuristic utility of the dualism between community and society is found to be decisively wanting when confronted by the occasional, community-like outbreaks of patriotic enthusiasm of modern societies, specifically when one chooses to sacrifice oneself in war (Grosby 2011). Recognition of complications of this kind led Talcott Parsons and Edward Shils (1951) to further differentiate human action through their formulation of the "pattern variables"; and shortly thereafter Shils ([1957] 1975) introduced another characterization of the types of social relation as primordial, personal, sacred, and civil.

Greater familiarity with this tradition of investigation into human action might keep the analyses of those economists (for example, Arrow, Davis, Hodgson) who have rightly recognized some of these complications from being unproductively diverted by those obfuscating descriptions of action like the temporally flat categories "interaction" or "structure," as if the social relation was devoid of meaningful referents, by pondering the individual as a *participant* in various, temporally deep symbolic complexes as traditions or "culture" (see Freyer [1927] 1998; Popper 1979; Shils 2006). By not indulging characterizations of action like "interacting," the analyst would recognize that the individual's participation in a tradition can, depending upon the social relation, contribute not merely or even primarily to the calculation of advantage, as if traditions were only accepted constraints on optimization, but also to the self-understanding of the individual – a self-understanding that may overlap with the self-understanding of other individuals, the recognition of which by those individuals is a crucial factor in the constitution of the social relation of a "we." This participation and its bearing on self-understanding is especially likely for non-commercial associations, because, unlike in the market place where criteria irrelevant to economic exchange are usually ignored, the significance of properties recognized in others (for example, one's nationality, religion) as arising from participation in a tradition is maintained, thereby having a bearing on actions and relations (Knight 1935a; 1935b). Furthermore, the phenomenon of participation may be key to understanding better what otherwise appears to be the paradoxical activity of when one acts for the benefit of others, when the individual has an interest in acting disinterestedly.

Implicit in this vantage point of participation is that the self, the individual, cannot be taken for granted, as if the mind is homogeneous in its seeking of an advantage accruing to that individual; rather, the mind participates in a multitude of different symbolic complexes. To be sure, as Arrow noted, while information (conveyed by those complexes) "may be supplied socially (as an externality), to be used it has to be absorbed individually" (1994, 8). In this regard, the principle of methodological individualism is rightly maintained: the "socially supplied information" – what has philosophically been characterized as "objective knowledge" (Popper 1979) or "objective mind" (Freyer [1927] 1998) or "objectivations" (Shils 1981) – must be grasped by the individual. However, with the concept of participation, the existence of that information or knowledge or mind is acknowledged, and, in contrast to the implication of the term "interaction," brought to the fore; but in no way does doing so imply a "group mind," for the individual must "absorb" (grasp or accept, even if only tacitly) that "information." Thus, as Hans Freyer ([1927] 1998, 206) felicitously observed, there is a "natural liberalism of the social situation"; for that participation never effaces the consciousness of the individual qua individual, even in a tradition-bound, highly integrated community (see Plessner [1924] 1999). But if so, as surely seems to be the case, we must then further acknowledge that because the mind of the individual participates in various symbolic complexes or traditions that are, in fact, heterogeneous, that is, there are a plurality of qualitatively different spheres of life (not only commercial, but also familial, artistic, even simply playful), then our very idea of the individual becomes problematic; for the mind (and actions) of the individual is now not merely an arena for the pursuit of advantage but also a dimension of potential, even unavoidable, moral dilemmas. An investigation into human action must analytically account for the existence of these dilemmas.

The idea of participation may go some distance in accounting for the "shared" motivation among individuals when they act as members of a group. Nonetheless, the relation between the individual and the "we" requires further clarification. The problem is complex; there are different ways to approach it. Let us continue by returning to the contrast between community and society, *Gemeinschaft* and *Gesellschaft*, in Hayek's writings on law.

## Further complications: the rule of law

In "Freedom and the Economic System," F. A. Hayek ([1939] 1997, 203) noted that the particular vision of social justice that is unavoidably conveyed by social planning requires a reversal of the historical tendency by which moral and legal rules have become formal and general. The generality of the law (general laws applicable to all), the equality before the law (laws must be the same for all), and the certainty of the law – these formal criteria of the "rule of law," necessary for individual freedom, subsequently analyzed by Hayek in *The Political Ideal of the Rule of Law* (1955) and *The Constitution of Liberty* (1960) – are undermined by central planning as it ineptly attempts to direct, in an unified manner, all individual activity in the service of a conception of public welfare that would, by preferentially treating some in contrast to others, putatively compensate for the place of chance in life, for example, familial affection and resources, or the unequal distribution of talent, or the greater initiative and ambition of one individual when compared to another, or new discoveries, or impersonal market forces, etc. In other words, the consequence of such an attempted compensation necessarily entails a view of the public welfare or social justice of a more comprehensive moral system at the expense of the freedom of the individual made more likely by the formal and general framework of law. Hayek thought that the attempt to implement such a vision represented for human civilization a disastrous step backwards: it was the road to serfdom, for

> the development of human civilization has been a movement from more to less comprehensive moral systems, from the member of a primitive tribe, whose daily life is a succession of acts regulated by a firmly established ritual, to the individual in the feudal society, whose fixed status determines the claims on life to which he is entitled, down to our times ... towards a life in which a constantly widening area [is] governed by individual tastes and preferences.
> ([1939] 1997, 203)

For there to be a widening area in which individual taste and preference can be pursued and expressed, moral and legal rules necessarily have to be formal and general.

In Hayek's analysis, we come across that familiar conceptual motif discussed above; for the recognition of a historical development from a more to a less comprehensive moral system was by no means unique to Hayek. It had become and still is a commonplace of sociological and legal observation, for example, Tönnies' contrast between the earlier *Gemeinschaft* and today's *Gesellschaft*, Durkheim's ([1893] 1997) distinction between mechanical and organic solidarity, Maine's ([1861] 1970, 165) formulation of a historical move from status to contract, and Gierke's ([1868] 1990, 113) admission that one of the greatest deeds of history was the emancipation of the individual as a result of the destruction of the medieval corporations. Thus, *Stadtluft macht frei*. The subsequent, welcomed refinements to what was and continues to be too often a simplistic dichotomy between the forms of action and attachment of antiquity and the middle ages, on the one hand, and those of modern life, on the other – by Weber in his formulation of multiple types of legitimate authority and different kinds of rationality; by Frank Knight ([1947]1982, 85), with his observation of the "fundamental error" of an excessive individualism that overlooks the fact of "some sort of family life, and far beyond that, some kind of wider primary-group and culture-group life, of a considerable degree of stability, must be taken into account as they are, as data"; and by Parsons and Shils' (1951) "pattern variables" – do not gainsay some merit to Hayek's argument. Nevertheless, there remain complications – complications that have to do with what Hayek (and, before him, Michael Polanyi) characterized as "the central theoretical problem of all social sciences" (1945, 528), namely, how to describe the existence of orders that have arisen not out of conscious direction but spontaneously. Our problem here is a better understanding of social phenomena of this kind beyond that of the market, and determining in what ways they have a bearing on human action.

While it is widely and rightly recognized that, when compared to the past, life today enjoys a "constantly widening area governed by individual taste and preference," the precise character, or variety, of that taste and preference is sometimes not considered. Although there is indeed wider latitude for the individual to pursue his or her taste and preference, for example, the choice of profession, or occupational mobility, and so forth, the question is, how distinctive is that individual pursuit? Perhaps this complication will come into sharper focus if we approach it through the lens of law. When doing so, the problem becomes whether or not the formality and generality of the law – consistently applied throughout the land such that we have equality before the law throughout a society (the rule of law necessary for individual liberty) – results paradoxically in a "flattening" of the expression of individual taste and preference by severely restricting, if not eliminating, the freedom of the individual to participate in any association of "special law." In other words, shall we take liberty to include not merely the wider latitude for the individual to pursue his or her tastes and preferences, but also freedom of association and especially freedom to participate in an association with its own rules and laws that may very well exist in tension with the formality and generality of the law of the land? And if so, what is the nature of the relation between such private associations with both other associations and especially the state? What are to be the limits of the idiosyncratic rules and laws of that association? Today, two examples (in fact, it seems as if the only remaining examples) of such associations are the natural association of the family and the voluntary association of the religious corporation. This problem deserves acknowledgment and discussion, even if it may be legally possible to address it with some degree of success, specifically, through some kind of basic law, for example, a version of the Bill of Rights. We shall return to this complication when we consider whether or not an association has rights and duties of its own, that is, whether or not a corporation has a "personality."

Returning to Hayek's analysis of the rule of law, how unequivocal has the movement from more to less comprehensive moral systems been? Perhaps the persistence of various traditions with their attendant attachments indicates that the movement cannot have been unequivocal; but if so, what has been its character? How are we to evaluate the "unevenness" of the movement? We know, for example, that nations and the patriotic attachment to them persist. How are we to judge this persistence? Are we to conclude that this persistence represents an evolutionary "residue": the continuation of an atavistic attachment that over time will disappear? Or should we be reluctant to draw this conclusion because we lack the evolutionary perspective of several hundred thousands of years? Should we instead consider the possibility that individual liberty, the generality and formality of the law that it requires, and the relatively less comprehensive moral system that provides greater scope for individual taste and preference all presuppose, in fact, a comprehensive moral system, a number of cultural (and even national) traditions; and that, without those traditions, it will be difficult to sustain freedom? If so, then we will face complications in our understanding of human action and attachment because we must take into account the influence of the culture (traditions) of what still is, albeit different from the past, a comprehensive moral system on the decisions and actions of the individual – what in the German tradition of the *Geisteswissenschaften* is called *Bildung*, the "cultivated character" of the individual.

This complication in our understanding of individual action in modern society was also raised, it seems to me, by Adam Smith ([1759] 1982, 188–193) in his recognition that at times human action is guided not by utility but by our sense of propriety, which may at times thwart even our desire for self-preservation.[1] But what are the sources of that sense of propriety, and what is their bearing on human action? This sense of propriety is not the creation of any particular individual; rather, the individual absorbs (to use Arrow's characterization) the meaning of what is right and wrong, as well as innumerable other meanings and symbolic complexes, through the individual's participation in the different, changing traditions of a society's culture. If there is merit to this line of deliberation, then we, once again, appear to face the likelihood of a differentiated, problematic constitution of the "self," where consideration of the advantage accruing to the individual of a particular action can be intermingled with other considerations of, for example, propriety, of conceptions of right and wrong. To resort to a spatial metaphor, the constitution of both the self and one's image of one's own self is multi-layered.

Putting aside for the moment this problem of the influence of traditions or culture on individual action – what Karl Popper (1979, 106–190) called the relation of "World 3" (the products of the human mind) and "World 2" (the subjective experience of the individual) – one faces the historical fact that the uniformity of the law, specifically its formal and general character, rests upon the consolidation of the sovereign state with a centralized judicial system. Two further complications arise from this historical fact. The first, analyzed so well by Tocqueville ([1840] 2012) that we need not explicate it here in any detail, is the extent to which one corollary of this consolidation is the helplessness of the individual vis-à-vis the state; for the existence of meaningful "intermediary" associations, especially those that encourage mutual aid, has been largely undermined precisely because of the monopoly of the state in promulgating law. As the French revolutionary convention, echoing Hobbes' ([1651] 1962, 245) earlier denunciation of independent associations as "worms in the entrails of a natural man," declared on August 18, 1792, "A state that is truly free ought not to suffer within its bosom any corporation, not even one dedicated to public instruction." And so, as Maitland ([1903] 1936, 230) characterized the result, "the absolute state faced the absolute individual." To Maitland's conclusion about this historical development we add that if there is to be assistance to the individual, it is not to be from the mutual assistance of the independent association of which the individual is a member, but only from the state, undertaken in the name of what is now understood as "public welfare" – a conception of public welfare (or in today's idiom, "social justice") defined, needless to say, by the state.

The second complication arising from the consolidation of the modern state is that since the rule of law, so necessary for the freedom of the individual, posits equality before the law of the land, it becomes increasingly unavoidable to set into motion the development of a conception of the public welfare of what is no longer a formal association of individuals but now a territorial community of law. If so, as the historical record indicates, then there are profound, albeit assuredly submerged, paradoxes lurking within Hayek's analysis of the rule of (formal) law in the constitution of liberty. Thus, it is precisely here, especially in light of these previously alluded to complications, that we encounter the attractiveness and forcefulness of Richard Cornuelle's (1991, 3) call for a better understanding of those associations that are "neither commercial on the one hand nor governmental on the other." Cornuelle's attention to these particular kinds of associations is significant; for the state has, for the most part, not been overly troubled by individuals joining together for the pursuit of economic gain, hence, partnerships, limited liability corporations, joint stock companies, and so forth. However, especially where the tradition of Roman law is dominant, as on the European continent, with associations of a different kind, the state has been far less tolerant, precisely because the existence of such independent associations represents a challenge to what actually is the relatively comprehensive moral system of the state. This is merely to observe that the associations of "special law" have been swept aside. Thus, taking modest steps to address Cornuelle's call for a better understanding of the voluntary social process will also require addressing the legal complications raised here.

## Corporate personality: mysticism or reality?

In his inaugural address, "The Nature of Human Associations" (*Das Wesen der menschlichen Verbände*), upon assuming the Rektorat of the University of Berlin in 1902, Otto von Gierke ([1902] 1935, 139–157) rightly observed that the character of the unity of associations was not only a problem for social philosophy but also necessarily a legal problem; for if associations have some kind of independent existence, whether they arise spontaneously or already exist, their ongoing activities are distinct from those of the state. The question then arises of whether, in fact, they have their own, autonomous rules and principles by which their activities are regulated. Thus, Gierke's problem is two-fold: (1) the philosophical problem of the nature of those associations that arise from the initiative and formative powers of its own members, and (2) the problem of how the independence of these associations should achieve, or necessarily implies, legal expression. In other words, does such an association have rights and duties specific to its own character? (To take one recent example that clarifies the problem: does a university have its own rules for hiring and promotion that are specific to the purpose of its existence – the teaching and discovery of truth – or must those rules be in accord with or even determined by the relatively comprehensive moral system of the state? This problem was the subject of Edward Shils' (1997, 177–233) "Jefferson Lectures" of 1979.) At stake in determining what it means for an association to have an "independent existence" is the very character of associational life; for only those associations that arise out of the initiative of its members are capable of satisfying the aspirations of those members.

Now, one need not entertain this problem and its implication at all if associations are viewed as merely a combination of individuals, each of whom keeps his or her contractual obligations and where the law recognizes the inviolability of the property of the individual. In this case, the "legal person" is and can only be the individual. Insofar as the law has to recognize various corporate bodies because, for example, they own property, the "personality" of the association is a "legal fiction," a *persona ficta* as formulated in the tradition of (the reception of) Roman law; the association has no substantive, autonomous existence; it has no rights of its own; it has no "life" of its own. Thus, there is the state and the individual. In such a state of affairs, as Maitland ([1903] 1936, 228–229) rightly noted, "all that stands between the state and the individual has but a derivative and precarious existence," for "if the personality of the corporation is a legal fiction, it is a gift of the prince," that is, of the sovereign state (for example, the requirement to be granted a charter by the state). Even so, the state may very well seek to facilitate a division of labor of the tasks to be performed, even encouraging the existence of numerous local associations to carry out those tasks, perhaps out of a concern for a more efficient delivery of some service. However, the very nature of those tasks will not and cannot be in dispute once decided upon by the sovereign; for to proceed otherwise runs the risk of undermining the formality and generality of the law of the sovereign authority, the jurisdiction of which is understood to hold sway throughout the land.

At issue here is whether the state is the sole creator of law, or whether there are other sources of law; in other words, whether the acceptable array of human action is determined by the state or it is left to individual initiative. There are obviously many complications of considerable significance here contained in the possibility of different sources of the objectives of human action and especially the heterogeneous directions they might take. But rather than pursuing these complications in an investigation of their consequences on the nature of sovereignty, even though implied by Cornuelle's call for a better understanding of voluntary community, let us return to Gierke's and our problem of the nature of the independent association.

The problem has now become whether or not an association is legally a "person" who, as such, has rights and duties. Or is it the case that only the individual is legally a person because only the individual is a free-willing creature who, as such, has rights and duties? If the latter is the case, then when we look upon an association, all that we should observe is a sum of individuals who stand in relation to, or "interact" with, one another. Thus, insofar as an association has some rights and duties or, for example, can sue and be sued as if it were a person, it is actually a fictitious person called into existence for a legal reason. However, note well that in the preceding observations the reality of the facts has forced these formulations: "insofar as the law has to recognize various corporate bodies" and "an association ... called into existence for some legal reason." There is manifestly a necessity of the law to recognize an association when it owns property; but how is this necessity to be understood? Is it possible that we face a reality more complicated than what limiting action to the individual takes for granted? Cornuelle's theoretical problem can now be reformulated: can it be that an association has "personality"?

Pollock and Maitland (1898, 488) thought that the crux of the problem of "corporate personality" was that:

> for more or less numerous purposes some organized group of men is treated as a unit which has rights and duties other than the rights and duties of all or any of its members. What is true of this whole need not be true of the sum of its parts, and what is true of the sum of its parts need not be true of the whole ... One of the difficulties that beset us at this point is that we are tempted or compelled to seek the aid of those inadequate analogies that are supplied to us by the objects which we see and handle. First we picture to ourselves a body made up of men as a man's body is made up of members. Then we find ourselves rejecting some of the inferences which this similitude,

this crude anthropomorphism, might suggest ... But all that is proved by the collapse of such analogical reasoning is that the social organization differs from, if it also resembles, that organization which the biologist studies; and this should hardly need proof.

Having granted the crude anthropomorphism of the use of the term "personality" in the phrase "corporate (or associational) personality," the fact remains that associations own property, act legally, usually have a representative, and many of their members act together. These characteristics, as well as others, convey rights and duties. If those rights and duties flow from the very nature of the association, why must they be granted? In other words, do various "we"s have independent existence? To generalize upon the problem of these observations, how are we to understand our ubiquitous use of the pronoun "we" instead of only "I"?

This problem of understanding "we" is, once again, the task before us when confronted by Richard Cornuelle's call for a better understanding of voluntary association. Cornuelle was by no means the first to see a need for a better understanding of associations out of a concern for liberty – an understanding that would not fall prey to an emphasis of an excessive individualism that, in fact, appears to misrepresent the reality of our existence. As mentioned above, Knight clearly saw the problem, although he did not pursue it; and obviously Gierke and Maitland forcefully did, too, by bringing to the fore what was for them the reality of "corporate personality." Edward Shils also struggled theoretically with the problem throughout his life, and pointedly so in a paper written a few years before his death, "Collective Self-Consciousness and Rational Choice" (Shils 2006, 195–216). This is how Cornuelle's call was formulated earlier by Gierke ([1902] 1935, 143) in the latter's following observation and rhetorical questions:

> We should have to endure [corporate persons] even if they were phantoms. Is it not, however, possible that their tough resistance [to being dissolved into individuals] demonstrates that they are by no means ghostly shadows, but living creatures? That law, when it treats organized associations as persons, is not disregarding reality, but giving reality more adequate expression? Is it not possible that human associations are real unities which receive through legal recognition of their personality only what corresponds to their real nature?

Clearly, we must proceed with care in addressing Gierke's questions. We acknowledge that an association of individuals cannot be the same as an individual. Thus, Maitland ([1903] 1936, 225) was obviously correct when he observed that "not all legal propositions that are true of a man will be true of a corporation." As but one example of how the corporation has to be different from a natural person, Maitland continued by observing that a corporation can neither marry nor be given in marriage. In seeking to take up Cornuelle's problem we must not lose sight of the elementary necessity of distinguishing between the individual (and the individual's mind) and the association, for otherwise we might wrongly drift into some mystical variant of a "group mind." Nonetheless, I think that Maitland (and Gierke before him) was correct to insist that "if there is to be group-formation, the problem of personality cannot be evaded" (230). And here, albeit in a legal idiom, is, again, Cornuelle's problem. It may very well be that "the word 'collectivity' is the smudgiest word in the English language" (237), still "if $n$ men unite themselves in an organized body, jurisprudence, unless it wishes to pulverize the group, must see $n+1$ persons" (235). If there is merit to Maitland's assertion, then the nature of this "$n+1$" should be explained in a manner that does not avoid the difficulties of the explanation through recourse to either descriptive evasions, as in the use of the word "collectively," or a doctrinaire reliance on an individualist emphasis that, in effect, dissolves the association. To proceed, we must return to that postulate of human action, methodological individualism.

## The social relation and methodological individualism

We may not know precisely what we mean when we use terms like "culture" or "tradition," but let us take for granted that these terms do, in fact, refer to some kind of social phenomenon. The phenomenon has over the years been described in various ways, depending upon the analyst, as "spirit," "psychic forces," "symbolic configurations," "World 3," "objective mind," and so forth. Whatever these terms actually refer to, we know that the creation and continued existence of the phenomenon occurs in and through individuals. Thus, we reaffirm the principle of methodological individualism. A group does not feel pleasure and pain; only individuals do. However, here is the complicating question: isn't it the case that the actions of individuals are often influenced by their involvement with or membership in an association that is organized around propositions and goals specific to that association?

Gierke formulated what I take to be the modest claim of an affirmative answer to this question in the following way:

> We feel ourselves to be self-sufficient beings, but we also feel ourselves to be parts of a whole which lives and acts within us. Were we to think away our membership in a particular people and state, a religious community and a church, a professional group, a family, and numerous other societies and associations, we should not recognize ourselves in the miserable remainder. When we think over all this, it becomes clear that it is not a matter merely of external chains and bonds which bind us, but rather a matter of psychological relations which, reaching deep within us and integrating us, form constituent elements of our

spiritual being. We feel that part of the impulse which determines our action comes from the community which permeates us.

([1902] 1935, 150)

The facts of our existence, in particular the evidently irrepressible urge of the individual to form and to participate in associations, require assent to the general point of Gierke's above observations. That urge is just as characteristic of human action as is the individual's calculation and subsequent pursuit of his or her own self-interest in the commercial relations of the market. In fact, the merit of Cornuelle's call and his earlier work, *Reclaiming the American Dream*, is the recognition that one expression of the individual's value of independence and self-propulsion is the formation and continuing existence of independent associations. Even so, certainly necessary is more careful formulation of the consequences of that urge than what appears in Gierke's above observations about "psychological relations"; for the continuing existence of "a whole which lives and acts within us" and "the community which permeates us" to which he refers is dependent upon the assent, at times tacit, and subsequent action of the individual. If that assent ceases then the association and the principles around which it is formed cease to exist. Thus, given that the creation and continued existence of an association can only occur through the actions of individuals, Gierke's formulations mask the problem of how we are to understand the "sharing" between individuals such that the association exists. Does "sharing" involve a more complicated process than some kind of simultaneous convergence of (or adjustment to) the pursuit of any number of individuals' interests?

Before turning our attention to this "sharing" and its bearing on the principle of methodological individualism, let us make clear that those "psychological" or "spiritual" relations that Gierke and so many others have referred to can be understood to be "invisible hands." As is well known, Adam Smith in *The Wealth of Nations* employed the expression "invisible hand" to account for the unintended result benefiting society at large arising from the individual's striving to better his or her own condition. However, James Otteson is surely correct when he observes an invisible hand in relations that are not commercial:

> Our strong desire for mutual sympathy of all our sentiments leads to reciprocity and mutual sympathy, thereby creating an invisible-hand mechanism that Smith thinks generates commonly shared standards of behavior and judgment, indeed, a commonly shared system of morality. It is an invisible hand because the agents in question do not intend to create a shared system of morality – they intend only to achieve mutual sympathy here, now, with this person. In so doing, however, they (unintentionally) create the behavioral habits, precedents, and protocols that will generate and maintain a shared system

of expectations and sentiments, with their correlated judgments, reproaches, and praises.

(2011, 39)

If this is so, then another way to understand the problem Cornuelle has set before us is to give the achievements of these truly invisible hands – the mechanism and its shared standards – their due.

We must employ the plural "hands" because, unlike the calculation of the price mechanism to signal preferences, desires, and the supply of objects to satisfy those preferences and desires, the objects of our sympathy are often incomparable, that is, they are not susceptible to being substituted for one another. Moreover, it is precisely because those "spiritual" objects – the meanings or symbolic configurations – are invisible (or not measureable) that there has been a tendency to dismiss them as mystical. However, to do so is incorrect. Thus, the entire problem before us can be reduced to this seemingly straightforward question, "Is human action sometimes influenced by numerous ideas, many of which are incommensurable?" If one answers this question with a "no," that is, action is to be understood as a behavioristic calculus of preference, the pressing nature of Cornuelle's problem of accounting for associations beyond the commercial dissolves.

Since we answer "yes" and assert that the action of the individual can be influenced by ideas, let us return to the problem of understanding the "sharing" of various meanings, conveyed by ideas, that takes place in associations. It is the case that life exists in actions that are individually centered. This is merely to recognize the self-dependency or the self-centeredness of every individual action. This recognition is why it makes sense to speak of the personality of the individual; and why, consequently, in the legal sphere, there has been skepticism about the existence of the "corporate personality" of an association. And it is this recognition of the facts of human experience that accounts for our acceptance of the methodological obligation to analyze any association, any social relation, as individually self-dependent actions. Moreover, this "natural liberalism of the social situation," this individual distinctness of all action, is an essential and permanent character of the human being, qua human. We, thus, reject any historical analysis that views the individual at some earlier time as being so immersed in a community (*Gemeinschaft*) that he or she might be lacking the capacity to express his or her own will, the capacity to say "no" to any given situation, to any association to which he or she might have been a member. This is not to deny, as previously observed, that there have been times, such as those we designate as "modern," when the exercise of that capacity has been easier, even welcomed or expected. Even so, in historically earlier periods, the individual is "neither abrogated nor effaced, only immersed, but, in fact, detachably immersed" in a social relation (Freyer [1927] 1998, 107). There is, once again, a natural sovereignty of the individual.

I wish these immediately above comments to be taken for granted. They are merely the starting point in addressing the problem of the nature of the independent association. But what of the sharing that makes the association possible, the consideration of the nature of what is shared, and the merit of Gierke's and Maitland's insistence on the existence of a "corporate personality" not merely as a legal status but as a reality justifying that status?

As a way into addressing these questions, consider this elementary example of a social relation between two individuals, where each, with their own interests and preoccupations, happen upon one another. These two individuals are "interacting," as they have randomly encountered one another; there is no social relation. However, as one extends his or her hand to the other, these two individuals are no longer interacting. They are now "participating" in that custom of greeting and solicitude known as the handshake. There now exists a social relation – the association of greeting and its performance – between these two individuals. What are the components of this temporally episodic association? Firstly, there is the meaning of this custom of greeting that both individuals find. Where is the meaning found? It is located within the consciousness of each of many individuals who recognize and accept the meaning of the handshake as a tradition signifying acknowledgment between two individuals. Secondly, the material out of which the social relation is formed is the living, individual human beings who make actual the custom by performing it.

This is a most elementary form of association because it is one where there is no institutional embodiment of the meaning acknowledged and performed, for example, a court for law, or a university for the teaching and discovery of truth, or a sacred text and church for a religion; nor is there any differentiation among the members of the relation, for example, a representative of an association with its own rules and regulations – a corporation. Nonetheless, the methodological problem is clear even in this elementary example: on the one hand, the action and the decision to act are individually centered; and yet, on the other hand, there is a trans-individual meaning (the custom of the handshake) that is acknowledged and accepted by each of the individuals. If we do not take into account the reality, albeit an invisible reality, of this second factor – the existence of various trans-individual meanings and the goals they convey – then we misrepresent the nature of a great deal of human action; and, by doing so, we fall further prey to what Cornuelle, and Knight before him, characterized as an excessive individualism. Many associations exhibit the character of having an inter-individual meaning and trans-individual structure. Many associations, even the most temporally fleeting, are structures of participation.

The recognition of the existence of an inter-individual meaning in which the individual of an association participates does not point to some mystical group mind; but it does point to the problem of the place of tradition in the action of the individual. Consider what takes place when the mind of the individual encounters the achievements of another individual or group of individuals, for example, when a musician performs a musical score, or when one reads a book or teaches a course at a university or spreads the gospel – examples where the inter-individual meaning has, unlike the previous example of the custom of the handshake, been embodied in a physical form (a musical score or a book). Here, the achievement of another "pulls," if you will, the individual up to heights that otherwise he or she would not have been able to achieve from merely his or her own experience. What takes place is not a phenomenon of group mind; and yet this previous achievement of another person exerts an influence on the actor, as the actor participates in the achievement, even, depending upon what is being done, creating a new achievement either by himself or with others. Moreover, another musician performing the same musical score, or another reader of the same book, or another missionary spreading the good news also participates in the same achievement. To be sure, this second person does not participate in exactly the same way as the first; nonetheless, there is an "overlap" of experience – an overlap that we can designate as "sharing." Each of the individuals participating in this trans-individual meaning recognizes in the other individual this participation. The result of this recognition by each of the individuals about those other individuals is a bond of commonality between them. We shall later consider variation in the bond that leads to distinguishing an association from when an association becomes a community.

Yet again, none of this points to the existence of a group mind. The animation, if you will, of the meaning conveyed by the inanimate physical object, for example, a musical score or a book, is dependent upon the action of the individual. If that action does not take place or cannot take place because the individual is not capable of understanding the meaning conveyed by the object, for example, the inscriptions of a dead language that have not been deciphered, then that meaning does not become a part of the life of the individual. In this instance, the meaning is either dormant or, if you will, "dead"; and, as such, it is not capable of being "activated," performed, that is, spoken and shared, hence, the phenomenon of the "dead language." However, when the individual does involve himself or herself in that meaning, then the distinctiveness and even the scope of the initiative of the individual has to be qualified if we are to understand what takes place. Herein is the compelling reason to qualify – by no means to reject – the principle of methodological individualism.

Let us consider another, more complicated example of this "overlap" of experience in order to clarify the phenomenon of "sharing" implied by the existence of an association. Two individuals attend a performance of Mozart's *Don Giovanni*. On the train ride home, having recognized that they both were at the opera, they talk about how they both were so favorably moved when they heard the tenor Luigi Alva sing "il mio Tesoro."

(They experienced an expansion of the self. Although a metaphor, perhaps the phrase "expansion of the self" is not merely a metaphor.) In the course of their conversation, they realize that they had many times seen one another at the neighborhood coffee shop. There was previously no relation between them at that coffee shop; but the following Saturday, when they do see each other, they sit down together to finish their morning coffee while discussing classical music. There is now a relation between them. *Key to this new relation is that each of them now recognizes a similar property about the other*, namely, their love of opera. They further discover that each of them has a child in the local high school and that they both are unhappy about the music appreciation and programs at that school. They, thus, both decide to form a parental arts association dedicated to raising money to improve musical education and opportunities at that school. A voluntary association has been formed around their shared appreciation for classical music and the task of improving appreciation for classical music, even though neither them, nor their children, sings or plays a musical instrument. And to further and appropriately complicate this example, frustrated by the state-mandated regulations at their children's school, they turn to the local opera company to assist them more productively in promoting appreciation for classical music among otherwise culturally wayward teenagers.

These examples and the earlier discussion lead us to recognize not only a more complex view of knowledge but also its corollary: a more complicated structure of the constitution of the self, as the individual participates in various, heterogeneous complexes of meaning. There evidently is a layered structure of consciousness, corresponding to the individual's pursuit of his or her own preferences and tastes, the components of which co-exist in a shifting combination with various aspects of the individual's self-understanding arising out of his or her decision to participate in correspondingly various meanings and goals. Thus, there is (1) individual consciousness; (2) individual self-consciousness, that is, the awareness of one's self; and (3) a plurality of "we"s constituted around any number of heterogeneous, trans-individual meanings arising out of the individual's attachments to goals and the individuals who share them that, in turn, have bearing on how one understands one's self. This description is a restatement of Popper's (1979) "three worlds," except that I have shifted its emphasis away from "objective knowledge" to how the self, in particular, self-consciousness, is constituted.[2] The self-dependency of all action, this "natural liberalism" conveyed by the principle of methodological individualism, forces us to take up what is now the problem of the constitution of the self. In other words, the principle of methodological individualism is to be viewed not only in terms of analyzing human action, but also in terms of understanding the development of self-understanding arising from the individual's participation in different traditions. The methodological obligation to begin with the individual applies not only in the analysis of the relation of one individual to another, but also in the relation of the mind of the individual to objective knowledge or tradition.

Here, I have presented merely the barest of outlines of the problem. In doing so, I have no doubt about the behavioral primacy of the first two of the above layers of awareness. However, we are born into a world not of our own making in which we must find our way, often in collaboration with others; and when doing so, it is this third layer or component of consciousness, unevenly shared with others, which has an influence not only on our decisions and actions, but also on our understanding of the self. It is with this latter, complicated relation where one finds experiences of regret, honor, shame, heroism, patriotism, awe, and so forth: those sentiments of approbation involving what Smith characterized as a "sense of propriety distinct from utility" ([1759] 1982, 188). We add to Smith's observation two considerations. First, the objects of approbation may differ qualitatively, for example, the experience of heroism when compared with that of awe, thereby indicating complexes of meaning that differ in kind and that, as co-existing, provide the potential for moral dilemmas. Second, bonds of commonality – the social relation of an association – between individuals are recognized by those individuals as a result of their participation in cultural complexes of meaning.

Of course, many associations revolve around utility – to achieve a common, practical goal, the pursuit of which may be limited in time or of an ongoing duration. In our previous example of the two opera goers, they both adopt the goal of improving appreciation for classical music among younger people. When the existence of the association is viewed as being limited to achieving a particular, practical, goal, it is easier to detach oneself from the association for any number of reasons, for example, if others join the association, making your contribution less necessary, or if the goal is achieved, and so forth. However, to return to our example, in addition to pursing the goal of improving appreciation for classical music, each of these individuals recognizes a property – a devotee of classical music – about the other that is also a part of their individual self-understanding. Thus, while they remain distinct individuals, there is also a bond of similarity between them arising from their participation in the tradition of classical music; and that bond of similarity is expressed in the nature of the association. In this case, since the association conveys a part of the individual's self-understanding, the association is viewed not only as existing for the pursuit of that practical goal but also as an extension of the personality of the individual as a member of the association. As a result, the individual's commitment to the association is likely to be stronger and more lasting. Moreover, there are other recognized properties shared with others that are perceived to have great existential significance far beyond the shared property of, in our example, being a devotee of opera. Examples of organizations of this kind are religious and patriotic associations. In these instances, the form of association is a community because the strength or intensity of the bond (that is, the individual's attachment to the complex of meanings around which the community is constituted, to the goal conveyed by that complex, and to others who are perceived as sharing in that meaning and goal) of the community indicates that it is resistant to being substituted for another meaningful attachment.

The bearing of already existing complexes of meaning (traditions), as in our previous examples, the custom of the handshake, classical music, and clearly those that I have characterized as existential, is not to be confused with traditionalism. For a tradition to continue to exist, to be a part of life, it must be acknowledged, even if only tacitly, by each of a number of individuals. In the course of that acknowledgment, traditions undergo unpredictable changes in response to always different circumstances. Those circumstances include changes in how the individual understands himself or herself, how other individuals respond to those changing circumstances, and how individuals respond to one another. The attempt to frustrate these kinds of changes represents traditionalism. To attempt to do so is to undermine what Cornuelle (1991, 4) referred to as "the value of independence and self-propulsion" that includes the human propensity to experiment. Although rarely seen as traditionalism, this is what central planning represents, as it must frustrate not only individual initiative but also, above all, the exercise of that initiative with others in pursuit of always-changing goals not authorized by the state. Thus, Cornuelle's observation of the need for a better understanding of community is also not to be seen as some variant of traditionalism; rather, it is recognition of the value of individual initiative in collaboration with others about matters which they understand best in response to problems that they understand best. In doing so, the individual, along with other individuals, will draw upon the resources at hand. Those resources include traditions and associations, already existing or newly created, that are organized around those developing traditions as bearers of shared, but also changing meaning. The phenomenon of sharing has these two components to it: the individual's participation in this always-changing meaning, and the recognition by the individual that other individuals also participate in that meaning in pursuit of what is now a common goal.

Human action is the action of an individual, but usually that individual participates in changing traditions; and when he or she does, symbolic properties that are constitutive of the individual's self-understanding are recognized in other participants of what is now a social relation. Sometimes, especially when the association is formed to pursue a specific goal for a limited amount of time, those recognized properties have little or no significance; they may be disregarded as being irrelevant to the specific goal being pursued by the association. Other times, however, the recognition of those properties is a referent (or one of the referents) around which the social relation is formed. In this latter instance, as Davis (2002) rightly observed, there is a "we," and it is a "we" that expresses a part of the self-understanding of the individual.

While all action is purposive, and in this sense there is an interest being pursued, some action also involves, or is a consequence of, the self-understanding of the actor. Rather than rejecting methodological individualism as not being a useful heuristic principle (so, Hodgson 2007), accepting it as a valid proposition opens up the pressing problem of clarifying the relation between the mind of the individual and qualitatively different kinds of objective knowledge. That this problem is avoided by an excessive individualism, wrongly assumed to be exclusively characteristic of modern life, has been often acknowledged and recently so in interesting ways by the economists Arrow (1994) and Davis (2002), and by some theorists of public choice, for example, when Ostrom observed that "presuppositions of methodological individualism need to be related to communities of shared understanding as a fundamental element in a framework for the analysis of decision situations" (1993, 171). However, while rightly recognizing shared understanding as an "externality," or that "individual behavior is always mediated by social relations" (Arrow 1994, 5) or "socially embedded" such that there are "shared intentions" (Davis 2002, 19), or "structured" (Hodgson 2007, 218–21), still avoided and thereby obfuscated are the phenomena of participation, the bearing of that participation and attribution on the understanding of the self, and the attribution of properties to others by virtue of which a relation of similarity is recognized.

## Conclusion

Even if it were possible for a central authority to understand well any number of problems confronting a society, it is better for local, voluntary associations to address them wherever possible. This is because the individuals of those associations will likely do so more energetically and effectively insofar as they understand that the problems being addressed, including those new problems that have unpredictably arisen as a consequence of addressing the original problem, directly impinge upon their lives and in ways that no central authority could foresee. This has been observed often enough.

What has not been often observed is that one reason why energetic involvement is likely is because addressing a perceived problem may have a bearing on how the individual understands himself or herself, as in our previous example, no longer as someone who merely enjoys attending the opera but now as someone who understands himself or herself as sharing in the responsibility for musical education. The understanding of the self may very well change as a result of both the individual's involvement and the influence of other, involved individuals on one another. In this way, both new understandings, including understanding of the self, and new problems emerge. In these circumstances, it is not merely or even primarily a matter of a more efficient allocation of resources or maximization of advantage, but rather an expression of one's developing understanding of the self, for example, donating to a university because a part of one's self-understanding is as a graduate of that university. Moreover, over time, a greater involvement that includes collaboration with others in making the donation may result in changes in the donation, as how one understands one's self and the university change. The benefits of such a donation do not accrue directly to the donor, except as some kind of "psychic reward." But focusing on the reward to account for the action obscures both the development of one's self-understanding and the attachment to others who share that understanding as factors in the decision. What has to be accounted for is not only the extension or expansion of the self in the social relation of the "we" but also how that extension or expansion may sometimes include physical objects as designated by the possessive pronouns "my" or "our," as in my (or our) university.

All the more significant would this attachment to others (and physical objects) be when the association of which one is a member has emerged from one's own initiative to create it or participate in it. It is here and only here where the dynamism of experimentation becomes possible, precisely because the association has arisen out of the initiative and subsequent, ongoing experience of each of any number of individuals by themselves and together. It is here and only here where responsibility (and the knowledge of what the responsibility entails) for one's own environment becomes possible. However, note well that one's (immediate) environment is also often a component of one's understanding of the self. Thus, local knowledge is not only a necessary factor for the individual's response to other individuals. It is that, but it may sometimes be more. It may be that the individual understands himself or herself in terms of the locality as a member not merely of a "we" but of a "we" constituted around the locality. In this case, local knowledge is not just crucially important for what economists, following Hayek (1945), refer to as the "knowledge problem." Knowledge is not just between individuals, mediating their actions, for example, the price signals of the market or the perceived immediate changes in demand and supply or changes in taste. The local knowledge of the immediate environment may also be a part of the understanding of the self, which may, in turn, be perceived as a property characteristic of others as members of a local association; and, as such, membership in the local association, because it is perceived as an extension of the self, may elicit actions of loyalty and self-sacrifice, where the benefits of an individual's actions accrue to others who are members of the association.

In considering these kinds of associations, we again encounter the problem of their relation to other associations and, above all, to the state, especially so when the association is independent precisely because it is substantively distinctive. By the use of the terms "substantive" and "distinctive," I mean the degree to which the independence of the association indicates that it has its own orientation and regulations distinct from, and even possibly in tension with, those of the state.

In considering the problem of this relation, we can put aside the arguments over whether or not it is appropriate to use the term "personality" in the characterization "corporate personality" by turning our attention to what is actually at stake in those arguments: do associations have rights and duties specific to the purpose of the association? If they do, then the problem of their relation to the comprehensive moral system, even where the laws are formal and general, is posed. It seems to me that Cornuelle "backed into" this problem when he observed, "perhaps there needs to be a rigid, even constitutionally defined and protected doctrine of separation of the independent sector and the state" ([1965] 1993,194). Implicit in Cornuelle's recognition of this need is that an association does indeed have its own "pre-political" rights and duties. By "pre-political" rights and duties, I intend merely to reformulate Cornuelle's observation that independent associations have "a *prior*, more powerful moral franchise than the state" (193, my emphasis); that is, the "personality" of the association is not exclusively a matter of legal recognition. And if so, then, as Gierke realized, we again face the problem of Johannes Althusius' *Politica* ([1614] 1995), of formulating a basic law of the land that allows for, by carefully adjudicating between, the expansive scope of individual freedom, about which Hayek wrote so compellingly, made more feasible by the formality and generality of the law, on the one hand, and the rights and duties of independent, voluntary associations with their "special laws," on the other.

If, in fact, the formation and existence of associations do sometimes have a bearing on the self-understanding of the individual as a member of a "we," and if that "we" has "personality," then, once again, the dichotomy or dualism of the socially embedded individual of the (local) community and the socially unencumbered individual of the (territorially extensive) society is simply too crude. As conceptual categories of analysis, they remain useful; but they certainly cannot be easily segregated historically. Furthermore, they and their respective forms of action interpenetrate one another. The individual today not only pursues his or her own interests, the benefits achieved by doing so accruing directly to individual, but also understands himself or herself as a participant in the traditions of various associations. With the latter, the individual undertakes actions, the benefits of which sometimes accrue not to himself or herself but to the association or other members of the association. This is merely to state the obvious; but it is an obvious state of affairs that, as Cornuelle argued, has to be explained and, when doing so, by refusing to resort to tautologies or by being content with a flimsy explanation like "psychic reward."

## Notes

1 A more recent, similar recognition is Ostrom's rejection of a methodologically doctrinaire reliance on utility: "Without commonly accepted standards of right and wrong, there is no basis for assuming autonomy to individuals to exercise responsibility for the actions they take in the governance of their own affairs and in relating to others. The use of extreme rationality assumptions runs the risk of stripping away and ignoring essential epistemic features that are constitutive of human affairs" (1993, 167).
2 The knowledge is "objective" because various meanings, for example, the significance of the handshake or a musical score, once created out of the flow of life achieve a *relative* independence. The independence is "relative" because the continued existence of the meaning, as a part of life, rests upon its acknowledgment by any number of individuals.

## References

Althusius, Johannes. [1614] 1995. *Politica*. Indianapolis, IN: Liberty Fund.
Arrow, Kenneth J. 1994. "Methodological Individualism and Social Knowledge." *American Economic Review* 84 (2): 1–9.
Cornuelle, Richard. [1965] 1993. *Reclaiming the American Dream: The Role of Private Individuals and Voluntary Associations*. New Brunswick, NJ: Transaction.
Cornuelle, Richard. 1991. "New Work for Invisible Hands." *The Times Literary Supplement* (April 5): 1–4.
Davis, John B. 2002. "Collective Intentionality and Individual Behavior." In *Intersubjectivity in Economics: Agents and Structures*, edited by E. Fullbrook, 11–27. London: Routledge.
Durkheim, Emile. [1893] 1997. *The Division of Labor in Society*. New York: Free Press.
Freyer, Hans. [1927] 1998. *Theory of Objective Mind: An Introduction to the Philosophy of Culture*. Athens: Ohio University Press.
Gierke, Otto von. [1868] 1990. *Community in Historical Perspective* (from vol. I of *Das deutsche Genossenschaftsrecht*). Translated and edited by Antony Black. Cambridge: Cambridge University Press.
Gierke, Otto von. [1902] 1935. "The Nature of Human Associations." In *The Genossenschaft-Theory of Otto Von Gierke*, edited by John D. Lewis, 139–57. Madison, WI: University of Wisconsin Press.
Grosby, Steven. 2011. "Nationalism and Social Theory: The Distinction between Community and Society." In *Handbook of Contemporary Social and Political Theory*, edited by Gerard Delanty and Stephen Turner, 280–289. London: Routledge.
Hayek, F. A. [1939] 1997. "Freedom and the Economic System." In *Socialism and War*, 181–211. Chicago: University of Chicago Press.
Hayek, F. A. 1945. "The Use of Knowledge in Society." *The American Economic Review* 35 (/4): 519–530.
Hayek, F. A. 1955. *The Political Ideal of the Rule of Law*. Cairo: Bank of Egypt.
Hayek, F. A. 1960. *Constitution of Liberty*. London: Routledge.
Hobbes, Thomas. [1651] 1962. *Leviathan*. New York: Macmillan Publishing.
Hodgson, Geoffrey M. 2007. "Meanings of Methodological Individualism." *Journal of Economic Methodology* 14 (2): 211–226.

Knight, Frank H. 1935a. "The Ethics of Competition." In Frank H. Knight, *The Ethics of Competition and Other Essays*, 41–75. New York: Harper and Brothers.
Knight, Frank H. 1935b. "Economic Theory and Nationalism." In Frank H. Knight, *The Ethics of Competition and Other Essays*, 277–359. New York: Harper and Brothers.
Knight, Frank H. [1947] 1982. *Freedom and Reform*. Indianapolis, IN: Liberty Fund.
Maine, Henry Sumner. [1861] 1970. *Ancient Law*. Gloucester, MA: Peter Smith.
Maitland, Frederic William. [1903] 1936. "Moral Personality and Legal Personality." In *Maitland: Selected Essays*. Cambridge: Cambridge University.
Ostrom, Vincent. 1993. "Epistemic Choice and Public Choice." *Public Choice* 77: 163–176.
Otteson, James R. 2011. *Adam Smith*. London: Continuum.
Parsons, Talcott and Edward Shils. 1951. *Toward a General Theory of Action*. Cambridge, MA: Harvard University Press.
Plessner, Helmuth. [1924] 1999. *The Limits of Community*. Amherst, MA: Humanity Books.
Polanyi, Michael. [1951] 1998. *The Logic of Liberty*. Indianapolis, IN: Liberty Fund.
Polanyi, Michael. 1962. "The Republic of Science." *Minerva* 1: 54–74.
Pollock, Frederick and Frederic William Maitland. 1898. *The History of English Law Before the Time of Edward I*. Cambridge: Cambridge University Press.
Popper, Karl R. 1979. *Objective Knowledge*. Oxford: Oxford University Press.
Schmalenbach, Herman. [1922] 1977. "Communion: A Sociological Category." In *Herman Schmalenbach on Society and Experience*, 64–125. Chicago: University of Chicago Press.
Schumpeter, Joseph A. 1909. "On the Concept of Social Value." *Quarterly Journal of Economics* 23 (2): 213–232.
Shils, Edward. [1957] 1975. "Primordial, Personal, Sacred, and Civil Ties." In Edward Shils, *Center and Periphery: Essays in Macrosociology*, 111–126. Chicago: University of Chicago Press.
Shils, Edward. 1981. *Tradition*. Chicago: University of Chicago Press.
Shils, Edward. 1997. *The Calling of Education*. Chicago: University of Chicago Press.
Shils, Edward. 2006. "Collective Self-Consciousness and Rational Choice." In *A Fragment of a Sociological Autobiography: The History of My Pursuit of a Few Ideas*, 195–216. New Brunswick, NJ: Transaction.
Smith, Adam. [1759] 1982. *The Theory of Moral Sentiments*. Indianapolis, IN: Liberty Fund.
Tocqueville, Alexis de. [1840] 2012. *Democracy in America*. Indianapolis, IN: Liberty Fund.
Tönnies, Ferdinand. [1887] 2001. *Community and Society*. Cambridge: Cambridge University Press.
Weber, Max. [1921] 1978. *Economy and Society*. Berkeley, CA: University of California Press.

# 8 Comment: Don't forget the barter in "truck, barter and exchange"!

*Shaun P. Hargreaves Heap*

## Introduction

What kind of individuals are we? It is common to think that we have two options and that we have neatly devised social arrangements to permit both Mr. Jekyll and Mr. Hyde, so to speak, to prosper. There is the "selfish me" who has an eye for the bargains in the market and there is the "communitarian me" who acts in associations of love, friendship and solidarity. The boundary between the anonymous and the cuddly versions of our selves may change with a country's institutional architecture, and some individuals may be largely either Mr. Jekyll or Mr. Hyde, but our options are formed by some version of this dualism. This is the common target of the preceding papers by Luigino Bruni, Paul Lewis, and Steven Grosby.

These authors have different ways of attacking this dualism but all seek to undermine it by problematizing the relation between the "I" and the "we" when we act in concert. All three papers are right on this point.

Bruni and Lewis share a particular argument; and I am going to focus on this. They want to make the "acting in concert" that is participation in the market involve a commitment among the market participants to a shared project of mutual benefit. This is what distinguishes the institution of the market and what makes the rise of the market so important. It encourages us to think more generally of social life as a shared project for mutual benefit. This is the market's virtue.

For both, this commitment to a project of mutual benefit in the market involves an individual having recourse to "we-intentionality," and this is why it forms part of an attack on the dualism that opposes selfishness (and the market) with solidarity (and the associational life). I am usually not persuaded that this use of collective intentionality really adds much to an older story about the role of norms, but I have to admit that the more I hear it, the more persuasive it becomes. I shall return to this briefly when I consider Grosby's chapter at the end, because he offers the kind of norm-based account of associational life that I usually favor. For the most part, I am going to focus on the substantive claim that the normative principle guiding behavior in markets is mutual benefit.

I shall argue that Bruni and Lewis are half right and half wrong on this point; and that one of the challenges for them is also a challenge for Grosby.

## Half right

Markets are an institutional form that is distinguished from planned arrangements by the way that each party involved in an economic outcome agrees to the actions that yield that outcome. This is why the market is connected with the exercise of liberty. If one adds to this a picture of the individual agreeing to do things because they offer him or her a net gain over some relevant set of domains, then it is easy to see how participation in the market is the same as participation in a project of mutual benefit.

Nevertheless it matters on the Bruni and Lewis accounts that people recognize the market as such an institution. Otherwise there would be no difference for individuals between their participation in the market and, say, going for a swim in the sea. They would both simply be actions taken in response to the opportunity for individual benefit. Since the person who sells me a pound of apples in the market does not have a gun pointed at their head, and it would be clearly nonsense to think of the sea making decisions (under duress or otherwise), I see no great difficulty with assuming that most people do understand this difference at some level.

In addition, there is the *longue durée* evidence of history where the rise of the market is associated with an extraordinary growth of material prosperity and individual life expectancy. The contrast in such a *longue durée* is with the command-and-control institutions of feudalism where pinching stuff is what went on. The lords and kings pinched or tried to pinch each other's territory, and the lords did the same with the output of the peasant. Feudalism institutionalizes a zero-sum mentality, and so it is no surprise that material living standards and life expectancy only bump along. Whereas, when markets, through being premised on mutual benefit, institutionalize a positive-sum mentality ... capow! In the course of the 300 years since markets became pervasive, our life span has doubled, we now work much less than we play, and we have several changes of clothes in our wardrobes. This background fact about the history of markets seems bound to seep into our understanding of what markets do.

Of course, this does not necessarily mean that when we participate in the market, we are committed to the project of engaging in activities for mutual benefit such that the description of our motives for participating in the market must take account of this commitment. Bruni and Lewis both argue, in effect, that this is the case (or at least that we are encouraged in this direction). I think both are right, but I am not concerned here with this final bit of their argument. My interest is more simply in what is necessary for this to be the case: that the normative principle of mutual benefit is encoded in the institution of the market and that this principle might plausibly be apparent to those who participate in the market. On both counts, as I have suggested, I think Bruni and Lewis are right. This is the sense in which they are half right. They have identified a conspicuous virtue of the market: as an institution organized around voluntary exchange it encourages us to think of economic (and social) life as a project in mutual benefit.

Further, I think it is plausible to argue, as they sometimes do and as Alexis de Tocqueville famously did, that the market through this commitment to mutual benefit encourages further virtues: we treat each other equally and we are inclined to trust each other.

Equality in the sense of equal treatment is entailed by the mutuality of "mutual benefit." This connects with later arguments by Becker (1957), for instance, that market forces drive out discrimination. There is even some experimental laboratory evidence that points in the same direction (Hargreaves Heap et al. 2013).

The encouragement to trust is not entailed in the same way by mutuality. It is more that markets and dispositions towards trust are handmaidens. The payment and the receipt of whatever is purchased are typically imperfectly synchronized and the gap cannot be covered by contracts as they are necessarily incomplete when there is uncertainty. Trust fills that gap. As a result, the expansion of markets goes hand in hand with the development of trust, and the success of one encourages the further development of the other. Or so the argument goes. Knack and Keefer (1997) offer supporting evidence. In a cross-country study of twenty-nine countries they find that high income levels are associated with high trust, and, to the extent that high income is in turn an indicator of the economic importance of the market, this makes the connection to the market.

## Half wrong

Let me turn to where I think Bruni and Lewis are half wrong by retracing the argument from Adam Smith. Smith argues that our propensity to "truck, barter and exchange" helps explain the rise of the market. The "truck" and "exchange" parts of this triptych connect with how markets involve a commitment to a project of mutual benefit that is rooted in our natures. It is the "exchange" part that is crucial for the mutuality, and it is supported by the wonderful observation that you never see dogs haggling over a bone. This is, in part, why I think Bruni is a bit tough on Smith as he seems to me to belong in the *Civile* tradition that Bruni wishes to juxtapose with Smith. Nevertheless, this is a minor disagreement. My first real concern with the Bruni and Lewis argument is that it overlooks the "barter" part of Smith's "truck, barter and exchange": that is, the haggling over the terms of the exchange.

Of course, Smith could be wrong. Indeed, neither our nature nor the experience of markets, perhaps, need essentially involve us in negotiation.

However, for the latter to be the case, the price has to be given by the market, and this only happens in a competitive equilibrium. This would be an unusual assumption to make, given the explicit Austrian twist to Lewis's argument, and I suspect few would want to defend its generality. The more general case has agents (and not markets) setting prices, and in setting or negotiating a price they are deciding how the mutual benefit from the exchange is to be divided. In this way, negotiation seems essential to actual market systems. However, the point about such surplus division is that it is *not* about mutual advantage: it is about who gets the advantage. In other words, markets are not just oriented to the project of creating exchanges of mutual benefit; they also have to solve a problem about how to divide that benefit. To connect this to the "we-intention" argument, while the commitment to mutual benefit obviously fits with team-like thinking, how to divide the team's spoils is less obviously covered by a general kind of team ethos unless it specifically brings with it some heavier normative baggage.

Markets have two further potentially important effects that might plausibly be regarded as an entailment of market exchange. The first follows from Smith's analysis of the market. It encourages a division of labor (and from this it generates dynamism). Smith thought this was all a part of the magic of the market system: it created coordination problems through such an encouragement to specialization and solved them through the market's price mechanism. Arguably, however, market systems have had as much recourse, in practice, to an alternative coordination device. We have seen the extraordinary rise of the large-scale commercial organization over the last 300 years. The question, then, is to what extent does using the market entail a commitment not just to exchanges where there is mutual benefit (and to haggling over how to distribute this benefit) but also to participation in non-market organizations like firms. And if it does, is there a tension between the principle of mutual benefit in the market and its likely absence in these large-scale, often command-and-control-like organizations?

The traditional answer to this question is that, although the principle of mutual benefit does not reign inside most organizations, it governs the choice of whether to join such an organization and thus governs intra-firm relationships and processes indirectly. Or to put this differently, one can always leave an organization. That is, one's continued employment always depends on the condition of mutual benefit in continuing to be satisfied. The trouble with this line of argument is that people do, through investing in organization-specific skills and through the difficulty of moving to new geographic areas, become hostages to an organization. An organization can behave differently now to the way it did twenty years ago. Had the person foreseen such a change they might not have joined. So the question in some sense becomes whether it is reasonable to assume that people can foresee changes in an organization's operating procedures. This is where the second feature of the market system that Bruni and Lewis overlook becomes important.

The market's dynamism is disruptive and such disruption is not always easy to anticipate. The point I wish to make about this is, however, slightly different. People strike deals in markets that are to their mutual advantage and a significant aspect of the disruption that ensues is to third parties. They can lose out. For example, one moment there are people working on the land; the next they are out of a job because the farmer bought a tractor. The farmer and the tractor supplier are both better off, but not the agricultural worker. Of course, the loss to the worker may be temporary. Nevertheless, the commitment to the principle of mutual benefit in a market is self-evidently partial in such circumstances. The team only forms for Bruni and Lewis between those engaging in the exchange. The market does not entail a wholesale commitment to mutual benefit. People who live in a society do not belong to the same team. Teams are formed opportunistically and they dissolve as easily.

To draw these threads together, it is wrong to imagine that markets are not riven with opportunism: that is, people acting in their interest at the expense of others. They are. One interest is constantly pitched against another in market exchanges. Furthermore, these conflicts have to be resolved without the settled morality of religion or the authority of Church, State and the Manor of feudal life. The wonderful trick of the market, really, is to yoke the settlement of these conflicts to the realization of the gains that come from only doing things that satisfy the test of mutual benefit. One might say that the rise of markets requires that we increasingly decide on how to divide the cake just as the institutions that might have helped get kicked away, but that markets also provide a powerful incentive to come up with some solutions because, unless we do, there is no cake at all.

In this task, it seems to me that there is a very natural slide from the equal treatment entailed by the mutuality of "mutual benefit" to equal division. Equality with respect to the zone of indeterminacy in economic exchanges becomes, as it were, the natural focal point for those parties to the exchange. Of course, there may be normative considerations that are shared by the parties and which provide reasons for departing from this, but the default position is an equal division of the cake. There is some experimental evidence that the market is associated with substantive equality: that is equality of outcome (and not just equal treatment). For example, Henrich *et al.* (2001) find that generosity (and hence proximity to an equal share) in an ultimatum game is more pronounced in societies where market integration is most advanced. There is also evidence that equality matters in the sense that the other virtue of markets, trust, dwindles in the presence of inequality. This is the finding of Knack and Keefer (1997) in their cross-country study, and it is also sometimes found in laboratory experiments (see Hargreaves Heap *et al.* 2013, where the damage to trust from inequality is stronger in market than non-market settings).

The slide from equal treatment to substantive equality does not, however, extend to the opportunism of the farmer and the tractor supplier in relation to the farm laborer. The point about markets is that they do not extend the same right to third parties: the farm laborer does not have to find it in his or her benefit for the deal to go through. So there is no initial presumption of equal treatment that can help the resolution of *this* conflict of interest that is inherent in markets. In practice, when trickle-down can be relied on, the workings of a market system guarantee mutual benefit for all and so the scope of the principle of mutual benefit is not visibly harmed. But this is only contingently the case. In turn, this is why the growth that some countries like the United States and the United Kingdom have experienced over the last 10–30 years, where median incomes have not changed, is so potentially challenging. For large segments of society, "trickle-down" has stopped as the gains of individuals at the top end of the income distribution have been accompanied by actual losses for those at the bottom (OECD 2012). The partial sense of mutuality in "mutual benefit" has become apparent: we are not all in it together.

## Associations

Grosby comes at some similar issues from a different angle. He is concerned (in part) with how to account for the importance of associational life for individuals while retaining a version of methodological individualism. Like Bruni, he returns to Smith for part of his argument. Only this time it is the Smith of *The Theory of Moral Sentiments* (and not the Smith of *The Wealth of Nations*). The individual in this Smith pursues the "special pleasure" of "mutual sympathy" and so has reason to enter into associations with others where norms of behavior enable such judgments of mutual sympathy to be enjoyed. The individual thus becomes socially embedded and this qualifies methodological individualism. This is Grosby's approach to what in the Bruni and Lewis argument becomes the move to "we"-intentionality. I have a residual preference for Grosby's way of, in effect, appealing to norms and norm-guided behavior, as I suggested at the beginning. But that, as you will have now guessed, is in part because I'm such a fan of Smith.

The observation that I wish to make on Grosby's chapter is, however, rather different, and it relates to my comment on markets in Bruni's and Lewis's chapters. It can again be traced to Smith, this time when he argues that the dynamism of markets disrupts the settled communities in which associations develop. He was thinking of the move from rural to urban areas, but the point is more general. To participate in associations, as in markets, is to participate in a transient social arrangement that is both done and undone by the exercise of individual liberty.

There is an interesting further question raised by the three chapters taken in conjunction as to whether associational life is qualitatively different from market life. The thought is provoked by Bruni and Lewis, who want market activity to be a form of participation in a joint project, just as participation in an association is for Grosby. If this is the case, then the endogenous dynamism (and disruption) of markets seems as likely to apply to associational life as it does to life in a market. Hence, the disruption to associational life (and markets) may be as much internal as it is external to an association (or a market). My observation, therefore, is this. To engage in associations is to engage in activity that is disruptive, and sometimes this disruption hurts people. To return to Smith's way of putting this that echoes where I left Bruni and Lewis, what happens to the "mutual" of "mutual sympathy" when this happens?

## Conclusion

I am not concerned here to decide between whether "barter" is a part of human nature, as Smith would have it, or emerges developmentally through the experience of market society. My point is that in so far as participation in the market involves a commitment to the normative operating principles of the market (whatever the reason), then those principles are something more than mutual benefit. They include normative principles for guiding how to distribute the benefits of exchange; and the default principle seems to be substantive equality with respect to the distribution of these benefits.

This is my first argument. My second is that there is a tension between the normative principles of mutuality and substantive equality and the disruptive nature of markets when it leaves some people worse off. The partial or contingent nature of the normative principles in markets is in tension, so to speak, with the principles themselves because the principles seem naturally to press for greater inclusivity. This tension is part of what it also means to embrace markets. I have concentrated on Bruni's and Lewis's argument in this respect, but the tension, I think, also arises for Grosby's argument with respect to associational life.

To put this second point in the language of "we"-intentionality, can the idea of being in a team withstand such disruptions? Is "we"-intentionality going to prove distinct from "I"-intentionality if the team is contingently created and dissolved in such self-serving ways? I am not sure about the answer to this question, but I am certain that the tension is felt more acutely when "trickle-down" demonstrably stops, as it has now in some countries.

## References

Becker, Gary. 1957. *The Economics of Discrimination*. Chicago: University of Chicago Press.

Hargreaves Heap, Shaun, Jonathan Tan, and Daniel Zizzo. 2013. "Trust, Inequality and the Market." *Theory and Decision* 74: 311–333.
Henrich, Joseph, Robert Boyd, Samuel Bowles, Colin Camerer, Ernst Fehr, Herbert Gintis, and Richard McElreath. 2001. "In Search of Homo Economicus: Behavioral Experiments in 15 Small-Scale Societies." *American Economic Review* 91 (2): 73–78.
Knack, Stephen and Philip Keefer. 1997. "Does Social Capital Have an Economic Payoff? A Cross-Country Investigation." *Quarterly Journal of Economics* 112 (4): 1251–1288.
OECD. 2012. *Going for Growth*. Paris: OECD.

# Part III
# Human(e) economics

# 9 Between *Gemeinschaft* and *Gesellschaft*
## The stories we tell

*Emily Chamlee-Wright and Virgil Henry Storr*

## Introduction

We live, simultaneously, in two worlds. On the one hand, we live in a world occupied and defined by our close relationships – those of family, neighborhood, and community – in which we cooperate with others who are very much known to us, sometimes in intimate detail. At the same time that we inhabit this world, we inhabit another world in which the food we eat, the garments we wear, the buildings we inhabit, and the technology we deploy are produced by multitudes of others distant and unknown to us. As producers in this world, we cooperate with countless others, again unknown to us, to bring about the goods and services we offer. Depending on the kinds of goods and services we produce, we may never directly encounter those who benefit from our efforts.

The first world, the world that the German sociologist Ferdinand Tönnies called "*Gemeinschaft*," is the sphere in which solidarity and the moral approbation of one's fellow men matters. It is the world that the Austrian economist F. A. Hayek described as the "intimate order" or "micro-cosmos" – the world in which people possess a great deal of local knowledge about those with whom they interact. Both Tönnies and Hayek tended to associate this world with the pre-modern era, a world that has diminished in importance with the emergence of the modern forms of association.

The second world, the sphere of social interaction Tönnies called "*Gesellschaft*," is the context in which social relationships are means of satisfying individual aims and purposes through impersonal mechanisms, such as those found in market capitalism. Hayek described this world as the "extended order" or "macro-cosmos" – the world in which people make increasing use of knowledge they do not possess directly, but that is instead fundamentally dispersed across countless producers, suppliers, financiers, investors, and consumers. Although both thinkers described distinguishable spheres of social life as well as the tensions their juxtaposition suggest, it is fair to say that Tönnies and Hayek viewed this second world differently.[1] Tönnies was concerned that the forces of *Gesellschaft* were eroding the solidarity we find in smaller communities. Hayek was concerned that the rules and attitudes fashioned within the intimate order would erode the marvelous productivity of the extended order.

As some scholars have pointed out, however, the intimate sphere of *Gemeinschaft* is far from retreating into a dim historical past (Garnett 2008; Storr 2008; Boettke and Storr 2002; Lavoie and Chamlee-Wright 2000; Cornuelle 1965, 1991, 1996). While the global extended order has indeed become increasingly complex and extends farther than it ever has in the past, individuals are still embedded within (admittedly changing) local, intimate orders in which solidarity matters a great deal. Critics have also challenged the notion that these two spheres are clearly distinct and separate from one another (Garnett 2008; Storr 2008; McCloskey 2010). As McCloskey notes, "The market is not the monstrously disembedded monster that both left and right have imagined. 'Market society' is not a contradiction in terms. *Gemeinschaft* intertwines with *Gesellschaft*" (368). Elements associated with the intimate order, such as the nuclear family, extended kin groups, neighborhood, ethnic and religious groupings, and so on, are essential nodes within the extended order, providing the local on-the-spot knowledge that is necessary for broader patterns of impersonal social cooperation (Granovetter 1985, 2005). Likewise, operations within the extended order can foster closer connections within the intimate spheres (Gudeman 2001). For example, the development of telecommunications as well as social media has dramatically lowered the costs of maintaining connections in the intimate sphere (Storr 2008).

It is thus problematic to view particular social contexts as being typified by *Gemeinschaft* and *Gesellschaft*. It is, however, still beneficial to use these distinctions to mark different modes of social engagement and human cooperation.

One of the important ways in which these two worlds differ from one another is in how people navigate them. Different narratives (or paradigms, or mental models) guide our thinking and action in these two spheres. Obviously, our motivations will tend to be different across the two spheres. For example, direct beneficence toward close friends and kin is often the driving motivation within the intimate sphere, whereas the search for profit is a common motive operating within the extended order. But the *motivation that inspires* an individual to act is not the same as the *narrative that guides* the individual's thinking and strategizing. The motivation tells us what the aims and purposes are; the narrative shapes the strategy and therefore the course of action by which one aims to achieve one's goals.

For the sake of argument, suppose that we possessed a single motivation, which is to benefit others. The question would then be how to achieve this aim. But the answer would depend upon whether we were operating within the intimate order or the extended order. Within each of these spheres, a different set of narratives would guide us. In the world of the intimate order, the narratives might include moral prescriptions such as "do unto others as you would have them do unto you," or "treat every man as your brother." The narratives that guide our action in the intimate sphere might also include personal stories recollecting experience with hardship, or stories of how the intended beneficiary of our action is particularly deserving of our beneficence. In the world of the extended order, on the other hand, the narratives that are likely to guide our way will be quite different, even if the motivation – to benefit others – is still the same. In the extended order, the narrative may include moral prescriptions such as "benefit others by lowering the cost of acquiring something they desire," or "benefit others by developing a new product or service they never before imagined." The narratives that guide our action in the extended order might also include personal stories recollecting examples of others who benefited others and became wealthy through their hard work, or stories of how innovative and successful entrepreneurs are held in esteem. The point we wish to emphasize is that the narratives that tell us what particular course needs to be taken are different depending upon whether we are operating within *Gemeinschaft* or *Gesellschaft*. As described above, this is the case even when the motivation is the same. The narratives guiding our action in each sphere will be all the more distinct when different motivations are taken into consideration.

Most of the time, we switch between these spheres without thought or effort. The production or purchase of a T-shirt calls forth one sort of narrative. The choice of a gift bestowed upon a loved one calls forth another sort of narrative. And, in the territory between *Gemeinschaft* and *Gesellschaft* (e.g., our responsibilities towards others within a moderately sized city), we make reasonable judgments about which set of narratives is most applicable. In daily life, this sort of navigation becomes so routine that it tends to escape our investigative eye.

There are moments, however, when the terrain between *Gemeinschaft* and *Gesellschaft* appears to us as less well-worn, less familiar. The puzzle of how we navigate effectively under such circumstances becomes more pronounced. During these moments, the narratives we would ordinarily call upon no longer seem to fit. As we argue below, the aftermath of catastrophic disaster is one such circumstance. The post-disaster moment is one in which the social systems that make ordinary life "work" no longer function. Operations of the market, for a time, do not function in the manner we ordinarily expect. Similarly, the operations of government and civil society are often incapacitated. The narratives that guide our thinking and action often no longer serve us. Though our capacity to help others known to us may be severely diminished, suddenly so many of the "unknown others" of the extended order seem intimately close both in terms of their need and our responsibility to them. Our narratives that would ordinarily set a course of action fail us.

And yet, we do act in such moments. How are we able to act in the post-disaster moment? What guides us as we navigate this unfamiliar terrain between *Gemeinschaft* and *Gesellschaft*? As we argue below, storytelling – the drawing upon and cultivation of narratives that fit the new context – guide us as we navigate this unfamiliar terrain. The analysis presented here is part of a multi-year ethnographic study of the political, economic, and social factors affecting disaster preparedness, response, and long-term recovery. Much of the empirical work conducted for the project took the form of in-depth qualitative interviews across multiple communities in the Greater New Orleans area and the Mississippi Gulf Coast. Combined, the field studies involved 301 subjects in the greater New Orleans area and in Hancock and Harrison Counties, Mississippi, and interviews and/or surveys of 103 New Orleans evacuees who were still living in Houston, Texas, three years after Hurricane Katrina in 2005, one of the deadliest hurricanes in the history of the United States. The New Orleans field studies included Central City, Gentilly, the Upper and Lower Ninth Wards, New Orleans East, Broadmoor neighborhoods, and St. Bernard Parish, a community that lies to the east of the Lower Ninth Ward. A principal theme of this project is how residents and other stakeholders leverage socially embedded resources in their redevelopment efforts (Chamlee-Wright 2010; Chamlee-Wright and Storr 2009a, 2009b, 2010b). As we argue below, the stories residents and other community stakeholders heard, told, and created were among these resources.

In the next section we briefly review the various literatures that address the role that stories play in guiding human action, with particular attention directed toward the middle ground between *Gemeinschaft* and *Gesellschaft*. The third and fourth sections present narratives that guided the strategies of people who returned to participate in the rebuilding of their communities following Hurricane Katrina. Specifically, we describe how returnees developed narratives with plots emphasizing their resilience and their damaged communities as central characters as a means of navigating the newly problematized middle ground between *Gemeinschaft* and *Gesellschaft*. The final section offers concluding remarks.

## How stories define who we are and guide our way

*We are all storytellers and we are the stories we tell.*
(McAdams, Josselson, and Lieblich 2006, 3)

Across the social sciences, interest in the role that narrative and story play in the development of self and perspective, in our understanding of how we as individuals connect to the broader social world, and in how such narratives guide our actions has grown significantly since the 1990s. Narrative scholars from a variety of disciplines seem to agree that stories help us filter and make sense of the complex and conflicting information we encounter; that stories help us gain clarity around our aims, purposes, and identities; and that storytelling and story listening are essential to civic life (Berger and Quinney 2005; McAdams *et al.* 2006; Nussbaum 1997).

Economists frustrated by the extremes of rational choice theory are among those who pay attention to the ways in which narrative frames our perspective, guides our action, and ultimately shapes the world. New institutional economists such as Denzau and North (1994) and North (1981, 1990, 2005), for example, draw our attention to the mental models through which human beings decipher their environment. Pre-existing beliefs about how the world works even more so than pure reason, they explain, guide our action. As North (1990, 20) points out, "we find that people decipher the environment by processing information through preexisting mental constructs through which they understand the environment and solve the problems they confront." These "preexisting mental models" may be passively conveyed through an unconscious process of enculturation, a process of deliberate ideological investment, or some combination of passive and deliberate transmission mechanisms (North 1981).[2]

Economic anthropologists have also investigated the role that mental constructs play in shaping economic choices and socio-economic outcomes. Gudeman (1986) and Bird-David (1990, 1992) have argued that dominant metaphors within a community shape exchange and production with one another and with the ecological environment.[3] Storr (2004) has imported this concept of the "primary metaphor" to his analysis of Bahamian economic culture. Storr (76–77) describes the primary metaphor of the master pirate.

> [I]n the Bahamas piracy evolved as a dominant model for attaining economic success and a primary metaphor for doing business. Many of the successful industries in the Bahamas (piracy, wrecking, gun smuggling, and rum running) were piratical in nature. And, at various times in the Bahamas' economic narrative, the *master pirate* has been the principal figure in the plot (the driving force of the economy and the primary agent of change in the tale).

Storr observes further that because slaves in the Bahamas enjoyed greater autonomy than their counterparts in Barbados, Trinidad, Jamaica, Haiti, or Cuba, they could contract out their labor, securing them a higher standard of living and health. Storr argues that these peculiarities of Bahamian slavery meant that the *"enterprising slave* [also] evolved as a dominant figure in the Bahamas' economic story" (77). Together, Storr argues, the primary metaphors of master pirate and enterprising slave have shaped economic culture since the colonial period.

According to McCloskey, the economic effects of narrative can be powerful indeed. In *Bourgeois Dignity*, McCloskey (2010) argues that narrative, not technology, not science, not trade, not Protestant accumulation, not geography, not human capital, not even social institutions like private property rights, is responsible for the sixteen-fold increase in prosperity we have experienced over the last two to three centuries. The narrative of dignity (with its requisite accompaniment liberty), she explains, allowed for the acceptance and even praise of bourgeois experimentation and innovation. As McCloskey writes, "It is not science that was the key to the door to modernity, but the wider agreement to permit and honor innovation, opening one's eyes to novelty, having a go" (371). Of course, the European Enlightenment was part of the story of this astonishing rise in the standard of living. "Yet, without a radical change in attitudes toward innovation for optimistically hoped-for glory in a society newly admiring the bourgeois virtues, with (for you) a little monetary profit on the side, the sheer intellectual awakening in Europe would not have enriched the world" (372). And, as McCloskey argues, the narrative worked its magic from within as well as from without, leading to a new bourgeois economic self-identity. "The new bourgeois society was pragmatic and nonutopian, but also a little mad – the madness that overcame European men and women once they came to believe that they were free and dignified and should have a go" (372).

Economics is clearly not the only social science discipline to awaken to the power of narrative in understanding complex social phenomena. Narrative psychologists, for example, use the phrase "narrative identity" to describe the ways in which people deploy stories to construct their identity and convey that identity to others. Some narrative psychologists theorize that stories serve an integrative function, providing, over time, a sense of unity, and purpose (Erikson 1963). McAdams (1985, 1997) argues that by bringing together different strands of one's experience, narrative identities lend a sense of coherence to one's life as a whole.[4] Major life events, such as illness, the death of a family member, divorce, or a catastrophic disaster, how we reacted to such events, and the lessons we draw from them, help to make up our narrative identity. This identity, in turn, helps to shape the way we understand and respond to future events.

In the interdisciplinary terrain investigating the development of moral capacity, Nussbaum (1997), MacIntyre (1981), and Coles (1989) emphasize the important role the stories of our childhood and the stories of great literature play in connecting us to others within our circle, to our community, and to the broader social world. After describing the archetypical characters and lessons of fairytales, MacIntyre asserts, "Deprive children of stories and you leave them unscripted, anxious stutterers in their actions as in their words. Hence there is no way to give us an understanding of any society, including our own, except through the stock of stories which constitute its initial dramatic resources" (1981, 216). Drawing upon this narrative stock, our lives become our own great stories, "stories in which characters must overcome great obstacles to find something of great value" (Taylor 2001, 21).

Herein lies an important clue as to how stories help us navigate the unfamiliar terrain that is created when our *Gemeinschaft* narratives and our *Gesellschaft* narratives no longer seem to fit the circumstances. Nussbaum (1997) argues that by encountering stories of others in vastly different circumstances than our own, whether it is Sophocles' *Antigone* or Toni Morrison's *Beloved*, we develop our narrative imagination, extending our capacity for compassion beyond what our immediate intimate-sphere experience would afford. For example, as Nussbaum describes,

> The tragic festivals of the fifth century B.C. were civic festivals during which every other civic function stopped, and all citizens gathered together ... Tragedies acquaint the young citizen with the bad things that may happen in a human life, long before life itself does so. In the process they make the significance of suffering, and the losses that inspire it, unmistakably plain to the spectator; this is one way in which the poetic and visual resources of the drama have moral weight. By inviting the spectators to identify with the tragic hero, at the same time portraying the hero as a relatively good person, whose distress does not stem from deliberate wickedness, the drama makes compassion for suffering seize the imagination.
>
> (1997, 93)

This increased capacity for compassion, Nussbaum argues, is essential for robust civic life. Civic life requires the ability to imagine one's self in the place of the unknown other. Stories serve as a bridge that extends the reach of our imagination and allows us to apply what we know about acting in the intimate sphere to action taken beyond the intimate sphere, at least to some point.

Beyond the content of stories, narrative scholars have emphasized also the important role storytelling (and story listening), and the practiced art of each, play in the development of the moral imagination that builds toward social cohesion (Coles 1989; MacIntyre 1981; Taylor 2001), or, for our purposes, builds a bridge between *Gemeinschaft* narratives and *Gesellschaft* narratives. As Taylor (2001) argues, the telling and hearing of stories not only allows us to form our character and identity; shared stories serve as a sort of social glue that connects us to one another as the storyteller and listener co-create meaning. As Taylor observes, everyday storytelling, such as gossip, nostalgia, and reminiscence, is an attempt at being understood within the social context. Sometimes, this kind of storytelling can rise to the level of the richest stories found in the great works of literature and can profoundly shape the moral imagination and identity of a community.

Elsewhere, we examine the role that collective narratives such as these have played in community rebound after disaster. Stories of displacement, relocation, and rebuilding within New Orleans' Vietnamese-American community, for example, rendered the post-Katrina context more familiar and less daunting and paved the way for a remarkably robust recovery (Chamlee-Wright and Storr 2009a, 2010a). Further, stories that captured a particular cultural trait or set of values at work within the community, such as adherence to a strong work ethic, affirm for the storyteller and impart to the listener lessons of "who we are" as a community. For example, stories celebrating St. Bernard Parish's working-class roots, attitudes, and values were a source of resilience within that community (Chamlee-Wright and Storr 2011).

Thus, stories wield an incredible force in the social world. The stories we hear and the stories we craft and tell shape who we are, give us perspective that helps us make sense of the world, directs our action, and connects us to one another. As we will discuss in greater detail below, the stories we craft, tell, and hear also help us navigate the unfamiliar terrain that emerges when the old stories no longer fit the context.

## The development of plot in the Katrina narrative

Ethnographic researchers, particularly those who deploy in-depth interview techniques, are essentially asking their subjects to tell their stories. This research methodology is particularly well suited to a post-disaster context because people often come to terms with a major life event by weaving it into the arc of their life story (McAdams 1985, 1997). How, for example, have the disaster and their responses to it interrupted and/or fit within the plot of their life story?

When conducting the fieldwork that informs this chapter, our practice was to tell our interview subjects that we had some specific questions we wanted to ask about their neighborhood, their life, and community before Katrina, and the steps they had taken and the frustrations they had encountered after Katrina. "But mostly," we would say, "we want to hear your story," so that the interview subject would know that they were welcome to deviate from the "script" of the interview questions if those questions were not the questions that would tap the relevant details of their lives and circumstances. In the early stages of our fieldwork, it became clear to us just how accurate the "storytelling" frame actually was. We were in fact asking them to be storytellers – to not merely offer the flow of events leading up to, during, and after the storm, but to help us make sense of those events. We were indeed eager listeners seeking to understand why, for example, an interview subject ignored calls to evacuate, or why a pastor chose landscaping as his first priority in the effort to rebuild his church, or how an elderly woman of modest means managed to be among the first in her neighborhood to rebuild her home. And, for the most part, they were also eager in their storytelling – an eagerness (often mixed with anger, anxiety, frustration, and sorrow) to articulate a coherent plot that made sense of all that had happened and rendered their own actions intelligible.

Consider the Katrina narrative of James Ray Cox in Waveland, Mississippi.[5] Situated in Hancock County along the Gulf Coast, the city of Waveland was considered "ground zero" for Katrina's landfall and the 26-foot storm surge that ravaged Mississippi's coastline. Cox lived with his wife and three children in Waveland and worked as the manager of the Waveland Wal-Mart Supercenter. Assistant manager Jessica Lewis had won this particular Wal-Mart a certain celebrity status in the days following the storm after using a bulldozer to break through the ruins of the store, pushing undamaged merchandise into the parking lot for residents to take what they needed. Unable to reach her supervisors, Lewis also took it upon herself to break into the pharmacy in order to supply the local hospital with critical prescription medications (Rosegrant 2007; Horwitz 2009). In the telling of his own Katrina story, however, Cox focused his attention on the longer-term recovery of the community. The plot of Cox's story centers on the reopening of the Wal-Mart under a tent in the store's parking lot just 19 days after the storm, which paved the way for a fully functional supercenter by Thanksgiving two months later.

Cox's home was destroyed by heavy wind damage and nine feet of water and, at the time of the interview, he and his family were living in a trailer on their property. Cox could have asked Wal-Mart to assign him to a different store in another part of the country but he decided to stay in Waveland. Cox had become an entrenched part of the business community, serving on the board of directors of the Chamber of Commerce.

A significant aspect of Cox's narrative is that he traverses and weaves together what might otherwise be considered three fairly distinct spheres. As the manager of a Wal-Mart store, he acted on behalf of what is arguably the ultimate symbol of the impersonal forces of *Gesellschaft* and he never conveys any doubt that those interests must be served. At the same time, Cox was concerned for his own family and the close network of personal and business ties we would associate with the intimate order of *Gemeinschaft*. He was also concerned with the middle ground between *Gesellschaft* and *Gemeinschaft*, the Waveland community as a whole.

One way to interpret this is that for Cox, Waveland was part of what he considered the intimate sphere – that it was perfectly natural in the post-disaster situation to extend a sense of solidarity to other members of his community. We should keep in mind that pre-Katrina, however, Waveland's population was 6,674. Arguably, had one of those 6,674 people come into the store asking for special assistance prior to Katrina, Cox would have likely called upon the narratives of the extended order to guide his response. In a post-disaster context, however, the narratives we might ordinarily call up often don't seem to fit. As Cox describes,

> You see [your fellow business] people, they've lost their homes and they totally lost their business. And now, *they're* self-employed. ... If you don't do something to help this community and give them a place to buy groceries and give them a place to buy the necessities of life to rebuild their lives, ... it probably would not be worth your while to [rebuild]. Would you as an individual expect someone to live here? You know, if you have to drive twenty, thirty, forty miles every three or four days? Is it worth your time to rebuild what was destroyed? ... So that's one of the things we looked at, you know, we have to do something. Granted, you know, our customer base probably was cut more than in half. But it probably would be decreasing today had our store and other businesses not decided, you know, just take a stance and come home, you know, and build this thing and get it back up and running as fast as they can ... You have to take a stance, because you have a vested interest in the community. You have a home.
>
> Both of my children have been – they were born in New Orleans in Tulane Hospital – but they've both been raised here, are being raised here. I have a son who's four, will be five ... and my daughter turned two in November. My wife and I chose to have children here and we want to raise our children here. There's some days we second-guess that now. But I mean it's fine, I mean it's gonna be fine. And I think the resilience of the people here in Hancock County will help to beat that.

In describing the murky post-Katrina social context, Cox borrows mechanisms and metaphors from both the extended and intimate spheres in an effort to attend to the middle ground that lies between. Here, the focus of Cox's narrative is on how he was able to serve his fellow businessmen and the broader Waveland community, but his means for doing so is to sell them groceries and supplies. He frames the reopening of a box store as "taking a stance" in favor of community. He is, in essence, deliberately extending the impersonal mechanisms of *Gesellschaft* to foster the rebirth of community. Further, Cox's narrative uses the metaphor of "home" to connect the intimate sphere of family and personal ties to the broader Waveland community, noting that costs have been borne by one (the intimate sphere of his own family) in his efforts to serve the other (the Waveland community). Thus, Cox is navigating this middle ground between *Gemeinschaft* and *Gesellschaft* by drawing upon the mechanisms and metaphors of each.

According to Cox's narrative, then, Wal-Mart has become a key player in Waveland's civic life. But, recalling Nussbaum (1997), robust civic life requires that we are capable of extending our narrative imagination beyond our immediate experience and relationships.

Soon after he returned to Waveland following the storm, Cox recalled feeling as though his dreams had been shattered – that he had worked tremendously hard and had been so proud to be the manager of a gleaming new supercenter, only to be wading through muck and devastation. He then noticed a woman with an infant who had asked to borrow a shopping cart. As Cox recounts,

> … to see a lady carry a baby that didn't have clothes. The lady didn't have any shoes on and she was asking to borrow plastic bags so she could make shoes out of it. And then she asked to borrow a shopping cart, so instead of carrying her baby four miles home she could roll him … Things like that will teach you, when you see a person just in shambles. I'll never forget my son crying when we walked back home to take his things [to the dump]. Things like that will teach you.

The sight of the woman in his store plays two roles in Cox's narrative. First, it was a reminder to him that feeling sorry for his own plight was not what should be occupying his attention. Second, and we see this in the seamless transition from the woman and her child to thoughts of his own, he has extended his narrative imagination enough to gain a sense of empathy and compassion for this person who is unknown to and socially distant from him. The cultivation of an extended sense of compassion, which Nussbaum (1997) attributes to great works of literature, unfolds for Cox in this bit of real-life drama played out in his store. It is in moments such as this that Cox can imagine what role a Wal-Mart supercenter can play in rebuilding civic life, in traversing that middle ground between *Gemeinschaft* and *Gesellschaft*.[6]

When asked to follow up on his observation that people in his county were particularly resilient, Cox describes the excitement that he and his staff felt in the days running up to the tent opening. Here again Cox borrows values ordinarily associated with *Gesellschaft* to attend to the needs of the community that is at the center of his Katrina narrative. As Cox recalls,

> … within days after the storm when all the law enforcement from Florida and all over the US and Virginia and all those guys were here, they're like, how in the world is it that y'all are excited about putting up a tent knowing your store was destroyed and your house was destroyed and you should be home working on your house and you're doing this with a smile and enjoying what you're doing. I don't know. We just get up and do it again. You know, you just do it. I mean you just do it. And maybe it's because our hearts are big. I don't know. We just do it. We got up, pulled up our bootstraps and just went to work. You do that, because you see your friends and neighbors and they're in [trouble] and in some ways, they might not be able to provide for themselves. So you gotta help them and provide.

Notice that immediately after describing an ethos of self-reliance, i.e., they "pulled up [their] bootstraps and just went to work," he connects that work ethic to a responsibility to provide for others within the broader community (known and unknown) who cannot provide for themselves. Here, Cox is creatively weaving self-reliance and work ethic, often associated with individual achievement, with "having a big heart" and providing for others. This formula works because the sense of solidarity and intentional beneficence usually associated with the intimate sphere has been extended up to the broader community.

Cox concludes the narrative by drawing our attention back to the important role the store played in the community's rebound and recovery. As he explains, "In my opinion, we made a statement when we decided to open the tent and move back into this store – that we were committed as a company to this community and helping rebuild. I mean, in my opinion, that's a very strong commitment."

Here again, the traversing of the middle ground between *Gemeinschaft* and *Gesellschaft* is accomplished by reimagining a business as a civic leader. With the store badly damaged and the future of the city in considerable doubt, such an outcome was not preordained. It was likely that Cox's deft adaptation of narratives from the intimate and extended orders had a great deal to do with Wal-Mart playing this role.

## New Orleans as a character in the Katrina narrative

As we describe elsewhere, the vast majority of interview subjects who had returned to New Orleans after Katrina professed an overwhelming devotion to their city and neighborhood (Chamlee-Wright and Storr 2009a, 2009b, 2011). This was true of those who lived in fashionable upscale neighborhoods in the heart of the city, stable (but architecturally uninspiring) neighborhoods in the outlying suburban tracts, and some of the poorest neighborhoods of the city. The pronounced sense of place was commonly expressed by white, black, Arab, and Latino residents and by members of the Vietnamese-American community who considered their New Orleans neighborhood to be their "second homeland." Such expressions of devotion were as common among business professionals and pastors as they were among working-class residents. In short, most of our interview subjects believed, as was often repeated, "There's no place like New Orleans."

But, of course, Katrina and the flooding that followed devastated New Orleans. Eighty percent of the city experienced significant flooding. More than 200,000 homes were destroyed either from the immediate surge of floodwaters or the standing water that remained for weeks before it could be pumped out. Upon their return, residents more often than not found their homes in ruins, some incurring flood depths of eight feet or more, all festering from the effects of toxic floodwaters and the ensuing mold.

In many communities, municipal services were completely absent for months (in some cases years) following the storm. This meant that storm debris (which might include boats, downed trees, parts of wrecked homes, and a countless variety of other materials) blocked road access and littered the community. The debris from gutted houses sat for many months on the roadside. Safety was a constant concern. Given this level of devastation, it would have been understandable if the sense of place residents had attached to their neighborhoods and city pre-Katrina had been wiped out completely.[7] And yet, at least for most residents who chose to return, this did not seem to be the case. The city of New Orleans was, thus, a key character in the narratives that displaced residents deployed after Katrina.

The cost–benefit analysis of a return to New Orleans was anything but clear. While it is true that for many residents their home was their only asset and therefore might inspire a return if this were the only consideration, a decision to return and rebuild came with significant costs. This was particularly true for those who returned early on. Remediation and renovation were expensive in terms of time, materials, and professional services, public and private services were meager at best, insurance payouts (if any were forthcoming) were bogged down in bureaucratic wrangling, employment opportunities within one's own profession were often non-existent, the post-disaster policy environment left residents confused around the basic questions of whether and how they would be allowed to rebuild, and it was early returnees who bore the costs of uncertainty, as only time would tell if their neighborhoods would be viable in the long term (Chamlee-Wright 2007; Chamlee-Wright and Storr 2009c). In short, on a narrowly rational basis, the cost–benefit calculation did not generally favor a decision to return and rebuild.

And yet, many did return. Clearly a pronounced sense of place was a reason for returning, but such a choice is difficult to understand within the narratives we customarily deploy in the context of *Gemeinschaft* and *Gesellschaft*. According to the narratives of the intimate sphere, for example, narratives of solidarity and shared purpose, it makes sense to endure great hardship and personal cost for a loved one. In this sphere it makes sense to engage in a strategy of intentional beneficence. But as we discuss above, commitment to the rebirth of a city reaches beyond the scope of what many of us consider to be the intimate sphere of *Gemeinschaft*, either in terms of our ability to extend our compassion or our ability to make a demonstrable impact on the eventual outcome. On the other hand, it was not clear that the decision to return fit the narratives of *Gesellschaft* either, as for most people bearing the costs associated with the decision to return and rebuild (particularly an early return) just didn't make sense based on cold rational calculation.

Interview data suggests, however, that following Katrina, an alternative common narrative seemed to emerge. This common narrative cast New Orleans as a central character in returnees' Katrina stories. Described by words and phrases like "love," "devotion," "commitment," "part of who I am," the character that was New Orleans possessed qualities reminiscent of a beloved family member, placing it firmly within the context of the intimate sphere. In some Katrina stories, New Orleans took on a matriarchal quality as the provider of home, food, nurturing, and comfort. As a beloved and intimate character within one's story, the narratives of solidarity, commitment, and sacrifice made sense.

When asked to recall what their community was like pre-Katrina, many interview subjects responded like Catherine Parker[†],[8] a resident of New Orleans East, who notes,

> There's nothing like New Orleans. Nowhere else is nothing like New Orleans ... There's an aura about New Orleans that you can't get anywhere else. You really can't.

Or as Broadmoor resident Kate Lyons[†] observes,

> New Orleans is much more than a city to us. It's more like a facet of your personality. It's part of who you are. I just love everything about the city. I love the spirit and the attitude of the people. I love the diversity of the city, which is totally unrecognized nationally. I love the blend that makes it unique. I love the music, the food, the festivals, Mardi Gras ... It's just the best place on earth.

In their recollections of pre-Katrina life, New Orleans as a character played a particular kind of role for New Orleanians that was different from the role she played for visitors. To a visitor, New Orleans had long been a place in which one's ordinary responsibilities could be suspended for a time. But to New Orleanians, New Orleans was much more than that. New Orleans was indeed the hostess, but the gatherings were the block parties of neighborhoods, the Mardi Gras balls, and after-church socials, as much as the nightlife on Bourbon Street. Like the family matriarch, New Orleans provided food that could be found nowhere else.

Most importantly, like the family matriarch, New Orleans provided a sense of home. After describing her extended family as possessing a rich bond that was both "familial and familiar," Central City resident Renee Lewis[†] observed,

> Well, the city that I love and the reason that I don't want to live nowhere else – it's not a perfect place – [is that] it is extremely unique in that its history and its culture kind of keep saying these two descriptive [terms]: familial and familiar. There is so much oldness that informs today, like the music and like the food and like the traditions that every New Orlean's commercial or public view puts forward in a very one-dimensional kind of way. But it's so much deeper

than that … When we were away from the city for a long, long time and were able to come back just for an evening, something that was going on at the Ashe Cultural Arts Center … [W]e went to this event and [with] the drums [and music] … it was like the heartbeat had got started again and I didn't realize how much of that I missed or how it was missing in my life. I guess what I didn't realize was how important it was for me to hear that – to kind of enliven my spirit, to quicken my heart.

For Lewis[†], New Orleans possessed the same familial and familiar qualities that her deeply connected extended family possessed.

Of course, any good story needs an antagonist. And, in the post-Katrina context, there were plenty of characters to fill this role. Not surprisingly, the hurricane itself served as a principal antagonist. As Lewis[†] describes, "The storm took effect. It casts us out like stray pennies in your purse that you just throw up on … a dresser … [A]s Katrina passed and the levees broke, our home was stolen from us."

The disaster as antagonist would fit any post-disaster context, but New Orleanians also perceived that their city was the target of unprovoked attacks from powerful corners, such as the national media that portrayed New Orleans as a city of welfare recipients and thieves. Among New Orleanians, the narrative that emerged was one in which a cherished member of the family – the matriarch, no less – was being picked on and bullied by forces far more powerful than she. Such a story tends to inspire, in any morally upright listener, a desire to leap to the victim's defense, save the beloved character, and vanquish the enemy. Describing his response to a State Farm Insurance agent who mocked New Orleans, for instance, Pastor Jack Green[†] recalls,

> I just ripped into him coz I [was] so angry. He said "do you think that people in other parts of the country should have to help New Orleans, you know, by paying more for insurance?" I said absolutely! I said without the city of New Orleans, the rest of the country [would suffer because], a) this is one of the only cities with unique character and b) it was one of the most important ports in the entire country. Absolutely!

Political elites at all levels served as another set of antagonists that helped to explain the slow pace by which recovery assistance was getting into the hands of residents (poor residents, in particular), the slow return of municipal services, and the uncertainty related to the redevelopment planning process. Eleanor Shaw's[†] Katrina story includes a political economy analysis that helps her understand and explain why city officials have stepped up eminent domain proceedings against her neighbors who have not yet returned to New Orleans. As she describes,

> If [homeowners] don't come and do something with the property, [the city is] going to give them a deadline and all this type of thing. ... I think [the city] just wants to confiscate their property.

When asked to clarify why she thinks the city is taking these actions, Shaw† explains,

> That's money. For instance my house here, if somebody can come along and confiscate my house. My husband and I have worked all our lives and spent money and deprived ourselves in order to have [this]. And then somebody is just going to take it? That's not right. And come time for taxes and what not, we paid taxes ... And [the city says,] "you didn't take care of your property, so we're going to take it." Then [the city will] turn around and sell it for three times what I paid for it. And that's what's going to happen to the money.

When pressed to explain what she believes will happen to the money, Shaw† concludes, "They're going to pocket it. What do you think is going to happen? It's not [like] they've done nothing worthwhile with it." More than a political economy critique, however, Shaw's† analysis helps to explain her own stubborn defiance. By deploying resources embedded within her extended family, this 88-year-old woman was among the first residents to return to her Lower Ninth Ward home (while the question of whether people should be *allowed* to rebuild in the Lower Ninth Ward was still under heated debated). Her Katrina story is clearly one that illustrates the important role of socially embedded resources, but it also explains why she was not willing to bow to what she perceived to be the will of powerful elites to take over the neighborhood she loved.

With New Orleans cast as a treasured member of the family, and an extensive cast of antagonistic characters in play, many of the storytellers felt it incumbent on them to help to save the city. Some returnees framed their role as part of a Divine plan, such as the owner of a diner who declared that God would give her the tools to start her own nonprofit. "I'm gonna raise money and I'm gonna build at least so many of these homes myself and show the government that, 'This is what you should be doing.'" Or, as Pastor Randy Millet of the Adullam Christian Fellowship pledged,

> I can tell you it's a closely-knit community, and for me, if this is what God's chosen for me to do, then so be it, because I want to see our community returned. Now, I'm one pastor doing one small part, but whatever I'm called to do, I want to be faithful to do my part ... And I believe it like this: great men are put in circumstances and they have to make choices.

In the name of rescuing their city and neighborhood, some of these heroes achieved astonishing results, such as the St. Bernard Parish school superintendent who drew people home by rebuilding the parish schools, or the registered nurse who drew people back to the Lower Ninth Ward by building a health clinic, the first facility of its kind in the community (Chamlee-Wright 2010). But most of the heroes were ordinary citizens who saw their own return as a small but significant step in the rebirth of the city, such as the Ninth Ward businessman who understood that his laundromat and convenience store served as a safe and hospitable social space for his neighbors; or the retired couple Jordan and Irene Walker[†], who returned to their Ninth Ward home to, in their words, keep their home and community alive. They observed that as long as people stayed away, it would only be "half a New Orleans."

IRENE WALKER[†]: You need your neighbors to come back and redo their houses. I want my neighbors back. I really do.

JORDAN WALKER[†]: For a house to be alive, it needs people living in it. A house that doesn't have people living in it is gonna deteriorate. And if people are living in it, then it's gonna have life and it's gonna survive.

And thus, with every neighbor that returns, this narrative asserts, another step is taken to save the central character of many returnees' Katrina story.

While solidarity, personal sacrifice, and intentional beneficence would not ordinarily fit the *Gesellschaft* context of a large metropolitan area, such narratives fit perfectly if the central character is drawn from the *Gemeinschaft* sphere of family.

## Conclusion

Scholars have long posited that we live simultaneously in two very different spheres: the sphere of the intimate order of *Gemeinschaft*, in which narratives of solidarity and intentional beneficence toward known others guide our actions, and the sphere of the extended order of *Gesellschaft*, in which narratives of narrowly focused self-interest guide our action and result in patterns of unintentional beneficence through impersonal signals and market mechanisms of exchange. Under ordinary circumstances, our ability to switch between these two spheres, to navigate the murky territory in between, and to deploy the appropriate narratives tends to escape our notice. Because it blurs the boundaries defining *Gemeinschaft* and *Gesellschaft* so dramatically, and renders unclear the territory between these spheres, a post-disaster context offers a particularly robust opportunity to understand this navigation process.

In this chapter, we discussed how people deploy narrative as a means of navigating these two spheres of social life. Further, we examined how people cultivate and deploy new stories when the boundaries defining and the territory between *Gemeinschaft* and *Gesellschaft* are problematized. Building from interview data gathered in the post-Katrina context of New Orleans and the Mississippi Gulf Coast, the analysis presented above suggests that when external events disrupt the boundaries that define the intimate and extended spheres of social life, people deploy their capacities for story craft and storytelling in order to find new narratives that guide their way. In the context of the post-Katrina environment, such capacities were a significant source of community resilience.

## Notes

1 Gudeman (2001) employed a similar distinction. For Gudeman, the economy is divided into two transactional realms, each governed by different kinds of relationships (9). On the one hand, there is market epitomized by the corporation, where relationships are characterized by anonymous exchange and rational calculation. On the other hand, there is community epitomized by the house, where relationships are characterized by sociality, reciprocity, and mutuality. According to Gudeman, these two spheres can, do, and must exist simultaneously but the growth of one is necessarily at the expense of the other (22).
2 In essence, the mental models that guide our interpretation of circumstances and our action in response to them function exactly in the way that humanists have described the role stories play. As Taylor (2001, 29) observes, "even those of us most committed to logic and rationality do not so much reason our way to our views and values as *use* reason to justify what we find ourselves believing and valuing. And those beliefs and values are likely to have been formed by our stories."
3 For example, Bird-David (1990) examines the metaphor dominant within the South Indian hunter-gatherer Nayaka community, who cast the forest in the role of "parent" and one another in the role of "siblings." This metaphor, in turn, dictates a variety of specific rule-following behavior intended to keep the community in balance with its environment.
4 For examples of narrative psychology that emphasize narrative identity as being multi-vocal, see Gergen (1991) and Hermans (1996).
5 For ethnographic details related to the field studies conducted for the broader project, see Chamlee-Wright 2010.
6 The central role that Wal-Mart's reopening played in Waveland's recovery was acknowledged by residents as well. As Waveland resident Jessica Fallows[†] observed, "It was Wal-Mart under a tent. We were all thrilled. Oh, we can go buy pop, or we can get, you know, our essentials. So we were really happy about that. That was a forward motion. And then Sonic opened. We had the busiest Sonic in ... the whole United States. It made more money in a shorter period of time than any Sonic did for a year in the United States. Amazing. It was like fine dining. Ooh, this is wonderful, you know, coz there was nothing else then. There was no stores. There was nothing that was even halfway resembling normal. I guess when businesses open up and they start being fully operational, it reminds us what normalcy used to be like" (Chamlee-Wright 2010, 50–51).
7 In fact, this was the reaction of some former New Orleans residents who evacuated to Houston following the storm and were still there three years later. Approximately half of the Houston-based respondents said that they preferred

New Orleans over Houston; 22% of these respondents said that they had not returned because the city no longer had the character, amenities, and appeal of the pre-Katrina New Orleans (Chamlee-Wright and Storr 2009b).
8 Whenever possible, we protect the identity of the interview subject. Names with the '†' superscript are pseudonyms. Because of the details of their narrative, it is sometimes impossible to obscure the identity of interview subjects. In such cases, we obtained permission to use the subject's real name.

## References

Berger, Ronald and Richard Quinney. 2005. *Storytelling Sociology: Narrative as Social Inquiry*. Boulder, CO: Lynne Reinner.

Bird-David, Nurit. 1990. "The Giving Environment: Another Perspective on the Economic System of Gatherer-Hunters." *Current Anthropology* 31 (2): 189–196.

Bird-David, Nurit. 1992. "Beyond 'The Original Affluent Society': A Culturalist Reformulation, and Discussion." *Current Anthropology* 33 (1): 25–34.

Boettke, Peter and Virgil H. Storr. 2002. "Post-Classical Political Economy: Polity, Society and Economy in Mises, Weber, and Hayek." *American Journal of Economics and Sociology* 61 (1): 161–191.

Chamlee-Wright, Emily. 2007. "The Long Road Back: Signal Noise in the Post-Katrina Context." *The Independent Review* 12 (2): 235–259.

Chamlee-Wright, Emily. 2010. *The Cultural and Political Economy of Recovery: Social Learning in a Post-Disaster Environment*. London: Routledge.

Chamlee-Wright, Emily and Virgil H. Storr. 2009a. "Club Goods and Post-Disaster Community Return, with Virgil Storr." *Rationality and Society* 21 (4): 429–458.

Chamlee-Wright, Emily and Virgil H. Storr. 2009b. "There's No Place Like New Orleans": Sense of Place and Community Recovery in the Ninth Ward After Hurricane Katrina." *Journal of Urban Affairs* 31 (5): 615–634.

Chamlee-Wright, Emily and Virgil H. Storr. 2009c. "Filling the Civil Society Vacuum: Post-Disaster Policy and Community Response." *Mercatus Policy Series*, Policy Comment 22.

Chamlee-Wright, Emily and Virgil H. Storr. 2010a. "Community Resilience in New Orleans East: Deploying the Cultural Toolkit within a Vietnamese-American Community." In *Community Disaster Recovery and Resiliency: Exploring Global Opportunities and Challenges*, edited by Jason David Rivera and DeMond Miller, 99–122. Boca Raton, FL: Auerbach Publications.

Chamlee-Wright, Emily and Virgil H. Storr. 2010b. *The Political Economy of Hurricane Katrina and Community Rebound*. London: Edward Elgar.

Chamlee-Wright, Emily and Virgil H. Storr. 2011. "Social Capital as Collective Narratives and Post-Disaster Community Recover." *Sociological Review* 59 (2): 266–282.

Coles, Robert. 1989. *The Call of Stories: Teaching and the Moral Imagination*. Boston, MA: Houghton Mifflin.

Cornuelle, Richard. 1965. *Reclaiming the American Dream: The Role of Private Individuals and Voluntary Associations*. Piscataway, NJ: Transaction Publishers.

Cornuelle, Richard. 1991. "New Work for Invisible Hands: A Future for Libertarian Thought." *Times Literary Supplement* April 5.

Cornuelle, Richard. 1996. "De-Nationalizing Community." *Philanthropy* (Spring): 10–33.

Denzau, Arthur and Douglass North. 1994. "Shared Mental Models: Ideologies and Institutions." *Kyklos* 47 (1): 3–31.
Erikson, Erik H. 1963. *Childhood and Society*. 2nd edition. New York: Norton.
Garnett, Robert F. 2008. "Positive Psychology and Philanthropy: Reclaiming the Virtues of Classical Liberalism." *Conversations on Philanthropy* V: 1–16.
Gergen, Kenneth. 1991. *The Saturated Self: Dilemmas of Identity in Contemporary Life*. New York: Basic Books.
Granovetter, Mark. 1985. "Economic Action and Social Structure: The Problem of Embeddedness." *American Journal of Sociology* 91: 481–510.
Granovetter, Mark. 2005. "The Impact of Social Structure on Economic Outcomes." *Journal of Economic Perspectives* 19 (1): 33–50.
Gudeman, Stephen. 1986. *Economics as Culture: Models and Metaphors of Livelihood*. London: Routledge.
Gudeman, Stephen. 2001. *The Anthropology of Economy*. Malden, MA: Blackwell.
Hermans, Hubert J. M. 1996. "Voicing the Self: From Information Processing to Dialogical Exchange." *Psychological Bulletin* 199: 31–50.
Horwitz, Steven. 2009. "Wal-Mart to the Rescue: Private Enterprise's Response to Hurricane Katrina." *The Independent Review* 13 (4): 511–528.
Lavoie, Don and Emily Chamlee-Wright. 2000. *Culture and Enterprise*. London: Routledge.
McAdams, Dan P. 1985. *Power, Intimacy, and the Life Story: Personological Inquiries into Identity*. New York: Guilford Press.
McAdams, Dan P. 1997. "The Case for Unity in the (Post)modern Self: A Modest Proposal." In *Self and Identity: Fundamental Issues*, edited by Richard Ashmore and Lee Jussim, 46–78. New York: Oxford University Press.
McAdams, Dan P., Ruthellen Josselson, and Amia Lieblich. 2006. *Identity and Story: Creating Self in Narrative*. Washington, DC: American Psychological Association.
McCloskey, Deirdre. 2010. *Bourgeois Dignity: Why Economics Can't Explain the Modern World*. Chicago: University of Chicago Press.
MacIntyre, Alasdair. 1981. *After Virtue*. Notre Dame, IN: University of Notre Dame Press.
North, Douglass C. 1981. *Structure and Change in Economic History*. New York: W.W. Norton.
North, Douglass C. 1990. *Institutions, Institutional Change and Economic Performance*. Cambridge: Cambridge University Press.
North, Douglass C. 2005. *Understanding the Process of Economic Change*. Princeton, NJ: Princeton University Press.
Nussbaum, Martha. 1997. *Cultivating Humanity: A Classical Defense of Reform in Liberal Education*. Cambridge, MA: Harvard University Press.
Rosegrant, Susan. 2007. *Wal-Mart's Response to Hurricane Katrina: Striving for a Public Private Partnership*. Kennedy School of Government Case Program C16-07-1876.0.
Storr, Virgil H. 2004. *Enterprising Slaves and Master Pirates*. New York: Peter Lang.
Storr, Virgil H. 2008. "The Market as a Social Space: On the Meaningful Extra-Economic Conversations That Can Occur in Markets." *Review of Austrian Economics* 21 (2 & 3): 135–150.
Taylor, Daniel. 2001. *Tell Me a Story: The Life-Shaping Power of Our Stories*. St. Paul, MN: Bog Walk Press.

# 10 Community, the market, and the state

## Insights from German neoliberalism

*Samuel Gregg*

## Introduction

The effect of market relationships upon non-market forms of human association – and vice versa – is a subject that has long occupied supporters and critics of free-market economies. It was a theme that, for example, engaged the attention of Scottish Enlightenment thinkers ranging from Adam Ferguson to Adam Smith. Markets, they understood, do not exist in a moral or sociological vacuum. In more recent times, much of this discussion has been conducted in terms outlined by the German sociologist Ferdinand Tönnies (1855–1936). He employed the terms *Gemeinschaft* (community) and *Gesellschaft* (society) to conceptualize what he regarded as the two types of human relationships (Tönnies 1912). *Gemeinschaft* concerned those forms of association in which individuals participated and valued as much as for the sake of the group itself as for their own individual good. Ethnic groups, guilds, and churches are good examples – though so too, in particular circumstances, might be the state. Such groups are often bound together by common values; they may also embody certain forms of status which are attributed to individuals by the group rather than earned or merited. For Tönnies, the family with its internal ascribed roles of father, mother, husband, wife, son, and daughter (as well as more extended relations such as grandparents and cousins) epitomized *Gemeinschaft*.

*Gesellschaft*, on the other hand, denoted those relationships and forms of association formed on the basis of people pursuing their individual self-interest and which do not presume to assert strong values or goals other than those chosen by the individuals that belong to such groups. Membership of such groups is more fluid, based on free association (implying that people can leave these forms of association much more easily than they leave, for instance, a family). They are often mediated through the legal mechanism of contract. Many types of commercial enterprises, in Tönnies' view, were essentially organizations based upon *Gesellschaft* expectations and through which people pursued their particular and individual (particularly economic) self-interests.

When Tönnies posed these as ideal types, he was not suggesting that all social activities could be rigorously segmented into *Gesellschaft* and *Gemeinschaft* relationships. That said, there is no shortage of scholars who have argued that, historically speaking, there have been tensions between *Gesellschaft* and *Gemeinschaft* forms of social relationships. In his masterly *Guild and State* (2003), the British historian and sociologist Antony Black traces the long history of conflict between groups and sets of values associated with *Gemeinschaft* and *Gesellschaft* expectations from Roman times onwards. While being careful not to draw excessively artificial lines of conflict (he notes, for example, that bishops and theologians were among the harshest critics of medieval guilds, while merchants numbered among some of the guilds' most ardent defenders), Black presents a formidable case to suggest that much of the social, economic, and political history of the West can be read in terms of the ongoing rise and fall of *Gemeinschaft* and *Gesellschaft* priorities and concerns in various political, economic, and social settings. Put in simplified terms, those promoting *Gemeinschaft* priorities typically complained that market-orientated relationships had a tendency to undermine non-economic forms of community. Likewise, those promoting *Gesellschaft* associations and relationships often argue that *Gemeinschaft* communities can have a suffocating effect upon commercial forms of social interaction and may even limit legitimate expressions of individuality and creativity.

One organization that does not fit neatly into the *Gemeinschaft*/*Gesellschaft* division is the state, especially the modern state. The state's unique capacity to provide legal substance – and, if necessary, enforcement – to contractual relationships may be considered as an essential contribution to the capacity of *Gesellschaft* relationships to be sustained over time. Yet when associated with, for instance, strong expressions of non-commercial community such as the nation, the state's power has been employed in ways that have unduly limited expressions of *Gesellschaft* forms of association. Likewise, those wishing to protect and extend free associative commercial relationships have been willing to call upon the state to break up monopoly control of sections of the economy by guilds and some of their modern successors such as trade unions. Similarly, those concerned with limiting the societal space occupied by commercial activity have not hesitated to lobby for restrictions on trade, such as limiting the number and type of businesses open for trade on days traditionally associated with rest and the pursuit of non-commercial activities, such as worship and recreation.

For a number of reasons, these conflicts between the priorities of *Gesellschaft* and *Gemeinschaft* (or what we might call "associations" and "communities") and their implications for state power particularly manifested themselves in Germany from the mid-nineteenth century onwards. One purpose of this paper is to examine the way in which a particularly influential group of German economists – specifically Walter Eucken (1891–1950), Franz Böhm (1895–1977), Alfred Müller-Armack (1901–1978),

Alexander Rüstow (1885–1963), and Wilhelm Röpke (1899–1966) – approached these issues. Their manner of doing so helps to explain why they are often called "neoliberals" and underscores some of their differences with what might be described as more traditional classical liberal approaches to social and economic problems. But by illustrating the number of contradictions left unresolved by the neoliberal approach – many of which flow from the way the neoliberals sought to use the state to resolve apparent tensions – this paper also raises questions about the usefulness of the *Gesellschaft–Gemeinschaft* distinction and sketches some ways forward beyond this form of ideal-type reflection.

## Between modernity and tradition

The nineteenth century is often described as the century of liberalism insofar as the Western world rapidly transitioned away from conditions of monarchial absolutism and mercantilist economies towards more representative forms of government and market economies. These developments were not, however, without their difficulties, especially in Germany. The challenges of German liberalization form an indispensable backdrop to the German neoliberals' engagement with the question of the most optimal relationship between the market economy, non-market forms of community, and the state.

Although the Kingdom of Prussia is most often associated with militarism, some of its political leaders were among the foremost promoters of classical liberal economic ideas in Europe after the end of the Napoleonic wars in 1815. The abolition of internal customs barriers between most German states at the end of 1833 (known as the *Zollverein*) was pioneered, for instance, by Prussian government officials who had been heavily influenced by reading Adam Smith's *Wealth of Nations* ([1776] 1981). The same Prussian state later concluded a tariff-reducing commercial treaty with France in 1862. The competition facilitated by these developments, along with the passing of legislation in Prussia and a number of other German states that forbade restrictive trade practices, helped accelerate the disappearance of the hundreds of guilds that had hitherto dominated large swaths of German economic life.

After 1870, however, the trend towards the growth of *Gesellschaft* forms of association and the demise of certain expressions of *Gemeinschaft* community underwent a reversal. One contributing factor was the long association of nineteenth-century German liberalism with nationalist sentiment. This made many German liberals otherwise inclined to support the growth of market-orientated relationships somewhat susceptible to market-restrictive laws and policies implemented in the name of national cohesion. Another *Gesellschaft*-inhibiting development was the rise of the German Social Democrats and trade unions as major political and economic forces in the wake of Germany's rapid industrialization. These groups were intent upon using the state to sharply restrict economic liberty and its supporting cultural and legal institutions throughout Germany. The situation was exacerbated by the financial and commercial crash that afflicted Imperial Germany in 1873, a subsequent severe industrial recession, and declining profitability on the part of Germany's formerly very productive agricultural sector after exposure to foreign competition.

Many German business leaders and political leaders became doubtful of the economic benefits of competition and free trade. Their concern was matched by rising worries among German intellectuals, Protestant and Catholic clergy, civil servants, and traditional Prussian elites about the ways in which the spread of *Gesellschaft* relationships was changing German society. The move of millions of Germans from agricultural settings and small towns to large cities and employment in industrial capitalist settings in a relatively short period of time resulted in considerable upheaval in families as well as social and religious communities that had existed for hundreds of years. The same developments also resulted in the growth of a large urban proletariat that increasingly voted Social Democrat and joined trade unions in large numbers. Ironically, these new formations embodied, often in a highly secularized form, many of the values of brotherhood and solidarity that had previously found expression in many pre-existing communities. They were also highly antagonistic to market liberalism and inclined to view institutions such as free exchange and contract as mechanisms for oppression.

One reaction of the Imperial German government to these developments was to introduce the world's first modern welfare state programs in 1884. The welfare state was understood by its architects to be focused upon ameliorating the social and economic condition of industrial workers so as to lessen the attraction of Social Democracy and trade unions. The ongoing growth of trade unions and the Social Democrats after 1884, however, underscores that such measures failed in their objective. After World War I, pressures upon – and antagonism towards – market economic arrangements increased. Many Germans (and not just Marxists) associated the war with the workings of market capitalism. Further discrediting of market liberalism followed in the wake of the Great Depression – an event that many Germans on the left and the right associated with capitalism's apparent failure. Towards the end of the 1920s, the German electorate became radicalized between the extremes of left (the German Communists) and the nationalist-right (the National Socialists). But, as Alexander Rüstow was later to observe, the economic views of Germany's Communists and Nazis enjoyed surprising similarities, especially concerning the dominant role they believed should be assumed by the state in the German economy of the future (1980, xiii).

The forces unleashed by Germany's shift towards economic modernity consequently created a range of new challenges for German economists inclined to support market approaches to economic policy on both empirical and normative grounds. How, for example, did one protect commercial organizations and market relationships from being suppressed by an economically and politically expansionist state often acting in the name of *Gemeinschaft* values? And could one do so while simultaneously preserving those *Gemeinschaft*-like communities that limited state power? What role, if any, should be played by the state in realizing these ends?

## Neoliberal responses

The responses of German neoliberal thinkers to these dilemmas reflected their determination to be as attentive to sociological concerns as they were to preserving basic social and institutional prerequisites required for market economies. On questions of economic policy, German neoliberals were usually in basic agreement with the Austrian School of economics, personified by figures such as Ludwig von Mises and F. A. Hayek. This was especially true with regard to their explanation of the causes of the economic problems afflicting Western nations and their criticisms of proposed socialist solutions.

But the term "neoliberal" – originally coined by Alexander Rüstow – underscored the fact that these market-orientated German economists were not entirely satisfied with nineteenth-century liberal responses to some of the problems associated with economic modernity as well as the crisis into which liberal capitalism was plunged after 1914. The neoliberal response, however, was far from uniform. Among the neoliberal economists, a variety of intellectual approaches and recommendations prevailed (Gregg 2010, 17–44).

Often known as the school of ordoliberalism and strongly associated with the University of Freiburg, Walter Eucken (1952) and Franz Böhm (1933) focused their attention upon the question of how to preserve and promote liberty in the complex conditions of modern social orders. Neither Eucken nor Böhm were convinced by traditional laissez-faire arguments that the spontaneous interaction of people usually sufficed to produce a secure and prosperous economy and secure a free society. They were especially attentive to the ways in which private actors, in the pursuit of their self-interest, often tried to use the power of the state to compromise essential market mechanisms such as a free price system. Eucken and Böhm especially had in mind the practice of cartelization that had become widespread throughout the German economy from the 1890s onwards.

As a civil servant working in Germany's economics ministry in the 1920s, Böhm had observed how different actors, ranging from industrialists to farmers, had built alliances with politicians of all parties with the goal of securing legal privileges for their particular businesses. "The experience of the last decades has shown," Böhm contended, "that business associations and interest groups have mastered the art of turning every politically influential ideology to their own purpose in a most effective manner" (1933, xi). To limit, if not prevent, such practices, the ordoliberals outlined a set of legal principles designed to obstruct the ability of private actors to co-opt state power against their competitors, thereby preserving if not expanding the space available for genuinely free associative activity.

To this end, Eucken specifically identified one "fundamental," seven "constitutive," and four "regulative" principles. The fundamental principle, Eucken stated, for genuinely free competition was a free price system. Without people able to buy and sell goods and services at prices freely agreed upon by all parties to an economic transaction, the very basis of free associative activity in the economy would be compromised. The constitutive principles highlighted by Eucken were designed to protect the free price system. They included a commitment to a stable monetary system (inflation being a major distorter of prices); the protection of private property; freedom to contract (without allowing people to contract in ways that diminished others' freedom to contract); open markets into which people could enter without obstruction and leave without compulsion; liabilities for people's formal commitments and choices (thereby tying risk to responsibility); constancy of economic policy (in the sense of avoiding decisions that created uncertainty); and, lastly, acknowledging the interdependence of all the aforementioned constitutive principles (Eucken 1952, 254ff).

This schema was not, however, as uncompromising as it seems. Under the heading of regulative principles, Eucken was willing to permit various forms of government economic intervention, provided they were consistent with, rather than undermined, any of the fundamental and constitutive principles. On one level, this translated into policies that sought to maintain open markets. A good example of such a policy would be the formal prohibition of the establishment of monopolies (291–294).

But some of Eucken's regulative principles also reflected an interest in using the law and the state to limit what Eucken considered the often socially disintegrative side effects of market relationships upon non-economic forms of community. He was willing, for instance, to allow a certain degree of wealth redistribution when the outcomes of market exchange were socially problematic. By this Eucken appeared to mean the type of vast wealth disparities that, to his mind, created cleavages within a society that facilitated a breakdown in solidarity between different income groups. For this reason, Eucken considered progressive taxation to be justified. Eucken was also willing to entertain policies that tried to address the external and social costs of the technological development associated with market progress, such as the redundancy of particular occupational groups. To this extent, ordoliberalism involved some effort to constrain the market's negative side effects – the type of side effects that were often used as the basis for calls to use the state to sharply constrict the market in the name of *Gemeinschaft* values.

A somewhat different approach to these subjects was adopted by Alexander Rüstow and Alfred Müller-Armack. While attentive to the legal-constitutional ideas developed within ordoliberal circles, they also sought to bring insights from historical sociology to bear upon similar questions. A professor of economics at the University of Cologne from 1939 onwards and later a senior official in West Germany's economics ministry, Müller-Armack believed it was a "mistake to expect that the mechanism of the market itself will create the ultimately worthwhile social order" (1947, 85). Instead, governments needed to design economically and socially interventionist policies that preserved the competitive order's fundamental institutions, but which also addressed modern industrial society's peculiar social needs (1971, 51).

Interventions that did not violate indispensable prerequisites for free markets such as free prices, Müller-Armack maintained, would help to realize some degree of security amidst the turmoil of free markets. Thus Müller-Armack was willing to consider "open direct subsidies" to particular groups and communities negatively affected by free markets (1947, 109). Examples of such policies included direct subsidies to farming communities as well as income supplements to families on low incomes. Müller-Armack's approach was grounded upon his conviction that it was possible for the government to pursue what he called a "stylistic coordination" of the life of the market with that of what he called "societal groups" ([1962] 1974, 149). The values and formations associated with *Gesellschaft* and *Gemeinschaft* need not, he thought, exist in perpetual tension with one another.

In attempting to realize such coordination, Müller-Armack looked carefully at how different schools of thought, often developed within the sphere of particular religious traditions, had tried to reconcile *Gemeinschaft* and *Gesellschaft* expectations and priorities. Here he was especially attentive to the various corporatist theories developed by particular Protestant and Catholic economists and social thinkers and how they might be synthesized with the free market. This helps explain why Müller-Armack was open to embracing codetermination arrangements – meaning formal employee participation in the management of a company or industry through means such as work councils or requiring some representation of employees on the boards of companies – for businesses that exceeded a certain number of employees and subsidizing certain industries (especially agriculture) and small businesses ([1960] 1982, 53–61). Central to Müller-Armack's approach was his conviction that unless the state took active measures to promote social cohesion (without impairing free prices), widespread support for the market economy would quickly diminish.

A similar approach manifests itself in the thought of Alexander Rüstow. Although he returned from World War I as a socialist, Rüstow's experiences working in Germany's economic ministry after World War I and his involvement in plans for nationalization of particular industries convinced him that *dirigiste* economic policies were doomed to failure. After resigning from the economics ministry, Rüstow became research director for the German engineering association. Here he witnessed how businesses involved in this industry were negatively affected by the state's implementation of import duties and direct financial assistance designed to protect the German coal and steel industry from competition. Like Böhm, he had been disillusioned by the collusion he witnessed between ostensively private commercial interests and civil servants in building up monopolistic control of sections of the economy (1980, xiii–xxix).

But besides being concerned about the damage done to principles of free association and competition, Rüstow was equally worried by what he regarded as the corrosive effects upon the rest of society of market forces. He argued that "competition as such, appealing as it does solely to selfishness as a motivating force, can neither improve the morals of individuals nor assist social integration; it is for this reason all the more dependent upon other ethical and sociological forces of coherence" (1942, 272). Like Müller-Armack, Rüstow went further and maintained that part of the problem was the culture that he believed was associated with laissez-faire liberalism (1945), specifically a type of "sociologic blindness" to the non-economic preconditions that permitted markets to function (1980, 455). The long-term stability of market arrangements, he insisted, depended heavily not only upon particular legal institutions but also on a host of *Gemeinschaft* communities.

Rüstow's approach to rectifying the situation was two-fold. First, he insisted that the state had to be insulated from the influence of those groups seeking legal privileges in order to maintain a genuinely competitive market economy ([1932] 1982, 3–186). Second, he maintained that the state could help to limit the impact of market competition upon society's non-economic social fabric. Here he had partly in mind redistributionist policies in order to reduce wealth disparities that to his mind had nothing to do with merit. More significantly, however, Rüstow advocated for a distinction between what he called compatible and incompatible interventions of the state into the market. In his important 1932 essay "Liberal Interventionism," Rüstow called for

> interference in precisely the opposite direction to that in which we have hitherto proceeded, i.e., not contrary to the laws of the market but in conformity with them: not to maintain the old situation but to bring about a new one, not to delay the natural course of events but to accelerate it. With this in mind, our recommendation is for a form of liberal interventionism under the motto of *fata volentem ducunt, nolentem trahunt* [Fate leads the willing, and drags the unwilling].
>
> ([1932] 1982, 184–185)

Thus when, for instance, a particular form of domestic agriculture (around which were often located a host of communities and social formations) started to lose competitiveness, Rüstow maintained that while a government should not embark upon the path of tariffs and subsidies (which, he argued, rarely worked and usually resulted in unhealthy collusion between interest groups and government officials), it could not do nothing whatsoever. Using the same example, Rüstow argued that the state should immediately offer educational and financial aid to affected communities *in order that* they could begin moving to a less fragile sector of the economy ([1932] 1982, 185). The point was not only to minimize (within reason) the break-up of long-standing communities (or at least facilitate their transformation in a less socially corrosive manner); it was also to limit such interventions to addressing clear instances of impending and significant social distress, but without undermining the workings of free prices and competition. To that extent, it also involved keeping people connected to the market order and avoiding the development of long-term dependence on the state.

## Markets and community: Wilhelm Röpke

Rüstow's "liberal interventionism" and his strong interest in integrating sociological concerns into economic policy recommendations influenced the neoliberal economist who invested the most intellectual energy in reconciling the demands of *Gemeinschaft* and *Gesellschaft* forms of association: Wilhelm Röpke. Röpke, however, went beyond all the thinkers considered above in terms of developing a framework to think about this question and specific policies that might facilitate these ends.

Most of Röpke's most concrete thinking on this subject occurred during the 1940s. It was primarily directed towards influencing the direction of economic and social policy in a post-war Germany. The National Socialists had, Röpke believed, exalted the nation at the expense of all other forms of community and subordinated the workings of the market to the state – a development that achieved its apotheosis in the form of the German war economy. The consequent weakening of both *Gemeinschaft* and *Gesellschaft* arrangements necessitated, in Röpke's mind, a two-fold response.

In Röpke's schema for the restoration of healthy economic and social arrangements, the *first* step to a sustainable market economy involved a basic decision *for* the market and *against* collectivism. This translated into a choice for free exchange, private initiative, genuine competition, free prices, flexible costs, and consumer sovereignty; and a choice against monopoly and efforts by interest groups such as businesses and trade unions to use state power to protect themselves from competition ([1944] 1948, 26–27, 32).

The second step, Röpke argued, involved the promotion of what he called *positive economic policy*. This was further divided into the subsets of *framework policy* and *market policy*. Röpke's framework policy drew upon Böhm and Eucken's work (38–39), specifically their emphasis upon establishing the rules for market competition and the institutions that enforced these rules impartially (28). In outlining what he called market policy, Röpke applied a variant of Rüstow's liberal interventionism. He distinguished between "'compatible' and 'incompatible' interventions: i.e., those that are in harmony with an economic structure based on the market and those which are not" (28–29). Interventions that undermined the price mechanism were considered incompatible; those, however, which appeared not to interfere with the price mechanism were worthy of consideration as market-compatible (1941).

The third element of Röpke's strategy – *economic and social policy* ([1944] 1948, 40) – focused upon realizing particular social-economic objectives. Here Röpke's thinking was plainly motivated by a concern to maintain and protect certain forms of economic life that he thought might be difficult to sustain in the conditions of full-blown market competition. Broadly speaking, economic and social policy translated into choices that favored the development of "small and medium-sized business in every branch of economic life, in favor of moderation, of what can be overseen and of what is suited to human dimensions, in favor of the middle classes, of the re-establishment of property for the widest circles, in favor of that policy which can be described in the catch-phrases 'deproletariatization' and economic decentralization" (30).

Here Röpke acknowledged parallels between his thought and a market-friendly interpretation of the 1931 papal encyclical *Quadragesimo Anno* (38) as well as distributivist ideas associated with thinkers such as G. K. Chesterton (39).

The fourth component of Röpke's approach was what he called *social policy*. Here Röpke explicitly stated that he was concerned with protecting and promoting non-market forms of community (1951, 49). The person who competes in the market was also someone who was a citizen, belonged to a family, and was often a member of civil associations. Such sociological realties, Röpke claimed, needed to be taken into account when thinking about economic policy. He acknowledged that it placed him at odds with what he called "unregenerate Liberals of the old school" and "unregenerate illiberals" ([1944] 1948, 32–33). Röpke's objective was to enhance the ability of long-standing social traditions to reintegrate society over and against what he considered competition's socially disintegrative side effects ([1942] 1992, 181).

Here Röpke went further than some of his neoliberal colleagues inasmuch as he was willing to spell out what this might mean in terms of specific policies. They included decentralizing industry in the name of deproletarization, federalism (99–114), integrating factories and industrial workers into non-urban settings, tax and credit policies that incentivized the acquisition of land property and the growth of small and medium-sized businesses (218–222), and revitalizing agriculture and artisanal and smaller trading industries (201–217).

A number of these policies reflected Röpke's interpretation of particular developments that he believed had helped smooth Germany's way towards National Socialist totalitarian policies, and his determination to ensure adequate protections for liberty against the threat of Communist totalitarianism. His encouragement of small and medium-sized businesses flowed from his observations concerning the ways in which large German businesses had colluded with governments before World War II to reduce market competition and eventually found themselves subsumed into the National Socialists' economic policies ([1944] 1948, 169–181). Likewise, Röpke believed that land redistribution would give more people a degree of non-state-based economic security beyond wages ([1942] 1992, 159) – something he considered essential for deproletarization. Wider property ownership, he argued, would also awaken awareness of the importance of property rights among sections of society previously disinclined to understand their importance (159).

## Neoliberal contradictions

A moment's reflection soon indicates that any government that decided to pursue social policy along the lines suggested by Röpke would be committing itself to extensive intervention in the economy. Perhaps because he was conscious of this, Röpke himself attached strong qualifications to the means by which governments might seek to realize such goals. He insisted, for instance, that the long-term future of a prosperous agricultural sector of the economy was not compatible with subsidies or protectionism ([1942] 1992, 184–193). Röpke also wondered whether he was burdening the state with too many tasks; he even asked his readers to consider whether he was making "the frequent mistake of turning the state into an ideal which does not correspond to sober reality" (191).

More generally, there are a number of contradictions pervading Röpke's approach to these issues – and by extension that of other prominent German neoliberals. It was, for instance, entirely possible that some of Röpke's social policy proposals could facilitate counterproductive ends. Seeking to encourage wider understanding of the importance of property rights may well be a worthwhile goal. But does permitting the state to engage in widespread land redistribution – which presumably requires taking property from some people (albeit with compensation for their loss) and giving it to others – actually increase appreciation of the importance of property rights? The bigger problem, however, with many of these proposals advanced by Röpke and some of the other neoliberals is that they seem to contradict principles that all the neoliberals discussed above underscore as essential. As Razeen Sally notes, many of the specific interventions proposed by neoliberal scholars "inevitably involve favoring one group over another by means of discretionary state-power, thus posing problems for the general rules of conduct in the classical conception of the law" (1998, 120–121).

In their defense, a number of neoliberals believed many of these measures designed to balance market forces with what they regarded as the needs of non-economic communities were designed to forestall the spread of what Röpke, for instance, regarded as a significant threat to liberty in post-war Europe: the welfare state. Röpke was conscious that the global march toward welfare states had begun in Imperial Germany ([1944] 1948, 146). Families and communities played an important role, in his view, in dealing with questions associated with unemployment, old age, and education. There was thus at least one market-friendly purpose to the neoliberals' ideas for promoting communities. The nurturing of a social cohesion through such communities would, Röpke believed, help nullify some of the reasons that many Germans – and Westerners more generally – were becoming attracted to the welfare state as a way of softening the rigors of market-oriented activities. Without such associations, Röpke maintained, people would inevitably look to the state to provide direct forms of social cohesion from "above" ([1958] 1998, 155): a tendency that would have negative implications not just for the market but also for a host of non-state communities whose immediate purpose was neither economic nor political.

In this connection, Röpke was especially influenced by some of Alexis de Tocqueville's concerns about the social and economic leveling effects of modern democracy. To the extent that democracy had undermined the power of hereditary castes, Röpke welcomed the advent of democracy. He had, however, thoroughly absorbed Tocqueville's warnings about modern democracy's potential to facilitate centralization (Röpke [1958] 1998, 7). Röpke warned that the French revolutionaries had managed to create (in the name of Rousseau's "General Will") a tyranny more centralized and ruthless than that of absolutist monarchs and far more willing to violate moral boundaries in the name of the national interest. The same developments, he stated, had facilitated the spread of mindsets that embodied a type of hostility towards "any manifestation of independence and autonomy ... whether it be the free market, free local government, private schools, independent broadcasting, or even the family itself" (226–227). Sometimes these tendencies also condemned these freedoms and communities in democracy's name (1963). The same outlook lent itself to a growing welfare state, full employment policies, and a willingness to employ inflationist policies – again, in the people's name.

It was, Röpke argued, a form of democracy that did not view itself as constrained by "the ultimate limits of natural law, firm norms, and tradition" ([1958] 1998, 220). In short, it seemed to subordinate all other normative concerns to the demands of political equality. Moreover, modern democracies provided public opinion with the means to force elected governments to pursue policies that diminished the economic liberties secured by institutions such as private property as well as shifting the onus for addressing welfare issues from the sphere of non-state communities towards the state (Röpke 1950, 65–75) – again, with negative consequences for non-state communities and the market. Citing Tocqueville, Röpke maintained that the post-war welfare state's growth was such that "it presses every nation to the point where it becomes nothing more than a herd of frightened beasts of burden whose shepherd is the government" ([1957] 1987, 82).

This being the case, however, Röpke's cultural-economic ideas underline an unresolved general dilemma in neoliberal thought. In the name of renewing the market economy and the moral, social, and political culture that they thought necessary to restrain collectivist tendencies, Röpke and other neoliberals were willing to contemplate government interventions that had the potential to undermine important corollaries of market liberties, such as the freedom of companies to grow beyond an-impossible-to-ascertain optimal size. In Röpke's case, his neoliberal theory does not indicate how a government's pursuit of active economic social policies can be aligned with the principles of framework and market policy, which, in many instances, would appear to rule out some of Röpke's proposed social policies. Here one cannot help but be struck by how often Röpke noted that the value of any policy is highly dependent upon the wisdom of those responsible for its realization. Prudence is, of course, indispensable for the implementation of public policy – social or economic – and should therefore be highly valued in any government official. But the first and second elements of Röpke's neoliberalism, as well as the fundamental and constitutive principles identified by Eucken and Böhm, were designed to restrict any government's ability to engage in discretionary social policies in the realm of the economy. Likewise, Eucken's regulative principles, ranging from minimum wages to income policies with a redistributive edge and anti-monopoly controls, provided considerable opportunity for a variety of interest groups to undermine the workings of free prices and competition with the assistance of government officials.

In the end, there may be no simple way to reconcile the neoliberal emphases upon binding rules and legal frameworks with the desire of neoliberals to address socio-economic problems that, if left to fester, might undermine market economies as well as all non-economic forms of association. At different points, Röpke changed his position concerning the compatibility of particular interventions in economic life with the overall functioning of market economies ([1958] 1998, 241). With the passage of time, Röpke's skepticism about the efficacy of various interventions seems to have increased. This suggests that Röpke either became more rigorous in applying the criteria of compatible intervention, or found the results unimpressive (Gregg 2010, 114–115).

## Beyond ideal types

The response of the neoliberals, be they ordoliberals like Eucken and Böhm or sociological liberals such as Müller-Armack, Rüstow, and Röpke, to these criticisms might be that they were trying to develop a framework for governments to think through various economic and social policies in a manner that enabled them to preserve free markets as well as *Gemeinschaft* forms of communities. The same framework, they might argue, also allowed them to try to address the type of social problems that, to their mind, had (1) helped to severely discredit – fairly or unfairly – nineteenth-century classical liberalism and the market economy more generally, and (2) consequently facilitated the rise of forms of collectivism that had undermined both *Gesellschaft* and *Gemeinschaft* forms of human association while creating the state as the primary form of community. Though not blind to the possible counterproductive effects of their policies, the German neoliberals' position was that those market-oriented liberals who cared about preserving freedom really had no choice but to integrate constitutional and sociological concerns into their work. Twentieth-century totalitarianism and collectivism, they believed, made ignorance of or disregard for these dimensions of human life not an option for market-oriented economists. In some respects, the post-war expansion of classical liberal thought into exploring how factors such as legal frameworks and cultural norms shape economic life is a vindication of the neoliberals' approach.

But in many respects, the German neoliberal effort to resolve what many European intellectuals perceived to be significant tensions between two ideal types of human group-life points to a larger issue. Could it be that Tönnies' association/community distinction has proved more of a hindrance than a help with regard to thinking through the economic and political implications of different forms of human association and the undying motivations that shape them?

Though Tönnies himself never presented these as ideal types, it is difficult to dispute that the *Gesellschaft–Gemeinschaft* paradigm quickly developed in this direction and continues to exercise considerable influence, not least because of the long-term influence of Continental (especially German) thought on this subject upon others reflecting on these matters. But while ideal types can be helpful in clarifying a number of issues, they also have their disadvantages. One of these is the manner in which they can direct people away from considering viable alternatives to thinking through complex phenomena such as the nature of different forms of community. In the case of the *Gesellschaft–Gemeinschaft* distinction, it is arguable that it encourages people to assume that market associations can *only* be undergirded by relationships based on self-interest (and a rather narrow conception of self-interest), while non-market communities are *essentially* altruistic in their character. A moment's thought, however, indicates that we should be careful about making such assumptions. Relationships of friendship that go beyond utility can, for instance, develop within and between businesses. Likewise, even something as non-market in character as the family can reflect elements of exchange.

Moreover, in actual life, most people are involved in many forms of association. People who participate in the same religious group are often competitors in the marketplace. People form friendships within commercial settings and with work colleagues. There is even a long history of businesses being founded on family relationships. When he visited the United States in the early 1830s, Alexis de Tocqueville marveled at how many American businessmen in cities such as New York, who spent much of the day engaged in competitive business activity, would gather in clubs in the evening for conversation about such non-commercial subjects as literature and poetry (Jardin 1998, 109).

Of all the German neoliberals, Röpke was the most influenced by and aware of Tocqueville's thought, and then primarily with regard to Tocqueville's warnings about the soft despotism that flows from the welfare state – a problem that became a major preoccupation of Röpke's in the last twenty years of his life. Yet in surveying Röpke's specific thoughts about markets and community, one finds that Tocqueville is rarely cited. On one level, this relative inattentiveness to Tocqueville is curious, given that market liberals (especially those associated with the Mont Pelerin Society such as Röpke and Friedrich Hayek) had identified Tocqueville as one who had insights to offer when it came to understanding and resisting the deeper cultural reasons for the shift towards economic interventionism that accelerated throughout Europe in the aftermath of World War II.

Tocqueville's *Democracy in America* was written in the 1830s – a time in which the "social question" associated with the rise of industrial capitalism (a question that was at least partly dominated by discussion of its effects upon long-existing forms of human community) was only just beginning to receive attention in European intellectual circles.

Americans, Tocqueville soon grasped, were a commercial people (1959, 271). At first, Tocqueville thought Americans were obsessed by the pursuit of wealth. Yet after a few weeks, he noticed something else about American society. For all their apparent concern with acquiring riches, Tocqueville realized that American merchants were quite religious, unfailingly polite, family-orientated, and possessed of strong philanthropic instincts, and a taste for fine art and good conversation.

Such a vision of society is difficult indeed to fit into a *Gemeinschaft–Gesellschaft* ideal-type dichotomy. But Tocqueville also underscored two other elements that implicitly raise questions about rigid market/community distinctions. The first was the relative absence of government from day-to-day American life. In short, despite the dynamism and social instability that went along with the Americans' embrace of activities such as entrepreneurship and their willingness to take risks, Americans perceived no consequent need to expand the size and role of the state (let alone develop a theory of state economic intervention). The second element noted by Tocqueville was that Americans dealt with these problems through the habit of free association. Rather than looking to the state, Americans turned to any number of communities – especially those based on religious convictions – to resolve any number of social and economic difficulties. For Tocqueville, the contrast with France, where a highly centralized state was seen as the first port of call for help, was astounding:

> Americans of all ages, all conditions, and all dispositions constantly form associations. They have not only commercial and manufacturing companies, in which all take part, but associations of a thousand other kinds, religious, moral, serious, futile, general or restricted, enormous or diminutive. The Americans make associations to give entertainments, to found seminaries, to build inns, to construct churches, to diffuse books, to send missionaries to the antipodes; in this manner they found hospitals, prisons, and schools. If it is proposed to inculcate some truth or to foster some feeling by the encouragement of a great example, they form a society. Wherever at the head of some new undertaking you see the government in France … in the United States you will be sure to find an association.
> 
> ([1835/1840] 2000, 513)

There is, however, another dimension to Tocqueville's analysis of these questions, which arguably contains the seeds of a research agenda that takes us beyond the *Gesellschaft* and *Gemeinschaft* discussion. And this concerns the *motivations* for the way that people engage in different forms of social relationship. Tocqueville noted that Americans tended to explain their propensity to address such social and economic problems under their own volition by reference to the promptings of *self-interest* rather than on the basis of sympathy or even love.

This was, of course, a rationale that surprised Tocqueville as well as the predominately European readership of *Democracy in America*. Even more interestingly, however, Tocqueville indicated that there was often more going on beneath the surface than might otherwise be supposed, because Tocqueville did not take Americans' explanation for their reasons for banding together to resolve problems at face value. Many people, he suggested, who claim to be acting on the basis of self-interest are not in fact doing so. This, Tocqueville commented, was quite characteristic of the Americans he observed:

> Americans enjoy explaining almost every act of their lives on the principle of self-interest properly understood … I think they often do themselves less than justice, for sometimes in the United States, as elsewhere, one sees people carried away by the disinterested,

spontaneous impulses natural to man. But the Americans are hardly prepared to admit that they do give way to emotions of this sort. They prefer to do more honor to their philosophy than to themselves.

([1835/1840] 2000, 526)

Americans, at least from Tocqueville's perspective, were much less self-interested than they presented themselves. Here one could add that the inverse is also often true: not everyone who says he is being charitable may actually be concerned about his neighbor.

Compared to the dualist outlook that seems to be encouraged by the *Gemeinschaft–Gesellschaft* distinction, Tocqueville's thinking about people's motivations and the way these shape the formation of different types of community arguably sidesteps the rigidities that European thinkers such as the German neoliberals struggled to escape – both in terms of the intellectual conceptualization of social conflict or problems (real and imagined) and in the design of policies that seek to address such difficulties. Even more broadly, it enjoys a certain resonance with the efforts of scholars such as James Otteson (1998) and Ryan Patrick Hanley (2009) to demonstrate the appreciation of Adam Smith and other Scottish Enlightenment thinkers of the complex set of intentions and motivations that people bring not only to the marketplace, but also to family, educational, civil society, and political settings.

Certainly, Tocquevillean-like approaches to political economy that touch some of the questions that preoccupied German neoliberals and many others in the twentieth century may not lead to the development of conceptual frameworks that are as "neat" as the paradigm proposed by Tönnies. And it may also be the case that a Tocquevillean framework is excessively influenced by particularly American or even more broadly "Anglo-American" experiences. That said, it does point to a way beyond the dualism that presently shapes so much of a discussion about political economy that, in many respects, may well have run its course.

## References

Black, Antony. 2003. *Guild and State: European Political Thought from the Twelfth Century to the Present*. New Brunswick, NJ: Transaction.
Böhm, Franz. 1933. *Wettbewerb und Monopolkampf*. Berlin: Heymann.
Eucken, Walter. 1952. *Grundsätze der Wirtschaftspolitik*. Tübingen: J.C.B. Mohr.
Gregg, Samuel. 2010. *Wilhelm Röpke's Political Economy*. Cheltenham, UK: Edward Elgar.
Hanley, Ryan P. 2009. *Adam Smith and the Character for Virtue*. Cambridge: Cambridge University Press.
Jardin, André. 1998. *Tocqueville: A Biography*. Translated by Lydia Davis with Robert Hemenway. Baltimore, MD: Johns Hopkins University Press.
Müller-Armack, Alfred. 1947. *Wirtschaftslenkung und Marktwirtschaft*. Hamburg: Kastell.

Müller-Armack, Alfred. [1960] 1982. "The Second Phase of the Social Market Economy: An Additional Concept of a Humane Economy." Reprinted in *Standard Texts on the Social Market Economy*, edited by Horst Wünsche; translated by Derek Rutter, 53–61. Stuttgart: Gustav Fisher.

Müller-Armack, Alfred. [1962] 1974. "Das gesellschaftliche Leitbild der Sozialem marktwirtschaft." Reprinted in *Genealogie der sozialen Marktwirtschaft*, 90–107. (Bern: Haupt., 1974).

Müller-Armack, Alfred. 1971. *Auf dem Weg nach Europa. Erinnerungen und Ausblicke*, Tübingen: Wunderlich.

Otteson, James. 1998. *Adam Smith's Marketplace of Life*. Cambridge: Cambridge University Press.

Röpke, Wilhelm. 1941. "Interventionismus." *Neue Zürcher Zeitung*, 30–31 July.

Röpke, Wilhelm. [1942]. *Gesellschaftskrisis der Gegenwart*. Erlenbach-Zürich: Reutsch. Translated by P.S. Jacobsohn as *The Social Crisis of our Time*. New Brunswick, NJ: Transaction, 1992.

Röpke, Wilhelm. [1944] 1948. *Civitas umana: Grundfragen der Gesellschafts und Wirtschaftsform*. Erlenbach-Zürich: Rentsch. Translated by C. S. Fox as *Civitas Humana: A Humane Order of Society*. London: William Hodge.

Röpke, Wilhelm. 1950. *Mass und Mitte*. Erlenbach-Zürich: Rentsch.

Röpke, Wilhelm. 1951. "Liberal Sozialpolitik." *Der Volkswirt* 5: 51–52.

Röpke, Wilhelm. [1957] 1987. *Welfare, Inflation and Freedom*. Reprinted in *2 Essays by Wilhelm Röpke: The Problem of Economic Order; Welfare, Freedom and Inflation*, edited by Johannes Overbeek. Lanham, MD: University Press of America.

Röpke, Wilhelm. [1958] 1998. *Jenseits von Angebot und Nachfrage*. Leinen: Eugen Rentsch. Reprinted in *A Humane Economy: The Social Framework of the Free Market*, edited by Dermott Quinn, translated by Elizabeth Henderson. Wilmington, DE: ISI Books, 1998.

Röpke, Wilhelm. 1963. "Die Planifikation, ein neues Etikett für eine überholte idée." *Neue Zürcher Zeitung*, 20 July.

Rüstow, Alexander. [1932] 1982. "Liberal Intervention." Reprinted in *Standard Texts on the Social Market Economy*, edited by Horst Wünsche, translated by Derek Rutter, 53–61. Stuttgart: Gustav Fisher, pp. 183–187.

Rüstow, Alexander. 1942. "Appendix." In *International Economic Disintegration*, Wilhelm Röpke. London: William Hodge.

Rüstow, Alexander. 1945. *Das Versagen des Wirtschaftsliberalismus als religionsgeschitchtliches Problem*. Istanbul: Istanbuler Schriften.

Rüstow, Alexander. 1980. *Freedom and Domination: A Historical Critique of Civilization*. Edited by D.A. Rüstow. Princeton, NJ: Princeton University Press.

Sally, Razeen. 1998. *Classical Liberalism and International Economic Order: Studies in Theory and Intellectual History*. London: Routledge.

Smith, Adam. [1776] 1981. *An Inquiry into the Nature and Causes of the Wealth of Nations*, 2. vols., edited by R.H. Campbell and A.S. Skinner. Indianapolis IN: Liberty Fund.

Tocqueville, Alexis de. 1959. *Journey to America*. Translated by George Lawrence. New Haven: Yale University Press.

Tocqueville, Alexis de. [1835/1840] 2000. *Democracy in America*. Edited by J.P. Mayer and translated by George Lawrence. New York: DoubleDay.

Tönnies, Ferdinand. 1912. *Gemeinschaft und Gesellschaft*. 2nd edn. Leipzig: Fues's Verlag.

# 11  Bourgeois love

*Deirdre McCloskey*

Modern social science, and especially in economics in its Samuelsonian forms, has become expert in simple human motivations, such as Max U and his simple consequences. But meaning is missing, which is to say that language and ethics are. Economists are slowly learning what other social scientists, not to speak of poets and novelists, have long known – that people cooperate, mainly, and when they do they talk, and when they talk they inscribe the social world with meaning good and bad, sacred and profane, right and wrong. The inscriptions then make their firms and churches and governments work. We need a science of such matters, what Vernon Smith and I call (borrowing Bart Wilson's term) "humanomics" (McCloskey 2011; Smith 2012).

Gatherings of humans are held together by language games. The games are empty, "cheap talk," in a society of a tyrant surrounded by slaves. But in a free society we must converse. Sweet talk, which merely in the paid sector is fully a quarter of earnings, holds us to our tasks, inspires us to charity and courage, illuminates our discoveries. One can see it working (to give what Herb Gintis once demanded of me, the killer app of humanomics) in the rise of conversation in the eighteenth century in Europe, and especially in those hives of the bourgeoisie in Amsterdam and Edinburgh and Philadelphia. Free people speak their minds, we say. The image is apt. Free speaking produced conversations that yielded amazing institutional and technological innovations, and the modern world.

Proving such propositions is both easy and hard, easy because evidence for it is littered over every human civilization, hard because economists have persuaded themselves that Prudence Only is all there is to human civilization. But let me try.

So-called Samuelsonian economics is the main sort at American universities today. It says that all human behavior can be captured in a utility function characterizing that sociopathic fellow, Max U. Max treats everyone as a vending machine. His pleasure tops everything.

The only way Samuelsonian economics can acknowledge anything else, such as love, is to reduce it to food for the implicitly male and proud lover, on a par with the other "goods" he consumes, such as ice cream cones or apartment space or amusing gadgets from Brookstone. In C. S. Lewis's *The Screwtape Letters*, the senior devil Screwtape is in fact suspicious of the very existence of "love," and reinterprets it as interest. God's "love" for human beings, "of course, is an impossibility ... All his talk about Love must be a disguise for something else – He must have some *real* motive ... What does he stand to make out of them?" ([1943] 1961, 86).

A Samuelsonian economist will say, "Oh, stop it. It's easy to include 'love' in economics. Just put the beloved's utility into the lover's utility function, $U_{Lover}(Stuff_{Lover}, Utility_{Beloved})$." Neat. Thomas Hobbes, who seems to have had little to do in his life with love, wrote in the economistic way in 1651: "That which men desire they are also said to Love ... so that desire and love are the same thing ... But whatsoever is the object of any man's appetite or desire, that is it which he for his part calleth Good" (I, Ch. 6, 24). Or, the modern economists say, "goods." But to adopt such a vocabulary is to absorb the beloved into the psyche of the lover, as so much utility-making motivation. A certain kind of Marxist economist makes the same reduction to interest, such as class interest. The grumpy but great libertarian economist Murray Rothbard was incensed when some decades ago I called him and George Stigler "Stalinists." George, I think, got the joke: that old line Marxists and new line Chicago Schoolers and medium-line Misesians have in common a faith that Interest Rules. Every time (except of course in their own often courageous academic careers).

St. Thomas Aquinas called love-in-a-utility-function "concupiscent love" – "as when we love wine, wishing to enjoy its sweetness, or when we love some person for our own purposes of pleasure" ([c.1269–1272] 1999, section on "Hope"; cited in Pope 2002, 237).[1] It can be virtuous or not, depending on its object. But it is not the highest love unless it ascends to love of the other for the sake of their own being. "Rare is the love of goods," the theologian David Klemm remarks, "that remains true to the love of God as the final resting place of the heart's desire" (2004, 224). You don't need to be a Christian to see Klemm's point.

The philosopher Michael Stocker notes that a psychological egotist of the sort commended in modern economics could get the pleasure from the thing lovers do, "have absorbing talks, make love, eat delicious meals, see interesting films, and so on, and so on," but would not love: "For it is essential to the very concept of love to care for the beloved ... To the extent that I act ... towards you with the final goal of getting pleasure ... I do not act for your sake ... What is lacking in these theories is simply – or not so simply – the person. For love, friendship, affection, fellow feeling, and community all require that the other person be an essential part of what is valued" ([1976] 1997, 68–69, 71).

And the beloved must be a living value in himself. If you love him out of pride or mere vanity he is reduced to a thing, a mirror, no longer a person. Love is therefore not the same thing as mere absorbing altruism. You need to explain this to the economists and other utilitarians.

## Bourgeois love 197

Your mother loves you, in one restricted sense, for the altruistic pleasure you provide to her. When you got your PhD she got utilitarian pleasure in two ways. First, she got some pleasure directly – that she is the mother of such a brilliant child. It reflected on her own brilliance, you see, or on her own excellence in mothering. It added to her utility-account some points earned, straightforward pleasure, like frequent-flyer mileage. And, second, she got some pleasure indirectly, because you did so well – for yourself, to be sure, *yet as a pleasure to her*. It is not for your sake. It is as though you were happy and accomplished *for her*. Even if no one else knew that you had your PhD, she would know, and know the material pleasure and higher satisfactions your education would give you, and would be glad for *her* sake. It was "on her account," as the revealingly bourgeois expression says. That is, she absorbs your utility into hers. If you are happy, she is happy, but derivatively. It is a return on her capital investment in motherhood. It's still a matter of points earned for her utility.

Economists think this is a complete description of your mother's love. Hallmark could make a card for the economist to send to his mother: "Mom, I maximize your utility." The great Gary Becker of the University of Chicago, for example, seems to think in this fashion, as do his numerous followers. "We assume that children have the same utility function as their parents," Becker wrote in a classic paper with Nigel Tomes, "and are produced without mating, or asexually. A given family then maintains its identity indefinitely, and its fortunes can be followed over as many generations as desired. Asexual reproduction could be replaced without any effect on the analysis by perfect assortative mating: each person, in effect, then mates with his own image" (1979, 1161).

Well. So much for happy and loving families; Tolstoy be damned.

Becker is rather more careful than his followers, actually, noting in an earlier paper that "loving someone usually involves caring about what happens to him or her" ([1974] 1976, 233). He realizes that love – or as he usually styles it, with embarrassed male scare quotes, "love" – entails more than "caring" in his restricted sense: "If M cares about F, M's utility would depend on the commodity consumption of F as well as on his own" (234). This is an attempt to acknowledge the evident truth that much of consumption and income-earning is *on behalf* of someone not the direct purchaser or income earner. After all, in the average American family with children, roughly 35 percent of expenditure is directed at the kids (Folbre 2001, 112). Moms are not buying all those frozen pizzas to feed *themselves*. How do we explain commercial engagement in the context of a community bound by such strange gifts?

But, anyway, Becker in this paper is willing to reduce a family to the husband's – sorry, I mean "M's" – utility, using a methodological twist characteristic of Chicago economics: "if one member of the household – the 'head' – cares enough about other members to transfer resources to them, this household would act *as if* it maximized the 'head's' preference function ([1974] 1976, 236–237)." That's nice so long as you are not worried about reinventing the common-law doctrine of *feme covert* in mathematical form. Believe me, as a Chicago School economist myself I attest that such a strange view has its uses for science. Really, it does. I've written whole books, scores of professional papers, going further, triumphantly concluding that *all* you need for historical explanation is "maximum utility."

But I was wrong. The economist's theory is not complete. For one thing, the behaviorism and positivism that often go along with utilitarianism are an unnecessary narrowing of the scientific evidence. Whitehead remarked in 1938 that "in such behavioristic doctrines, importance and expression must be banished and can never be intelligently employed." He added cleverly: "A consistent behaviorist cannot feel it important to refute my statement. He can only behave" ([1938] 1968, 23). In 1982 Stuart Hampshire declared that our knowledge of our own minds, including ethical intentions, "deserves the title of knowledge no less than the kind of knowledge of past, present and future states of the world we derive from perception, from memory and from inductive inference" (274).

As the feminist philosopher Virginia Held notes, relationships "are not reducible to the properties of individual entities that can be observed by an outsider and mapped into a causal scientific framework" (1993, 8). She may be giving too much away: the *meaning* of a relationship, I repeat, is just as "scientific" as is a budget constraint. We do not have to go on forever and ever accepting the definition of "scientific" that happened to be popular among certain English and Austrian academic philosophers around 1922. Your love for your son is real and scientific and motivational, though in some circumstances a behaviorist psychologist watching you from a great height might have quite a lot of trouble "observing" it.

More important, treating others as "inputs" into a self's utility function, as Becker and Tomes (1979) put it, is to treat the others as means, not as ends. Immanuel Kant said two centuries ago in effect that your mother, if she is truly and fully loving, loves you *as an end, for your own sweet sake*. You may be a rotten kid, an ax-murderer on death row. You're not even a PhD. You give her "nothing but grief," as we say. In all the indirect, *derivative* ways you are a catastrophe. And yet she goes on loving you, and stands wailing in front of the prison on the night of your execution. Economists need to understand what everyone else already understands, and what the economists themselves understood before they went to graduate school, that such love is of course commonplace. It is common in your own blessed mother, and everywhere in most mothers and fathers and children and friends.

You see it, too, in the doctor's love for healing, in the engineer's for building, in the soldier's for the fatherland (or mother country), in the economic scientist's for the advance of economic science, down in the marketplace and up in the cathedral. As the economist Andrew Yuengert puts it, "Without ultimate ends, there is no reason to be an economic researcher:

economics is *for* ethics" (2004, 12). Frank Knight understood this eighty years ago. To be sure, there is routine form-filling in being a doctor and insincere uses of statistical significance in being an economic scientist, but without loving and transcendent ends such lives would have no point. The philosopher Alasdair MacIntyre makes a distinction between goods "internal to a practice," like being a good scientist, and those that are external, such as winning the Nobel Prize, or getting rich. He notes that utilitarianism, even in so saintly a utilitarian as John Stuart Mill, cannot admit the distinction (1981, 185).

Such loves, or internal goods, defeat the economistic view that all virtues can be collapsed into utility. Utility is the measure of an ends-means logic, what I call Prudence Only. *Loving* an end goes beyond means. Whatever happiness of identity a painter earns may be measured by the income he gives up. But that does not make the happiness the same thing as the income (Abbing 2002). The happiness is comparable to the happiness of identity a skillful truck driver earns or a skillful tennis player, whether poorly or well paid.

Amartya Sen (1987) speaks of a "duality" in ethics between what he calls "well-being," which is the utilitarian idea of people as pots into which pleasure is dumped, and "agency." Agency is "the ability to form goals, commitments, values, etc." It "can well be geared to considerations not covered – at least not *fully* covered – by his or her own well-being" (41). But I would call this "agency" the virtues of faith and hope and justice and, above all, love.

The philosopher David Schmidtz likewise speaks about two separate "rational" sources of altruism. (He means "economistic" when he writes "rational.") One source he calls "concern" for others, "which is to say [that the beloved's] welfare enters the picture through our preference function," that is, through our tastes for pleasures. It is the Beckerian notion of "caring." Schmidtz observes that there is quite a different altruism, too, a nobler one on its face, which he calls "respect," by which we constrain ourselves in regard to the beloved. "We manifest *concern* for people when we care about how life is treating them (so to speak), whereas we manifest *respect* for people when we care about how *we* are treating them, and constrain ourselves accordingly" ([1993] 1996, 164), italics mine). An economist would say that one has preferences over bundles of goods to be consumed ("concern"), but also over the constraints to be observed ("respect").

But to these usefully distinguished sources of caring, which fit into Samuelsonian economics, I would add a third and a glorious one – one Schmidtz would acknowledge, of course, if he were not intent in the article on showing a "selfish" rationale for love. The third is *sheer* love, appreciation for the beloved, the expression here below of *agape/caritas*/holy charity. That it is sheer does not make it unanalyzable. The political scientist Joan Tronto analyzes the ethics of care as politics, seeing in the ethical use of sheer love an attentiveness, a responsibility, a competence, and a responsiveness (1993, 127–137). Attentiveness is temperance and humility in the face of the plight of others. Competence is a species of prudence. Responsibility arises from human solidarity, keeping faith with who we are. And responsiveness is the justice of attending to others. That is, Love is not reducible to Utility, and is a virtue only when in context with other virtues: temperance, humility, prudence, justice, solidarity, faith.

Of course. Only an economist or an evolutionary psychologist would think otherwise and put embarrassed quotation marks around the very word "love," and then reduce it to gain. The most extreme of the evolutionary psychologists claim that love itself is an evolutionary result of Prudence Only, this time of the very genes themselves. Consider Steven Pinker (1997) on the rationality of friendship: "now that you value the person, they should value you even more ... because of your stake in rescuing him or her from hard times ... This runaway process is what we call friendship" (508–509).

No, Steven, it is what we call self-absorption. The cognitive philosopher Jerry Fodor remarks of Pinker's one-factor theory:

> A concern to propagate one's genes would rationalize one's acting to promote one's children's welfare; but so too would an interest in one's children's welfare. Not all of one's motives could be instrumental, after all; there must be some things that one cares for just for their own sakes. Why, indeed, mightn't there be quite a few such things? Why shouldn't one's children be among them?"
>
> (1998, 12)

He quotes Pinker on the evolutionary explanation for why we humans like stories, namely, that they provide useful tips for life, as, for example, to someone in Hamlet's fix: "What are the options if I were to suspect that my uncle killed my father, took his position, and married my mother? Good question." Startlingly, Pinker does not appear to be joking here. It's unintentionally funny, this "scientific" attempt to get along without sheer love, or sheer courage, or to get along without the aesthetic pleasure of stories reflecting faith and hope.

Even the admirable philosopher the late Robert Nozick fell prey to the reductionism of socio- and psycho- and evolutionary- and brain-science-biology. But characteristically he had wise doubts. "Someone could agree that ethics originates in the function of coordinating activity to mutual benefit, yet hold that ethics now is valuable because of additional functions that it has acquired" (2001, 300). She certainly could.

In the analysis of the philosopher Harry Frankfurt, sheer Love has "four main conceptually necessary features." It must be "a *disinterested* concern for the well-being or flourishing of the person who is loved" (2004, 79, italics supplied). That's the main point, and is the way the utility-driven mother imagined by economists is less than perfectly loving. Her utility function reflects precisely, and only, self-interest.

Frankfurt, by the way, equivocates between "love" as love of persons and "love" also of non-persons such as The Revolution or Art or God. Thus he adds that love is "ineluctably personal" (2004, 79), which I believe would be better expressed as "ineluctably *particular*." Anyway, the person [or transcendent thing] "is loved for himself or for herself as such, and not as an instance of type" (80). One loves *Harriet* particularly, not incidentally as a type of "woman" or "Vermonter," however much one might admire those types. As Nozick puts it, "the love is not transferable to someone else with the same characteristics ... One loves the particular person one actually encountered ... Love is historical" (1974, 168).

And "the lover identifies with his beloved." The two share so much that the line between their selves is forgotten. A friend, said Aristotle, is another self. And finally "loving entails *constraints* on the will. It is not simply up to us" (Frankfurt 2004, 80). Our love for our children, though involuntary and often enough unreciprocated, is glorious. But it must be a give-and-take, acknowledging the constraints imposed by the children. "No, Ma. We'd better have Thanksgiving this year at my mother-in-law's house." The constraining is not *simply* up to us, observe, though it can and should be *self*-disciplined, too, if it is to be a virtue rather than merely an unrestrained and animal passion.

So: disinterested, particular, identifying, and constraining. None of these four fits an epicurean, utilitarian, pleasuring definition of love. The economist's Maximum-Utility Man, Mr. Max U, is, above all, self-interested. He couldn't care less if the item satisfying his interest is this particular one. He has no identity himself to project onto the beloved. And he regards all constraints on utility maximization as bad. "The hedonistic conception of man," Thorstein Veblen thundered in 1898, "is that of a lightning calculator of pleasures and pains, who oscillates like a homogenous globule of happiness under the influence of stimuli that shift him about the area, but leave him intact. He has neither antecedent nor consequent. He is an isolated, definitive human datum" (389).

If the kid cries too much, declares our Max U, the isolated, self-interested man, regardless of whether he is the father, let us send him to probable death in an eighteenth-century orphanage, since this particular kid is fungible with others. A house "filled with domestic cares and the noise of children" would make a poor place for discoursing on social justice and the raising of children (Coulson and Pearcey 2001, 36). Thus on five occasions did Jean-Jacques Rousseau act, that great pre-Romantic teacher of good behavior in love and education.

Samuelsonian economics takes need-love, or more narrowly goods-and-services-concupiscence, as all love, and calls it pleasure or utility. But, as has been repeatedly discovered in experimental and observational studies, the argument fails even in its own terms. For example, suppose a

Samuelsonian economist says that contribution to public goods – say, the British lifeboat service – is utility-based, in the sense that it is motivated *altruistically*, by a desire to make sure there are enough lifeboats. That is, the economic agent gives to the lifeboat fund *not* to cover the highly unlikely event that he himself might otherwise drown – *pace* Steven Pinker – but because many *other* people will. He is public spirited, altruistic.

Yet he is still a Max-U fellow: he gets utility from contemplating the ample provision of lifeboats. It's like your mother Maxine U getting pleasure from your graduation. If she could get the graduation without spending a dime on you, all the better, right? Now such an attitude is an ethical improvement over screw-you individualism of a Steinerian or Randian or Pinkerian sort. But it seems to be empirically false. In 1993, Robert Sugden, for example, noted that a plain implication of Max-U altruism is that £1 given by Max U would be a perfect substitute for £1 given by anyone else, at least in Mr. U's opinion. So Max U would *of course* free ride on other people's contributions to lifeboats. Every time. According to Sugden's (1993) empirical work on the lifeboat fund, however, many people in Britain do not so free ride.

Which is evident: there *is* such a fund, and it does very well in bequests and in coins dropped into collection jars in pubs. Evidently British people feel that free riding in such a case would be bad – which is not a sentiment that would motivate a Max U-er. Sugden and others have shown repeatedly that people do not view the contributions of others as fungible £-for-£ with their own contributions. People take the view that there is something ineluctably particular about *their* giving. So also in blood donations and in going over the top at the Somme. Altruistic hedonism does not look like a very good explanation of human solidarity and courage (Sugden 1993).

You could reply that the lifeboat-giver or the blood donor or the voter down at the polling place get utility from the sheer act of giving their money or time without recompense. The love for God, in the altruistic hedonist view, is no different from satisfying an itch or buying a rugby shirt. Therefore economists studying the economics of religion, even if believers themselves, sometimes stop their concerns at explaining church attendance with the same tools one would use for explaining visits to the mall. But *that* is merely a pointless renaming of love – or justice or faith or some other virtue of steadfastness. As C. S. Lewis remarks, "one must be outside the world of love, of all loves, before one thus calculates" ([1960] 1991, 120).

Lewis offers a ladder of love. The four loves human and divine are, climbing upward: affection, human sexual desiring (*eros*), human friendship (*philia*), and finally charity, that is, *agape*. The lowest is one's love for non-humans, such as a dog or a thing. The highest includes, Aquinas says, a sacred version of friendship, the astonishing friendship between unequals of humans and God. *Agape* is God's gift, notes Lewis, following orthodoxy since Augustine, for God "can awaken in man, towards

Himself, a supernatural Appreciative love" ([1960] 1991, 140). The proud blasphemy that we are loved *for our evident merits* dissolves into "a full, childlike and delighted acceptance of our Need ... We become 'jolly beggars'" (131).

The other three loves for humans, and I suppose also the best love for non-humans, Lewis would group under "natural loves." These are not to be disdained. But they need to have that touch of transcendent *agape*, transcendent "charity," if love "is to be kept sweet" ([1960] 1991, 7, 116). "Whatsoever love elects to bless," says Richard Wilbur, "Brims to a sweet excess / That can without depletion overflow" ([1971] 1988, 61). The overflow gives a *point* to a virtuous life, whether medieval or socialist or bourgeois.

At this juncture, the male, prudent, scientific, economistic, and materialist stoic breaks into indignant rhetorical questions: "Who cares about *sweetness*? 'Sour' tastes fine to me. Point, schmoit. What possibly could *love* have to do with the hard world of a commercial economy? Let's get practical here. Can't we do just fine in a world of bourgeois business without love? Isn't that the, uh, *point* of economics? Isn't love something for weekends and the Home?" Or as Yeats said, "The Catholic Church created a system only possible for saints ... Its definition of the good was narrow, but it did not set out to make shopkeepers" ([1909] 1965, entry 51, 334).

Economics since its invention as a system of thought in the eighteenth century has tried to "economize on love," that is, to get along without it, that is, to justify shopkeepers far removed from saintly or poetic Love. Economics has elevated Prudence, an androgynous virtue counted good in both men and women as stereotypically viewed, into the *only* spring of action. Tracing it back to Epicurus, Alfred North Whitehead complained that "this basis for philosophical understanding is analogous to an endeavor to elucidate the sociology of modern civilization as wholly derivative from the traffic signals on the main roads. The motions of the cars are conditioned by these signals. But the signals are not the reason for the traffic" ([1938] 1968, 31).

The way most economists do their job is to ask, Where's the prudence? "The rudimentary hard-headedness attributed to them by modern economics," as Sen puts it, is the only virtue in the economist's world (1987, 2). When in the 1960s I wanted to show that Victorian Britain did not fail economically I used Prudence-Only calculations of productivity to calculate that there was no residual to be accounted for by causes other than Prudence. When in the 1970s I wanted to show that medieval English open fields were insurance in an age of terrifying uncertainty I used Prudence-Only calculations of portfolio balance to show that Prudence sufficed to explain the scattering of a peasant's plots of land. When in the 1980s I wanted to show how to teach economics through applied examples rather than useless theorem-proving – which unfortunately has since then triumphed in advanced economic education – I used Prudence-Only arguments throughout, though I was beginning in that decade to worry that they might not suffice.

Adam Smith asserted in 1776 that "what is prudence in the conduct of every private family can scarce be folly in that of a great kingdom" ([1776] 1981, 457). A splendidly useful principle. Hard-headed. No talk of love, or of any other virtue than prudence. Smith, however, understood well what later economists have gradually come to forget. After all, said Smith as early as 1759 (Smith [1759] 1984), we want people to have a balanced set of virtues, including even love, not *merely* prudence, and this for all purposes, sacred, profane, business, pleasure, the Good, the Useful, the wide world, and the home, too. All. The legal philosopher Annette Baier argues in "What Do Women Want in a Moral Theory?" that love and obligation, which are both necessary for a society to survive, arise from "appropriate trust" (1994, 10).

One of our crowd, the economist and historian Alexander Field, has based a similar argument on biology. He notes that on meeting a stranger in the desert with bread and water you want, you do not simply kill him. Why not? Sheer self-interest implies you would, and if you would, he would, too, in anticipation, and the game's afoot. Once you and he have chatted a while and built up trust, naturally, you will refrain. But how does trust get a chance? How did it *originate*? Field argues that it originates from "modules inhibiting intraspecific violence," that is, from a very long evolution of a taboo on hurting one's own kind (2004, 300). The "failure to harm" non-kin is hardwired into animals. It evolved from selection at the level of the group, Field argues, not the individual. It's better for you as a behavioral egoist to kill the man you meet in the desert. But of course you are inhibited in doing so, because you are not in fact such an egoist: *that's* best for the human species.

I remember driving once in Amherst past a woman walking towards me on the verge, and the strange thought entering, "Suppose I run her down?" I didn't, I am very glad to report. But there it was, the potential for intraspecific violence even in a very peaceable and law-abiding woman. André Gide's novel of 1914, *Lafcadio's Adventures*, turns on the utterly pointless murder of a stranger, pushing him off a speeding train, just to see it done. It happens.

But Field's observation is that usually it does *not* happen. Considering the opportunities to harm, the inhibitions to doing so must be powerful indeed. For my purposes it doesn't matter whether the inhibitions come from socialization or from biology. Anyway – and perfectly obviously – we are equipped with desires for both the sacred and the profane, mutually reinforcing and completing. One of the sacred computer chips in our brains or one of the sacred virtues in our characters is "being nice and trusting."

Adam Smith was not, it seems, a particularly religious man. But he was in his only regular academic job, at Glasgow University ages 28 to 41, a professor of moral philosophy, and he took his assignment seriously. After his death, however, his followers came to believe that a profane Prudence, called "Utility," rules. Jeremy Bentham and his followers, and especially his twentieth-century descendants Paul Samuelson, Kenneth Arrow, Milton Friedman, and Gary Becker, are to blame. These are good men, great scientists, beloved teachers and friends of mine. But their confused advocacy of Prudence Only has been a catastrophe for the science that Adam Smith inaugurated. No need, declare the economists of the late twentieth century, for the non-Prudent virtues – well, maybe a little Justice and Temperance on the side to keep the Prudence on track, but certainly not any need for the sacred, transcendent virtues, such as spiritual love. As Field writes, "To build a discipline on the proposition that [behavioral egoisms] exhaust the range of essential human predispositions is to lead to the unsustainable conclusion that there are no cartels, no racial discrimination, no voting, no voluntary contributions to public goods, and no restraint on first strike (defect) in single play Prisoner's Dilemmas" (2003, 313). And no nationalism, no honor, no love, no courtesy between strangers.

In our time the Prudence-Only ethic has become "Maximize stockholder wealth, and by the way make sure that you as the CEO or CFO have a good chunk of it, and a little inside knowledge about its present value." You will find some ethicists in business schools arguing that the reason to be just or loving or temperate is precisely that it is prudent. Your stock options will be worth more if you do not sexually abuse your employees and cheat your customers. Virtue makes more money, doing well by doing good.

This is to miss the point of being virtuous. The point of a life exercising the virtue of love, for example, is its transcendence, not the stock options conferred on one who successfully lies about his commitment to the transcendent. In a famous article, Milton Friedman argued, as the title supplied by a *New York Times* editor put it, that "the social responsibility of business is to increase its profits" (1970, 32). Milton argued that a society with more wealth can better pursue its transcendent goals, and more wealth is produced by maximizing profits. That's right, and is one crucial argument for capitalism. He further argued that a hired manager for Boeing who improves his social standing in Chicago by getting *the corporation* to give to the Lyric Opera is stealing money from the stockholders. That's right, too, though there is a contrary economic argument, namely, that the ability to play the noble lord with the stockholders' money is part of executive compensation. The stockholders would have to pay the manager more in cash than they do if they insisted that he not be allowed to give away the corporation's money to worthy causes. But most people who have expressed shock or pleasure at Milton's article have not noticed that he adds a side constraint to the manager's fiduciary duty to the stockholders: "make as much money as possible *while conforming to the basic rules of the society, both those embodied in law and those embodied in ethical custom"* (1970, 33, italics added).

The opposite argument is that being honest makes money. As it was expressed in a book on managerial economics, "unethical behavior is neither consistent with value maximization nor employee self-interest" (Arce M. 2004, 265). Wouldn't that be nice if it were true? The journalist Bennett Daviss wrote in 1999 in the magazine *The Futurist* an article entitled "Profit from Principle," with the headline, "Corporations are finding that social responsibility pays off." "In the new century," Mr. Daviss believes, "companies will grow their profits only by embracing their new role as the engine of positive social change" (2003, 203, 209). Image ads spread the Good News.

It's a tough-minded, American idea. A study in 1999 by the Conference Board found that 64 percent of American codes of ethics in businesses are dominated by profits. By contrast, 60 percent of the European codes are dominated by "values" (Donaldson [2000] 2003, 100). When many years ago the Harvard Business School was given more than $20,000,000 to study ethics it initiated courses that collapsed the virtues into the one good of Prudence, the utility of "stakeholders." Harvard has since then taught thoroughly all the virtue that money can buy.

The point is that Smith got it right and the later economists and calculators have got it wrong. You can't run *on prudence and profit alone* a family or a church or a community or even – and this is the surprising point – a capitalist economy. In far-away Japan some decades before Smith, one Miyake Shunro (also known as Miyake Sekian), the director of a newly formed academy for 90 bourgeois students in the merchant city of Osaka, gave his inaugural address on the theme. Tetsuo Najita explains that in Miyake's discussion a profit is

> nothing other than an extension of human reason ... Indeed, merchants should not even think of their occupation as being profit seeking but as the ethical acting out of the moral principle of "righteousness" [*gi*]. When righteousness is acted out in the objective world, Miyake went on, "profit" emerges effortlessly and "of its own accord" without passionate disturbances.
>
> (1987, 91)

In 1726 Japan, as only a little less urgently in Europe at the time, the task was to elevate the status of merchants, the lowest of the four classes of the Tokugawa regime. The elevation entailed leveling.

In Europe the priesthood of all believers cast doubt on God-given hierarchy in general, and yielded the radical egalitarianism of, say, Smith or Kant, with precursors a century before in the literal Levelers. One's position in the great chain of being came to be seen as a matter of nurture, not of Nature. Thus Smith in that egalitarian year of 1776:

The difference of natural talents in different men is, in reality, much less than we are aware of ... The difference between ... a philosopher and a common street porter, for example, seems to arise not so much from nature, as from habit, custom, and education ... [F]or the first six or eight years of their existence ... neither their parents nor their playfellows could perceive any remarkable difference ... [T]hey come to be employed in very different occupations ... till at last the vanity of philosophers acknowledge scarce any resemblance ... By nature a philosopher is not in genius as disposition half so different from a street porter as a mastiff is from a greyhound.

(I. ii. 28–30; compare to Peart and Levy 2005)

Similarly in Japan, Conrad Totman notes, the seventeenth and especially the eighteenth century witnessed a nascent if minority "belief in universal human potential" and a "defense of callings other than rulership." The merchant's son, Itō Jinsai (1627–1705), declared in 1683 that "all men are equally men." Another scholarly merchant's son, Nishikawa Joken (1648–1724), wrote even more startlingly, "when all is said and done, there is no ultimate principle that establishes superior and inferior among human beings: the distinctions result from upbringing" (Totman 1993, 181, 359). Obvious, yes? Not to the men of the seventeenth century, in Europe or Japan.

As also for Smith and the other pro-bourgeois intellectuals of the Enlightenment, the philosophical elevation of the bourgeoisie in Japan was achieved by showing business to be consistent with ethical behavior. As in Europe, it took two centuries or so to become widely accepted. From small beginnings in the late seventeenth and early eighteenth centuries the Japanese gradually reversed the ancient Confucian contempt for merchants, as the Europeans at about the same time reversed their own classical and Christian anti-commercial prejudices.

At length in the new East and in the new West you did not need to be a Chinese general or a Confucian bureaucrat, a Buddhist priest or a samurai, a Christian monk or a duke, to be honorable. Najita explains that *gi* (recall Benedict on *gi-ri:* social obligation) meant in Western terms "justice," but with a prudent emphasis on its calculative side, "the mental capacity to be accurate and hence fair, principled, and thus non-arbitrary, ... the human capacity to know external things, evaluate them, and make intellectual judgments as to what was, or was not, just" (1987, 88). A few decades after Miyake Shunro had lectured on bourgeois virtues to the school in Osaka, its new leader declared that "human beings are endowed by heaven at birth with a virtuous essence consisting of compassion, righteousness, propriety, and wisdom" (Nakai Chikuzan [around 1760] as quoted in Totman 1993, 359). It was a Confucian-based egalitarianism, from which Miyake deduced – as Confucius himself, hostile to merchants, did not – "like the stipend of the samurai and the produce of the farmers, the profit of merchants is to be seen as a virtue" (359).

Adam Smith, had he known of these contemporary developments in Japanese thought – though it was, I repeat, a minority movement there – would certainly have agreed, as his latter-day followers in the business-ethics movement do, Robert Solomon, for example. Business needs, Solomon declares, "both ethics and excellence," a motto that would serve for Japanese and American business nowadays on its sweetest behavior (1992, 21). No greed. No crony capitalism. "Less money, fewer clients," as Tom Cruise says in *Jerry McGuire.* No avarice.

A hardened Chicago economist, or just a Chicagoan, might reply, "So? Call me 'greedy' or 'avaricious' if it makes you feel better, but I like my SUV and my mink, and if screwing other people gets me such toys, fine. What do I care about my so-called 'soul'?" To which Zeno the Stoic replied, as Gilbert Murray put it, "Would you yourself really like to be rich and corrupted? To have abundance of pleasure and be a worse man? Apparently, when Zeno's eyes were upon you, it was difficult to say you would" (1915, 30). Zeno's Roman-Greek follower Epictetus said, "No man would change [honorable poverty] for disreputable wealth" ([c.AD 130] 1920, 286).

It seems so, by the Deathbed Test: what would you wish to remember on your deathbed, more diamond rings consumed or more good deeds done in the world? *Drek* or *mitzvoth*? Aristotle wrote that things good by nature are those that "can belong to a person when dead more than alive" (1991, 1367a, 81). "Although therefore riches be a thing which every man wisheth," wrote Hooker in 1593, "yet no man of judgment can esteem it better to be rich, than wise, virtuous, and religious" (Book One, Chap. 2, X. 2. 189). Unto death.

Leave off, if you wish, the religious part or the death talk. "The virtuous person's reward is … an entire life of satisfying actions," writes Daryl Koehn, "while the vicious person's punishment is a life of actions that produce both unexpected and unintended consequences for himself and others" (2005, 536). Even in consequentialist terms, in other words, an instrumental and materialist view of love is a scientific mistake. A loveless economy would not work. And it would be hell. The secular meaning of the Christian word "hell" is personal corruption, which in truth makes ruling in such a figurative place worse, not better, than serving in heaven. "We must picture Hell," writes C. S. Lewis, "as a state in which everyone is perpetually concerned about his own dignity and advancement, … where everyone lives the deadly serious passions of envy, self-importance, and resentment" ([1943] 1961, ix).

David Schmidtz sees again into the core here. He notes a mental experiment imagined by another philosopher that we could "pull a lever" to decide whether or not to have scruples. "Many of us would pull a lever that would strengthen our disposition to be honest" (1993, 169). But as we actually are after Eden we are weak. If you profess an Abrahamic religion you can call the weakness "original sin." Or you can argue as Schmidtz does that natural selection has made people, alas, "built to worry about things that can draw blood, not about the decay of their characters" (170).

In *The Invisible Heart* (2001), a finely crafted "economic romance" (*sic*), Russell Roberts makes a similar point about the limits of instrumentalism. He improves upon a famous mental experiment of Nozick's in which you are asked whether you would like to be hitched up to an "experience machine."

"Superduper neuropsychologists," Nozick had posited, in a tradition going back through Huxley's *Brave New World* and Descartes' thought experiments to Plato's cave, "would stimulate your brain so that you would think and feel you were writing a great novel, or making a friend, or reading an interesting book. All the time you would be floating in a tank, with electrodes attached to your brain ... Would you plug in?" (1974, 42–44).[2] In other words, "what else can matter to us, other than how our lives feel from the inside?" Apparently there's something more than instrumental feeling, more than what our good friend Max U cares about. As Nozick remarks in another book, "We are not empty containers or buckets to be stuffed with good things" (1989, 102).

Or imagine a "transformation machine," which would take us at the flick of a switch into the lives and characters of Albert Einstein or Queen Elizabeth I, "really." If you were starving on the streets of Calcutta you would instantly agree. But among you, you comfortably bourgeois readers, any takers? Roberts sharpens the questions by making clear, in his economist's way, the opportunity cost. His character Sam Gordon is discussing the matter with his class of high school seniors:

> But there's one detail that I neglected to mention. This imaginary life that you get to experience while on the Dream Machine *must replace your actual life*. You will never wake up. You enter the room today as the teenager you are. You win the Masters, the Nobel Peace Prize, surpass the popularity of The Beatles, then you grow old and die. It can be a painless death, preceded by [the dreamt experience of] a glorious old age ... But after they unhook the last electrode, ... they put you into the ground ... They cart you away and bring on the next?
> (Roberts 2001, 138)

"Still interested?" Sam asks his kids. Of course not. Max U would leap at such a chance to achieve – well, at least to "experience" – utility. But you as your actual self would not do so, because you intend to go on being *you*. "While a cat will be satisfied leading an animal's life of sensation and appetite," remarks Daryl Koehn, "a human being needs something more" (2005, 535).

The *difficulty* of life, within limits, is its charm. Sen makes the point with the use of his somewhat veiled term "agency" (1987, 43).[3] He speaks of an "agency achievement" that is not reducible to "enhancement of well-being" in a utilitarian sense. His way of putting it sounds like David McClelland's old idea of "need for achievement," that is to say, the need for an identity that strives. No striving, no identity. You would agree to a magic spell to stop a cancer, surely. If you could repeat your life you might do so, especially if this time you had a chance to get it right. In stories in books and on TV you temporarily enter into imagined lives, perhaps not temporarily enough for your own good.

But scarcity in *your own* life seems essential for a real human life. Imagine you were an Olympian god. Being immortal, you would have no need for the virtues of hope, faith, courage, temperance, or prudence. These make no sense if you, like the Devil, cannot die. Othello stabs Iago, who replies in defiance, "I am cut but do not die." Though then he does. Most virtues are useless to someone who really cannot die. Even on Olympus, admittedly, the virtues of love and justice might have political rewards. But what gives human love its special poignancy, and gives human justice its special dignity, is the limit to life. You love a man *who will die*. You help a woman *who is a mere mortal*. Not being either a cat or an Olympian god you want a real life with real hazards and rewards, not an experience machine. You wish to retain an identity, a Faith and Hope, as you might put it, named You.

You might as well give in and call it a soul.[4]

The late eighteenth-century impulse and especially the utilitarian impulse was to force ethics into a behaviorist and naively scientific mode, reducing it to some "immensely simple" formula, as one of the virtue ethicists put it. For example, many utilitarians and some Kantians do not want to acknowledge the force of words and free will and inner light. I myself acknowledged these un-behaviorist motivations late, finally realizing that the meaning of a human action, not merely its external appearance, is important for its scientific description.

Virginia Held argues that in ethics "we should pay far more attention … to relationships among people, relationships that we cannot see but can be experienced nonetheless" (1993, 8). We would not call a mother "virtuous" who felt no emotion in carrying out her duties towards her children. Nor would we call a good Samaritan "good" who saved the drowning victim in order to achieve fame.[5] Or call a business person "ethical" who followed the law out of fear of jail time. Virtue is not merely a matter of observable action. It is dispositional – feeling, for example, love and regret and anguish and joy for our acts of will.

That is, it is a matter of character, *ethos*, exercising one's will to do good, to *be* good. It is a matter of one's soul.

## Notes

1 Quoted in Cessario, "Hope," 2002, in Pope, *Ethics of Aquinas*, p. 237. See the similar analysis in Aquinas, *Summa theologiae*, *c*.[1270] 1920, Ia IIae, q. 26, art. 4, objection 3, "On the contrary."

2 William James posed a similar question in *Pragmatism* ([1907] 1949).
3 "Self-interested behavior can scarcely suffice when agency is important on its own" (Sen 1987, 55).
4 As Nozick asks, "For ethics, might the content of the attribute of having a soul simply be that the being strives, or is capable of striving, to give meaning to its life?" (1974, 50).
5 Compare White, "Kantian Critique" (2006, 239). The example is Kantian.

## References

Abbing, Hans. 2002. *Why Are Artists So Poor? The Exceptional Economy of the Arts*. Amsterdam: Amsterdam University Press.
Aquinas, St. Thomas. [c.1269–1272] 1999. *Disputed Questions on Virtue [Quaestio disputata de vertibus in commune* and *Quaestio … cardinalibus]*. Translated with a preface by Ralph McInerny. South Bend, IN: St. Augustine's Press.
Aquinas, St. Thomas [c.1270] 1920. *Summa Theologia. Secunda Pars Secundae Partis*, questio 161. Translated by the Fathers of the English Dominican Province. 2nd edn. Online edition 2000. www.newadvent.org/summa/316101.htm.
Arce M., Daniel G. 2004. "Conspicuous by Its Absence: Ethics and Managerial Economics." *Journal of Business Ethics* 54 (3): 261–277.
Aristotle. [c.350 BC] 1991. *Rhetoric*. Translated by George A. Kennedy. Oxford: Oxford University Press.
Baier, Annette C. [1994] 1998. "Ethics in Many Different Voices." In *Renegotiating Ethics in Literature, Philosophy, and Theory*, edited by Jane Adamson, R. Freadman, and D. Parker, 247–268. Cambridge: Cambridge University Press. Originally published in *Moral Prejudices: Essays on Ethics*. Cambridge, MA: Harvard University Press.
Becker, Gary and Nigel Tomes. 1979. "An Equilibrium Theory of the Distribution of Income and Intergenerational Mobility." *Journal of Political Economy* 87: 1153–1189.
Becker, Gary S. [1974] 1976. "A Theory of Marriage." In *The Economic Approach to Human Behavior*, 205–250. Chicago: University of Chicago Press. Originally published in *Journal of Political Economy* July/August 1974.
Coulson, Charles and Nancy Pearcey. 2001. *Developing a Christian Worldview of the Problem of Evil*. Carol Stream, IL: Tyndale House.
Daviss, Bennett. [1999] 2003. "Profits from Principle: Corporations Are Finding That Social Responsibility Pays Off." *Futurist*. March 28–32. Reprinted in *Annual Editions: Business Ethics*. 15th edn., edited by John E. Richardson, 203–209. Guilford, CT: McGraw-Hill/Dushkin.
Donaldson, Thomas. [2000] 2003. "Adding Corporate Ethics to the Bottom Line." *Financial Times*, Nov 13. Reprinted in *Annual Editions: Business Ethics*. 15th edn., edited by John E. Richardson, 98–101. Guilford, CT: McGraw-Hill/Dushkin.
Epictetus. [c.130 AD] 1920. *The Book of Epictetus, Being the Enchiridion, together with Chapters from the Discourses and Selections from the Fragments of Epictetus*. Edited by T. W. Rolleston and translated by Elizabeth Carter. London: George G. Harrap.
Field, Alexander. 2004. *Altruistically Inclined? The Behavioral Sciences, Evolutionary Theory, and the Origins of Reciprocity*. Ann Arbor, MI: University of Michigan Press.

Fodor, Jerry. 1998. "The Trouble with Psychological Darwinism." Review of *How the Mind Works*, by Steven Pinker, and *Evolution in Mind*, by Henry Plotkin. *London Review of Books* 20 (2): 11–13. Reprinted at http://humanities.uchicago.edu/faculty/goldsmith/CogSciCourse/Fodor.htm and at http://www.homestead.com/flowstate/files/fodor.html.

Folbre, Nancy. 2001. *The Invisible Heart: Economics and Family Values*. New York: The New Press.

Frankfurt, Harry. 2004. *The Reasons of Love*. Princeton, NJ: Princeton University Press.

Friedman, Milton. 1970. "The Social Responsibility of Business Is to Increase Its Profits." *New York Times Sunday Magazine*. Sept. 13.

Hampshire, Stuart. [1959] 1982. *Thought and Action*. New edn. Notre Dame, IN: Notre Dame University Press.

Held, Virginia. 1993. *Feminist Morality: Transforming Culture, Society, and Politics*. Chicago: University of Chicago Press.

Hobbes, Thomas. [1651] 1914. *Leviathan*. Everyman edition. London: J. M. Dent.

Hooker, Richard. [1593] 1907. *On the Laws of Ecclesiastical Polity*, vol. I (Books 1–4). Everyman edition. London: J. M. Dent.

James, William. [1907] 1949. *Pragmatism: A New Name for Some Old Ways of Thinking*. New York: Longmans, Green.

Klemm, David. 2004. "Material Grace: The Paradox of Property and Possession." In *Having: Property and Possession in Religious and Social Life*, edited by William Schweiker and Charles Mathewes, 222–245. Grand Rapids, MI: Eerdmans.

Koehn, Daryl. 2005. "Virtue Ethics." *The Blackwell Encyclopedia of Management*. 2nd edn., vol. II, *Business Ethics*, edited by Patricia Werhane and R. E. Freeman, 535–538. Oxford: Blackwell.

Lewis, C. S. [1943] 1961. *The Screwtape Letters, and Screwtape Proposes a Toast*. London: Macmillan.

Lewis, C. S. [1960] 1991. *The Four Loves*. Orlando, FL: Harcourt, Brace & Company.

McCloskey, Deirdre N. 2011. "Ethics, Friedman, Buchanan, and the Good Old Chicago School: Getting (Back) to Humanomics." Paper presented at 12th Summer Institute for the History of Economic Thought, University of Richmond, June 24–27.

MacIntyre, Alasdair. 1981. *After Virtue: A Study in Moral Theory*. Notre Dame, IN: University of Notre Dame Press.

Murray, Gilbert. 1915. *The Stoic Philosophy*. London: Allen & Unwin.

Najita, Tetsuo. 1987. *Visions of Virtue in Togugawa Japan: The Kaitokudō Merchant Academy of Osaka*. Honolulu: University of Hawai'i Press.

Nozick, Robert. 1974. *Anarchy, State, and Utopia*. New York: Basic Books.

Nozick, Robert. 1989. *The Examined Life: Philosophical Meditations*. New York: Simon & Schuster.

Nozick, Robert. 2001. *Invariances: The Structure of the Objective World*. Cambridge, MA: Harvard University Press.

Peart, Sandra J. and David M. Levy. 2005. *The "Vanity of the Philosopher": From Equality to Hierarchy in Postclassical Economics*. Ann Arbor, MI: University of Michigan Press.

Pinker, Steven. 1997. *How the Mind Works*. New York: Norton.

Pope, Stephen J., ed. 2002. *The Ethics of Aquinas*. Washington: Georgetown University Press.
Roberts, Russell. 2001. *The Invisible Heart: An Economic Romance*. Cambridge, MA: MIT Press.
Schmidtz, David. [1993] 1996. "Reasons for Altruism." In *Altruism*, edited by Ellen Frankel Paul, Fred D. Miller, and Jeffrey Paul, 52–68. Cambridge: Cambridge University Press. Reprinted in *The Gift: An Interdisciplinary Perspective*, edited be Aafke E. Komter, 164–175. Amsterdam: University of Amsterdam Press.
Sen, Amartya. 1987. *On Ethics and Economics*. Oxford: Blackwell.
Smith, Adam. [1759] 1984. *The Theory of Moral Sentiments*. Glasgow edition. Edited by D. D. Raphael and A. L. Macfie. Indianapolis, IN: Liberty Fund.
Smith, Adam. [1776] 1981. *An Inquiry into the Nature and Causes of the Wealth of Nations*. Glasgow edition. 2 vols. Edited by Roy H. Campbell and Andrew S. Skinner with assistance from W. B. Todd. Indianapolis, IN: Liberty Classics.
Smith, Vernon L. 2012. "Adam Smith on Humanomic Behavior." *The Journal of Behavioral Finance and Economics* 2 (1): 1–20.
Solomon, Robert. 1992. *Ethics and Excellence: Cooperation and Integrity in Business*. New York: Oxford University Press.
Stocker, Michael. [1976] 1997. "The Schizophrenia of Modern Ethical Theories." *Journal of Philosophy* 73: 453–466. Reprinted in *Virtue Ethics*, edited by Roger Crisp and Michael Slote, 66–78. Cambridge: Cambridge University Press.
Sugden, Robert. 1993. "Thinking as a Team: Toward an Explanation of Non-Selfish Behavior." *Social Philosophy and Policy* 10: 69–89.
Totman, Conrad. 1993. *Early Modern Japan*. Berkeley, CA: University of California Press.
Tronto, Joan C. 1993. *Moral Boundaries: A Political Argument for an Ethics of Care*. New York: Routledge.
Veblen, Thorstein. 1898. "Why Is Economics Not an Evolutionary Science?" *Quarterly Journal of Economics* 12: 373–397. Available online at http://cepa.newschool.edu/het/profiles/veblen.htm.
White, Mark A. 2006. "A Kantian Critique of Neoclassical Law and Economics." *Review of Political Economy* 18 (2): 235–252.
Whitehead, Alfred North. [1938] 1968. *Modes of Thought*. New York: Macmillan, Free Press.
Wilbur, Richard. [1971] 1988. *New and Collected Poems*. New York: Harcourt Brace.
Yeats, William Butler. [1909] 1965. *Estrangement: Extracts from a Diary Kept in 1909*. Reprinted in *The Autobiography of William Butler Yeats*. London: Macmillan.
Yuengert, Andrew. 2004. *The Boundaries of Technique: Ordering Positive and Normative Concerns in Economic Research*. Lanham, MD: Lexington Books.

# 12 Comment: Behind the veil of interest

*Laurent Dobuzinskis*

We live complex lives. Economists have wrongly assumed that Max U, to use Deirdre McCloskey's amusing play on words, personifies economic agents, i.e., individuals making choices guided by economic competition and constrained by property rights. But this is fast changing. While political philosophers have long argued that the liberal order is not merely utilitarian, economists are now beginning to acknowledge that market processes also depend on a set of institutions and practices that are structured by a wider range of motivations and norms than a narrowly construed notion of self-interest. The three papers that I am commenting upon here drive this point home with extraordinary force and brilliance. They must be read in conjunction with many similar explorations in what is fast becoming a new field of scholarship (e.g., Gérard-Varet *et al.* 2000; Kolm and Ythier 2006; Bruni and Zamagni 2013). This literature includes theoretical and empirical streams. On the theoretical side, one could argue that it is precisely this new interest in the values sustaining economic life that warrants revisiting the works of an earlier generation of scholars, such as the German "neoliberals" of the post-war years (see Samuel Gregg's paper). On the empirical side, behavioral economics has relied advantageously on experimental methods, but Emily Chamlee-Wright and Virgil Storr's paper exemplifies the usefulness of narratives in that regard.

Having begun by underlining what is common to all three papers, I shall continue with that theme for a while, before turning to what I see as possible lines of tension among them, and offering a few critical comments on some of the key points raised by the authors. I am intrigued in particular by McCloskey's profoundly original but, as I explain below, somewhat counter-productive plea for recognizing the importance of "bourgeois love" in the economic sphere.

One does not have to be a dogmatic utilitarian to think that self-interest goes a long way toward explaining the choices made by economic agents, nor to find some merit in Tönnies' *Gesellschaft–Gemeinschaft* dichotomy. None of the three papers discussed here categorically refutes the truism that self-interest is at work in market exchanges and, indeed, in many other purposeful interactions among strangers in modern societies. Even if McCloskey strongly objects to the idea that "Prudence Only is all there is to civilization," she does not go as far as claiming that Prudence is irrelevant.[1] But these papers warn us not to take Tönnies' dichotomy too literally, and that often real human beings inhabit a gray area somewhere in between the desolate *Gesellschaft* and the cozy *Gemeinschaft*. While F. A. Hayek worried about the perverse effects that values and expectations, forged in pre-modern times in the sphere of face-to-face relations, might have on his market-based "Great Society," the German "neoliberals" analyzed by Gregg were troubled by the reverse danger. They feared the corrosive effects that materialism and nihilistic individualism might have upon the very foundations of a free society; thus the state might be called upon to shore up traditional institutions in order to sustain the moral values that prevent economic competition from degenerating into a dehumanizing force, provided that this can be done with the appropriate restraint and foresight. As Gregg points out, this was a concern that Tocqueville had voiced in an earlier era; and he aptly remarks that Tocqueville was not fooled by the rhetoric of self-interest in America, for often it is used as a veil for actually engaging in philanthropic and other socially constructive enterprises. Although not explicitly, McCloskey's allusion to language games perhaps conveys a similar idea. Utilitarians could be guilty of taking too literally the vernacular of ordinary business life; if one digs a little deeper, more complex motivations are revealed that are shaped by a range of emotions that may well include love. These emotions underlie choices that are made in all kinds of settings, from the family to the marketplace. And, of course, when disaster strikes, the veneer of utilitarian, tough-minded business realism gives way to a more humane and generous discourse, as Chamlee-Wright and Storr have found. Thus all three papers reinforce the point that dichotomies have no purchase on reality.

Let me now consider instances of divergence. I perceive at least two lines of cleavage: one that runs between Gregg's paper and the other two; and one that distinguished McCloskey's paper from the other two. The first concerns the role of the state in mediating between *Gesellschaft* and *Gemeinschaft*; the second has to do with the significance of "enlightened self-interest" (or love of our better self) for an appreciation of the altruistic side of human nature.

State actors do not figure prominently in Chamlee-Wright and Storr's paper, and are remarkably absent from McCloskey's own. The German theorists that Gregg revisits, however, were very much concerned with the role that state institutions can play in mediating tensions between *Gesellschaft* and *Gemeinschaft*. As he also explains, they expressed different degrees of confidence in the capacity of state authorities to carry out this task (or they changed their mind somewhat, as in the case of Wilhelm Röpke, who became more skeptical about social policy in his more mature years). But the questions they posed had in common that they belonged to the tradition of *political* economy. By contrast, it is remarkable that the narratives presented by Chamlee-Wright and Storr pay so little attention to state authorities. Admittedly, resentment toward political elites is mentioned, but the focus is clearly on the spontaneous and local community-based initiatives rather than on the notion of citizenship, i.e., participation in the broader *political* community. This is not surprising considering that Katrina can be cited as a classic example of government failure, especially in comparison to the far more efficient response that city, state and federal authorities gave to the devastation caused by Hurricane Sandy. It would be interesting in a future project to compare narratives drawn from residents from the New Jersey shore with those of the Mississippi Delta in that regard, and whether, in the case of the former, state assistance reinforced or, on the contrary hindered, spontaneous, local "boot-strapping" initiatives.

At first sight, McCloskey's apparent neglect for public policy does not pose a problem. The state, after all, has little to do with love; or rather it has little to do with nurturing it and everything to do with controlling it! But if her purpose is read more broadly as having something to do with character formation, and how we learn to behave as true human beings rather than as robotic incarnations of Max U, then this neglect becomes a little more problematic. John Stuart Mill (2001, 35) arguably went out on a limb when he claimed that the function of the state is "to enhance the sum of the good qualities in the governed." This could clearly become an invitation to intrude in all sorts of areas where the state has no legitimate reasons for intervening. Nevertheless, in contemporary societies, the subject of education is inevitably a political issue. Even libertarians concede that the responsibility to educate children cannot fall one-hundred-percent on the parents – for example, they may need to receive school vouchers. And education always involves more than merely learning the "three Rs." In fact, learning to become virtuous citizens of the Republic has always been seen in America as one of the main responsibilities of schools.[2] This is not to say, of course, that school is the only or the best instrument for teaching virtue and civility; but it is not a negligible one. It could be retorted that in a short paper there is no space for veering off into that sort of tangent; but it is somewhat puzzling that in her much larger work, *The Bourgeois Virtues* (2006), with which I find myself in agreement more often than not, the subject of schooling also remains untreated. (By contrast, and as is well known, Smith discusses it at some length in *The Wealth of Nations*.)

McCloskey's paper is unique in another respect. While the other two papers are critical of the assumption that market-based economic and political systems are reducible to the concept of *Gesellschaft* – in other words, they reject the hypothesis that self-interest rules supreme – they do not preclude the possibility that a more enlightened form of self-interest could be at work in *Gemeinschaft*. Indeed, many institutions and social practices constitutive of *Gemeinschaft* give opportunity to those who are part of them to build a *reputation* as a good neighbor, volunteer, community leader, or whatever. Now a reputation is in some sense a reciprocal relationship based on trust; but being reciprocal means that mutually beneficial relationships can take place. Because someone has a good reputation, I trust her to carry out some task or to fulfill some obligation, but in return she may expect from me to be called upon again in the future, to be recommended to someone else, or praised in some other form, and each of these interactions usually involves some tangible or symbolic benefit (e.g., gaining recognition as a means of being granted a higher social status). Although such forms of cooperation can be exploitative or cynically manipulated by dishonest persons, in general it is not inappropriate to describe them as virtuous. (It seems more than plausible that James Ray Cox, whose account is central to Chamlee-Wright and Storr's paper, was not indifferent to his reputation when he chose to mobilize Wal-Mart's resources to provide assistance to the residents of his neighborhood.) There is indeed a long tradition of moral theory, going back to the eighteenth century (e.g., Etienne Bonnot de Condillac or Adam Smith), that relies on self-love to accomplish the goals of the moralist. Smith's "impartial spectator" suggests to us ways of acting that make others think highly of ourselves, and thus is complicit in the pursuit of our own self-satisfaction. In more recent times, the paradigm of *homo reciprocans* (Bowles and Gintis 2002) has been gaining ground in normative economics, although it is in a sense a rediscovery of a very ancient paradigm analyzed by anthropologists such Bronisław Malinowski and Marcel Mauss. (Interestingly, however, the reciprocity at stake in the works of several behavioral economists is often negative, consisting of the "altruistic punishment" of free riders who, obviously, work against our long-time interest in the voluntary provision of public goods.) According to Serge-Christophe Kolm (2008, 25):

> reciprocity … plays a fundamental role in the constitution, cohesiveness and existence of societies. It can by itself be the main or sole relationship underlying some social or economic systems. It has a major importance in the working of the economy and of political systems. It has an essential normative role in various ways. It often has an intrinsic normative value related to fairness or rewarding merit for balance reciprocity, and to altruism and liking in various forms for liking reciprocity. Reciprocity is also very commonly a necessary condition of altruism, respect, helping behaviour, affection, kindness, truth telling, promise keeping, trustworthiness, and cooperation.[3]

In other words, reciprocity sometimes becomes almost indistinguishable from love, even if we may still wish to place love or pure altruism on a higher level. By insisting, however, on the admittedly rarely discussed relevance of love to economic and social analysis, McCloskey sets the bar too high. She seems to find little value in enlightened self-interest, which she considers to be hardly different from self-interest *tout court*. Few saints walk among us, and even Saint Martin gave only half his coat to the shivering beggar whom he encountered. The many layers of meaning that Kolm discerns in the notion of reciprocity should give pause to McCloskey. Yes, Max U is a soulless character, but instead of aiming straight for "bourgeois love" to transcend his limitations, a detour through bourgeois gift-giving – which encompasses pure and disinterested gifts but also takes on board more balanced and reciprocal relations – probably offers a better chance of success. Elsewhere, McCloskey (2006) has shown herself to be largely in agreement with this view, but in denouncing the flaws of simplistic utilitarianism with the verve she displays here, she puts the contrast in somewhat starker terms than I suggest is warranted.

## Notes

1 As she makes quite clear in McCloskey (2006, ch. 21).
2 Stephen Macedo (2000) offers thoughtful views on this topic.
3 To clarify a few things in this quote, Kolm distinguishes between at least two forms of reciprocity: (i) "balance reciprocity," which typically involves strangers or individuals who may be familiar to each other but are not affectively close, and is motivated by fairness; and (ii) "liking reciprocity," which may not be very different from McCloskey's notion of love, except that it stresses the fact that love grows with the love that is given back, so to speak.

## References

Bowles, Samuel and Herbert Gintis. 2002. "Homo Reciprocans." *Nature* 415: 125–128.
Bruni, Luigino and Stefano Zamagni, eds. 2013. *Handbook on the Economics of Reciprocity and Social Enterprise*. Cheltenham, UK: Edward Elgar.
Gérard-Varet, L.-A., S.-C. Kolm, and J. Mercier Ythier, eds. 2000. *The Economics of Reciprocity. Giving and Altruism*. New York: St. Martin's Press.
Kolm, Serve-Christophe. 2008. *Reciprocity: An Economics of Social Relations*. New York: Cambridge University Press.
Kolm, Serge-Christophe and Jean Mercier Ythier, eds. 2006. *Handbook of the Economics of Giving, Altruism and Reciprocity*, vol. II. New York: Elsevier.
McCloskey, Deirdre. 2006. *The Bourgeois Virtues: Ethics for and Age of Commerce*. Chicago: University of Chicago Press.
Macedo, Stephen. 2000. *Diversity and Distrust: Civic Education in a Multicultural Democracy*. Cambridge, MA: Harvard University Press.
Mill, John Stuart. 1861/2001. *On Representative Government*. London: Electric Books.

# Part IV
# Entangled spheres

# 13 How is community made?

*Colin Danby*

## Introduction

Richard Cornuelle recognized that community falls into a blind spot between market and state. His work tries to understand and rally an independent "third sector" capable of addressing social ills and shows that charitable and service organizations share some of the virtues of enterprises in their ability to put innovative ideas into action.

Robert Garnett shows that, despite these efforts, Cornuelle remained wedded to a "separate spheres" approach, distinguishing

> the commercial sector and the "independent sector," the latter defined as a pluralistic array of noncommercial institutions. ... Cornuelle's rendering of these two sectors is careful and nuanced. Yet he posits a distinct human propensity – the desire for profit or the desire to serve others – as the driving force of each sector. ... his dual-system theory struggled to find a way beyond a principal pillar of the Progressive edifice, namely *the narrow view of commerce as an amoral engine securing social cooperation by wholly impersonal means (wherein tender sentiments of sympathy, solidarity, and benevolence play no necessary role)*. ... So even as Cornuelle extolled the scope and virtues of the independent sector, the force of his argument in the 1965 book was undercut by his unwitting retention of a narrowly conceived economy.
> 
> (2011, 3; emphasis in original)

In this paper I want to extend the discussion of what it means to study community – the kinds of organization and activity in Cornuelle's "third sector" – when we drop the assumption that we inhabit a "modern" society split between blindly amoral commerce on the one hand, and charity and love on the other. What we really inhabit, I contend, is a single, mixed, underdetermined, and often confusing world in which people and institutions attempt to structure an uncertain future in overlapping and sometimes contradictory ways. They may do that in modes we label "commerce" or "family" or "charity," but those are cleanly separable neither in their effects nor in their motives.

A corollary of lifting the aprioristic assumption of a modern society with institutionally separate spheres is that we can no longer assign moral values to entire sectors. A basic move in modernist[1] thought has been to try to divide society into spheres with distinct motivations (or propensities) and to let the alleged motivation of each sphere define its moral character. Instead, I propose to start with observable networks of inter-relation and obligation, without assuming ethical essences.

To deepen this distinction, I pull apart two different accounts of how community is made, a "holist" account, in which a large, discrete "culture" shapes all its members, and a more bottom-up "intersubjective" account, in which people hash out meanings for themselves. In the next section I expand on the "holist" understanding of community, bringing in Hayek to make the stakes clear. After that, I develop the alternative "intersubjective" account of community-making, and then work out some of its implications.

This paper emphasizes knowledge. My guiding question, introduced in the next section, is how social individuals understand each other, whether as customers or suppliers, borrowers or lenders, colleagues, co-religionists, kin, neighbors.

## How is community possible?

David Hume ([1748] 2006) and Immanuel Kant ([1783] 1949) raised a fundamental critique of the conditions under which we can claim that our ideas correspond to things in the world. The critique applied as much to social as to scientific knowledge: How do we understand each other? How do individuals within any society interpret their social environment? This is a question not just about the knowledge of social scientists but, more profoundly, about how any and every human being copes socially: How are we able to understand our social surroundings (including our economic milieu) well enough to function properly in them? What is the relationship between the social world outside our heads and our internal understandings of that world?

On the whole, British political economy looked for psychological propensities (e.g., Smith [1759] 1976, [1776] 1979) and institutions (chiefly markets) that minimized the interpretive problem individuals faced. Instead of having to figure out too much, we could rely on certain standards and patterns of behavior in the people we had immediate dealings with, and markets would fill in the rest, releasing us from having to perceive or understand people and material conditions at a distance. While Smith valued friendship, remember also his jaundiced view of associations of workers *or* capitalists in *The Wealth of Nations*, and his lack of interest in religious institutions: his Stoic social ontology did not leave a problem for community to solve.[2]

It was left to Romantic[3] thinkers and their descendants to further develop theories of community. They tried to solve the Hume–Kant problem differently. If society is *already in* our minds, then we avoid the problem of the correspondence of external phenomena to our internal ideas about them.[4] How might society already be in our minds? Either it made our minds, or our minds made it. The first argument stresses the hegemony of a larger cultural unit that people are born into. The second argument stresses the active engagement of people in making lives together and hashing out meanings among themselves: they know their society because they have made it. It is vital to my argument to distinguish the two resulting conceptions of community and knowledge, which I will shorthand "holist" and "intersubjective."

The *holist* conception assumes a discrete cultural whole into which people are born and raised as social human beings, which provides their basic categories of thought. It emphasizes common lore, shared religion, and standard processes of making people into fully acculturated members of a given society. This is a foundational idea in cultural anthropology: if you live among the X people long enough, learning their language and joining their rituals, you gain insight into the *common* X culture, a structure of meanings and understandings that make their lives together thinkable, possible. Culture is unitary, discrete, and bounded (from other cultures). While the transmission of X culture may involve priests and teachers, they are the servants of the culture rather than its masters. In the stronger versions of this concept of culture/community, particularly the stereotype of "traditional society" that served as a foil for Enlightenment thinkers and modernization theorists, the common culture not only facilitates communication and knowledge, but actually does much of people's thinking for them.

Hayek[5] relies on this conception of culture when he writes of "tradition" as a set of understandings and practices that shape thought and understanding:

> What we call mind is not something that the individual is born with … but something that his genetic equipment … helps him to acquire, as he grows up, from his family and adult fellows by absorbing the results of a tradition that is not genetically transmitted. Mind in this sense consists less of testable knowledge about the world, less in interpretations of man's surroundings, more in the capacity to restrain instincts – a capacity which cannot be tested by individual reason since its effects are on the group. … It may well be asked whether an individual who did not have the opportunity to tap such a cultural tradition could be said even to have a mind.
>
> (1991, 22–23)

In Hayek's account, world history has been the scene of competition among multiple cultural/moral traditions. Each tradition is a sort of social operating system, preceding and shaping the individuals brought up in it. The successful traditions secure wealth and power for their societies, who out-compete inferior systems. He borrows Herder's notion of separate cultural universes, but not Herder's cultural relativism. In Hayek's story, "tradition" has been pluralized and given an evolutionary dynamic: laissez-faire capitalism is the winner, while socialism is revealed as dangerous atavism cloaked in reason, a regression to the most primitive of traditions which more advanced traditions have overcome.

But even those advanced traditions have only *contained* collectivism, not extirpated it:

> Part of our present difficulty is that we must constantly adjust our lives, our thoughts and our emotions, in order to live simultaneously within different kinds of orders according to different rules. If we were to apply the unmodified, uncurbed, rules of the micro-cosmos (i.e., of the small band or troop, or of, say, our families) to the macro-cosmos (our wider civilisation), as our instincts and sentimental yearnings often make us wish to do, *we would destroy it*. Yet if we were always to apply the rules of the extended order to our more intimate groupings, *we would crush them*. So we must learn to live in two sorts of world at once.
>
> (Hayek 1991, 18; emphasis in original)

Has any literary modernist ever written with more plangency about our divided selves? Not only do we inhabit distinct spheres, but the spirit of each threatens to annihilate the other! In Hayek's world there are households, little islands of the truly primitive, there is the private sector, humming away on the basis of inherited principles it does not fully understand, and there is government. That's it.[6]

Richard Cornuelle saw the thinness of this imagination. But he kept the underlying modernity, the distinction between commerce and community, postulating a robust human propensity to "serve" that would distinguish community both from the cold amorality of commerce *and* from the dangerous atavism of the Hayekian micro-cosmos. He is at pains to describe a "third sector" peopled by sensible, rock-ribbed American individualists (Cornuelle 1965, 1983). But, trapped by the dualism of asocial commerce versus community, he is unable to develop a clear account of the knowledge that this third sector produces, one that would address the critiques that Hayek and Friedman raised about philanthropy (Garnett 2010). Much of his recommendation boils down to a call for the independent sector to become more independent and self-confident, coupled with a recurrent complaint that government, in attempting to address social problems itself, has sapped private initiative.

Cornuelle is most persuasive when he points out that the broad philanthropic sector shares some of the characteristics that commend free enterprise. It gives individuals – including individuals with limited means – the capacity to act directly in the world. It encourages experimentation. It is large, diverse, and unmanaged.[7] Note that none of these insights depend on the idea that the philanthropic sector is imbued with a different spirit than the business world. If anything, they point in the opposite direction.

To recapitulate my argument: I have distinguished two broad responses to the Hume–Kant problem of social knowledge, those of British political economy and those of the Romantic theories of community. I have further pulled the Romantic theories apart into two traditions, holism, described above, and intersubjectivism, elaborated below. The larger argument is that we should favor the intersubjectivists if we want to build on Cornuelle's work, not least because they can dispense with the modernist assumptions just described.

## Intersubjective accounts

For the ground-level *alternative* to the holist approach to community, think about someone you know well. You will never have direct access to their mind, nor they yours. But you know from experience that prolonged interaction can generate workable and even subtle shared understandings.

What I am calling the intersubjective concept of community and knowledge starts with two propositions about interpretation. The first is what Isaiah Berlin calls "expressionism" in his discussion of Johann Georg Hamann and Johann Gottfried Herder:

> *Expressionism*: The doctrine that human activity in general, and art in particular, express the entire personality of the individual or the group, and are intelligible only to the degree to which they do so. Still more specifically, expressionism claims that all the works of men are above all voices speaking, are not objects detached from their makers, are part of a living process of communication between persons and not independently existing entities.
>
> (2000, 176)

This concept covers much more than acts of speaking and writing. It says that all activity that brings us into contact with other people is expressive: the way we hold our bodies, our dress, our gestures, our acts of care or violence, the work that we do with others. It also points to what people produce – goods, services, art – as interpretable expression.

The second, related proposition is that to be socially human is to be an interpreter of these expressive acts. Interpretation, here, is not a simple matter of turning codes into clear signals. The concept of interpretation is instead *hermeneutic*, which is to say that we understand expressions not by decoding them into something else, but by working out their relationships to other expressions. Precisely because there is never an authoritative "clear" message that is encoded, but instead a mere circulation of signs, interpretation may be contested and uneven. We have all had the experience of being misunderstood, of discovering that we have transmitted a message we did not intend. Sharing a "culture" is not enough to prevent this. In other words, to be *shaped* by culture is not the same thing as to be *determined* by it or have it do your thinking for you.

So, in the *intersubjective* conception, to be a social human being is to be a maker and interpreter of meanings. To be a social human is to (try to) understand and (hope to) be understood. These meanings are not just words, but also movement, dress, the exchange of food, acts of care, commercial transactions. The intersubjective approach is *embodied*, as we might say in contemporary academic language, because it speaks to all the ways that our common lives as physical beings influence each other through interpretation. Further, in a robustly intersubjective social ontology, people are not just idly communicating but building communities of interpretation through their efforts to engage with others and develop ties.

Here is the critical argument: precisely to the degree that you emphasize people's *embodied* and long-accustomed closeness to each other, the ways they get used to each other, learn to read each other, share parts of the physical world, provide for (or thwart) each other's needs and desires – precisely as you emphasize this, you move *away* from a holist, top-down notion of culture. The simplest way to distinguish the holist and intersubjective versions is to ask whether people are substitutable in roles. In the most basic version of holism, one acculturated member of society X is as good as another, and once members of it are culturally shaped (learning the language, undergoing coming-of-age rituals and so forth), little further maintenance is required because culture does the work of interpretation. In the basic intersubjective version, by contrast, ties are personal and take ongoing work by the individuals involved: you cannot switch people in and out of roles. If I am hit by a bus a colleague could take over my class the next day, but not my family relationships.

A key logical distinction: if you *start* with the holist account of community, it is easy enough to fit intersubjectivity *into* that account as a mechanism by which the whole reproduces itself, or reveals itself. Romantics like Hamann and Herder saw a fundamental reality like God or the nation manifesting itself through a thousand daily details of food, poetry, gesture, and speech: the intersubjective was merely a channel for the manifestation of the whole. More materialist social scientists (Giddens 1979; Bhaskar 1979; Geertz 1973) have explained the transmission and stability of large cultural wholes as the result of the work of individual meaning-makers who, in the pursuit of their individual projects, unwittingly reproduce the larger system. An intersubjective account of community is not necessarily inimical to a holist account. But if we give up the impulse to fit all actions into structural reproduction, then we can see that the intersubjective account does not logically *imply* holism. The intersubjective conception can point instead toward a rhizomorphic (Deleuze 2013) social organization of extended root systems, shaggy networks, and possibly significant patterns of exclusion even among people who live close together.

To put it another way, I do not deny the existence of languages, religions, regional cuisines, systems of etiquette, or other cultural phenomena that exist on much larger scales than personal networks. What I *am* questioning is the central explanatory role that such systems/structures have in so much social analysis. I contest the reduction of ground-level intersubjectivity, in many holist accounts, to a mere feature or expression of large systems or structures. Such reduction is clear even today in the anthropological literature on intersubjectivity (Jackson 1998), which, for all its nuance, still sees the intersubjective as pointing to the whole – as symbolizing it, manifesting it, helping people think about it. In a similar way, Austrian intersubjective theorists Lavoie and Chamlee-Wright retain the idea of "culture" as a social operating system working at the national level and influencing economic outcomes *as* a bounded and discrete national whole. Their hermeneutic sophistication shows up in their effort to distinguish their approach from crude theories of culture by arguing that *each* national culture is a complex and dynamic thing, not a set of fixed inherited values. But the hermeneutics are still subsidiary, in social-ontological terms, to the holist theory of culture. (Chamlee-Wright and Lavoie 2000, 65).[8]

## Entangled lives

How important are these shaggy networks, these rhizomorphs of personal connection that the field of the intersubjective brings to view? There is no killer argument here: committed modernists are confident that they can explain this meso level either from the bottom up (as the result of individual maximization) or from the top down (as a consequence of structure). I can only hope to persuade by reference to observation and experience, highlighting the elements of social life that are brought into view when we take the intersubjective as a ground for analysis. In addition, it may be worth pointing out that one reason the world appears modernist is that data has been built that way: the concept of measurable "population," for example, rests on the command to the census-taker that people be assigned uniquely to bounded "households," rather than larger kin networks, so that the *work* of making family units in and through the practices of intersubjective relations across familial units disappears from view (Danby 2012). I use the metaphor "entangled" for two purposes: first, as an opposite of "separate," of the modernist assumption of separate spheres; second, as a way of signposting a social ontology in which people

## Entangled individuals

We inhabit multiple social frameworks at the same time. We live in large kin structures, networks of friends and colleagues, firms and organizations, religious communities, and other more diffuse nets of affiliation, at the same time and in the same place. We produce care services and goods like family dinners. Even in "business," we develop social ties within firms as well as to customers and suppliers (Granovetter 1985). Graduates of US business programs are counseled to network directly and electronically, to develop and cultivate ties. Aside from these observable facts, I appeal to the reader's internal experience of love, responsibility, even guilt and individual conflict. It may be possible to set up our lives so that we owe nothing to anybody. But most of us go to great lengths to establish ties of long-term, open-ended responsibility, including the production of new socialized human beings. It is a rebuke to economics, orthodox or heterodox, that it has so much to say about idle pleasure-seeking but lacks a theory of responsibility.[9]

## Entangled firms

There is a broad classical tradition, going back to Adam Smith and notably including Allyn Young (1928), which emphasizes relations of complementarity between enterprises, rather than theorizing units as exclusively competitive. In Brian Loasby's (1976, 1998, 1999) work, firms have internal organizations that take into account the ongoing uncertainty of their business, and they also enter into a variety of formal and informal relations and understandings with other businesses. Inter-firm relations are not limited to market transactions and contracts; substantial complementarity exists between businesses (1998; see also Granovetter 1985). Loasby vastly expands the more traditional Austrian emphasis on market signals, and by his approach to the day-to-day and year-to-year work of a firm he also begins to challenge the idea that firms themselves are neatly bounded or independent entities. The more one moves in the direction of networks or sets of relations, whether between households, between firms, or between households and firms, the less free-standing the nodes of that network become. This does not imply that businesses are solidaristic: the same kinds of tensions, imbalances of power, and betrayals that occur in families happen between firms. But we end up with a richer and more consequential range of business interconnection than either the neoclassical imagination of firms as arms-length market transactors, or more structural imaginations in which firms form part of a single capitalist bloc. Relatedly, there is a large and fascinating literature on family firms (e.g. Oxfeld 1993; White 1994; Yanagisako 2002) that suggests that kin ties are routinely useful for providing finance and recruiting labor, particularly for small businesses.

As I have argued elsewhere (Danby 2004a) this interconnection and complementarity comes into much clearer view if we start with the post-Keynesian insight that in contemporary economies most consequential transactions are forward, not spot, and that, as a result, both individuals and firms live enmeshed in obligations to others. This fact does not tell us what the institutional or ethical character of these meshes of obligation are, but it opens up an object of investigation that is obscured if we assume that such an economy can be modeled as though it used only spot transactions, or that some automatic level of state or cultural machinery takes care of undergirding these long-term ties between economic units. I start with Shacklean priors that the future is radically underdetermined, and that it is made through the interactions of individual efforts to plan and structure it – not all of which, of course, succeed. But I keep the point, emphasized by some critical realists (Lawson 2003, 2012), that people pull off a great many of their plans: planning matters. Recognizing that the future is uncertain, people typically make efforts to build robustness into their plans – one reason to diversify and enlarge our social networks.

## Entangled knowledge

Carol Gilligan (1982) reinterpreted the result, in studies of ethical reasoning among children, that girls resisted applying universal principles to ethical dilemmas, and instead inquired about the particular social relationships in which ethical problems arose. Gilligan argued that rather than showing a failure to rise to abstract reasoning, this approach demonstrated alternative and arguably more sophisticated approaches to social reality. Instead of abstracting the problem away from specific social ties, she showed that female respondents typically took into account the effect that different possible resolutions of a dilemma would have on those social ties. Theirs was a situated, socially curious, and socially minded response. Gilligan's results support an intersubjective social ontology: it is not so much that the female respondents were peculiar or essentially feminine (an interpretation Gilligan herself has resisted) as that they were simply more aware of the social reality around them (Larrabee 1992).

What the literature on care has illuminated is the extensive, ongoing *labor* of building social connections: those connections do not spring into existence on their own or maintain themselves without work; they are not simply given to us by tradition (or by the state or any variety of social structure, for that matter).[10] And this labor, as I have argued elsewhere

(Danby 2004b), is remarkably consistent across social realms: we find it in business, in government agencies, in volunteer organizations, among friends, in kin systems, in households. Because this labor is often self-concealing, we may fall into the error of thinking that it is "natural" or a mere reflex of a larger structure or tradition. Networks have to be consciously built and maintained. Culture or tradition or the state may give you tools and categories, and may thwart or enable certain kinds of connection, but they do not do the work of making them.

Holist accounts tend to portray the culture or tradition as the unit that does the important thinking and coordinating. This is evident in nineteenth-century Romanticism, in Levi-Straussian structural anthropology, and in Hayek's account of tradition in *Fatal Conceit*.[11] Consider Hayek's "Most knowledge – and I confess it took me some time to recognise this – is obtained not from immediate experience or observation, but in the continuous process of sifting a learnt tradition" (1991, 75). This extraordinary statement may summarize Hayek's own intellectual practice. But in his determination to drive away the evil spirit of planning, Hayek has also tossed out the functions of attention, inquiry, discovery, and reflection that accompany entrepreneurial action – functions that also accompany independent sector action in Cornuelle's account.

## Entangled ethics

Neither business, nor community, nor family, nor any other category, is inherently virtuous or vicious. Modernist arguments tend to assign moral values to entire sectors: for example, Romantic anticapitalism disdains all business as selfish and crude and celebrates community as loving and whole. One can invert these values to make the opposite argument. There is an enduring (and endearing) Whiggishness in Cornuelle that praises both and hopes that with the right allocation of tasks we will achieve the best of both worlds in a prosperous and caring society. (For examples, see 1965, 106–124, 1983, 173–189.) His is a world with very little active evil. I do not want to dismiss the ethical, but to argue, on the contrary, that the work of ethical analysis has barely begun.

It is an obvious and unavoidable consequence of the intersubjective approach that we will find uneven patterns of connection, including outright exclusion. Note that this insight disappears if we see the intersubjective as mere training, as nothing but our point of access to a larger "culture" or tradition that all its members share alike. (This is, not to put too fine a point on it, the reactionary use of the concept "culture," which turns it into a warm sea in which all can bathe, rather than a system of distinction, exclusion, and power.) It is for this reason that feminist philosophers like Claudia Card (1990) and Sara Ruddick (1995) have resisted the idea of inflating "care" into a general ethic, arguing that whatever the benefits of care, it also lends itself to exclusion and domination. Close, even loving, familial ties can be power-laden and exploitative; feudalism functioned through personal ties and individual relationships. Organized crime works along personal and often familial connections. It is futile to expect any concept of "community" to provide the moral high ground, the ethical purity, the wholeness and love that we imagine we have lost in the modern world. The trope of recovering something lost is powerful, and recurs in Cornuelle's work, but it leads us into simplistic categorizations.

## Conclusions

I have argued for a robustly ground-level, intersubjective, interpretive social ontology and sought to distinguish it *both* from high modernity (pure *Gesellschaft*, an atomistic society) *and* from the holist, traditionalist conceptions of "culture" as a single, bounded system that strongly shapes individual members. Dropping the modernist assumptions of holism and drawing on the feminist, Austrian, and post-Keynesian insights about the close concatenation of people and firms, we are led to an unevenly networked world. This is an alternative account of how community is made, and how knowledge functions within it.

The anthropologist James Ferguson writes (1999, 207) that "the ethnographic project of 'cross-cultural' interpretation has too often assumed coherent and semiotically pure communities, systems of shared meanings within which signification and interpretation are unequivocal and unproblematic." Mulling over the confusing scene in a Lusaka bar, he asks,

> But what happens if we replace the archetypal image of the anthropologist dropped into the middle of a culturally homogeneous village community with that of a crowded, noisy city street scene, where different languages, different cultures, diverse social microworlds, and discordant frames of meaning are all thrown together in the normal course of things? Here there is much to be understood, but none of the participants in the scene can claim to understand it all or even to take it all in. Everyone is a little confused (some more than others, to be sure), and everyone finds some things that seem clear and others that are unintelligible or only partially intelligible …
>
> Neat lines between the locals who know what's going on and the foreigner who doesn't proved hard to maintain on the Copperbelt, where everyone seemed to be coming or going, where nearly everyone spoke of their home as some place other than where they lived, where languages and cultures ran together in a cryptic hodgepodge to which no one seemed to hold any definitive interpretive key. Miscommunication and partial communication were not simply temporary obstacles in

the methodological process of the ethnographer but central features of the "authentic" cultural experience.

(1999, 207–208)

Could this be what the world is like? Is it possible that the world has never been tidy or transparent, and that we have been over-impressed by twentieth-century efforts to make it appear tidier than it is (Danby 2012)? A robust intersubjectivity that is *not* yoked to the assumption of cultural homogeneity opens up a wider sphere of action and difficulty. Interpretation is necessary; interpretation is difficult. People may have reasons "not to establish a bond of communication but to rupture it" (Ferguson 1999, 210); there may be a politics to unintelligibility and to refusals to interpret.

But if we cannot depend on one or another unified "culture" to make us happy, whole, or prosperous, we also open much greater scope to individual action, and action by smaller groups. Once we drop the modernist assumption that individuals have limited ability to build their own worlds, and bring into view extensive individual efforts to craft their social surroundings, philanthropy (like entrepreneurship) becomes less odd: like many of our actions, it is an effort to shape our surroundings with uncertain results.

Cornuelle's work brought into view a large, shaggy, and diverse "independent sector," not always intelligible to others or even to itself, and indeed strengthened by the fact of its internal diversity: part of his lament about the governmentalization of this sector is that a wide range of different projects are brought under a single state logic and thus pulled out of their own quirky circuits of knowledge and action. These are insights upon which we can continue to draw, even if we drop the modernist frame.

## Notes

1 Modernism is essentially the idea that human history follows a path from cozy, primitive "tradition" to dynamic, alienated "modernity." I present a more extended description of modernist thought in Danby (2009). It should be emphasized that the underlying modernist template can generate a wide range of stories. Thus Friedrich Hayek, Fredric Jameson, Anthony Giddens, and Naomi Klein are all modernists in that they accept that this is the fundamental story of human history, although they assign different ethical values to the sphere of commerce.
2 See Fitzgibbons (1995). You can see the Stoic ethic of accepting an uncaring universe, and not unduly troubling each other, as a criticism-in-advance of Romanticism. There is a fascinating further discussion of this difference in John Stuart Mill's 1840 essay on Coleridge (1950), in which he distinguishes the kinds of phenomena (in particular, nationalism) on which a thinker like Coleridge has an advantage over political economists.
3 By which I mean the tradition of Goethe, Hamann, Herder, Coleridge, Carlyle, and Ruskin. Romanticism for our purposes is essentially the doctrine that

accepts the modernist story that history moves from traditional to modern, but laments it (Berlin 2001).
4 Pribram (1983, 209). See also Winch (2009) and Waterman (2003) for discussions of Romantic political economy.
5 For more on Hayek's relation to the Romantic School see Caldwell (Bruce Caldwell 2004) and Hayek's own discussion of Herder (Hayek 1991). See also (Mirowski 2002, 234–241).
6 Hayek's account is thus an ingenious modification of the standard modernist story that depicts human history moving from close traditional community (*Gemeinschaft*) to distanced modernity (*Gesellschaft*). He retains the idea that the inevitable loser in human history is sentimental *Gemeinschaft* (the "micro-cosmos"). But in his account, the winner is *another* tradition of similar antiquity, that of commerce and enterprise.
7 See (Cornuelle 1965, 31–33, 96–101; 1983, 21–32) on the creativity, adaptability, and close-to-the-ground nature of the independent sector, all keys to his overall argument for its superiority to government.
8 For example, "The issue in economic comparative advantage is not which country, say Mexico or the US, is better in more things, but which of each culture's strengths are those most suitable for *it* to focus on" (Chamlee-Wright and Lavoie 2000, 65). The entire chapter is written as though it were reasonable to treat national cultures as discrete wholes.
9 Nel Noddings (2003) is one of the most persuasive theorists of the kind of "care" that is not generalizable to an abstract principle but is only meaningful when it is personalized and specific. Important work has been done in feminist scholarship in care (Irene van Staveren 2001). The key point in relations of responsibility and care is that the well-being of specific other people matters: this is larger than the individual, but much smaller than "society" or any large-scale structural constraint (Danby 2004b).
10 This meso approach to care provides a robust, Austrian-friendly, critique of macro-scale policy. Again, see Nel Noddings (2003), who is particularly eloquent on the point that "care" for an individual is quite a different thing from "care" for any large abstraction.
11 One could make the same criticism of "Volume-1 Marxism": your position in the class structure tells you what to do.

## References

Berlin, Isaiah. 2000. *Three Critics of the Enlightenment: Vico, Hamann, Herder*. Princeton Paperbacks 372. Princeton, NJ: Princeton University Press.
Berlin, Isaiah. 2001. *The Roots of Romanticism*. Princeton, NJ: Princeton University Press.
Bhaskar, Roy. 1979. *The Possibility of Naturalism: A Philosophical Critique of the Contemporary Human Sciences*. Philosophy and the Human Sciences 1. Brighton, Sussex: Harvester Press.
Caldwell, Bruce. 2004. *Hayek's Challenge: An Intellectual Biography of F.A. Hayek*. Chicago: University of Chicago Press.
Card, Claudia. 1990. "Gender and Moral Luck." In *Identity, Character, and Morality*, edited by Amelie Ocksenberg Rorty and Owen J. Flanagan. Cambridge, MA: MIT Press.
Chamlee-Wright, Emily and Don Lavoie. 2000. *Culture and Enterprise: The Development, Representation and Morality of Business*. London: Routledge.

Cornuelle, Richard C. 1965. *Reclaiming the American Dream*. New York: Random House.
Cornuelle, Richard C. 1983. *Healing America*. New York: Putnam.
Danby, Colin. 2004a. "Toward a Gendered Post-Keynesianism." *Feminist Economics* 10 (3): 13–42.
Danby, Colin. 2004b. "Lupita's Dress: Care in Time." *Hypatia* 19 (4): 23–48. doi:10.2307/3811055.
Danby, Colin. 2009. "Post-Keynesianism without Modernity." *Cambridge Journal of Economics* 33 (6): 1119–1133. doi:10.1093/cje/bep007.
Danby, Colin. 2012. "Postwar Norm." *Rethinking Marxism* 24 (4): 499–515. doi:10.1080/08935696.2012.711052.
Deleuze, Gilles. 2013. *A Thousand Plateaus: Capitalism and Schizophrenia*. London: Bloomsbury Academic.
Ferguson, James. 1999. *Expectations of Modernity Myths and Meanings of Urban Life on the Zambian Copperbelt*. Berkeley, CA: University of California Press.
Fitzgibbons, Athol. 1995. *Adam Smith's System of Liberty, Wealth, and Virtue: The Moral and Political Foundations of The Wealth of Nations*. Oxford: Clarendon Press.
Garnett, Robert F. 2010. "Hayek and Philanthropy: A Classical Liberal Road Not (Yet) Taken." In *Hayek, Mill and the Liberal Tradition*, edited by Andrew Farrant. Hoboken, NJ: Taylor & Francis.
Garnett, Robert F. 2011. "Cultivating Conversations." *Conversations on Philanthropy* VIII: 1–6.
Geertz, Clifford. 1973. *The Interpretation of Cultures; Selected Essays*. New York: Basic Books.
Giddens, Anthony. 1979. *Central Problems in Social Theory: Action, Structure, and Contradiction in Social Analysis*. Berkeley, CA: University of California Press.
Gilligan, Carol. 1982. *In a Different Voice: Psychological Theory and Women's Development*. Cambridge, MA: Harvard University Press.
Granovetter, Mark. 1985. "Economic Action and Social Structure: The Problem of Embeddedness." *American Journal of Sociology* 91 (3): 481. doi:10.1086/228311.
Hayek, Friedrich A. 1991. *The Fatal Conceit: the Errors of Socialism*. Chicago: University of Chicago Press.
Hume, David. [1748] 1999. *An Enquiry Concerning Human Understanding*. Oxford: Oxford University Press.
Jackson, Michael. 1998. *Minima Ethnographica: Intersubjectivity and the Anthropological Project*. Chicago: University of Chicago Press.
Kant, Immanuel. [1783] 1949. *Kant's Prolegomena to Any Future Metaphysics*. Reprint edn. Chicago: Open Court.
Larrabee, Mary. 1992. *An Ethic of Care: Feminist and Interdisciplinary Perspectives*. London: Routledge.
Lavoie, Don. 1994. "The Interpretive Turn." In *Elgar Companion to Austrian Economics*, edited by Peter Boettke, 54–62. Aldershot: Edward Elgar.
Lawson, Tony. 2003. *Reorienting Economics*. London: Routledge.
Lawson, Tony. 2012. *Economics and Reality*. London: Routledge.
Loasby, Brian J. 1976. *Choice, Complexity, and Ignorance*. Cambridge: Cambridge University Press.
Loasby, Brian J. 1998. "Ludwig M. Lachmann: Subjectivism in Economics and the Economy." In Koppl, R. and Mongiovi, G. (eds), *Subjectivism and Economic Analysis: Essays in Memory of Ludwig M. Lachmann*. London: Routledge

Loasby, Brian J. 1999. *Knowledge, Institutions and Evolution in Economics*. London: Routledge.
Mill, John Stuart. 1950. *Mill on Bentham and Coleridge*. London: Chatto & Windus.
Mirowski, Philip. 2002. *Machine Dreams: Economics Becomes a Cyborg Science*. Cambridge: Cambridge University Press.
Noddings, Nel. 2003. *Caring: A Feminine Approach to Ethics & Moral Education*. Berkeley, CA: University of California Press.
Oxfeld, E. 1993. *Blood, Sweat, and Mahjong: Family and Enterprise in an Overseas Chinese Community*, Ithaca, NY: Cornell University Press.
Pribram, Karl. 1983. *A History of Economic Reasoning*. Baltimore, MD: Johns Hopkins University Press.
Ruddick, Sara. 1995. *Maternal Thinking: Toward a Politics of Peace*. Boston, MA: Beacon Press.
Smith, Adam. [1759] 1976. *The Theory of Moral Sentiments*. Oxford: Clarendon Press.
Smith, Adam. [1776] 1979. *An Inquiry into the Nature and Causes of the Wealth of Nations*. Oxford: Clarendon Press.
van Staveren, Irene. 2001. *The Values of Economics: an Aristotelian Perspective*. New York: Routledge.
Waterman, A. M. C. 2003. "Romantic Political Economy: Donald Winch and David Levy on Victorian Literature and Economics." *Journal of the History of Economic Thought* 25 (01): 91–102. doi:10.1080/1042771032000058334.
White, Jenny. 1994. *Money Makes Us Relatives: Women's Labor in Urban Turkey*. Austin, TX: University of Texas Press.
Winch, Donald. 2009. *Wealth and Life: Essays on the Intellectual History of Political Economy in Britain, 1848–1914*. Ideas in Context 95. Cambridge: Cambridge University Press.
Yanagisako, Sylvia. J. 2002. *Producing Culture and Capital: Family Firms in Italy*. Princeton, NJ: Princeton University Press.
Young, Allyn. 1928. "Increasing Returns and Economic Progress." *Economic Journal* 38 (152): 527–542.

# 14 Commerce, community, and digital gifts

*Dave Elder-Vass*

Digital gifts are ubiquitous on the internet: web pages, blog entries, social media posts, photographs, videos, and contributions to advice forums, for example, are widely made available for anyone to use without payment or reciprocation. And they are becoming increasingly important in the lives of an increasing number of internet users, with the International Telecommunication Union reporting that 2.7 billion people are now online (ITU 2013, 2). It may be tempting to see all this digital giving as occupying a social space in which commerce is absent and community therefore present, but this would be to fall into the trap of the commerce/community dualism that this volume seeks to question.

In the terms of this dualism, commerce, on the one hand, represents the commodity economy as it is understood in neoclassical economics, in which actors assume rational personae and engage in asocial exchanges at market prices with a view to optimising over their preference functions. Community, on the other, represents a space about which this tradition of economics is largely silent, a space that acts for it as a kind of dumping ground for all those social activities that can be dismissed as uneconomic, activities that might be of interest to sociologists and anthropologists, but activities that these economists assume they can safely ignore. In this space, for example, people have emotions, they have values, they are socialised into normative patterns of action, they have relationships with each other, they resemble each other or differ from each other, they support each other or undermine each other, and they sometimes give to each other without calculation or reciprocation. This is, no doubt, a straw binary, a caricatured representation, and there are certainly many economic studies that depart from it, such as those on pro-social behaviour documented by Meier (2006), yet it is still one that is worthy of critique if it resonates closely with the assumptions really (if not necessarily consciously) made by many economists.

In this context, community has an essentially negative function: it is the other of commerce, and it must be kept strictly separated from commerce in order to preserve the purity and the mathematical tractability of the economy as it is represented in mainstream economics. To question the dualism, then, is to pose a threat to the integrity of the work done in that tradition.

In the context of this straw binary, we could arguably replace the word *community* with any other that would encompass those aspects of human social behaviour that are to be excluded from economics. Yet it is a word with a history, a word that has symbolised the social side of this distinction, or some variant of it, at least since the work of Ferdinand Tönnies (2003 [1887]). For Tönnies, and for many others, *community*, or rather *Gemeinschaft*, usually translated as *community*, not only indicates a range of social phenomena that are excluded from most representations of the commercial economy, but also ties them together into a kind of romantic ideal type: "a spontaneously arising organic social relationship characterized by strong reciprocal bonds of sentiment and kinship within a common tradition" (Merriam-Webster 2013). Such conceptions of community function as cover for an imaginary ideal of interpersonal harmony based on multiple congruent affiliations and affinities, but these understandings of community are at least as problematic as the concept of a purely rational asocial economy. They miss, for example, the diversity of communities in contemporary society, their exclusionary nature, their radical intersectionality in the sense that any individual may belong to multiple communities, the decreasing importance of kinship and locality as a basis for community, the socially constructed nature of the cultural affinities that many communities are built around, and the existence of commercial relationships alongside relationships of affect between the same people. Most social life and most economic life, which I take to be a part of social life and not somehow distinct from it, conform to neither the mainstream economic model of commerce nor the romantic model of community. Actual commerce and actual community are both more complex and more interwoven than the commerce/community binary suggests.

This chapter explores those relationships by considering the increasingly important phenomenon of digital gifts. In the commerce/community dualism, gifts would seem to belong firmly on the side of community, with the implication that they are given only to those with whom we have close existing relationships, in a normatively endorsed process that is often seen as making and strengthening connections within the community. But one of the striking characteristics of digital gifts is that they are often gifts to strangers, gifts that entail no obligation to reciprocate. Another is that they are by no means always divorced from commercial interests: many digital gifts are given in the pursuit of profit.

Digital gifts thus prompt us to question multiple implications of the commerce/community binary, and point the way towards an alternative understanding of the economy, in which it is understood as deeply social, with both commercial and non-commercial aspects, and deeply entangled with communities: but communities that take diversely unromantic forms. This chapter also seeks to contribute to a number of wider yet related arguments: first, that giving is an economic activity and an important one in contemporary societies; second, that there is a diverse range of giving practices, which do not all function in the same way or have the same implications; third, that in some contexts, certain giving practices are a promising alternative to commodity exchange; but fourth, that giving is often entangled with other economic practices in complex and interesting ways.

## Gifts and digital gifts

For mainstream economics, the economy is precisely coextensive with the commodity economy: it essentially consists of *transfers of goods and services that take the form of exchange and productive activity that is undertaken with the intention of exchanging the product*. There may be grudging extensions for the state sector, which is brought back into the exchange economy by measuring it in terms of the purchase of inputs as commodities rather than in terms of the value of its outputs, but giving, and production for giving, is generally excluded without even an acknowledgement that the exclusion has taken place. The exceptions are (1) gifts of money and (2) products that are produced and purchased as commodities in order to be given as gifts, which are of interest to economists only in their role as commodities and cease to be of interest as soon as they have been purchased by the eventual giver of the gift.

Yet many of our needs, material and otherwise, are met by activities that fall outside the commodity economy. If the economy is to be defined in terms of the function it performs, then, rather than in terms of a self-confirming dogma about the form the economy should take, it cannot be identical with commerce, or with the commodity economy, but must also include those other activities. Instead, it is more coherent and plausible to understand the economy in terms of the provisioning of goods and services, as economic thinkers from a range of heterodox traditions have done (Boulding 1973, 1986; Dugger 1996; Garnett 2007; Gruchy 1987; Nelson 1993; Sayer 2004, 2). When we do think of the economy in these terms, it becomes clear that giving is an economic activity in much the same sense that exchange is an economic activity, and producing to give is an economic activity in much the same sense as producing for sale. And when we look at the vast range of provisioning activity that occurs in contemporary society, we quickly find that an enormous proportion of it occurs outside the commodity economy. That provisioning activity includes, for example, a broad range of gift economy practices such as charitable giving, volunteering, blood and organ donation, ritual gifts on birthdays and other occasions, assistance to friends, neighbours, co-workers and indeed unknown passers-by, bequests, and perhaps most substantially of all, sharing of resources and caring labour within the household.[1]

Although the literature on the gift economy (which can be found predominantly in anthropology) is plagued with attempts "to construct a single image or type or form of 'the gift' that can be counterposed to neoclassical exchange" (Danby 2002, 27), not all of these gift economy practices work in the same way. Some may seem to fit quite comfortably into the conventional commodity/commercial dualism, such as sharing and caring within the family. But others do not, and this paper illustrates the point with some examples from the wide range of digital giving practices that have become increasingly important and prevalent in recent years.

Digital gifts have become ubiquitous on the internet. Indeed the web is *based on* digital gifts: almost every web page we load into our browsers is a complex text offered for downloading without any requirement for, or expectation of, any return to be made in exchange for viewing the content concerned (Barbrook 2005 [1998]; Berry 2008, 12).[2] Web pages, blog posts, videos on YouTube, photographs, advice offered in a vast range of forums, and status updates on Facebook, for example, are products of labour that are given freely by their creators, and although sites like Facebook may allow creators to restrict who may access their creations, much of this material is freely available to anyone. These digital gifts entail no obligation to reciprocate, and furthermore, unlike charitable gifts, they entail no sense that the recipient is *unable* to reciprocate or is in any way inferior to the donors: there is no stigma entailed in loading a web page without reciprocating the gift that it constitutes. These are free gifts, often to strangers, given to their recipients as equals.

At this level, there is no obvious connection between digital gifts and *either* commerce *or* community. Say, for example, a steam train enthusiast spends a number of hours creating a web page containing useful information and rare photographs that relate to a certain kind of steam engine. Once the page is published, it is freely available to anyone who wishes to view it. No commodity changes hands and commerce is utterly absent when another web user views the page. Yet there is little trace of community at work here, either. Granted, both the author and the reader presumably have some shared interest in steam engines, but typically the authors and readers of web pages have no previous personal connection, have never met and may never meet each other, and may have very different backgrounds and interests beyond the minimal affinities implicit in the act of viewing the page. The presumed association of giving with community implicit in our straw binary is nowhere to be seen.

## Digital communities

This is not to say, however, that there is *no* connection between digital gifts and communities (nor is it to say that there is *no* connection between digital gifts and digital commerce, as we shall see in later sections). The web is also a site of community interaction, and inevitably, given the central role of gifts in the web, these interactions are fuelled by digital gifts.

Social networking sites like Facebook and Twitter, for example, rest on a constant flow of material that is freely shared by their users: status updates, tweets, links to interesting web pages, photographs, and even videos. On Facebook, in particular, a high proportion of such sharing occurs between people who already know each other offline (Ellison et al. 2007, 1155) and thus serves to consolidate and sustain existing relationships that have roots in face-to-face interaction. It is a little counterintuitive to think of status updates and tweets as gifts: the closest offline parallel is arguably conversation rather than gift-giving.[3] Yet we may also compare them to newspaper stories, which have traditionally been supplied as (parts of) commodities and by contrast with these status updates and tweets are a de-commodified form of media: a gift form.

There are, however, multiple kinds of community on the internet. On Facebook, offline communities of interaction are reproduced (and sometimes expanded) online. Elsewhere, communities are constructed that have less, or even no, prior basis in offline interaction. Again, giving, as the characteristic form of interaction on the web, plays a central role, but there are important differences between the ways in which giving operates to build community ties online and offline.

To understand these phenomena we must engage briefly with the long tradition of economic anthropology of the gift centred on the notion of reciprocity and in particular on the work of Marcel Mauss (Mauss 2002 [1950]).[4] In counterposing the pre-modern gift economy to the modern commodity economy, Mauss arguably mirrored the community/commodity dualism that mainstream economics is so enamoured of, but there are nevertheless valuable elements in his work. Among these is the argument that gifts create social ties and help to build and sustain communities, because they tend to create a sense of obligation in the recipient towards the giver of the gift (Godbout and Caillé 1998, e.g., 10, 12). My view is that different kinds of gifts, in different social contexts, have different effects, but that many contemporary gifts do *not* create a firm obligation to reciprocate the gift with one of equivalent value, as Mauss tends to argue they do (Elder-Vass 2014a). Nevertheless, gifts may help to sustain communities. Thus, for example, personal presents in contemporary Western societies are often given as tokens of a desire to sustain and perhaps deepen the relationship between giver and recipient. In accepting such a gift, the recipient signals acceptance of that continuing relationship, and their intention to reciprocate the *relationship*. Reciprocation of the *gift* with something vaguely equivalent at some point in the future may indeed occur, but this is entirely secondary to the larger commitment.

The digital case is different, I suggest, for reasons that derive in part from the technical characteristics of digital gifts. Once a digital product has been created and placed in an accessible location on the internet, and unlike non-digital physical goods and services, the marginal cost of giving away further copies of it is effectively zero. This is one of the reasons that the originators of digital goods are often willing to share them so freely, but one consequence is that the donor's gift is no longer a sign of a personal commitment to the recipient, whose degree of disconnection from the giver is so complete that most remain utterly anonymous. Equally, and unlike the recipients of gifts of physical goods and services, those who receive digital gifts may reasonably feel that their receipt of a copy imposed no burden or sacrifice on the originator and thus feel little sense of obligation towards the originator, little sense that reciprocation in some form might be required or expected. The acceptance of a digital gift need not, therefore, lead to any further commitment to a relationship between giver and receiver, and may do nothing to develop or sustain a community.

Nevertheless, such gifts *may* sometimes act as a step in the development of an online community. The recipient may feel moved to reciprocate directly, perhaps in the form of some sign of appreciation – a 'like' on a Facebook page, or an appreciative comment in an online forum, for example. Or the recipient may feel moved to make a more substantial contribution of their own. Conversations may begin, connections may be made, recognition of contributions may be made public, and contributors may feel valued for their work. This is the stuff of real communities, though their members may never meet or even know each other's names, let alone whether they share any affinities beyond the single topic that brought them together. But, unlike the case of offline present giving, there may be hundreds or thousands of free riders, taking these gifts without reciprocation, for every recipient who by responding becomes part of an online community. These are communities to which only the givers belong, and not those recipients who take without giving or giving back.

A particularly attractive case of such a community is provided by Wikipedia.[5] Wikipedia is created entirely by unpaid volunteers, and indeed anyone can edit a Wikipedia page (with a few exceptions). It is run with minimum levels of hierarchy, with disputes being resolved largely by the achievement of consensus under the guidance of a well-developed set of normative standards, and only rarely by the intervention of administrators, who are themselves volunteers selected on the basis of their previous contributions to the project (Forte *et al.* 2009). Its product is freely available to anyone who chooses to make use of it. Its running costs are relatively low given the enormous levels of usage – at the time of writing it is the seventh most visited site on the web (Alexa.com 2013) – and are met entirely by soliciting voluntary donations from users; indeed, the site does not even accept advertising.

The users of Wikipedia hardly form a community: their relationship with the pages it provides is essentially instrumental. But the contributors to Wikipedia are a different matter. They contribute partly for reasons of personal satisfaction, as Clay Shirky has stressed in a fascinating account of his reasons (as far as he can tell by introspection) for making his first Wikipedia edit. His first reason – "a chance to exercise some unused mental capacities" (Shirky 2009, 132) – is reminiscent of unalienated labour: work that is done for the sheer pleasure of exercising our creative powers. His second, he describes at first as "vanity" but then as the desire to "make a meaningful contribution" to changing the world (Shirky 2009, 132) – another aspect of unalienated labour: work in which we can exercise our creativity by determining for ourselves what the product of our work will be and how it will impact on the world. And his third reason, which he considers "both the most surprising and the most obvious" was "the desire to do a good thing" (Shirky 2009, 133): to do something for the benefit of humanity at large. O'Sullivan suggests that although these motivations may indeed be significant, for many contributors to Wikipedia there are also others that Shirky misses, notably "the attractions of belonging to a community, and of being recognized and valued by that community, especially one which offers a non-hierarchical and collaborative form of organization. Membership gives participants a sense of belonging, a common purpose, and offers mutual support in achieving the aims of the group" (O'Sullivan 2009, 87).

This sense of participation in a community comes not only from the feeling of having made a contribution to a common endeavour, but also from participation in processes of interaction with other contributors (Lessig 2008, 159–160). These processes are highly public, though unseen by most Wikipedia users, and anyone can obtain a flavour of them by simply clicking on the 'Talk' tab of any Wikipedia page. Wikipedia editors contribute under pseudonyms, with real names actively discouraged, which severely limits connections between users that extend beyond the scope of Wikipedia itself (O'Sullivan 2009, 88). Yet editors can interact with other editors through the Talk tabs and build up significant prestige within the Wikipedia community under their pseudonyms (indicated, for example, by being awarded *barnstars* by other users) as a consequence of making valuable contributions (Reagle 2010, 10), and can also take on more responsible roles as a result (Forte *et al.* 2009). This is a community that is driven by giving, though a very different kind of community than the traditional stereotype.

## Entanglement

The phenomenon of open-source software is a less pure case of the gift economy in action but an equally interesting one.[6] This is software that is supplied (generally for free) along with its humanly readable program code so that anyone with the appropriate skills can modify or extend it, and under licence conditions that permit users to do exactly that (Stallman 2010, 3). This provides the basis for cooperative development of the software, as any programmer can make improvements. Programmers who are interested in contributing to a product are free to choose what work to do on it, and then offer their improvements back to the open-source community. An element of hierarchy does exist in these communities, as groups exist that consolidate the most successful modifications into new releases of the product, but despite this, there is an unusually low level of hierarchy and centralised control given the complexity of the product. Nevertheless, open-source communities have developed some of the most successful software in the world: an organisational feat that would previously have been considered impossible (Benkler 2013, 214). Benkler reports, for example, that such software accounts for "roughly three-quarters of web servers" and "more than 70 percent of web browsers" (Benkler 2013, 220). It also includes Linux, an operating system that is used by most of the major website providers, and Android, a variant of Linux that is now the most widely used smartphone operating system in the world (Linux Foundation 2012).

Each open-source software product develops through the work of an interacting community of programmers, who become part of that community by virtue of the gifts of labour they make to the community's joint project. Like Wikipedia editors, they engage in debate on how the product of their work should be used, and like Wikipedia editors, they may develop prestige and recognition within the community on the basis of their contributions. But unlike Wikipedia, these are not commerce-free communities. Many of those who contribute to these projects are not independent individuals: in the case of the Linux kernel, for example (which may not be representative), only 17.9 percent of the changes made between 2005 and 2012 were made by unaffiliated individuals (Corbet *et al.* 2012, 9). The vast majority were made by programmers working for commercial software companies, notably Red Hat, Novell, Intel, and IBM (these four contributed over 30 per cent of the changes). While the data collection method means that some of these programmers may have been working on the project in their own time, it is clear that most of it is paid work, done for commercial companies, who are the real donors of this work to the project.

Commercial companies, like individuals, are responsive to the normative environment they face, and one recent study found that one claimed motivation for these contributions was a sense of moral obligation to contribute to communities whose work benefited the donating companies (Anderson-Gott *et al.* 2011, 113). However, both this and other studies have found, as we might expect, that the predominant motivations are more profit oriented. Broadly speaking, these fall into two classes: (a) selling complementary products and services (Weber 2004, 195–203); and (b) benefiting from the rapid innovation cycle in successful open-source communities without needing to do all the software development themselves. IT services companies who are actively involved in developing an open-source product develop deep expertise that enables them to provide support and integration services to companies that wish to use that product, and can offer, for example, to write fixes and new function for a customer that will then become part of the open-source product (Anderson-Gott et al. 2011, 109). Red Hat, for example, market themselves as "The world's leading provider of open source enterprise IT products and services" (Red Hat 2012). The second type of benefit was nicely explained by Kevin McEntee, VP of Systems & ECommerce Engineering at Netflix:

> We benefit from the continuous improvements provided by the community of contributors outside of Netflix. We also benefit by contributing back the changes we make to the projects. By sharing our bug fixes and new features back out into the community, the community then in turn continues to improve upon bug fixes and new features that originated at Netflix and then we complete the cycle by bring those improvements back into Netflix.
>
> (McEntee 2010)

Conventional economists will not be surprised by these profit-oriented motives, but they are being pursued here in a way that has very little connection with the economics of markets. These companies are investing in work that is then released into the open-source community for free, in the hope that these contributions will reap returns that are themselves entirely voluntary and somewhat unpredictable. Indeed, the most successful of these companies recognise that their success depends on them actively supporting the open-source community and its ethos of sharing the software it produces freely, as Red Hat has recognised from the outset (Lessig 2008, 179–184). Once again, we find commerce and community not on opposite sides of a binary divide, but interacting, in this case to their mutual benefit.

Individual contributors to open-source projects have equally diverse motivations, many of them equally inaccessible to market-oriented understandings of human action. There is no wage for their contributions, nor do they exchange them for some contractually agreed return of value. Why, then, do they make these free gifts to strangers? Some of the motives include elements of self-interest, the focus of Lerner and Tirole's somewhat economistic analysis (Lerner and Tirole 2002). For example, programmers who make frequent or high-quality contributions to open-source projects achieve recognition from their fellow contributors and thus prestige within the project community – generally a virtual community, in the sense that face-to-face meetings are rare and largely peripheral to the community process, but nevertheless a source of interaction and validation for its members (213; what Lerner and Tirole call the "ego gratification incentive"). These reputational benefits – symbolic capital, in Bourdieu's terms – may be valued in their own right but they are sometimes also converted into more material benefits, as, for example, when a programmer gains a good reputation within an open-source community and is then able to secure a well-paid job, or independent consultancy contracts, or easier access to venture capital for a start-up, as a result (the "career concern incentive": 2002, 213, 217–220). It seems unlikely, however, that the distant prospect of such an outcome provides the initial motivation for many contributors – we must distinguish between career benefits that sometimes accrue and the question of whether the prospect of such benefits is a significant motivator.

Other motivations are more difficult for conventional economics to accommodate. As Benkler puts it, one is simply "the pleasure of creation" (Benkler 2002) – a factor that essentially contradicts economic understandings of labour as a cost that must be compensated for by some other reward. At least some of these programmers are people who enjoy programming, enjoy putting their brains to work at solving problems and creating something of value to a wider community. Theirs is the pleasure of unalienated labour, labour in which the worker chooses her task, controls her own labour process and product, can interact with others involved in the process as a free and equal individual, and can exercise her creativity for the wider benefit of humanity (by contrast with alienated labour as described in Marx (1978 [1844], 74–76). This is labour freed from the tyranny of the market, a kind of labour that is sometimes denigrated as a mere hobby, and yet a kind of labour that is intensely productive of the flourishing that our economies so often fail to generate.

## Inducement gifts

Cases such as the free development of open-source software by companies that sell complementary goods and services are a variety of a more general form of gift that we may call *inducement gifts*. In inducement giving practices the donor gives in order to induce a commercial transaction, or a series of such transactions, that are collectively of *greater* value to the giver than the original gift. This is another type of giving that is growing rapidly as a result of the possibilities opened up by digital technology (Anderson 2009). Unlike many other giving practices, which often represent economic forms that we may see as alternatives to, or in competition with, contemporary capitalism, inducement giving is giving turned to the service of capitalism. Within this cluster of practices we constantly find "an entanglement of gifts within the commodity form" (Fuchs 2008, 171).

Inducement giving is a set of non-exchange practices deep within the commercial economy (but also a set of practices with relatively little relation to anything resembling traditional conceptions of community). One implication is that even if our aim is only to understand the commercial economy we must also take account of other kinds of motivation and other kinds of practice than those analysed in commodity exchange models of commerce. At the same time, we can see here a tussle for control of important economic spaces, in which there is a kind of colonisation of giving going on, in which the commercial economy acts back on the form and usage of giving practices.

Inducement gifts are not themselves part of an exchange, nor is there a strong normative requirement for a reciprocal return of equivalent (or even different) value. Any return by the recipient is entirely voluntary, but the gift is nevertheless designed to produce such a return. So this is a variety of giving that may sometimes generate an element of reciprocation, but a very different kind of reciprocation than that involved in pure exchange, first because it is voluntary, and second because it is often far from equivalent in value. There are at least three significant varieties of inducement giving.

In the first variety the inducement gift is intended to induce subsequent exchanges in the market. We may call these *marketing gifts*. Anderson, for example, describes the strategy adopted in the USA in the early twentieth century to market Jell-O, a gelatine-based food product. Unable by law to sell their product door to door, the company's sales force gave away recipe books with recipes for using the product instead. The result was to encourage consumers to buy the product in order to try out the recipes (Anderson 2009, 9–10). This has long been a fairly widespread phenomenon in commercial economies, but it is one that has been given a new lease of life by digital developments. One contemporary digital case is the phenomenon of "advergaming", in which companies give away computer games that feature their products in ways designed to encourage the gamer to buy them (or ask their parents/carers to do so) (Lumpkin and Dess 2004, 166). This is also the logic behind the currently rapidly growing phenomenon of free computer games in which gamers can make accelerated progress or enhance their participation in other ways by making in-game purchases – a $2 billion market in the USA in 2011 (Cheshire 2012: 139).[7] Such gifts do not entail an obligation to reciprocate, but they *are* designed to induce a response that generates a return to the original giver. That response, however, is not a return gift but a market exchange in its own right, from which the original giver expects to make a profit.

The second variety of inducement gift is what I will call *solicitation gifts*. These gifts are linked to a request for a return gift that is nevertheless entirely voluntary. The origin of the name is the case of the beggar's flower: a gift given by a beggar that is then followed by a request for a return gift of money. In principle, the return gift is optional, but, if one accepts the flower, reciprocation may be strongly expected by the giver and the recipient may experience strong criticism from the giver if a return gift is not made. Such cases approach quite closely to the principle of reciprocity, despite being nominally free, and one clear reason for this is that the beggar's flowers are a limited resource. Whether the beggar has bought the flower, grown it, or picked it from the roadside, there is some cost to the beggar in replenishing their supply, so they need to ensure that they achieve a reasonably high rate of reciprocation. When potential recipients are aware of these expectations, accepting the flower is more or less a signal of intent to reciprocate.

Solicitation gifts depend in part for their effectiveness on the cultural associations they invoke: the sense discussed earlier in which gifts are signs of mutual commitment, and the expectation of fair reciprocity that is built into some types of giving. Such associations can be exploited in a variety of commercial contexts to provoke returns to the original giver that carry the outward form of market exchange (unlike the return gift to the beggar) and yet are motivated in part not by the purchaser's need for the thing purchased, but by a sense of normative obligation to the seller.

In the digital economy, the virtually costless nature of digital gifts changes the dynamic of solicitation gifts radically. When the digital gift is effectively free (at least at the margin) to the giver as well as the recipient, the giver can afford to give away vast numbers of gifts even if the rate of reciprocation is extremely low. In such circumstances, it is not necessary to pressure the recipient for a return and there can be a much stronger sense in which the return is voluntary for the original recipient. This is a practice that has mushroomed recently in the smartphone app market[8] (though it has roots in the PC shareware movement). Many software apps are available from the app markets in two forms: a free form and a paid form. Nominally, the paid form may be superior in some way – the 'freemium' business model (Anderson 2009, 26–27), but in practice the free version is often very close in functionality to the paid version – it may, for example, do everything that the paid version does but include a start-up screen encouraging the user to upgrade to the paid version, or it may be identical to the paid version except that advertisements are displayed on certain screens. Another feature of these apps is that even the paid versions are remarkably cheap – perhaps a twentieth or a fiftieth of the price of a console game.

In cases where the paid version is markedly superior to the free version, we may regard the free version as a marketing gift, designed to induce the recipient to purchase the paid version. But in cases where the paid version is very similar to the free version, why do users upgrade? No doubt there are many reasons, but one is simply the feeling that the suppliers of the app *deserve* a reward for providing something that we experience as having significant use value. Such feelings are encouraged, though fairly subtly on the whole, by introductory messages from the developers and by occasional comments by other users. For a purer case of this phenomenon, consider the launch of the album *In Rainbows* by Radiohead: "Rather than release its seventh album into stores as usual, the band released it online with the request that you pay as much or as little as you wanted. Some chose to pay nothing … while others paid more than $20. Overall, the average price was $6" (Anderson 2009, 153).

The return gift in these cases is itself a further free gift, but it is one that is motivated by a sense of the justice of paying something for what we have received. These are not reciprocal gifts in the sense that reciprocation is *required* by either gift in the sequence, yet they do share something of the spirit of reciprocity.

Let me call the third variety of inducement gift *loaded gifts*. These are gifts whose acceptance or use automatically entails a return gift that is in a sense hidden, or at least an implicit rather than an explicit element of the process. A prime contemporary example of this is Google Search. When a user searches the web using Google, the search results that are returned are a gift from Google, a service that has value to the recipient but for which there is no charge. Yet at the same time, the user returns two implicit gifts to Google: the gift of their attention, and the gift of information about their interests, in the form of the search terms that they have entered. Google in turn frequently makes use of these gifts to present advertising to the user, using the information supplied by the user to identify which adverts would be most relevant to the user's current interests. At this point, Google has not yet realised any value from the user's gift, but if the user then clicks on one of the ads, Google collects a commission from the advertiser.[9] This is what Anderson calls a "three party market" (Anderson 2009, 24–25) and, in some respects, the basic structure is similar to advertising in conventional media: the media publisher sells the attention of its readers to advertisers, thus generating a commercial transaction from that attention. One of the things that makes Google different from most conventional publishers (though not all)[10] is that the reader is acquired by giving a gift: in this case, free search results.

One might doubt whether Google's search results are really a gift at all, or perhaps a form of exchange. And are these search results, if they are a gift, a form of free giving – a gift that entails no obligation to reciprocate – or a form of reciprocal giving, since there is an element of reciprocation built into the nature of the process? It is tempting to think of Google Search as a mix of gift and exchange – a particularly clear example of the "entanglement" of the gift and commodity forms stressed by Fuchs (Fuchs 2008, 171, 185), or of what Lawrence Lessig calls "hybrid economies" (Lessig 2008, ch. 7).

Such hybrids are becoming increasingly important, but they do not rest on a single model of interaction between commerce and community; many such forms are possible, and they will continue to coexist with purer forms of the commerce and community models. These many forms of digital gifts and digital hybrid economies reinforce an argument that has been made particularly effectively by the feminist geographer J. K. Gibson-Graham: that the economy we occupy is not straightforwardly or overwhelmingly a capitalist (or commercial) one, but already a radically diverse economy (Gibson-Graham 2006). The new forms that are emerging in the digital economy simply increase that existing diversity.

## Conclusion

This paper has deployed examples of digital giving practices to support a series of interlinked arguments about the relations between commerce, community, and giving itself. Perhaps the most striking conclusion is that different giving practices stand in radically different relations to these phenomena. Consider community: contributions to Facebook help to sustain and extend existing offline communities; contributions to Wikipedia develop a virtual community that includes the givers but not the receivers; and Google's gifts of search results do not develop a community at all. Digital giving cannot be simplistically identified with *community* as if there were some simple, consistent, and universal relation between the two. Consider commerce: Wikipedia is a commerce-free environment; Facebook provides a space for individuals to share freely with each other, yet is provided for profit and disfigured by commercial advertising; while inducement gifts are given purely in order to generate linked commercial transactions. Digital giving cannot be simplistically separated from commerce, as if the two were utterly antagonistic, and yet some forms of giving offer real alternatives to commodity exchange as a form of organising our provisioning and thus our economy. And in some of these spaces, giving is implicated in both community and commerce, which coexist, overlap, and interact.

One reason for focusing on *digital* giving is to unsettle the common assumption that giving is in some way a pre-modern activity. Robert Garnett has argued that we must "undo the modernist separation of economic science from economic anthropology – to recognize that a market-based economy is characterized by the very 'premodern' qualities commonly ascribed to gift economies such as thick sociality, complex networks of interlocking obligations, and temporal separations of outlay and return" (Garnett 2010, 127). Garnett rightly problematises the assumption that such qualities are pre-modern with his scare quotes but I would also wish to move beyond the related assumption that it is only anthropology, with its focus on predominantly non-modern economies, to which economics needs to connect. Contemporary giving is not the same as non-modern giving; contemporary community is not the same as non-modern community; and it is the contemporary forms of these that economics needs to come to terms with. The commerce/community binary is above all a device for excusing economists from engagement with the thick sociality of actual economic practice, as Garnett suggests, and to my mind, this demands a thorough engagement with the *sociology* of economic life as well as with the lessons of anthropology. There is more than one modernist disciplinary wall that must come crashing down if we are to recognise the fully social, complexly determined, and culturally specific nature of commodity exchange as well as of the gift economy.

Rejecting the dualism of commerce and community is just one step towards a wider recognition that both are intensely social, that both are diverse, and that the mainstream tradition of understanding the economy as a set of highly stylised "markets" in which faceless optimising rational actors interact briefly at the moment of exchange is utterly inadequate for the explanation of any part of the economy.

## Acknowledgements

I would like to acknowledge the many ways in which my colleagues have contributed to the process of constructing this argument. These include, but are not limited to, conversations with Robert Garnett, Paul Lewis, Karen O'Reilly, and Balihar Sanghera, and the many useful questions and comments made in response to my presentations on giving at events in Moscow, Newport, London, York, and Nottingham during 2012–13.

## Notes

1. For related arguments, see, for example, Gibson-Graham (2006) and Negru (2010).
2. The primary exception is websites that only allow access on a paid basis, whether pay-per-view or through a subscription. Content provided on this basis is not a gift but a commodity.
3. I thank Dave Beer for making this point in a seminar at the University of York on 5 June 2013.
4. I have criticised the tendency of Mauss and his followers to see the gift economy as so firmly oriented to reciprocity that it becomes little more than an alternative form of exchange (Elder-Vass 2014a). Nevertheless, reciprocity does play a significant role in *some* giving practices.
5. This paragraph is based largely on material from O'Sullivan (2009) and Reagle (2010).
6. For more on open-source software as a form of gift economy, see Elder-Vass (2014b), upon which much of this section is based.
7. At the time of writing, many of these games are delivered through Facebook.
8. *App* is another word for a computer program or piece of software, usually used to refer to a program that can be used on a smartphone. I follow usual practice here in calling the sites from which apps can be acquired *markets*, although the term is thoroughly inappropriate when the apps are free.
9. This business model is explained thoroughly by Battelle (2005, ch. 5–7) and Levy (2011: part 2).
10. Free newspapers have become increasingly common in recent years.

## References

Alexa.com. 2013. "Top 500 Global Sites." http://www.alexa.com/topsites, accessed 16 July 2013.

Anderson, Chris. 2009. *Free: The Future of a Radical Price*. New York: Random House.

Anderson-Gott, Morten, Gheorghita Ghinea, and Bendik Bygstad. 2011. "Why Do Commercial Companies Contribute to Open Source Software?" *International Journal of Information Management* 32: 106–117.
Barbrook, Richard. 2005 [1998]. "The Hi-Tech Gift Economy." *First Monday*. http://firstmonday.org/htbin/cgiwrap/bin/ojs/index.php/fm/article/view/1517/1432, accessed 3 January 2012.
Battelle, John. 2005. *The Search*. London: Nicholas Brealey.
Benkler, Yochai. 2002. "Coase's Penguin, or, Linux and *The Nature of the Firm*." *Yale Law Journal* 112: 369–446.
Benkler, Yochai. 2013. "Practical Anarchism." *Politics and Society* 41: 213–251.
Berry, David. 2008. *Copy, Rip, Burn*. London: Pluto.
Boulding, Kenneth E. 1973. *The Economy of Love and Fear*. Belmont, CA: Wadsworth.
Boulding, Kenneth E. 1986. "What Went Wrong with Economics?" *American Economist* 30: 5–12.
Cheshire, Tom. 2012. "Test. Test. Test." *Wired UK* 01 (12): 132–139.
Corbet, Jonathan, Greg Kroah-Hartman, and Amanda McPherson. 2012. *Linux Kernel Development*. The Linux Foundation.
Danby, Colin. 2002. "The Curse of the Modern: A Post-Keynesian Critique of the Gift/Exchange Dichotomy." *Research in Economic Anthropology* 21: 13–42.
Dugger, William M. 1996. "Redefining Economics: From Market Allocation to Social Provisioning." In *Political Economy for the 21st Century*, edited by C. J. Whalen, 31–43. New York: M.E. Sharpe.
Elder-Vass, Dave. 2014a. "Free Gifts: Beyond Exchangism." Unpublished paper, available from author.
Elder-Vass, Dave. 2014b. "The Moral Economy of Digital Gifts." Unpublished paper, available from author.
Ellison, Nicole B., Charles Steinfield, and Cliff Lampe. 2007. "The Benefits of Facebook 'Friends.'" *Journal of Computer-Mediated Communication* 12: 1143–1168.
Forte, Andrea, Vanessa Larco, and Amy Bruckman. 2009. "Decentralization in Wikipedia Governance." *Journal of Management Information Systems* 26: 49–72.
Fuchs, Christian. 2008. *Internet and Society*. New York: Routledge.
Garnett, Robert F. 2007. "Philanthropy, Economy, and Human Betterment." *Conversations on Philanthropy* IV: 13–35.
Garnett, Robert F. 2010. "Philanthropy and the Invisible Hand." In *Accepting the Invisible Hand*, edited by M. D. White, 111–138. New York: Palgrave.
Gibson-Graham, J. K. 2006. *The End of Capitalism (As We Knew It)*. Minneapolis, MN: University of Minnesota Press.
Godbout, Jacques and Alain Caillé. 1998. *The World of the Gift*. Montreal: McGill-Queen's University Press.
Gruchy, Allan G. 1987. *The Reconstruction of Economics*. Westport, CT: Greenwood Press.
ITU. 2013. *The World in 2013: ICT Facts and Figures*. Geneva: International Telecommunication Union.
Lerner, Josh and Jean Tirole. 2002. "Some Simple Economics of Open Source." *Journal of Industrial Economics* 50: 197–234.
Lessig, Lawrence. 2008. *Remix*. New York: Penguin. http://archive.org/details/LawrenceLessigRemix, accessed 16 Sep 2013.
Levy, Steven. 2011. *In the Plex*. New York: Simon & Schuster.

Linux Foundation. 2012. "How Linux is built." https://www.youtube.com/watch?v=yVpbFMhOAwE, also available at http://www.linuxfoundation.org/, accessed 12 March 2013.

Lumpkin, G. T. and Gregory G. Dess. 2004. "E-Business Strategies and Internet Business Models." *Organizational Dynamics* 33: 161–173.

McEntee, Kevin. 2010. "Why We Use and Contribute to Open Source Software: Netflix." http://techblog.netflix.com/2010/12/why-we-use-and-contribute-to-open.html, accessed 12 March 2013.

Marx, Karl. 1978 [1844]. "Economic and Philosophical Manuscripts of 1844." In *The Marx-Engels Reader*, edited by R. C. Tucker, 66–125. New York: W. W. Norton.

Mauss, Marcel. 2002 [1950]. *The Gift*. London: Routledge.

Meier, Stephan. 2006. *A Survey of Economic Theories and Field Evidence on Pro-Social Behavior*, Working Papers: Federal Reserve Bank of Boston. http://www.bos.frb.org/economic/wp/wp2006/wp0606.pdf, accessed 16 Sep 2013.

Merriam-Webster. 2013. "Gemeinschaft – Definition and More." Merriam-Webster, http://www.merriam-webster.com/dictionary/gemeinschaft, accessed 5 August 2013.

Negru, Ioana. 2010. "The Plural Economy of Gifts and Markets." In *Economic Pluralism*, edited by R. F. Garnett, E. K. Olsen and M. Starr, 194–204. Abingdon: Routledge.

Nelson, Julie A. 1993. "The Study of Choice or the Study of Provisioning? Gender and the Definition of Economics." In *Beyond Economic Man*, edited by M. A. Ferber and J. A. Nelson, 23–36. Chicago: University of Chicago Press.

O'Sullivan, Dan. 2009. *Wikipedia: A New Community of Practice?* Farnham: Ashgate.

Reagle, John. 2010. *Good Faith Collaboration*. Cambridge, MA: MIT Press.

Red Hat. 2012. "The World's Leading Provider of Open Source Enterprise IT Products and Services." http://www.redhat.com/rhecm/rest-rhecm/jcr/repository/collaboration/jcr:system/jcr:versionStorage/fb405b2d0a0526023d2a9fc5eedad019/2/jcr:frozenNode/rh:resourceFile, accessed 12 March 2013.

Sayer, Andrew. 2004. "Moral Economy." Lancaster: Department of Sociology, Lancaster University. http://www.lancs.ac.uk/fass/sociology/papers/sayer-moral-economy.pdf, accessed 29 October 2009.

Shirky, Clay. 2009. *Here Comes Everybody*. London: Penguin.

Stallman, Richard. 2010. *Free Software, Free Society*. Boston, MA: GNU Press.

Tönnies, Ferdinand. 2003 [1887]. *Community and Society*. Mineola, NY: Dover.

Weber, Steve. 2004. *The Success of Open Source*. Cambridge, MA: Harvard University Press.

# 15 Classical liberalism and the firm
## A troubled relationship

*David Ellerman*

## Introduction

Richard Cornuelle has forcefully raised an issue that has been rather neglected in libertarian, Austrian, or market-process economics, namely that "lacking any analytical device but market theory" ([1965] 1993, 186), the market-based approach has trouble giving a satisfactory account of social associative action or even an account of what goes on inside firms. The lacunae in the Austrian approach are shared with the new institutional economics of neoclassical economic theory: "A fundamental feature of the new institutional economics is that it retains the centrality of markets and exchanges. All phenomena are to be explained translating them into (or deriving them from) market transactions based upon negotiated contracts, for example, in which employers become 'principals' and employees become 'agents'" (Simon 1991, 26–27).

Cornuelle was writing at the time when the socialist experiments of the twentieth century were collapsing. This was widely seen as a historical verification of the Austrian critiques of a socialist economy in favor of a market economy, and, more broadly, the critiques of planned organizations (*taxis*) in favor of spontaneous orders (*cosmos*). This leaves a big problem; accounting for the "visible hand" of the organizations that are so important in, if not characteristic of, modern industrialized market economy.

> As the dust settles on the ruins of the socialist epoch, a second crippling deficiency of libertarian thought is becoming more visible and embarrassing. The economic methodology that the Russians have lately found unworkable still governs the internal affairs of firms in capitalist and socialist countries alike. An economy presumably works best if it is not administered from the top; a factory presumably works best if it is.
> 
> (Cornuelle 1991, 3)

The overall topic of this volume is the relationship between commerce and community in various settings, with the focus in this paper on the firm. The analysis will use a number of polarities involving contrasting Weberian ideal types. In addition to the overarching contrast between commerce and community, there are the polarities of markets and/or firms, extrinsic and/or intrinsic motivations, exit and/or voice, and the legal roles of employee and/or member in a firm. Polarities are analytical tools. Their use does not imply the assumption that everything must fit on one end or the other of the polarity. It should be recognized at the outset that real-world cases will almost always involve some mixture of the ideal types – in contrast to more "idealized" intellectual models. But that recognition should not be taken as a license for the homogenizing thinking that just presents everything as a mixture so that "all cows are gray" and thus there are only different shades of gray.

## Markets in the firm

Herbert Simon has perhaps done the most to integrate organizational analysis into neoclassical economics and has even argued that the "economies of modern industrialized society can more appropriately be labeled organizational economies than market economies. Thus, even market-driven capitalist economies need a theory of organizations as much as they need a theory of markets" (Simon 1991, 42).

Our representatives of the Austrian treatment of the firm, Cowen and Parker, agree that "Simon correctly recognises that the modern market economy is an organisational economy" (1997, 14, fn. 4). Moreover, Cowen and Parker agree with the lack of any serious theory of the firm in the neo-classical theory.

> That the neo-classical "theory of the firm" is not a theory of the firm at all but rather a theory of perfectly competitive markets, is now well recognised. In this theory the firm is a 'black box' or void in which inputs are (somehow) frictionlessly converted into outputs. The theory does not address how these inputs are converted and under what decision-making process; instead, market participants react automatically and reliably to all price signals.
>
> (76)

This criticism is supposed to be addressed by the "new institutional economics" (e.g., North 1990 or Furubotn and Richter 1998). But Simon's as well as Cornuelle's criticism was not simply that the neoclassical or Austrian theory fell short, but that the theory relied on essentially one analytical device, namely "market theory," where all "phenomena are to be explained translating them into (or deriving them from) market transactions based upon negotiated contracts" (Simon 1991, 26). Hence, in Cowen and Parker's survey and restatement of the Austrian view of the firm, one would expect some new analytical device. But as the name, *Markets in the Firm*, of their booklet indicates, the focus is still on markets.

Wherein, then, does the Austrian theory of the firm (or, at least, in Cowen and Parker's treatment) or the neoclassical theory fall short? We consider three basic problems: (1) the implicitly assumed universal efficacy of extrinsic (usually pecuniary) incentives, (2) the contrast between the institutional logic of exit, exemplified by arms-length markets, and the logic of commitment, loyalty, and voice, exemplified by organizations, and (3) the assumed compatibility of the standard firm organized on the "legal relationship normally called that of 'master and servant' or 'employer and employee'" (Coase 1937, 403) with the underlying principle of classical liberalism "that individuals are the ultimate *sovereigns* in matters of social organization …" (Buchanan 1999, 288).

## The assumed universal efficacy of extrinsic motivation

Paraphrasing J. L. Austin, one is "tempted to see the overestimation of external motivation as an occupational disease of economists – if it were not their occupation" (Ellerman 2005, 27).[1] Indeed, if pecuniary motivation was so efficacious, then the "management problem" in firms, schools, and other organizations would be a rather simple problem in "human engineering" and solved long ago.

> Although economic rewards play an important part in securing adherence to organizational goals and management authority, they are limited in their effectiveness. Organizations would be far less effective systems than they actually are if such rewards were the only means, or even the principal means, of motivation available. In fact, observation of behavior in organizations reveals other powerful motivations that induce employees to accept organizational goals and authority as bases for their actions.
> (Simon 1991, 34)

Simon goes on to explain how the new institutional economics fails to take these non-pecuniary motivations into account, and his remarks apply as well to Cowen and Parker, who do not differ from the new institutional economists in this regard. "The attempts of the new institutional economics to explain organizational behavior solely in terms of agency, asymmetric information, transaction costs, opportunism, and other concepts drawn from neo-classical economics ignore key organizational mechanisms like authority, identification, and coordination, and hence are seriously incomplete" (42). For instance, "identification" raises the question of community. How can a company get its staff to identify with and be loyal to the company as a workplace community engaged in a cooperative activity? This is no problem for Cowen and Parker;

just set up bonuses to reward loyalty, teamwork, cooperation, and identification!

> People respond to the carrot as well as the stick and hence most firms appreciate the value of cultivating loyalty and high performance from their employees by using appropriate incentives.
>
> (1997, 47)

> (B)usinesses should use bonuses for different purposes, including … cementing loyalty to institutions, including customs that benefit the firm as a whole …
>
> (Ibid., 66)

> Collectively-based bonuses, which distribute some percentage of aggregate profits to managers and workers in the form of salary, encourage teamwork, co-operation, and identification with the goals of the firm.
>
> (Ibid., 67–68[2])

However, any "loyalty" bought with extrinsic incentives would not be genuine but would only be "loyalty-displaying behavior," and similarly for "teamwork, co-operation, and identification."

Another example of this breezy economistic treatment of the serious problems of management systems and organizational design is the treatment of Deming and Japanese management methods in general – "Our approach to the market and organisations has been influenced by the management philosophy of W. Edward Deming …" (Cowen and Parker 1997, 17), and to get those results, it is a matter of the "explicit application of market-based economic theory to managerial problems" (17). Yet Deming recommends precisely the *opposite* of this advice based on "market-based economic theory." Deming recommends abolishing "incentive pay and pay based on performance" (1994, 28), e.g., to pay sales people by salary rather than by commission, and to replace a system based on monitoring and quality bonuses with a system using trust based on self-esteem and pride in the quality of one's work.

Unfortunately, it is not simply a matter of extrinsic incentives being less effective than intrinsic motivation to motivate higher-order tasks and more subtle organizational virtues. Salient extrinsic incentives can override, crowd out, and atrophy the subtler forms of internal motivation. This type of phenomenon is sometimes called the "cost of rewards" and there is a large literature on it in social psychology (Lepper and Greene 1978), management theory (Follett [1926] 1992), and even in political theory (Grant 2012) – in addition to references in these and other fields (Ellerman 2005).

Moreover, the manipulation of staff by external incentives poses a threat to autonomy and self-efficacy and creates a form of reactance or "push-back" due to the human source of the pressure. This dependence on other human wills is familiar in the classical liberal notions of oppression or coercion. "'The nature of things does not madden us, only ill will does,' said Rousseau. The criterion of oppression is the part that I believe to be played by other human beings, directly or indirectly, with or without the intention of doing so, in frustrating my wishes" (Berlin 1969, 123). "In this sense 'freedom' refers solely to a relation of men to other men, and the only infringement of it is coercion by men. This means, in particular, that the range of physical possibilities from which a person can choose at a given moment has no direct relevance to freedom" (Hayek 1960, 12).

In a similar vein, Mary Parker Follett emphasized the "law of the situation"; "Our job is not how to get people to obey orders, but how to devise methods by which we can best *discover* the order integral to a particular situation" (Follett [1926] 1992, 70). Then it is the impersonal situation, not the boss, that requires something to be done. This is part of the old classical liberal idea of the rule of law, not of men. It also might be compared to Michael Polanyi's description of end-independence in a spontaneous order: "The actions of such individuals are said to be free, for they are not determined by any *specific* command, whether of a superior or of a public authority; the compulsion to which they are subject is impersonal and general" (1951, 159). The idea goes back to Rousseau's theme that it is not coercion if the "necessity [is] in things, never in the caprice of men" ([1762] 1979, 91).

The more subtle intrinsic motivations cannot be manipulated by the salient pecuniary incentives under the control of managers; it is more a question of identity, culture, and community in the workplace (see Dore 1987 about the company-as-community). The over-reliance on extrinsic incentives becomes particularly pernicious when managers try to "train" staff members to respond to their manipulable incentives – but that only buys a few short-term effects on the "behavior" market (which may, however, trigger manager bonuses). This not only leaves the sources of staff commitment and effort untapped, but probably does longer-term damage to the firm through all the costs of rewards and reactance effects.

## Market logic of exit vs. organizational logic of commitment, loyalty, and voice

We have seen that both neoclassical theory and Austrian economics focus on markets, and even when they try to analyze the firm, the primary effort is to find "Markets in the Firm." So far, we have focused on the inadequacy of essentially identifying motivation with extrinsic and pecuniary motivation. But markets and organizations also have different institutional logics.

Albert Hirschman has made the well-known distinction between two logics: the logic of exit exemplified by markets, and the logic of commitment, loyalty, and voice that might be exemplified by organizations. The point is that we now have a whole "science of economics" where the market logic of exit is the only logic. "The economist tends naturally to think that his mechanism (exit) is far more efficient and is in fact the only one to be taken seriously" (1970, 16).

There is an almost automatic reflex that mobility, liquidity, and the absence of frictions are to be preferred over immobility, illiquidity, and the presence of frictions. But the point is that in organizations where the logic of commitment comes into play, then the mobility, liquidity, and frictionless nature of markets may well have negative effects.

Moreover, Keynes was much concerned with the adverse effects of stock market liquidity (i.e., ease of exit) on real investment and enterprise. Real investment in productive enterprise should be stable, and the management of enterprise requires a long-term commitment in order for the application of "intelligence to defeat the forces of time and ignorance of the future" (1936, 157). But when investment is securitized as a marketable asset on the stock exchange, then it "is as though a farmer, having tapped his barometer after breakfast, could decide to remove his capital from the farming business between 10 and 11 in the morning and reconsider whether he should return to it later in the week" (151). The stock exchange panders to the "fetish of liquidity" and thus continually undermines the bonds of long-term commitment that are so important to problem-solving and productive enterprise. Keynes, of course, wrote this long before today's ultra-short-termism with quarterly reports, stock options, computerized trading, and the constant churning of mergers and acquisitions activity.

One way to make these points using a language of efficiency is to contrast the notion of X-efficiency (Leibenstein 1966) with the usual notion of allocative efficiency. Since the principal "factor" with variable characteristics is the people working in an enterprise, the "X" in X-efficiency is essentially "effort" (see Ellerman 2005). In the post-war era, the large Japanese firms have perhaps gone the furthest to develop the organizational logic of commitment and effort-efficiency and to contrast it with the market logic of exit. For instance, to one trained to think in terms of the logic of exit, any immobilities, frictions, rigidities, or barriers to exit would just seem inefficient and irrational. But Japanese economists have evoked the example of useful barriers to exit as in the maritime practice of a captain being expected to go down with his ship.

> The way in which underpayment of wages in the early years of service and the acquisition of firm-specific skills create barriers to exit is obvious. These exit barriers perform several important functions for

the firm as an organizational entity. The first is the incentive function whereby the interests of the firm and the interests of the individual are linked. Unable easily to exit, people can only protect their interests by working to ensure that the firm prospers. ... The interlinking of interests means that when crisis looms, efforts are redoubled. The option of leaving the sinking ship is not freely available, either to the crew or the captain.

(Kagono and Kobayashi 1994, 94)

Barriers to exit can enhance identification, loyalty, and commitment, and thus effort-efficiency. As scholars of Japanese industry put it:

Many of the investments made by employees and the assets they have developed over the long term are realizable only within the firm, and these assets would not be fully appreciated in the market place. Hence there is greater commitment, though not necessarily happy, satisfied commitment. Where the "logic of exit" prevails, however, the freedom of exit of uncommitted shareholders, and the insecurity thereby induced in managers by frequent takeovers, has a knock-on effect to reduce commitment, as much on the part of senior managers as on rank and file employees.

(Dore and Whittaker 1994, 9)

In Japan, the takeover market is virtually non-existent and "It's not just that the labour market for executive talent is imperfect: over large areas of the economy it just does not exist" (Dore 1994, 380).

We have already noted how engineering market-based incentives falls far short of developing the more subtle organizational virtues of loyalty, commitment, and identification. The company-as-community uses the alternative "internal" or non-market solution of developing a corporate culture[3] of mutual commitment and cooperation that leads to a high-level virtuous circle. This cooperative culture is feasible because the managers and workers see themselves as members of a commitment-based community and will reap the joint fruits of their cooperative efforts.

One logic or the other ramifies through all the aspects and structures of a firm. Sometimes a firm organized on the logic of exit is stereotyped as the "American firm," and a firm organized on the logic of commitment is the "Japanese firm" or "J-firm" (Aoki 1988). We will summarize and compare in Table 15.1 some of the ways that the two logics (essentially *Gesellschaft* and *Gemeinschaft*) affect firm structure.[4]

The two advanced industrial countries that have done the most to restructure in the direction of the firm-as-community are the two countries that lost World War II, so the old owners of the major companies were removed, and what eventually emerged from that freedom to restructure ownership was some corporate form with greater de facto internal

Table 15.1 Two firms

| | Firm based on logic of exit, a.k.a. firm as nexus of market contracts | Firm based on logic of commitment, a.k.a. firm-as-community |
|---|---|---|
| Efficiency | Allocative efficiency: moving resources to the use with the best return (high mobility). | X-efficiency: getting the best return from resources in the given uses (low mobility). |
| Change strategy | Replace what you have with something better. Problem is to improve choice among options with fixed characteristics. | Transform what you have into something better. Problem is the transformation of given option to improve its characteristics. |
| Source of flexibility and change | Exit (change takes place through entry and exit from the organization). Rather flight than fight. Error leads to replacement. | Voice (change takes place by transformation within organization). Rather fight than flight. Error leads to learning. |
| Labor mobility | High mobility so changes take place primarily by hiring workers embodying new knowledge. | Low mobility so changes take place primarily by workers learning new knowledge and skills. |
| Contractual relationships | Arms-length. | Relational. |
| Shareholder interest | Maximization of company profit (assumption that shareholders are normally unrelated to company). | Shareholding often representative of business relationships, the latter being the primary economic interest. Little attention to unrelated floating shareholders. |
| Model of supplier relationships | Competition between standardized producers with feedback through the market. | Cooperation with a small number of suppliers to continuously improve product through non-market feedback. |
| Stability in relationships | Low trust relationships ⇒ highly explicit contracts with competitive arms-length exit-oriented relationships so no need to invest in building trust ⇒ low trust relationships. | High trust relationships ⇒ incomplete relational contracts with voice-oriented relationships requiring investment in building trust ⇒ high trust relationships. |
| Job definition | Extensively specified job definition to limit opportunism since there is little commitment. | Job flexibility and low monitoring based on worker commitment to company. |

Table 15.1 (cont.)

|  | Firm based on logic of exit, a.k.a. firm as nexus of market contracts | Firm based on logic of commitment, a.k.a. firm-as-community |
|---|---|---|
| **Worker motivation** | Individual pecuniary self-interest (non-cooperative strategy). | Members expected to identify with firm and shared interest (cooperative strategy). |
| **Organized worker representation** | Trade union (adversary relation based on workers versus company) – my jam or your jam. | Enterprise union (oppositional relation loyal to company) – our jam today or our jam tomorrow. |
| **Response to decline** | Reduce employment and other direct costs to maintain profits. | Maintain employment, reduce hours, and retrain workers for new product lines. |
| **Business ownership** | Stock market liquidity. Firm as "investment." | Illiquidity of closely held business. Firm as enterprise. |

ownership/membership. The Japanese idea of the company-as-community (Dore 1987), outlined in the table, is the basis for a fully competitive "employee-favouring" (as opposed to "shareholder-favouring") model. Germany has also developed more responsible and even "employee-favouring" forms of enterprise. The German institution of *Mitbestimmung* or codetermination is harder to imagine in the American-style corporation, which sees the people in the firm as the labor-suppliers in an arms-length market relationship ruled by the logic of exit (Dore 2000).

## Classical liberalism and the hard cases of voluntary alienation contracts

We have so far contrasted the firm-as-market-nexus with the firm-as-community from the viewpoint of motivation (extrinsic versus intrinsic) and efficiency (allocative versus effort-efficiency). We would be remiss if we didn't also examine the legal structure of a firm from the viewpoint of classical liberalism (broadly speaking). One cannot analyze a firm, say, a cotton-producing farm, as a community independently of whether it is legally structured as a slave plantation or a kibbutz.

As a description of the core of classical liberalism, we might take James Buchanan's statement of the principles of normative individualism.

> The justificatory foundation for a liberal social order lies, in my understanding, in the normative premise that individuals are the ultimate

*sovereigns* in matters of social organization, that individuals are the beings who are entitled to choose the organizational-institutional structures under which they will live. In accordance with this premise, the legitimacy of social-organizational structures is to be judged against the voluntary agreement of those who are to live or are living under the arrangements that are judged. The central premise of *individuals as sovereigns* does allow for delegation of decision-making authority to agents, so long as it remains understood that individuals remain as *principals*. The premise denies legitimacy to all social-organizational arrangements that negate the role of individuals as either sovereigns or as principals.

(1999, 288)

Buchanan contrasts the view of Plato (and Aristotle), who saw a natural inequality where certain adult persons were considered of diminished capacity, if not as human instruments, with the view of Adam Smith, who began with the classical liberal assumption of natural equality before the law. "To Plato there are natural slaves and natural masters, with the consequences that follow for social organization, be it economic or political. To Adam Smith, by contrast, who is in this as in other aspects the archetype classical liberal, the philosopher and the porter are natural equals with observed differences readily explainable by culture and choice" (2005, 67). Thus a liberal social order would rule out any assumption of people of a certain race or sex as being of diminished legal capacity on account of their race or sex. That takes care of the easy cases, but what about the *hard cases* where, for whatever reason, adults of full capacity voluntarily agree to a contractual arrangement where they take on the *legal* role of a person of diminished capacity or even a human instrument (even though they are, of course, still de facto a person of full capacity)?

A historically recent case of such a legal institution would be the coverture marriage contract wherein an adult woman of full capacity voluntarily agrees to give up her independent legal personality in favor of that of her husband. As Blackstone put it:

> By marriage, the husband and wife are one person in law: that is, the very being or legal existence of the woman is suspended during the marriage, or at least is incorporated and consolidated into that of the husband; under whose wing, protection, and cover, she performs everything; and is therefore called in our law-French, a feme covert, and is said to be under the protection and influence of her husband, her baron, or lord; and her condition during her marriage is called her coverture.
> ([1765] 1959, 83; section on "Husband and Wife")

The *feme covert* could only make contracts or acquire property as an agent for her husband; she was not a sovereign or principal in her own name.

Thus the coverture marriage contract was clearly in violation of Buchanan's sovereign-or-principal statement of classical liberalism. But it was also a *voluntary* contract – unless one wants to argue that all marriages up to the beginning of the twentieth century in the liberal democracies (and many marriages elsewhere in the world today) were "not really voluntary" (an embarrassing attempt to dodge the hard case).

The coverture marriage contract was by no means the first example of a legal institution based on a voluntary contract for a fully capacitated adult to take on the *legal* role of a person of diminished or no capacity. For instance, only the crudest defenses of slavery, even in antiquity, were based on some notion of natural inequality (as in Plato and Aristotle). In the *Institutes* of Justinian, ancient Roman law provided three legal ways to become a slave, and all were explicitly or implicitly contractual. "Slaves either are born or become so. They are born so when their mother is a slave; they become so either by the law of nations, that is, by captivity, or by the civil law, as when a free person, above the age of twenty, suffers himself to be sold, that he may share the price given for him" (Lib. I, Tit. III, 4).

In addition to the third means of outright contractual slavery, the other two means were also seen as having aspects of contract. A person born of a slave mother and raised using the master's food, clothing, and shelter was considered as being in a perpetual servitude contract to trade a lifetime of labor for these and future provisions. Manumission was an early repayment or cancellation of that debt. In the early modern era, Thomas Hobbes clearly saw a "covenant" in the ancient practice of allowing prisoners of war to plea bargain their death penalty into a lifetime of servitude. It would be a "hard choice," but a voluntary one given the circumstances.

> And this dominion is then acquired to the victor when the vanquished, to avoid the present stroke of death, covenants either in express words or by other sufficient signs of the will that, so long as his life and the liberty of his body is allowed him, the victor shall have the use thereof at his pleasure. … It is not, therefore, the victory that gives the right of dominion over the vanquished but his own covenant.
> ([1651] 1958, Bk. II, Chap. 20)

Thus *all* of the three legal means of becoming a slave in Roman law had explicit or implicit contractual interpretations.

The other major hard case is the undemocratic constitution wherein people voluntarily give up and alienate their rights of self-governance to a sovereign person or group who rules in their own name (i.e., not as a delegate or representative of the people). Again we may start with Roman law. The sovereignty of the Roman emperor was seen as being founded on a contract of rulership enacted by the Roman people. The Roman jurist Ulpian gave the classic and oft-quoted statement of this view in the *Institutes* of Justinian:

> Whatever has pleased the prince has the force of law, since the Roman people by the *lex regia* enacted concerning his *imperium*, have yielded up to him all their power and authority.
> (Lib. I, Tit. II, 6, quoted in Corwin 1955, 4)

Hobbes made the best-known attempt to use this calculus of consent to found non-democratic government on the consent of the governed. Without an overarching power to hold people in awe, life would be a constant war of all against all. To prevent this state of chaos and strife, men should join together and voluntarily alienate and transfer the right of self-government to a person or body of persons as the sovereign. This *pactum subjectionis* would be a "covenant of every man with every man, in such manner as if every man should say to every man, I authorize and give up my right of governing myself to this man, or to this assembly of men, on this condition, that you give up your right to him and authorize all his actions in like manner" (Hobbes [1651] 1958, 142).

The American constitutional scholar, Edward S. Corwin, noted that questions arose even in the Middle Ages about the nature of the *lex regia*. "During the Middle Ages the question was much debated whether the *lex regia* effected an absolute alienation (*translatio*) of the legislative power to the Emperor, or was a revocable delegation (*cessio*). The champions of popular sovereignty at the end of this period, like Marsiglio of Padua in his *Defensor Pacis*, took the latter view" (1955, 4, fn. 8). It is precisely this question of *translatio* or *concessio* – alienation or delegation of the right of government in the contract – that is the key question, not consent versus coercion. Consent is on both sides of that alienation (*translatio*) versus delegation (*concessio*) framing of the question. The alienation version of the contract became a sophisticated tacit contract defense of non-democratic government wherever the latter existed as a settled condition. And the delegation version of the contract became the foundation for liberal democratic theory.

The German legal thinker Otto Gierke was also quite clear about the alienation-vs.-delegation question.

> This dispute also reaches far back into the Middle Ages. It first took a strictly juristic form in the dispute … as to the legal nature of the ancient "*translatio imperii*" from the Roman people to the Princeps. One school explained this as a definitive and irrevocable alienation of power, the other as a mere concession of its use and exercise. … On the one hand from the people's abdication the most absolute sovereignty of the prince might be deduced. … On the other hand the assumption of a mere "*concessio imperii*" led to the doctrine of popular sovereignty.
> (Gierke 1966, 93–94)

In view of this history of apology for autocracy based on consent, the distinction between coercion and government based on the "consent of the governed" was *not* the key to liberal democratic theory. The real debate was *within* the calculus of consent, and was between the alienation (*translatio*) and delegation (*concessio*) versions of the basic social or political constitution. Late medieval thinkers such as Marsilius of Padua (1275–1342) and Bartolus of Saxoferrato (1314–57) laid some of the foundations for modern democratic theory in the distinction between consent that establishes a relation of delegation and trusteeship versus consent to an alienation of authority.

> The theory of popular sovereignty developed by Marsiglio (Marsilius) and Bartolus was destined to play a major role in shaping the most radical version of early modern constitutionalism. Already they are prepared to argue that sovereignty lies with the people, that they only delegate and never alienate it, and thus that no legitimate ruler can ever enjoy a higher status than that of an official appointed by, and capable of being dismissed by, his own subjects.
> (Skinner 1978, vol. I, 65)

To secure these rights for democratic theory, the task was to develop arguments that there was something inherently invalid in the alienation or *translatio* contracts, and thus to decide always in favor of "delegation of decision-making authority to agents, so long as it remains understood that individuals remain as *principals*. The premise denies legitimacy to all social-organizational arrangements that negate the role of individuals as either sovereigns or as principals" (Buchanan 1999, 288).[5]

## Inalienable rights theory: treating the hard cases

With some anticipations by the Stoics, the notion of inalienable rights descends through the Scottish and German Enlightenments from the Protestant Reformation's notion of the inalienability of conscience. As the great English liberal, Lord John Morley,[6] put it:

> To what quarter in the large historic firmament can we turn our eyes with such certainty of being stirred and elevated, of thinking better of human life and the worth of those who have been most deeply penetrated by its seriousness, as to the annals of the intrepid spirits whom the protestant doctrine of indefeasible personal responsibility brought to the front in Germany in the sixteenth century, and in England and Scotland in the seventeenth?
> ([1874] 1928, 91–92)

Secular authorities may try to compel belief but they can only buy some external conformity on the market for behaviors. "For no matter how much they fret and fume, they cannot do more than make people obey them by word or deed; the heart they cannot constrain, though they wear themselves out trying. For the proverb is true, 'Thoughts are free.' Why then would they constrain people to believe from the heart, when they see that it is impossible?" (Luther [1523] 1942, 316).

Martin Luther was explicit about the de facto element; it was "impossible" to "constrain people to believe from the heart." In Morley's terms, their "personal responsibility" for their beliefs is "indefeasible."

> Furthermore, every man is responsible for his own faith, and he must see it for himself that he believes rightly. As little as another can go to hell or heaven for me, so little can he believe or disbelieve for me; and as little as he can open or shut heaven or hell for me, so little can he drive me to faith or unbelief. Since, then, belief or unbelief is a matter of every one's conscience, and since this is no lessening of the secular power, the latter should be content and attend to its own affairs and permit men to believe one thing or another, as they are able and willing, and constrain no one by force.
> 
> (Luther [1523] 1942, 316)

In the Scottish Enlightenment, the notion of the inalienability of conscience was translated into the doctrine of inalienable rights by Francis Hutcheson, Adam Smith's teacher and predecessor in the Chair of Moral Philosophy in Glasgow. Although intimated in earlier works, the inalienability argument is best developed in Hutcheson's influential *A System of Moral Philosophy*.

> Our rights are either *alienable*, or *unalienable*. The former are known by these two characters jointly, that the translation of them to others can be made effectually, and that some interest of society, or individuals consistently with it, may frequently require such translations. Thus our right to our goods and labours is naturally alienable. But where either the translation cannot be made with any effect, or where no good in human life requires it, the right is unalienable, and cannot be justly claimed by any other but the person originally possessing it.
> 
> (1755, 261)

Hutcheson contrasts de facto alienable goods where "the translation of them to others can be made effectually" (like the services of a shovel) with factually inalienable faculties where "the translation cannot be made with any effect." For instance, we may employ a shovel for our own purposes *or* we may alienate and transfer it to someone else to use it for their purposes. But the same cannot be said of our selves. We may act in our own name as "sovereigns" (to use Buchanan's phrase) but we cannot in fact alienate or transfer the employment of our selves to another person or persons, and thus, where "the translation cannot be made with any effect," the right is inalienable. Between persons, there is no alienation, only Buchanan's delegation where the person remains the principal.

In the American Declaration of Independence, "Jefferson took his division of rights into alienable and unalienable from Hutcheson, who made the distinction popular and important" (Wills 1979, 213). It is this theory of inalienable rights, which descends from the Reformation through the Scottish Enlightenment, that finally allowed classical liberal democratic thought to deal with the hard cases. A *pactum subjectionis* would pretend to alienate that which is inalienable; a democratic constitution would only sanction a delegation of powers to the people's representatives; the people remain the principals. And when slavery was abolished, it was both involuntary and voluntary slavery that was abolished. As the economist Paul Samuelson put it in his economics primer: "Since slavery was abolished, human earning power is forbidden by law to be capitalized. A man is not even free to sell himself: he must *rent* himself at a wage" (Samuelson 1976, 52, his italics).

## Classical liberalism and the employment firm

Samuelson brings us back around to the original question of the compatibility of hard-case classical liberalism, i.e., the Smith-inspired classical liberalism together with the Hutcheson-inspired theory of inalienable rights, with the legal structure of the conventional firm based on the "legal relationship normally called that of 'master and servant' or 'employer and employee'" (Coase 1937, 403).

A conflict immediately arises with hard-case classical liberalism, which rules out alienation contracts where "the translation cannot be made with any effect." We may employ a shovel and be de facto responsible for the results, and then we can rent out the shovel to another person and turn the shovel over to them to be employed by them and they will be responsible for the results. But the same "translation cannot be made with any effect" when the rental concept is applied to persons.

A person factually cannot stop "employing" themselves and voluntarily turn over that employment to another person as their "employer," who would then be responsible for the results. At most, the "employee" voluntarily cooperates with the "employer" by following the latter's instructions, but then they are both inexorably co-responsible for the results. This is, of course, legally recognized when the joint activity is criminous so the legal authorities have grounds to intervene to see who is de facto responsible so that the legal or *de jure* responsibility can be imputed accordingly. "All who participate in a crime with a guilty intent are liable to punishment. A master and servant who so participate in a crime are liable criminally, not because they are master and servant, but because they jointly carried out a criminal venture and are both criminous" (Batt 1967, 612). Since it can hardly be argued that "employees" suddenly become de facto non-responsible instruments when their actions are not criminous, exactly the same joint de facto responsibility for the results of the joint activity with the working employer holds in the conventional firm.

It is the reaction of the legal system that changes when no crime or tort is involved. Then there is no occasion to hold a trial to see who is de facto responsible. It is only a matter of the voluntary employment contract being fulfilled on both sides. On the employer's side, it is a matter of the payment of wages and the fulfillment of any other contractual obligations. But on the side of the rented persons, since the "employment" of the employees cannot in fact be transferred (unlike the rental of a thing like a shovel), the legal authorities in the human rental system accept a surrogate performance as "fulfilling" the contract, namely obeying the employer (even though the legal authorities are well aware from the hired criminal example that "obeying the employer" does not effect any translation of de facto responsible agency from employees to employer). Then with both sides of the employment contract "fulfilled" (and the same for the other input contracts), the employer has paid all the costs of the used-up inputs to production and thus has the undivided legal claim on the product that is produced.

Thus by violating the inalienable rights part of classical liberalism, i.e., by validating the human rental contract (for non-criminous activities), the employment system legally authorizes the type of firm where the people working in the firm are inexorably de facto co-responsible for the (negative and positive) results of their voluntary activities, and yet the "employees" have zero legal responsibility for the negative results (the input liabilities and thus costs of the used-up inputs) and zero legal ownership of the positive results (the assets that are the produced outputs). Thus fully capacitated de facto responsible human beings end up, by virtue of the voluntary contract for the "renting" or "employing" of persons, in the legal role of having zero legal responsibility for the negative or positive results of their inexorably co-responsible actions within the scope of their "employment," i.e., in the legal role of a rented instrument like a shovel.[7] A legal institution where fully capacitated adults have zero legal responsibility for the positive and negative results of their actions is a canonical violation of the "Kantian ethical precept" (Buchanan 2005, 15) that persons are always to be treated as ends in themselves and never simply as a means or as a thing.

The underlying juridical norm of imputing *de jure* responsibility in accordance with de facto responsibility when applied to private property rights gives the legitimation basis for the appropriation of property rights, namely people getting the fruits of their labor (which applies equally well to bearing the negative fruits of their labor by getting the legal or *de jure* responsibility for those liabilities). The mismatch between de facto and *de jure* responsibility in the employment firm shows that such a firm is based on violating the legitimate basis for appropriating private property; private property being the basis for the classical liberal order defining the natural system of liberty. As the Austrian economist, Friedrich von Wieser put it:

> The judge ... who, in his narrowly-defined task, is only concerned with the *legal imputation*, confines himself to the discovery of the legally responsible factor, – that person, in fact, who is threatened with the legal punishment. On him will rightly be laid the whole burden of the consequences, although he could never by himself alone – without instruments and all the other conditions – have committed the crime. The imputation takes for granted physical causality. ...
>
> If it is the moral imputation that is in question, then certainly no one but the labourer could be named. Land and capital have no merit that they bring forth fruit; they are dead tools in the hand of man; and the man is responsible for the use he makes of them.
>
> ([1889] 1930, 76–79)

Thus in a firm implementing the juridical principle of responsibility, the people working in the firm would have the "whole burden of the consequences," including the legal liabilities for using the "dead tools" of land and capital as well as the legal ownership of the positive fruits of their jointly co-responsible labor.

The Conservative diplomat and public servant Lord Eustace Percy summarized the situation well.

> Here is the most urgent challenge to political invention ever offered to the jurist and the statesman. The human association which in fact produces and distributes wealth, the association of workmen, managers, technicians and directors, is not an association recognised by the law. The association which the law does recognise – the association of shareholders, creditors and directors – is incapable of production and is not expected by the law to perform these functions. We have to give law to the real association and withdraw meaningless privilege from the imaginary one.
>
> (Percy 1944, 38, quoted in Goyder 1961, 57)

Such a firm, where the legal members are the people working in the firm, would thus implement the responsibility principle at the foundation of private property and would generalize the self-"employment" of the family farm or proprietorship to larger firms to make up the productive sector in the natural system of liberty implied by the deeper principles of classical liberalism. Examples of such firms include industrial cooperatives such as the Mondragon system of cooperatives in the Basque region of Spain (Whyte and Whyte 1991).

The same conclusions are obtained if we follow the governance principles of classical liberalism based on being a sovereign or principal, never just a subject (as in the *pactum subjectionis* that transforms people from citizens into subjects). "The postulate of natural equality carries with it the requirement that genuine classical liberals adhere to democratic principles of governance; political equality as a necessary norm makes us all small 'd' democrats" (Buchanan 2005, 69). Governance in the liberal democratic order cannot be based on an alienation contract but only on a delegation contract where the people remain the principals. "The premise denies legitimacy to all social-organizational arrangements that negate the role of individuals as either sovereigns or as principals" (1999, 288).

Here again we see that the social-organizational arrangement of the employment firm directly violates the principles of the classical liberal democratic order. The employment contract is a contract of alienation, not delegation. The employer is not the delegate or representative of the employees; the employer manages the workplace in his own name, not in the name of the people being managed as the ultimate principals.

Thus the legal structure of the firm that is consistent with classical liberal democratic theory is again the firm where the legal members or citizens of the firm are the people working in the firm (who are the ones being managed), and where the managerial power exercised by the managers is delegated to them from the workplace-citizens who are the principals in accordance with the sovereigns-or-principals doctrine of classical liberalism (see Ellerman 1992). A firm of member-owners would better exemplify the idea of the firm-as-community than a firm of employees.

## Concluding remarks

The results of applying the hard-case principles of classical liberal democratic theory to the human rental firm are, in a certain sense, shocking – just like the application of the principles of the American Founding Fathers to the "peculiar institution" of their day. We find it hard to understand how the Founding Fathers could, for the most part, avoid this issue, which was clear even at the time to other observers.[8] But when there is such a clash between the espoused principles and the dominant institution of the day, then there surely is almost complete cognitive dissonance.

At the outset, we noted that both neoclassical and Austrian economics indeed have something of a blind spot concerning the firm. The strength of both types of economics is the theory of the market. We also saw at the outset two other reasons for the neglect of the firm. Intrinsic motivation plays an important motivational role in any type of work that goes beyond the exercise of brute muscle power. Yet the market operates primarily on the basis of extrinsic motivation, so a market-oriented economics is inclined either to essentially ignore firms as human organizations (e.g., to model them as "production functions") or to primarily view the "markets in the firm."

In the Hirschmanian contrast between the logic of exit and the logic of loyalty, commitment, and voice, markets tend to operate by the former logic and organizations by the latter logic. While markets can foster "sweet commerce," firms can under the appropriate circumstances (e.g., with member-owners rather than employees) be a source of community, a community second only to the family and typically stronger than the residence-based community of political life.

When the underlying hard-case principles of classical liberal economic and political theory are applied to the typical employment firm, then we found the surprising results that such a firm directly violates those principles. Any hint of this discord leads to the cognitive dissonance that results in a certain incuriosity in applying the deeper (hard-case) liberal principles to the firm, a reluctance that echoes the Founding Fathers' reticence in applying their principles of inalienable rights to slavery. The relationship of classical liberalism to the (employment) firm is much troubled indeed.

## Notes

1 See Ellerman (2005), *Helping People Help Themselves,* where the shortcomings of the overestimation of extrinsic motivation are treated at book length – so only the main points can be made here.
2 Cowen and Parker have no doubt heard of the "1/N problem" but ignore it here.
3 On the question of the shortcomings of economic theory and game theory in dealing with the culture of organizations, see Kreps (1990).
4 See Dore (1987) for a similar table.
5 See Skinner (1978) for an extensive history of the alienation-vs.-delegation theme.
6 Friedrich Hayek lamented that Morley's liberalism was not better appreciated in his own country: "Men like Lord Morley ... who were then admired in the world at large as outstanding examples of the political wisdom of liberal England, are to the present generation largely obsolete Victorians" ([1944] 2001, 188).
7 It should be noted that the size of the rental payments or wages plays no role whatsoever in this analysis. Moreover, the analysis of the human rental contract, like the analysis of the coverture marriage contract, assumes the contract is perfectly voluntary.
8 As Dr. Johnson famously asked: "how is it that we hear the loudest yelps for liberty among the drivers of negroes?" ([1775] 1913).

## References

Aoki, Masahiko. 1988. *Information, Incentives, and Bargaining in the Japanese Economy.* New York: Cambridge University Press.
Batt, Francis. 1967. *The Law of Master and Servant.* London: Pitman.
Berlin, Isaiah. 1969. *Four Essays on Liberty.* Oxford: Oxford University Press.
Blackstone, William. [1765] 1959. *Ehrlich's Blackstone.* New York: Capricorn.

Buchanan, James M. 1999. *The Logical Foundations of Constitutional Liberty: The Collected Works of James M. Buchanan*, vol. I. Indianapolis, IN: Liberty Fund.

Buchanan, James M. 2005. *Why I, Too, Am Not a Conservative: The Normative Vision of Classical Liberalism*. Cheltenham: Edward Elgar.

Coase, Ronald. H. 1937. "The Nature of the Firm." *Economica* IV (Nov.): 386–405.

Cornuelle, Richard C. 1991. "New Work for Invisible Hands." *Times Literary Supplement* 5 April 1991: 1–4.

Cornuelle, Richard C. [1965] 1993. *Reclaiming the American Dream: The Role of Private Individuals and Voluntary Associations*. New Brunswick, NJ: Transaction Publishers.

Corwin, Edward S. 1955. *The "Higher Law" Background of American Constitutional Law*. Ithaca, NY: Cornell University Press.

Cowen, Tyler and David Parker. 1997. *Markets in the Firm: A Market-Process Approach to Management*. London: IEA.

Deming, W. Edwards. 1994. *The New Economics for Industry, Government, Education*. Cambridge. MA: MIT Center for Advanced Engineering.

Dore, Ronald. 1987. *Taking Japan Seriously*. Stanford, CA: Stanford University Press.

Dore, Ronald. 1994. "Equality–Efficiency Trade-offs: Japanese Perceptions and Choices." In *The Japanese Firm: The Sources of Competitive Strength*, edited by Masahiko Aoki and Ronald Dore, 379–391. Oxford: Oxford University Press.

Dore, Ronald. 2000. *Stock Market Capitalism: Welfare Capitalism. Japan and Germany versus the Anglo-Saxons*. Oxford: Oxford University Press.

Dore, Ronald and Hugh Whittaker. 1994. "Introduction." In *Business Enterprise in Japan: Views of Leading Japanese Economists*, edited by Kenichi Imai and Ryutaro Komiya, 1–15. Cambridge, MA: MIT Press.

Ellerman, David. 1992. *Property & Contract in Economics: The Case for Economic Democracy*. Cambridge, MA: Blackwell.

Ellerman, David. 2005. *Helping People Help Themselves: From the World Bank to an Alternative Philosophy of Development Assistance*. Ann Arbor, MI: University of Michigan Press.

Follett, Mary Parker. [1926] 1992. "The Giving of Orders." In *Classics of Public Administration*, edited by Jay Shafritz and Albert Hyde, 66–74. Pacific Grove, CA: Brooks/Cole.

Furubotn, Eirik and Rudolf Richter. 1998. *Institutions and Economic Theory: The Contributions of the New Institutional Economics*. Ann Arbor, MI: University of Michigan Press.

Gierke, Otto von. 1966. *The Development of Political Theory*. Translated by B. Freyd. New York: Howard Fertig.

Goyder, George. 1961. *The Responsible Company*. Oxford: Basil Blackwell.

Grant, Ruth W. 2012. *Strings Attached: Untangling the Ethics of Incentives*. Princeton, NJ: Princeton University Press.

Hayek, Friedrich A. 1960. *The Constitution of Liberty*. Chicago: University of Chicago Press.

Hayek, Friedrich A. [1944] 2001. *The Road to Serfdom*. London: Routledge Classics.

Hirschman, Albert O. 1970. *Exit, Voice, and Loyalty: Responses to Decline in Firms, Organizations, and States*. Cambridge, MA: Harvard University Press.

Hobbes, Thomas. [1651] 1958. *Leviathan*. Indianapolis, IN: Bobbs-Merrill.

Hutcheson, Francis. 1755. *A System of Moral Philosophy*. London.

Johnson, Samuel. [1775] 1913. "Taxation No Tyranny: An Answer to the Resolutions and Address of the American Congress." In *The Works of Samuel Johnson*, vol. XIV, 93–144. Troy, NY: Pafraets.
Kagono, Tadao and Takao Kobayashi. 1994. "The Provision of Resources and Barriers to Exit." In *Business Enterprise in Japan*, edited by Kenichi Imai and Ryutaro Komiya, 89–102. Cambridge, MA: MIT Press.
Keynes, John Maynard. 1936. *The General Theory of Employment, Interest, and Money*. New York: Harcourt, Brace & World.
Kreps, David. 1990. "Corporate Culture and Economic Theory." In *Perspectives on Positive Political Economy*, edited by James Alt and Kenneth Shepsle, 90–143. Cambridge: Cambridge University Press.
Leibenstein, Harvey. 1966. "Allocative Efficiency versus X-Efficiency." *American Economic Review* 56 (3): 392–415.
Lepper, Mark R. and David Greene, eds. 1978. *The Hidden Costs of Rewards: New Perspectives on the Psychology of Human Motivation*. Hillsdale, NJ: Erlbaum.
Luther, Martin. [1523] 1942. "Concerning Secular Authority." In *Readings in Political Philosophy*, edited by Francis W. Coker, 306–329. New York: Macmillan.
Morley, John. [1874] 1928. *On Compromise*. London: Macmillan.
North, Douglass C. 1990. *Institutions, Institutional Change and Economic Performance*. Cambridge: Cambridge University Press.
Percy, Eustace. 1944. *The Unknown State: 16th Riddell Memorial Lectures*. London: Oxford University Press.
Polanyi, Michael. 1951. *The Logic of Liberty*. Chicago: University of Chicago Press.
Rousseau, Jean-Jacques. [1762] 1979. *Emile or On Education*. Edited by Allan Bloom. New York: Basic Books.
Samuelson, Paul. 1976. *Economics*. New York: McGraw-Hill.
Simon, Herbert. 1991. "Organizations and Markets." *Journal of Economic Perspectives* 5 (2 Spring): 25–44.
Skinner, Quentin. 1978. *The Foundations of Modern Political Thought*, vol. I: The Renaissance. Cambridge: Cambridge University Press.
Whyte, William Foote and Kathleen King Whyte. 1991. *Making Mondragon*. Ithaca, NY: ILR Press.
Wieser, Friedrich von. [1889] 1930. *Natural Value*. Translated by C.A. Malloch. New York: Stechert and Company.
Wills, Garry. 1979. *Inventing America*. New York: Vintage Books.

# 16 Comment: Exploring the liminal spaces between commerce and community

*Martha A. Starr*

The three essays by Colin Danby, Dave Elder-Vass, and David Ellerman raise varied and interesting perspectives on interrelationships between commerce and community, both as they are represented in economic thought and as they manifest themselves in the real world. "Commerce" is the market economy, where firms compete in pursuit of profits, and all relationships between people – in their roles as business owners, managers, employees, shareholders, consumers, inventors, traders, borrowers, lenders, and so forth – are driven by commercial logic. These kinds of relationships are of course what economists have traditionally been trained to study; they represent only a subset of activities of production, consumption, investment, and exchange, which also take place in the home, in community groups, in private charitable and nonprofit organizations, and in public institutions, otherwise known as "community." As much as hardline neoclassical economists (like Gary Becker) sought to explain all economic activity – in or out of the business sector – as reflecting similar processes of individuals maximizing utility, it is obvious that relationships within families, social networks, community groups, private voluntary associations, and other types of organizations and entities, have logics to them that are not satisfyingly described as outgrowths of self-interested optimization. These three essays ask whether we can or should draw bright lines between "commerce" and "community," and whether they should be understood as operating according to distinct or overlapping types of logic.

Colin Danby rejects the idea of a dichotomy between commerce and community, arguing instead that we "inhabit a single, mixed, underdetermined, and often confusing world in which people and institutions attempt to structure an uncertain future in overlapping and sometimes contradictory ways." In Danby's view, we should resist the temptation to split the world into a business sector coldly focused on profits and a community sector that warmly revolves around caring and giving, as one finds both pro-sociality in the business sector and ruthless self-interested behaviors in the community (think the Ku Klux Klan). In the absence of a natural divide between commerce and community, Danby calls for a "robustly subjective social ontology" that takes into account the dynamic, overlapping, contradictory forms of entanglements between people and aggregations of people, where their own understandings of how these work both shape the characteristics of the communities in which they participate and are shaped by them. This strikes me as a promising approach, especially for studying entities like social enterprises and social businesses that operate in the borders between commerce and community (see, for example, Borgaza and Defourny 2001). Practically speaking, I worry that it is difficult to study people's self-understandings (what they are, where they came from, how they matter, how they change over time) in ways that are rigorous and yield insights of broad-based interest; grounded theory may provide a good approach. Nevertheless, the idea of examining how people themselves understand similarities and differences between commerce and community seems a highly worthwhile project.

Turning to questions about how and why people relate to each other in spheres seemingly outside of market relations, Dave Elder-Vass's essay analyses the "digital gift": all the things people produce and contribute to each other via the internet, ranging from advice, humor and recipes, to Wikipedia entries, free apps, and open-source software. It is hard to understand this outpouring of activity via traditional economic theory, except for the observation that digital "givers" must get intrinsic satisfaction from giving, as they often have no idea to whom their gift may go. More richly, Elder-Vass points to Benkler's "pleasure of creation" (or one could also reference Veblen's "instinct of workmanship") as providing wells of motivation and interest for people's digital gifts. As Elder-Vass explains, digital communities have features that make them unusual compared to normal ones, as relationships in digital communities are typically contingent, anonymous (or based on a digital identity), and activity-specific, rather than repeated, personal, and spanning multiple social spheres. More broadly, digital gift-giving also challenges the simple dichotomy between commerce and community because these are private voluntary exchanges of ideas and work products, but are also arms-length.

I think Elder-Vass is spot-on in asking us to look closely at the emergence of digital communities and at patterns of activity and interaction among people within them. Particularly interesting may be communities that sprout up to create and maintain innovative voluntary, distributed-computing projects, such as the widely dispersed group that collectively runs the crypto-currency Bitcoin (see Brito and Castillo 2013). The rules and procedures governing Bitcoin rest on familiar business logics of optimization and incentives. But they also incorporate principles of autonomy, self-governance, open participation, transparency, and power that is broadly distributed across the network. As such, they contrast with – and aim to contest – traditional monetary institutions premised on opposite values. This echoes Danby's point that people's subjective understandings of where their activities fit within the spectrum of commerce and community relations have an importance of their own.

Finally, David Ellerman focuses on questions of commerce and community as they relate to the firm. He argues that both new institutional and Austrian economics have blind spots when it comes to analyzing modern firms, both because they overemphasize the role of market logic in explaining firms' behavior and because they pay no attention to the unacceptable ethics of that logic. In theorizing the various facets of business life, both approaches focus on the extrinsic motivations of business owners, managers, workers, shareholders, suppliers, etc. – that is, what they do to best extract gains from the opportunities present in their environment. Here Ellerman refers to the *logic of exit*: If workers are not well paid relative to other jobs they can take, they will quit; if owners can boost their wealth by shutting down the business and selling off its assets, they will; if an incumbent supplier renegotiating a contract demands a large price increase, the firm can opt not to renew; if customers of a local business have found the quality of its products to have fallen, they can go elsewhere. If abilities to exit provide constant pressures that firms must always navigate, then properly conceptualizing how they operate, survive, and thrive in view of these pressures must rest on understanding the exit logic.

However, an alternative would be to understand firms to be communities of workers, suppliers, managers, and customers driven by a *logic of commitment*, where they are not constantly looking at the exit to see whether they can do better elsewhere, but rather are engaged in sustained processes of learning, feedback, and cooperation within contexts of enduring organizations that fight to do well with what they have. This sort of model describes corporations in Germany and Japan, but not so much in the USA, where the exit logic dominates. But we should challenge the exit logic, Ellerman argues, because employment relationships based upon it are ethically unacceptable: they reduce people to the labor they sell and make it impossible for them to take full responsibility for the positive and negative outcomes of their actions. In this sense, full realization of the idea of the corporation as community would require the emergence of firms in which workers have full voice and a share in ownership.

While the three papers provide rich and interesting perspectives on commerce and community, one longs a bit for the firm foundations of old modernist approaches, where businesses were single-mindedly profit oriented; people were rich in their motivations and cared for their families, friends, co-workers, and communities; and government either propped up businesses or supported people, depending on your view. Admittedly, these sorts of simplifications are caricatures and leave too much room for vilifying businesses and romanticizing people. But I worry that, in acknowledging how much more complex the realities of commerce and community are, we may turn our attention away from the larger unfolding scene. The contemporary trend among corporations and other larger-scale entities is in fact towards prioritizing logics of optimization and exit, on the grounds that competition, uncertainties, scarcities of resources, etc., force organizations to continually track how they are doing relative to their objectives and to exercise exit options when performance falls short. To be sure, their objectives vary across sectors: maximizing profits in the private firm, maintaining balance between revenues and costs in the private nonprofit organization, or maximizing outcomes for "stakeholders" from available resources in the public domain. But in broad-based ways, cheap computing and big data have increasingly fostered real-time monitoring of employees, divisions, programs, products, ad campaigns, etc., and enabled constant discourse about what business units to launch or fold, which employees to promote or fire, what product lines to redesign or discontinue, etc. (see, for example, Economist Intelligence Unit 2012, Lohr 2013, or Mathews 2013). As Ellerman outlines, progression of this sort of logic inexorably crowds out possibilities of alternatives, like the cooperative ones he has worked to advance. In this sense, it is a source of concern that, if we fail to acknowledge how different core commercial values and rationales are from the alternatives, we miss opportunities to contest logics that run against social and individual goods.

## References

Borgaza, Carlo and Jacques Defourny, eds. 2001. *The Emergence of Social Enterprise.* London: Routledge.

Brito, Jerry and Andrea Castillo. 2013. "Bitcoin: A Primer for Policy Makers." Mercatus Center.

Economist Intelligence Unit. 2012. "Big Data: Lessons from the Leaders." London: *The Economist*.

Lohr, Steve. 2013. "Big Data, Trying to Build Better Workers." *New York Times* (April 20).

Mathews, Amanda Wilde. 2013. "Hospitals Prescribe Big Data to Track Doctors at Work." *Wall Street Journal* (July 11).

# Part V
# Not by commerce alone

# 17 Reciprocity, calculation, and non-monetary exchange

*Steven Horwitz*

## Introduction

The standard textbook version of economics describes the allocation of limited means among unlimited wants as the central problem of economics. By contrast, a long-standing tradition in economics, including major twentieth-century figures such as Ludwig von Mises, F. A. Hayek, and James Buchanan, put *exchange* at the center of its vision of the discipline. All three thinkers made use of some version or another of the words "catallactics" (the science of exchange) or "catallaxy" (the nexus of market exchanges). For this tradition, markets were first and foremost about exchange, and exchange, particularly in the work of Buchanan, was also seen as at the core of other social processes such as politics. When the task of economics is reoriented away from questions of optimal allocation to questions about the role of exchange, a variety of new perspectives become available. With a catallactic view of economics, the set of institutions within which those exchanges take place becomes a central factor in both understanding the exchanges that occur and whether they are likely to enhance or detract from human well-being. A purely allocation-focused economics is unlikely to have the same concern with institutions as does an exchange-focused economics, and this point is evident in the near absence of institutional analysis in so much of modern economics.

Seeing economics as centrally about exchange also enables us to see economic ideas at work in non-monetary exchange contexts. For example, as more careful biological study has revealed, contrary to Adam Smith's claim that only humans have a propensity to truck, barter, and exchange, we now know that other animals do engage in forms of exchange. We also know that exchange and other forms of reciprocity more generally are important features of socializing processes in humans and other animals. Economists have long understood the way in which the division of labor and exchange create interdependencies among nations as well as individuals. Upon introducing the word "catallaxy" to describe the market order, Hayek wrote that the Greek root of that word meant "not only 'to exchange,' but also 'to admit into the community' and 'to change from enemy to friend'" (1977, 108). Exchange is not just a way we obtain goods and services in anonymous markets, but can also be a way we create and sustain communities, both intimate and anonymous.

The various forms of reciprocity and exchange that are found in the animal world are often found as strategies for group survival in the face of severe resource constraints. For human communities, non-market exchange and reciprocity are important ways in which humans improve their lives and the lives of others. Although they are not sufficient to facilitate the economic coordination and prosperity we associate with what Smith and Hayek called "the Great Society," non-market forms of exchange and production not only improve life in the Great Society, they have also been crucial tools for survival in difficult times. In what follows, I offer some theoretical underpinnings for understanding these issues of how exchange and reciprocity play out in intimate and anonymous orders through an extended discussion of Carol Stack's (1974) classic ethnography of poor, urban, African-American families in the late 1960s, *All Our Kin*. Looking at Stack's findings through the eyes of a more "catallactic" approach to economics suggests that exchange alone cannot be the distinguishing characteristic between more intimate communities and more anonymous market orders. Non-monetary exchange happens within the face-to-face world of small communities, and various forms of non-monetary exchange, reciprocity, and gift giving are important parts of the anonymous Great Society as well. Stack's work helps us see the complexities of the ways in which multiple forms of exchange in various contexts are at play in the Great Society.

## Reciprocity and exchange in nature

For decades the accepted view of animal behavior in an evolutionary context was to always think in terms of individual creatures struggling to survive against the pressures of the environment. Even as our understanding of genetics and natural selection improved, the focus was still on the level of the individual animal itself. In more recent years, the view of evolutionary biologists has broadened in two different directions. They have thought more completely about the ways in which animal behavior is really not about the survival of individual animals per se, but rather the passing on of genetic material. When seen in terms of ensuring the survival of genetic information, some previous behavior that did not seem to make sense in terms of individual survival was made intelligible in terms of the survival of parental genes. At the same time, and more important for the argument here, theories of group selection were developed as ways to account for what seemed to be altruistic behavior in some animals. Altruistic behavior was often reinterpreted as being an element of some form of reciprocity in animal societies, the result of which was to enhance the survival of the group. With the group better able to survive, the survival of any one member was that much more likely, suggesting that what looked like pure altruism was in fact reciprocal exchange that was good for both the individual animal and the group as a whole from an evolutionary perspective.

Biologists who investigate reciprocity in animals distinguish between two forms of apparently altruistic behavior: kin selection and reciprocity. The difference is the degree to which those engaged in the altruism are related. So when we see parents favoring their own offspring, or those of a close relative, we are observing kin selection. Such behavior has a more obvious evolutionary explanation as it clearly promotes the survival of the parental genes, even if it might be harmful to the parent as an individual animal. Parents who give up food for their offspring are accepting the risk to their own survival to promote that of their, perhaps numerous, children. The net result is positive from an evolutionary standpoint. Reciprocity, by contrast, is altruistic behavior that shows no favoritism to one's kin. It can include kin, but they are not treated any differently from non-kin. These latter forms of behavior are particularly interesting as they point toward the importance of group survival in the larger picture of the evolutionary process.

For forms of reciprocity in the animal kingdom to work, biologists have argued that several criteria have to be met, with three being of particular importance. One is that the role of donor and recipient must frequently reverse (i.e., there must be true reciprocity in pairs of animals). Second, "the short-term benefits to the recipient are greater than the costs to the donor" (Wilkinson 1990, 77). Finally, donors must be able to identify cheaters and have some mechanism for excluding them. In the language of economics, there must be an enforcement mechanism to eliminate free riders. As I will argue later, these three criteria are equally applicable to reciprocal non-monetary exchange processes among humans. Together, these three criteria distinguish reciprocal exchange from pure altruism. The first two together indicate that there is exchange taking place, though with the two halves being temporally distinct. If roles reverse and the benefits in each act are to one and not the other, over time we have mutually beneficial patterns of exchange. The third criterion helps to ensure that this is exchange and not altruism by identifying contributors and excluding free riders.

One example illustrating this in the animal kingdom is the practice of reciprocal food exchange among vampire bats (Wilkinson 1990). Vampire bats cannot make it through two consecutive nights without feeding. After about 60 hours, their lives will be seriously threatened without being able to ingest blood. The bats rely on larger animals as feeding sources and often those animals are able to fend them off before they can get a sufficient meal. As a result, some percentage of bats in any group of bats will go without food on any given night. Though some bats are more effective feeders than others, and young bats are often less capable, no bat is completely safe from the threat of starvation. Every bat therefore has an "interest" in making sure that the group as a whole has enough food. Bat societies that did not develop a way to share food would be at an evolutionary disadvantage as compared to ones that did, as such sharing would make it more likely that more bats would survive and procreate.

Vampire bats have developed a fairly sophisticated system of doing precisely that. Bats that have successful feedings will regurgitate the blood they have ingested as a way to feed other bats in the colony, and not just members of their kin. As Wilkinson (1990, 76) points out, sharing with non-kin is comparatively rare in the animal kingdom, so researchers had to be careful to demonstrate this was actually reciprocal exchange and not just kin selection. Wilkinson and his research team were able to do so through a complex process of observation, tagging, and tracking. They found that bats did indeed regurgitate for non-relatives, even preferring them sometimes. They also found that they preferred other bats who were frequent roost mates, with both kin and non-kin being recipients of regurgitated food. Blood sharing rarely took place among complete strangers and, in fact, tended to occur in a kind of "buddy system" of defined pairs. As Wilkinson points out, this is a "strong indication that their roles reverse on a regular basis" (80). In addition, they found that when sharing did take place, it almost always involved regurgitating for a bat with less than 24 hours to live. This suggests that bats were discriminating by the odds of dying, not by kin relation.

Wilkinson's work could not definitively establish that the bats had an exclusion mechanism, but he did point to several pieces of evidence that are highly suggestive. First, the buddy system observation indicates that the bats must have some way of identifying one another, which is a necessary piece of having some exclusion process. The belief is that the social grooming that bats do is what enables them to identify each other, and the mutual grooming takes on patterns with respect to known bats versus strangers that are similar to the regurgitation. Finally, researchers believe that bats can identify each other through the unique auditory signals they emit. With the ability to identify individual members of the group, and the fact that the reciprocal food exchanges have proven to have survival value, the implication is that there must be some process by which free riders are excluded, even if it has not been observed in natural settings.

The vampire bats and other, though limited, examples among animals suggest that reciprocity can play a key role in helping animal communities survive when resources are not sufficient to assure that all can have enough to eat. This sort of reciprocity can be seen, in Matt Ridley's (1998) words, as part of the "origins of virtue" in humans. As we learned the benefits of such exchange as a way to ensure survival, we also became accustomed to norms of sharing and reciprocity. Exchange continues to play a central role in human societies, but with one important difference: we exchange with both people we know and who are geographically proximate, and with anonymous other humans who can live thousands of miles away. Intimate and anonymous social orders involve different types of exchange with different consequences.

## Orders, organizations, and the role of economic calculation

Although exchange is ubiquitous among humans, how it takes place and its social consequences differ depending on the particular context. There are many ways one could carve up the social world to explore such differences, but for my purposes the relevant way is to distinguish between "intimate" and "anonymous" social orders. Exchange takes place in both, but intimate orders are most often characterized by forms of barter and relatively simple forms of implicit credit, along with very personal, informal forms of norm enforcement. By contrast, more anonymous orders are largely characterized by more geographically extensive, money-based indirect exchange, and more complex forms of explicit credit. Enforcement is not informal, but rather through formal legal processes.

The work of F. A. Hayek gives us a vocabulary for making these sorts of distinctions. Hayek is most known for his development of the concept of spontaneous order, which is the idea that many human practices and institutions evolved as the result of human action, but not intentional human design. That is, institutions such as money or language were not consciously invented by any one person, but are instead the products of processes of undesigned social evolution. Because of his emphasis on these forms of undesigned order, people frequently interpret him as saying that everything is a spontaneous order. In fact, Hayek's work is clear that not all social institutions are spontaneous orders and that a good number are better described as "intentional" or "made" orders, or what he sometimes terms "organizations."[1] The relationship between the distinction between undesigned orders and intentional organizations and that between intimate and anonymous orders is a complex one, and is at the heart of understanding the issues in front of us.

The distinction between spontaneous orders and intentional or instrumental organizations is important because the spontaneous order of the "Great Society" (or what Adam Smith called the "commercial society") comprises various instrumental organizations such as households/families, firms, and other made orders. These smaller made orders are characterized by strong elements of intentional planning, centralized direction of resources, and a unified goal. Their interaction within the broader social order, however, is unplanned and uncentralized. Individuals in the modern world must constantly move back and forth among a variety of social institutions and contexts, some of which more closely resemble made orders while others are spontaneous orders. Hayek argues that the challenge this poses is that the structure and moral rules of the two kinds of order are very different, requiring that we both recognize those differences and know how to behave appropriately in the relevant institutional environment.

Although, as I will argue later, there are problems seeing the distinction between spontaneous orders and instrumental organizations as a pure dichotomy, we can still identify a number of criteria that distinguish one from the other. One such criterion is the degree of complexity an institution entails. Made orders are sufficiently simple that the person(s) at the top can survey the entire institution and can thus structure it to serve whatever specific purposes they wish, hence the idea of an "instrumental organization" (Hayek 1973, 38). This contrasts with spontaneous orders, such as the market or the even more extended order that Hayek calls the Great Society, which can be of any degree of complexity, are rule-based, have structures that may not be obvious, and serve no particular purpose. Instead they serve as general processes by which the individuals who participate in them can achieve their myriad specific purposes. For example, a firm has a very specific purpose, which is to maximize profits, whereas something like a language or a market has no specific purpose; rather each exists to serve whatever purposes those who make use of them might wish.

At the core of the difference between the two types of order therefore is a difference in the scope of discretion possessed by individual actors. In made orders, where there is a unified goal or purpose determined by those who made the order, those at the top have the ability to ensure that other individuals are engaged in the pursuit of the order's goal or purpose and not pursuing purposes of their own. Individuals who participate in made orders also understand that they do not have a wide scope of choice and must follow the commands or specific rules set down by those in charge. Consider the way that employees, soldiers, or athletes act within each of the made orders that define the institution of which they are a part. Firm managers can direct employees to one or the other part of the factory or a military commander can direct troops toward one objective or another, or a baseball manager can ask a player to sacrifice bunt in a particular situation. In none of these three situations do the individuals have the discretion to decide what to do other than on a very moment-to-moment basis. Such a structure is not incompatible with rules playing a role, though these rules will simply describe the proper procedures for engaging in a particular function or task. They are means to a specific end.

Spontaneous orders, by contrast, are structured by abstract rules that guide the behavior of the individuals and organizations that comprise them. Importantly, those rules are, as Hayek terms them, "ends-independent," which means that they enable individuals to pursue a multiplicity of ends, rather than being geared toward a specific, agreed-upon end, as in organizations. These rules are most often framed negatively, as in "do not steal" or "do not coerce others." Where framed positively, they are sufficiently abstract to permit them to serve a variety of purposes, e.g., "respect property and live up to contracts." In neither of those cases does the rule specify what is to be done with the property or what is being contracted for. Ends-independent rules simply indicate that *whatever ends one has, these are the rules one must follow to pursue them*, i.e., the rules are independent of the particular ends that people have. The advantage of such a system is that it does not require the agreement of the participants on the value of any particular ends. Instead, we only need to agree on a smaller number of general rules in order for all of us to pursue our own ends. Spontaneous ordering processes work best when we have a large number of people with differing ends and no common purpose.

In contrast, in cases where a group is small and homogeneous and has an agreed-upon specific purpose in mind, making use of a made order might be more appropriate:

> In any group of men of more than the smallest size, collaboration will always rest on both spontaneous order as well as on deliberate organization. There is no doubt that for many limited tasks organization is the most powerful method of effective coordination because it enables us to adapt the resulting order much more fully to our wishes.
> (Hayek 1973, 46)

For the numerous limited and specific tasks that occupy most of our days, instrumental organizations work better than spontaneous ones because we are able to consciously construct them to achieve the agreed-upon goals. It is when coordination *among* these organizations, each having different purposes, is necessary that we must rely on spontaneous ordering processes. The Great Society, in Hayek's view, is the spontaneous order that emerges from the mutual interaction of these deliberate organizations as each pursues its plans within the rules of the legal order.

This sharp distinction is useful for analytical purposes, but the real world presents us with complications. In general, within instrumental organizations, we tend to have fairly face-to-face relationships with other members and this provides a level of intimacy that allows us to be more able to determine what each other might know or might prefer. Finding agreement upon the ends and employing the intentionally cooperative (as opposed to rule-based) structures that often characterize made orders are much easier if individuals have some degree of familiarity with each other that results from the intimacy of repeated face-to-face contact. As a result, made orders are often built around belief systems or aspects of one's identity that make the common goals of the organization more obvious and easier to agree on, e.g., a church or an ethnicity-based service organization. For non-monetary forms of exchange to be effective, actors must know a fair deal about the preferences of others or have some other effective (non-monetary) way of calculating the benefits and costs of their action. The more intimate the order, the more possible this is.

The market and other complex adaptive social systems, by contrast, are fundamentally processes of anonymous interaction. We do not know the vast majority of the "others" with whom we interact in sufficient depth in the Great Society to be able to appeal to their love for us or their knowledge of us when trying to get them to act in the ways we desire. We must rely on, as Adam Smith ([1776] 1976, 18) put it, their "self-love" and get them to cooperate through exchange. For example, the rules of the market, and the other institutions that comprise it, enable people to interact and cooperate without needing to know very much detail about others. The very nature of monetary exchange on the market is premised on the abstraction (or in sociological terms, the "ideal type") of the "money user." Money's anonymity is key to extending the range of exchange from the barter of smaller, more homogeneous, intimate orders to the broader Great Society.[2]

In understanding the role that exchange plays in both intimate and anonymous orders, we need to address the question of how parties to the exchange assess the value of the objects of exchange. Actors need some way of calculating which exchanges are worth engaging in before the fact and then assessing whether the exchange was worth it after the fact. Actors can attempt to make use of their own subjective values, which is fine for simple bilateral exchanges. However, if goods are going to have some sort of publicly accessible value, what we might call, following Mises ([1912] 1980), their "objective exchange value," then there has to be some common denominator of value that all can recognize. For any complex set of transactions where the ultimate exchange involves multiple parties, all must be able to have some value they can access. In the marketplace of the anonymous Great Society, money prices serve this function, as every good exchanging against money enables goods to have a single price reckoned in terms of that money. Money prices are the objective exchange values that facilitate complex, multiparty exchanges. If we wish to extend the benefits of comparative advantage and exchange and the social cooperation they promote to the widest range of people possible, markets, money, and money prices are necessary.

In reciprocal exchanges in intimate orders, something has to substitute for the role played by money prices. If the community is homogeneous enough, the problem can be solved by everyone having similar assessments of the value of various goods and services. If we think about a group of close friends who occasionally care for each other's kids or invite the adults over to dinner, we can imagine them having a pretty good consensus on the value of those two activities, especially if they find themselves in similar life situations, such as all being dual-income households. A similar process might be at work in a larger, slightly less homogeneous group. Admittedly, these common community evaluations will be notably less precise than what can be attained through monetary exchange. However, they can still be more than sufficient for the kinds of reciprocal non-monetary exchanges that take place in more intimate orders, particularly if actors are not that concerned with the ability to precisely measure the degree of their "profit" and "loss." In more informal systems, common community assessments of the subjective value of goods and services can provide a rough and ready objective exchange value. Similar "balance keeping" is true of gift exchanges as well.

The prior argument indicates that some process of economic calculation must be available if people really wish to engage in reciprocal exchange. An intimate order greater than the size of a family will, again, need something that approximates the role of money prices. In the debate in the interwar years over whether a planned economy that lacked private property, exchange, and money prices could rationally allocate resources, Ludwig von Mises (1920) argued that private property, specifically in the means of production, was a necessary condition for economic coordination and rational resource allocation. Mises' key point was that without monetary exchange and money prices, there was no way for producers in any economy beyond the size of the household to determine which inputs to use to produce a given output, or which outputs to produce from a given set of inputs. Does this mean that *all* production in a monetary economy must require monetary exchange and money prices? As noted earlier, the extended order of the Great Society comprises a whole variety of smaller-scale intentional organizations in which various forms of production take place. Of particular interest in the context of thinking about community responses to poverty and disaster are the group of activities normally labeled "household production."

Household production encompasses all of the tasks necessary for a household to function. These include cooking, cleaning, doing laundry, caring for children, mowing the lawn, and so forth. As Mises recognized in the context of the debate over economic calculation, the head(s) of the household are able to survey all of the various means and ends and decide what ends to pursue and how best to pursue them without the need for money prices. What happens in households, which are often (though not always) co-extensive with the social institution of the family, is certainly a core part of the extended order of the Great Society. The anonymous parts of that extended order will not function if, for example, children are not sufficiently fed and well-raised. Even beyond kids, the other things done by households do not have perfect substitutes on the market. Finally, the role played by parents in socializing children into the norms of the extended order is one, I have argued (Horwitz 2005), for which there is no sufficiently close substitute.

If households are sufficiently simple such that the heads of household can directly solve the problem of resource allocation without recourse to money prices, the broader concept of "the community" is not as fortunate. Communities are characterized by more intimate knowledge of other residents than would be true of a large city or a whole nation. However, most communities are not "top-down" in the way that the ideal type of a made order is, and they are still governed by rules that give individuals a great deal of latitude. As a consequence, we tend to see within communities more actions that look like what a household or a firm might engage in as the increased personal knowledge of other members allows for more altruism or other forms of interaction that are normally not seen in the anonymous marketplace. Communities thereby challenge the strict dichotomy of intimate versus anonymous orders. Instead, communities are frequently defined by their members as having a history or symbols that generate a common identity, which in turn generates a sense of what has been called "collective intentionality" (Lewis 2009). This shared identity, along with the greater intimacy that communities tend to have, might explain why it is often easier, for example, to get people to donate time and money to local causes, particularly if they are to help known neighbors, than it is for national or international causes with more anonymous recipients.[3]

Communities therefore have a degree of complexity greater than that of households but not of the degree that characterizes the market or Great Society. As such it will be difficult, if not impossible, to allocate resources in a rational way without the assistance of what Mises (1920) terms "aids to the mind" such as money prices. If communities are going to attempt to allocate resources by some form of non-monetary exchange, they will have to develop some substitute for the money prices of the market. Those substitutes will not be as powerful and precise as money prices (and the calculation of budgets and profits and losses they make possible), but they might be sufficient for fairly effective resource allocation in reasonably intimate communities, and particularly in fairly limited contexts. In examining how communities attempt to allocate resources outside of formal, monetary exchange, we should be looking for these analogues of prices, profits, and losses to understand how such non-monetary exchange systems could be sustainable.

This discussion of households and communities has another important implication: these institutions make the anonymous/intimate and extended order/organization distinctions much less clear. Often framed as a continuum from intimate to anonymous, these distinctions might be better conceived of as a series of concentric circles.[4] At the center might be the individual, with the next circle being the household, followed by the community, followed by the full extended order.

This way of conceptualizing matters allows us to see two important things. The first is that this enables us to see how individual action ripples outward to the household, community, and Great Society. Within those ripples will be the potential for numerous unintended consequences, both good and bad, depending on the institutions that each circle comprises. The reach of our intentions is distinctly local. Second is the way in which institutions, rules, and norms that emerge in the Great Society, and in communities, in turn structure the choices facing individuals and households. Beyond these structures, the values that drive the market order, and the wealth that they make possible, provide the motivation and means for resources to flow from the outer rings to individuals, households, and communities for both everyday concerns and situations of great need. What Deirdre McCloskey (2006) calls the "bourgeois virtues" are both causes and effects of the expansion of the market order. Those virtues are often instantiated in a desire to put the wealth that markets create to work in the form of gifts, grants, and other non-market forms of resource transfers or exchanges that are intended to improve the lives of those in the more inner circles. However, if this non-market resource allocation process involves exchange, it will have to have some way other than money prices that ensures that economic calculation is minimally possible. The rest of this chapter explores how this framework can be applied to the community described in Stack's *All Our Kin* and what some of the implications are for both poor communities and communities in crisis.

## Exchange and reciprocity in Carol Stack's *All Our Kin*

Carol Stack's *All Our Kin* is a classic piece of ethnography from the late 1960s. It is best read as a response to the Moynihan Report on the state of the African-American family produced by the US government in 1965. The report concluded that the African-American family was dysfunctional and in disarray. Stack and other social scientists began to investigate whether that claim was accurate, or whether the official data used to construct it had perhaps overlooked aspects of the lived lives of African-Americans, particularly poor ones, that might provide a more rich and complete picture of the way in which families functioned in that community. Stack's strategy was one of the most radical: she engaged in participant-observer research by becoming a member of a poor, urban, African-American community in the American Midwest. She spent several years living with the people she was researching, integrating herself into the community to the extent possible. This enabled her to see the workings of family structure from the inside in a way not possible when one looks only at the statistical data and similar forms of evidence. Her conclusion was that even though the families of poor African-Americans were not functioning ideally, they were not nearly as dysfunctional as portrayed in the Moynihan Report.

What *All Our Kin* suggests is that the residents of the community she observed, which she names The Flats, found very creative ways to adjust the form that families took in order to enhance their functioning in the face of significant poverty. The critique of the Moynihan Report, as well as much other writing on the family before and since, was that by not looking closely enough at the way poor, black families actually *functioned*, the report assumed that because the family did not have a particular structure (namely that of middle-class, white America), it must therefore be dysfunctional. This confusion of form and function is endemic in much writing about the family, and one of the contributions of Stack's work is to point out that one cannot make assumptions about functionality based only on form. Multiple forms of the family turn out to be reasonably functional, independent of whether those forms are the result of the resource pressures, such as in the case of The Flats, or of choices such as divorce, single-parenthood, or same-sex marriage.[5]

Of interest for my purposes here are some of the ways in which the families Stack described were able to make use of their limited resources to maximize their ability to function. To understand the strategies that they adopted, one must understand the circumstances they faced and the structure of their families and households. First, this was an extremely poor community, suffering under the legacy of segregation and lingering racism of the early- and mid-twentieth century. Employment was scarce, and jobs did not pay well. Many families were on various forms of government assistance. Family structure aside, individuals and families in The Flats faced significant resource constraints.

A common feature of families in The Flats was a large number of women who bore children of multiple fathers, without being legally married to any of them. Female-headed households were quite common, and this was one of the features of the African-American family that the Moynihan Report noted as evidence of its dysfunctionality. Many fathers did take on varying degrees of responsibility for their children, but this did not always, or even often, involve legal marriage. In contrast to a more nuclear model in which resources enter the family through the income-earning activities of a married couple who then use those resources to provide for themselves and their children all in the context of a single household, the families of The Flats (and this is true of families in other circumstances of poverty, both historically and around the world today) relied on persons outside the nuclear family and physical household to provide income and various forms of household production such as childcare. Where more comfortable, middle-class families could assume a near total overlap between "the family" as a biological and sociological unit, and the household as the organization through which income is earned and specific acts of production and consumption take place, the family structure of The Flats challenged that identification of family and household.

What is often termed "extended family" was central to this process. Mothers relied on their relatives to provide both physical resources and time. As is often the case with female-headed households, a network of female relatives was the core of these networks of kin. In addition, if the father stepped up and took responsibility for his child, even outside of a legal marriage, his extended family was brought into the kin network of the mother and child and could be drawn upon for various kinds of resources. Of additional importance is that the biological mother need not be the de facto mother for purposes of identifying whose extended family will be drawn upon. Motherhood, as well as a variety of other familial relationships, was defined within the community through a long-standing system of recognized norms. Stack argues: "The system of rights and duties should not be confused with the official, written statutory law of the state," and that these rights and duties are "enforced only by sanctions within the community" (1974, 46). Stack provides extensive detail on the nature of these kin networks and how they were formed and dissolved. Once such kin networks, or "personal kindreds" as Stack refers to them, are established, they become the basis for an extended household based on reciprocal exchange.

Stack devotes an entire chapter to what she terms "swapping." Faced with needs much greater than the available supply of resources, nothing can go to waste, whether a physical object or the time of residents. The solution is an "intricately interwoven" system of exchange through which resources, including time, are given to others in the community with the expectation that they will reciprocate at some point in the future. The swapping of The Flats is really a sophisticated form of credit rather than direct and immediate barter. It is tempting to see it as a form of gifting but, as Stack makes clear, providing resources for other members of the community comes with the expectation that the recipient will give back eventually. It is not a one-way pure gift, but more like a loan in which the repayment does not have to take the form of the same object or activity that was lent. Stack defines the swapping process as the exchange of "any object or service offered with the intent of obligating" (1974, 34). The nature of these exchanges could involve anything from household objects like a TV or coffeepot, to things like clothing or cash, but also to services such as childcare and housing. It was not unusual, Stack reports, for children to be moved from house to house over the course of their childhood as it became easier for one or another relative to care for them. The same was true to an extent of adults, who might require temporary housing in the home of a relative.

Stack argues that swapping had both an economic and sociological function. The economic function is clear enough, in that it became a way to reallocate resources to those who needed them most at any particular time. Economically, this sort of exchange behavior can be seen in three complementary ways. First, it is a form of credit, as Stack's phrase "with the intent of obligating" suggests. Those who have objects or time or space that is greater than their current needs can "save" by providing those resources to others with the expectation of being able to draw on that saving down the road in the form of a reciprocal act of saving/lending from the recipient. Second, it can be seen as a way of minimizing the "idleness" of resources. A typical middle-class family might think nothing of having a closet full of clothes, most of which don't get worn in a typical week but are there in case we want them. In a poor community, those can be seen as a sort of wasteful "idleness" that could be put to a more valuable use by being worn by other members of the community. Clothing not currently being used was fair game for swapping. One can extend this analysis to other household objects as well as household space and the time of community members. If some kin find themselves with the time to care for the child of other kin who are struggling, they will do so with the expectation of reciprocation down the road.[6]

Finally, all of this swapping is perhaps best understood economically as extending the effective size of a household to the entire network of kin with whom one might swap. What swapping does is to enable people to draw on a larger range of other people and resources to accomplish their various forms of household production. Whether taking the form of financial resources, objects like a couch or clothing, or time devoted to childcare, swapping enables residents of The Flats to not be limited to what is available within the four walls of their homes in engaging in household production. Living space, childcare, and other resources can come from anywhere within their personal kindred.

The extension of the effective household size in The Flats can be understood as a way to change the cost-effectiveness of household production. As discussed earlier, households are sites of non-market production. We can adapt the basic Coasean (1937) analysis of the firm here to observe that households face a trade-off between what we might call the non-monetary administrative or coordination costs of organizing resources within the household versus the explicit monetary costs of acquiring resources from outside the household. For the households of The Flats, this trade-off can be understood as between the costs of setting up and enforcing their sophisticated system of swapping, which amounts to an extension of the de facto household across a number of physical households, and the costs of acquiring new resources such as clothing or services such as childcare on the market, or perhaps at the opportunity cost of their own time. The goal of household production is to ensure that meals are cooked, houses are cleaned, errands are run, and children are raised. The organizational form that does so best will depend upon the relevant costs.

## Economic calculation in the impoverished community

Within a single physical household, the need for some system of accounting and calculation is far less pressing as the heads of household can make allocation decisions directly. However, when the size of the household expands as we see in The Flats, some process for keeping track of how resources are being drawn upon or provided becomes necessary. What we see in The Flats is that the residents have in fact developed a fairly sophisticated system of credit and calculation.

The Flats is a more systematic version of behavior we see frequently in intimate orders even when not faced with ongoing resource scarcity. A lighter version of this sort of swapping characterizes middle-class America, though not in the systematic and deeply embedded way we see in The Flats. Family members trade favors with regularity. Members of the same school or house of worship might trade-off carpooling or caring for children after school when their parents are in a bind.[7] Neighbors might trade objects or time with some regularity, e.g., the classic "may I borrow a cup of sugar?" This sort of behavior happens in good times and bad, though the struggles of friends and community members tend to produce more of it. We frequently bring meals to friends, neighbors, or co-religionists who are ill or who have had a death in the family. We might also volunteer to care for the children of the same people in a time of difficulty. We do all of this with the knowledge, or at least the belief, that those people would do the same for us were we in their situation.

Exchange is at the heart of both the more extensive swapping system of The Flats and the somewhat ad hoc processes we see in wealthier communities. Both involve what we might term as "barter credit" exchanges, as parties trade without money and do so asynchronously. The asynchronous nature of the exchanges is what makes them appear as forms of mutual gift giving rather than true exchanges. We know from The Flats, at least, that the actors themselves understood what they were doing as a form of exchange, not gift giving. They believed that "what goes around, comes around" and their willingness to give of their physical resources or time was a way of earning credit should they require help. The existence of a way of excluding free riders (see below) also indicates that this was not a mere gift exchange but a credit system. Spreading your willingness to give more widely also increased the number of people who you could draw on in the future. Of course, doing so increased the complexity of the process, and without money as a common denominator, this barter credit system requires some other way of keeping track of who has credit and debit balances.

As noted earlier, for reciprocal exchange to work with reasonable effectiveness in intimate orders, such systems will have to include some sort of substitute for the monetary calculation that characterizes anonymous orders. Stack reports that the residents of The Flats were aware of all of this and had developed some ways of engaging in substitutes for monetary calculation. As Stack describes it:

> A person who gives and obligates a large number of individuals stands a better chance of receiving returns than a person who limits his circle of friends. In addition, repayments from a large number of individuals are returned intermittently; people can anticipate receiving a more-or-less continuous flow of goods. *From this perspective, swapping involves both calculation and planning*
> 
> (1974, 40; emphasis added)

Again, without the ease of comparison that monetary prices provide us, the calculations that go into swapping and other forms of reciprocal exchange will not be as precise, but they exist nonetheless. Non-human communities cannot calculate in the way that humans can, but sufficiently intimate and homogeneous human communities can engage in this process without the aid of money to a degree sufficient for their purposes. What is clear is that exchange is not limited to market contexts and that reciprocal exchange, as opposed to gift giving, in the absence of money must develop some substitute process of pricing or valuation, as well as an analogue of profits and loss.

Dealing with free riders is one of the most fundamental problems such a system must solve. Stack's discussion suggests that residents of The Flats did have mechanisms for identifying and excluding cheaters. One's reputation for being a fair trader was paramount to being able to draw on the community in the swapping process. People who only received and did not donate quickly developed a reputation for doing so and were excluded. The primary process by which reputational information was spread was through the female gossip network. The women of The Flats used gossip as a way to inform the community of those who were and were not reciprocating. Stack reports: "Individuals who fail to reciprocate in swapping relationships are judged harshly" (1974, 34). One resident said of a relative who never reciprocated, "Well, lots of people talks about someone who acts that way" (35). Non-reciprocators would find themselves refused a swap when they were in need, providing the exclusion necessary to prevent free riding.

One can view these reputational effects as non-monetary forms of profit and loss. Those with good reputations for giving back when they have been helped will more easily get help from others when needed, which is analogous to profits. Those who do not "pay it forward" develop bad reputations and begin to be excluded from the swapping process, and find it hard to acquire goods or services when they might need them. That result is the analogue of monetary losses.

The residents of The Flats were also cognizant of the question of value and price. Stack notes that the value within the community was not the same as the market value of the object or service in question.[8] Instead, the value of an object for swapping purposes was "based upon its retaining power over the receiver; that is, how much and over how long a time period the giver can expect returns of the gift" (1974, 42). If we think in terms of both credit and subjective value, the value of a good was dependent on its value in the eyes of the recipient, which in turn established the indebtedness of that person to the giver and the community more broadly. For example, if it became known that you agreed to look after a friend's children for an extended period, that was of significant value to the friend and would have two consequences. First, it would enhance your reputation within the community and make it easier for you to draw upon others in the future. It would also significantly encumber the recipient, both to you and The Flats as a whole. Within an intimate and quite homogeneous community, there would also be widespread agreement on the swap value of various objects or activities. Within such a community, money is not necessary to achieve a fairly high level of uniformity of value.

The absence of money does point to the limitations of a non-monetary swapping system such as this one: the credit one earns for creating value for others by providing goods and services has no traction outside the specific community. The ability to calculate without money is limited to the relatively intimate and homogeneous community of The Flats, and even there it applies only to household production and a range of consumption goods. The advantage of the monetary calculation of the anonymous order of the Great Society is exactly that it dramatically extends the range of people to whom we can provide value and trade for their products in return. We are not bound to what we can do for those in the more inner of our circles.

However, when the forces of community and household obligation are strong enough, even the acquisition of a significant amount of money may not serve as a pathway out of poverty and thereby have little value outside the community. Stack notes how residents of The Flats who came into unexpected money were under a strong obligation to disperse it to kin in the community, leaving little for themselves. This phenomenon is known as "leveling" because of the way in which it made it so difficult for any one family to work their way up and out of The Flats. The intensity of this obligation is evidence of the power of money as compared to the non-monetary exchange system of The Flats. Residents understood that money gave them a degree of flexibility and an access point to the extended order outside The Flats. It enabled them to move to the outer rings of the concentric circles. Leveling worked to both give a limited version of that access to a wider number of people while also serving as a way to ensure that those with resources continued to be a source of wealth inside the community.

Even as leveling made it difficult to escape, the swapping system served very effectively as a way to improve the lives of The Flats community. At one point, Stack (1974, 33) refers to the limited supply of goods in The Flats being "perpetually redistributed" within the community. Members of the community note that "you not really getting ahead of nobody, you just get better things as they go back and forth." Others make similar observations about how this process does not really improve people's well-being. Economists might beg to differ. If trade is itself value-creating due to the subjectivity of value, straight swapping makes both parties better off, at least *ex ante*. This sort of internal-to-the-community trading is, like all trading, a way of reallocating resources to higher-valued uses. Even if the stock of goods were constant, swapping improves people's subjective well-being by enabling them to get goods they prefer to those they trade away. When we add the credit element in, we see additional benefits. Trading through time is mutually beneficial as well. If I swap away something now because I think I will need some other good or service later, I am better off as I have aligned my consumption through time more accurately. Presumably my swapping partner has the opposite set of preferences and is made better off by getting something from me now in exchange for the more open obligation to swap something back to the community later on. Note that swaps do not have to be between the same partners; the expectation of reciprocation is to the community as a whole, though specific trading partners can call on each other for reciprocation. All of this activity is wealth-enhancing, at least within the limits of the supply of resources in the community and the extent to which non-monetary calculation could function within it.

An important implication is that trying to analyze this community by looking at the behavior of individual households or families will provide a very incomplete picture as these categories, especially the "household," are so fluid and permeable that they do not play the same role as a constituent component of economic analysis as they do in communities where the Coasean trade-off alluded to above is different. In more heterogeneous communities, where the costs of non-monetary calculation are high and where there is sufficient access to money and monetary exchange, we will tend to see households that are more independent. That ring of the concentric circles will be less permeable and the individual household will be a much more obvious building block of social analysis. Where circumstances are different, whether more pervasive like The Flats or in particular cases within more heterogeneous and better-off communities, the community can be the relevant unit of analysis. As we see with The Flats, taking a larger-scale view of the community as a network of exchangers defined by complex kin relationships enables us to better understand their creative adaptation to poverty.

## But is it just kin selection?

Having described the world of The Flats, it is worth confirming that what we are observing is, in fact, reciprocal exchange and not kin selection by using the same criteria researchers have applied to the vampire bats. We need to show that donors and recipients must frequently reverse, that the benefits to the recipient exceed the costs to the donor, and that there is a way to identify cheaters and exclude them. The first two are clear from the previous section. Although the swapping process is not limited to pairs, no person plays only the role of donor or recipient. Members of The Flats community find themselves in both roles with frequency. The benefits clearly outweigh the costs and community members use that kind of language to explain why they swap. They understand that if they give up something they value less today, they will be able to draw on the community later on when their need is greater. That is, they understand that the immediate need of the recipient is greater than the immediate cost to the donor. And it is perhaps their inability to see an optimistic future beyond the relatively short run that enables them to calculate fairly effectively to meet their immediate needs yet not quite see the ways in which something like leveling prevents them planning effectively for the longer run.

One might object that what happened in The Flats really is just "kin selection" given that the exchange networks were based around kin. However, in the evolutionary literature, kin has to be understood in strictly biological terms. With the vampire bats, the question was whether or not they also reciprocated with genetic strangers, and they did, indicating this was reciprocal exchange not narrow kin selection. The implication is that reciprocal exchange is a strategy not just for ensuring the furthering of one's genes but for promoting the survival of the whole community. The same is true of The Flats. The kin networks that Stack identified as central to the swapping process were not purely biological. As noted earlier, the woman recognized for social purposes as the mother was not always the biological mother, and in some cases not even a blood relative. Swapping also took place among biological strangers, as members of a mother's network might swap with members of the network of her baby's father. Stack points out that the language of kinship was also used as a way to indicate close, reciprocal relationships among non-kin in the biological sense: "Non-kin who live up to one another's expectations express elaborate vows of friendship and conduct their social relations within the idiom of kinship" (1974, 40). It might be true that the residents of The Flats gave preference to people who they *called* kin and thereby chose to make part of their household/community, but that is not the same as preferring their biological kin, which is what is necessary for this to be kin selection. It would seem that the reciprocal exchange is here a strategy for community survival, analogous to that of the vampire bats. This suggests that reciprocal exchange has powerful evolutionary roots for populations faced with significant resource challenges.

## Calculation, community, and concluding thoughts

One of the lessons to draw from Stack's book is that in attempting to make sense of the behavior we see in any particular historical context, just working with the poles of the intimate–anonymous continuum is not enough, nor is treating exchange as exclusively a property of the anonymous extended order. Exchange does not necessarily require the use of money and the other formal structures of the marketplace to function, and often function very well, within the more inner rings of our alternative concentric circles model. Households and communities often rely on non-monetary exchange as an effective way to coordinate behavior. Mises, Hayek, and Buchanan were right in encouraging economists to think about markets as catallaxies, or networks of exchange, but as Buchanan's (1964) extension of the catallactic approach to the political world suggests, exchange is a more encompassing phenomenon than what we observe in formal markets characterized by monetary exchange. However, even non-monetary exchange, especially if it is to guide any form of production, must have some way of mimicking the process of monetary calculation that guides choices in monetary exchange in a more formal market. There must be some way, if weaker and less reliable, to provide incentives and signals about the desirability of actions as well as mechanisms for dealing with problems such as free riders. Without the ability to provide a proxy for monetary calculation, non-monetary exchange systems are unlikely to be sustainable forms of wealth creation.

A further implication of this chapter's discussion is that although the anonymity that comes with monetary exchange enables its reach to extend well beyond household and community (i.e., to the outer ring of the extended order), there may well be situations in which non-monetary exchange is preferred, perhaps due to poverty or a scarcity of actual money, or because monetary exchange is seen to be inappropriate given the role that the particular good or service plays within the community. One recurring situation in which non-monetary exchange might play a larger role is in post-disaster recovery. Actual money may be in short supply, or the formal institutions of the market may have been substantially weakened by the disaster, such that non-monetary exchange becomes a better option. More generally, monetary exchange might be possible and appropriate, but also come with greater costs than the sorts of non-monetary exchange we see in The Flats. Researchers exploring the ways in which households, communities, and markets operate should be mindful of the ubiquity of exchange among humans, even when money and more formal market institutions are weak or absent.

Finally, the experience of The Flats should also remind researchers of the flexibility and permeability of the rings of the concentric circles around the individual. What counts as a household or a community, and how much either mimics or complements "the market," will shift as contexts and constraints change. Although the concentric circles models and the Hayekian distinction between the intimate and anonymous are helpful organizing frameworks, the concepts of exchange, community, intimate orders, and anonymous orders are all arguably messier and less precise than they sometimes seem. The lesson of *All Our Kin* is that we need to look closely at what we are studying to make sure we understand whether and in what ways those terms apply. Beginning with how the actors themselves understand what they are doing and then bringing to bear carefully the relevant frameworks from social theory can render intelligible what otherwise might seem strange. Doing so requires, however, that we not get overly bound by dichotomies when social institutions and practices refuse to fit neatly into those concepts.

## Acknowledgments

I thank all three editors and participants at a seminar at King's College London for very helpful feedback on the first draft.

## Notes

1  The same distinction is also described as "catallaxy" vs. "economy" or "cosmos" vs. "taxis" to refer to spontaneous and made orders respectively.
2  The philosopher Georg Simmel ([1907] 1978) made this issue one of the central themes of his *The Philosophy of Money*.
3  Certainly, large-scale disasters, for example, can produce an outpouring of funds, but the number of small, local, community causes that find support in the US is almost endless. Of course, for others, shared national, intellectual, or political identities might explain more global level giving.
4  I thank Lenore Ealy for the concentric circles imagery.
5  As these are not the focal issues of this paper, let me note here that the claim is not that all family forms are *equally* functional. For example, the literature on the impact of divorce on children is clear that they are, on average, slightly worse off than children from intact marriages. The claim is more subtle: a variety of family forms are *sufficiently* good at the task of raising children to adulthood as functioning, responsible citizens while also serving the various needs of the parent(s). All other things being equal, we might wish every child was raised in a two-parent household with the attendant financial and human resources. Even if this is the best of all family structures, it does not mean it is the only functional one.
6  The analysis here is identical to the ways in which economists might talk about the role of a fire truck sitting in a fire station or the cash in one's wallet. It is tempting to consider it "idle," but in fact it is providing the service of being "available." That service is, of course, evaluated subjectively and, as we see with the clothing example, the value of availability might be less than the return expected from the "credit" gained by swapping the object today for the promise of reciprocation later on.
7  One of the interesting aspects of *All Our Kin* is that schools and especially churches are nearly non-existent in Stack's account of life in The Flats. It is hard to believe that the church in an African-American community was so peripheral to the everyday lives of the residents that it was not part of the regular rhythm of life and, particularly, to the attempt to share resources through swapping. Whether the omission of the church was really due to its peripheral role or some blind spot on the part of Stack is an interesting question. It might also be a difference between the lives of urban poor African-Americans and rural ones. I thank Sarah Skwire and Cathy Crosby-Currie for some discussion of this issue.
8  Stack is a bit confused in this section as she seems to adopt a cost of production understanding of an object's price, which she sees as distinct from its monetary value. An economist who reads *All Our Kin* will frequently wish that Stack had a better understanding of basic microeconomics, as it would have given her a clearer framework for understanding much of what she saw. Such a framework would have made the argument even more powerful, as I hope I am demonstrating in this paper.

## References

Buchanan, James M. 1964. "What Should Economists Do?" *Southern Economic Journal* 30: 213–222.

Coase, Ronald H. 1937. "The Nature of the Firm." *Economica* 4: 386–405.

Hayek, F. A. 1973. *Law, Legislation, and Liberty*, vol. I: Rules and Order. Chicago: University of Chicago Press.

Hayek, F. A. 1977. *Law, Legislation, and Liberty*, vol. II: The Mirage of Social Justice. Chicago: University of Chicago Press.

Horwitz, Steven. 2005. "The Functions of the Family in the Great Society." *Cambridge Journal of Economics* 29: 669–84.

Lewis, Paul. 2009. "Commitment, Identity, and Collective Intentionality: The Basis for Philanthropy." *Conversations on Philanthropy* IX: 46–64.

McCloskey, Deirdre. 2006. *The Bourgeois Virtues*. Chicago: University of Chicago Press.

Mises, Ludwig von. 1920. "Economic Calculation in the Socialist Commonwealth." In *Collectivist Economic Planning*, edited by F. A. Hayek, 87–130. Clifton, NJ: Augustus M. Kelley, 1935.

Mises, Ludwig von. [1912] 1980. *The Theory of Money and Credit*, Indianapolis, IN: Liberty Press.

Moynihan, Daniel P. 1965. *The Negro Family: The Case for National Action*. Washington, DC: Office of Policy Planning and Research, US Department of Labor.

Ridley, Matt. 1998. *The Origins of Virtue: Human Instincts and the Evolution of Cooperation*. New York: Penguin.

Simmel, Georg. [1907] 1978. *The Philosophy of Money*. Boston, MA: Routledge & Kegan Paul.

Smith, Adam. [1776] 1976. *An Inquiry into the Nature and Causes of the Wealth of Nations*, edited by Edwin Cannan (1904 edn.). Chicago: University of Chicago Press.

Stack, Carol. 1974. *All Our Kin*. New York: Basic Books.

Wilkinson, Gerald S. 1990. "Food Sharing in Vampire Bats." *Scientific American* 262, February: 76–82.

# 18 Kidneys, commerce, and communities

*Neera K. Badhwar*

## The problem

My topic is the relationship between kidney markets and communities. A group of people forms a community when, and to the extent that, it is animated by mutual goodwill and trust. A community may include all the residents of a country, or only those who share a common interest, purpose, status, origin, set of values, or religion. By this definition, nearly everyone belongs to more than one community. I will call the latter "special-interest communities," and the former simply "community." I will focus on community and kidney markets, or the lack thereof, in the USA and India, and on a special-interest community that I call the "International Transplant Community" (ITC). By "free market" I mean a system of voluntary exchange for mutual benefit, whether legal or illegal, between individuals or groups.

It is widely recognized by philosophers and economists that free markets can create a spirit of community where there was none before by eroding distinctions of class and caste and fostering mutual goodwill and trust (Friedman 1962; Anderson 1993; Badhwar 2008; Satz 2010). It is less widely recognized that a lack of community spirit – of mutual goodwill and trust – can also prevent free, non-exploitative markets from arising or flourishing (McCloskey 2006; Satz 2010; and Rose 2011 are notable exceptions here). As, of course, can communities that are hostile to markets, such as the ITC. This community consists of bioethicists, transplant surgeons and nephrologists; organizations that educate potential donors, procure organs, or match donors and recipients; and international organizations like the World Medical Association, the International Transplantation Society, and the World Health Organization. The exploitative, even involuntary, nature of kidney markets in India and many other developing countries is best explained both by the lack of community spirit between or even within the different strata of society, and by the power of the ITC and Western governments to prevail on governments everywhere to ban markets in kidneys.

The absence of legal markets in kidneys has also created a situation in which tens of thousands of people all over the world needlessly suffer and die. The number of kidney patients on the waiting list in the USA now is around 98,787 (The Organ Procurement and Transplantation Network, http://optn.transplant.hrsa.gov/data/annualreport.asp, accessed July 2013). Only 16,812 got a transplant in 2012 and 4,903 died for want of a kidney (The National Kidney Foundation [NKF]. http://www.kidney.org/news/newsroom/factsheets/Organ-Donation-and-Transplantation-Stats.cfm, accessed July 2013) – not including those who were never put on the waiting list because the doctors judged that, in their condition, they would never get a kidney in time. It is not, of course, only kidneys that are in short supply; so are other transplantable organs, such as livers and hearts. But the shortage of kidneys is special for two reasons: one is that nature has been unusually generous by endowing each of us with a spare kidney, and the other is that kidney removal and transplantation are now extremely safe for both parties, at least in the West. Yet most of us spend our lives carting around an extra healthy kidney, and take both of them with us when we die, even as those with kidney disease usually lose both kidneys and die for lack of a kidney. These facts make the issue of the kidney shortage especially urgent and poignant.

Many excellent articles and books defending kidney markets of one kind or another have been written (Cherry 2005; Taylor 2005; Epstein 2006; Satel 2012; Matas 2007; Hippen 2008; Radcliffe-Richards *et al.* 1998). My aim is not so much to add to these arguments as to show that free and non-exploitative kidney markets can flourish only if society is animated by a sense of community, and that in developing countries the best hope for such a society is allowing global free markets. It is a mistake to think that legalizing kidney markets would undermine community spirit in the USA or other countries. Most of the arguments against legalizing kidney markets, as I show below, are variations on the theme that commodifying the human body is fundamentally incompatible with human dignity and equality, which, in turn, are necessary for community. These arguments, however, while purporting to protect objective values, merely express some people's feelings or opinions. So using them to advocate that markets be banned is merely to impose one special-interest community's opinions on other communities. Another argument is that a market in kidneys would crowd out the altruistic motive behind kidney donations and, thereby, undermine community. I argue, however, that even if the crowding-out premise is true, the conclusion doesn't follow. Moreover, this insistence on altruistic motivations has become a fetish that is *morally* unjustified. I then challenge the claim that by crowding out altruistic motives, kidney markets would lead to fewer kidneys overall. This argument is contrary to everything we know about markets and human psychology. I also address another worry cited by opponents of kidney markets, which is that the rich will feed off the life and health of the poor. This claim has some merit in the case of poor countries, but none in the case of the USA or other Western countries. Moreover, banning markets and driving them underground only exacerbates the problem of involuntary or exploitative markets in poor countries. Some economists regard the very idea of a free, mutually beneficial, but exploitative exchange as mistaken, if not incoherent. I explain why this is not so, and argue that the best hope for non-exploitative markets in poor countries is foreign medical investment and global trade in kidneys. In concluding, I hypothesize that the ITC's continued opposition to kidney markets, in spite of the ban's tragic consequences and violation of potential sellers' and buyers' liberty, is best explained by the psychology of community membership and the phenomenon of "moral entrapment."

## The meaning(s) of the human body

A common cure for a persistent shortage in some good is to allow a free market in that good. But markets in solid organs, both cadaveric and *inter vivos* (from living donors), were outlawed in the USA in 1984 when Congress passed the National Organ Transplant Act (NOTA). As is often the case with legislation that stems from moral outrage or a public outcry, NOTA was written broadly enough that it banned not only money but all forms of compensation to anyone from anyone, whether poor, middle class, or rich, both in life and after death. (The NKF does support leave for live donors and reimbursement for their direct expenses [see http://www.kidney.org/transplantation/livingdonors/pdf/LDTaxDed_Leave.pdf, accessed July 15, 2013], but it still opposes compensation for non-living donations.) Since then, it has been held as an article of faith by most bioethicists and kidney organizations that the only morally acceptable kidney is an altruistically donated kidney, regardless of the dearth of such kidneys. According to some opponents of markets, selling body parts, whether *inter vivos* or cadaveric, somehow degrades the body and corrupts its "meaning," thereby weakening communal bonds (Sandel 2012; Kass 2002, ch. 6). Leon Kass adds that this corruption is evident in the repugnance "we" feel at the very thought of such an action.

Given the controversy over selling body parts, however, clearly not all of us feel such repugnance. The "meaning" of the body and its parts varies from context to context, from individual to individual, from community to community. Socrates thought that he was identical with his soul, and called the body a prison of the soul, the death of which could not possibly affect *him* – if, he clarified, his soul survived the death of his body. Till recently, the Zoroastrians of Iran disposed of their dead by exposing the corpses to the vultures and other birds of prey in "Towers of Silence." They did this both because they regarded burial or cremation as a pollution of nature by the dead body, and because they regarded letting the vultures feed on dead bodies as an act of charity. In India many Parsis, Zoroastrians of Iranian descent, still dispose of dead bodies this way. Tibetan Buddhists also engage in "sky burial," but go one better than Parsis, hacking and cutting the body to make the vultures' work easier (Logan 1997). As they do so, they laugh and chat.

Are Parsis and Tibetan Buddhists guilty of a perversion of some objective value that only those who bury or cremate their dead recognize and respect? It would be terribly parochial to think so. Many different evaluations of, and practices concerning, the body are compatible with the facts of human life and human dignity. Hence, agreeing to sell one's body parts after death to hospitals for transplantation, in exchange for a payment now or a bigger payment to one's estate after one's death, might be expressive of nothing more than a desire for reciprocity.

Attitudes towards the living body also vary widely. The Catholic Church holds that selling an organ uses the body as an "object" and, thereby, violates human dignity (John Paul II 2000). But most other religions disagree. On some interpretations, Jewish scriptures do not forbid the selling of a kidney even by a living vendor if it is meant to save a life (Tracy 2009). Neither do Hinduism or Buddhism, as far as I know, and, indeed, selling kidneys was legal in India till 1994 (Reddy 1993). Given the existence of thriving kidney black markets in most Muslim countries, and legal markets in Iran and, before 2007, in Pakistan, it seems that Islam also does not forbid such sales. True, some vendors have been ostracized for their act (Hippen 2008, 6), but some have also stated that they wish they had three kidneys so that they could sell another one (Scheper-Hughes 2002, 70).

In thinking about the meaning people attach to the body and its parts, it helps to remember that many practices we are comfortable with now were at one time seen by elites as degrading when done for money, including teaching in ancient Greece, which was frowned upon by Plato and Aristotle. Likewise, till very recently, the selling of plasma, eggs, sperm, surrogate motherhood, and bone marrow in the West were prohibited. (Sales of bone marrow were legalized only in March 2012, and only if collected by apheresis. See http://www.ij.org/bone-marrow-release-6-25-2012, accessed July 2013). The meaning-of-the-body argument, then, cannot justify the ITC and Western governments in pressuring non-Western governments to ban organ selling. Nor can it justify a ban in a pluralistic society such as the United States with its diverse communities. Doing so merely imposes one community's norms – the ITC's – on other communities. Even Kass, one of the leading voices in condemning organ sales, admits: "regardless of all my arguments to the contrary, I would probably *make every effort and spare no expense* to obtain a suitable life-saving kidney for my own child or grandchild – if my own were unusable ... [and] *I would readily sell one of my own kidneys*, were its practice legal, if it were the only way to pay for a life-saving operation for my children or my wife" (2002, 179, emphasis mine). So either Kass realizes that buying or selling kidneys is compatible with humanity and dignity, or he realizes that saving a child's life is more important than humanity and dignity.

## Crowding-out anxieties and altruism-fetishism

A second reason often given for banning kidney sales is that allowing them would "crowd out" the altruistic motive that undergirds communities. I will grant the crowding-out premise for the sake of argument and focus on the complaint that this will damage community spirit. On this view, even if kidney vendors are fully informed about the possible (in the USA now, minimal) risks of the surgery, guaranteed a kidney should they ever need one (or dialysis if they are not eligible for surgery), and offered an ample sum for their kidneys, transactions between them and recipients are incompatible with community spirit. Some proponents of altruistic donations even insist that reimbursement for lost wages and travel expenses for living donors, or funeral expenses for cadaveric donors, must be banned, lest the purity of the donor's altruism be tainted by the dark shadow of self-interest.

The quest for such Kantian purity, however, is elusive: human beings typically have multiple motives for their actions, a fact that led Kant himself to declare that we could never be sure that our actions came from a pure heart (1948). The many excellent arguments against this (what can only be called) altruism-fetishism have largely fallen on deaf ears. These arguments point out that many so-called altruistic donations are motivated by shame or guilt in the face of family pressure, rather than by, or in addition to, altruism. Moreover, most living donors are relatives or close friends of the recipients. Hence their motives are a mixture of self-interest and altruism. In addition, many live donations are actually paired or chain exchanges, in which the altruistic component of the donor's motivation is directed at someone other than the recipient. In paired exchanges, if A wants to donate to B, but cannot do so because her blood type is incompatible with B's, she makes an agreement with C, who is in the same situation vis-à-vis D, to donate her kidney to D in exchange for C's donating to B. When a paired exchange is not possible because either A or C or both are incompatible with both prospective recipients, a chain exchange involving more potential donors and recipients can save several people (Sack 2012). Both kinds of exchanges are arranged by the National Kidney Registry, founded by Garet and Jan Hil, whose longest chain was between thirty donors and thirty recipients. Purely altruistic live donations from one stranger to another are rare. Cadaveric donations, which in 2012 were more than twice as many as live donations (11,043 vs. 5,769, according to the NKF), are, of course, made largely for altruistic reasons, but are far from meeting the need for kidneys. In light of these facts, the claim by two nephrologists that we have a viable system of altruistic donations can only be regarded as wishful thinking: "Our greatest concern is that kidney selling would distort and undermine the altruism and common citizenship on which our whole organ donation system currently relies. The … moral commitment to do one's duty can be weakened by financial compensation and monetary reward" (Danovitch and Leichtman 2006, 14).

Not only is there very little altruism relative to the need, the altruism that does exist is largely confined to white Americans. In particular, although African-Americans are the most likely to need a kidney, they are far less likely to donate one, in part because they mistrust the medical system, or fear that their kidney will be used for a white patient instead of an African-American patient (Goodwin 2004, 2007). So it is an exaggeration to claim that the current system expresses a sense of "common citizenship." This claim is further undermined by the fact that we now have a commons in cadaveric kidneys to which everyone has an equal "right" but no one any obligation to keep stocked (Tabarrok 2002). In other words, the ban on markets has led to a tragedy of the commons, the very opposite of the ideal of common citizenship or community.

The most important objection to the crowding-out-of-the-altruistic-motive worry is a moral one: if altruism is a concern for others for their own sake, the insistence on altruistic-only kidneys is its very opposite, for it forcibly prevents patients and prospective vendors from saving their own lives or lifting themselves out of poverty, respectively, through peaceable, mutually beneficial exchanges. Both justice and compassion dictate that the important thing is to have enough kidneys, voluntarily and non-exploitatively donated or sold, and not the motive of the giver. There *are* some things that we ought to do for others without compensation: everyday acts of kindness and generosity, low-risk rescues in emergencies, such as the proverbial pulling out a drowning child from a pond, helping our adult children or aging parents if they need help, and so on. And in a good society – a society that constitutes a community – most people do do such things. A society in which people merely respected each other's negative rights, while being indifferent to their weal and woe (should it even be psychologically possible for rights-respecters to be thus indifferent), would not be much of a community. But becoming organ donors after death, in spite of the not-unreasonable fear that our lives might be prematurely terminated on the operating table, is not something we are morally required to do as an expression of our concern for others. A fortiori, donating a kidney to a perfect stranger *inter vivos* is far from something we are morally required to do. Indeed, not only is this not a duty, it is supererogatory, far beyond the call of duty. Moreover, a society in which most people did believe that they had a duty to offer their kidneys to strangers for nothing would be neither very happy nor very moral. For in such a society, most people would also believe that they were entitled to other people's kidneys. On a promiscuous theory of our duties to others, it can easily be argued, as one writer already has argued, that "the sick have a right, under some circumstances, to the body parts of the healthy," and that "the state has the moral power to enforce that right" (Fabre 2003, 131).[1] But a society in which people felt they had a right to each other's body parts would be a society in which they regarded each other and themselves as mere means to each other's ends – the very antithesis of a community.

The insistence on altruistic-only donations, legally enforced, amounts to a death sentence for the vast majority of kidney patients. Instead of treating people as ends in themselves by respecting their freedom to benefit themselves, the ITC has elevated *altruistic donation* to the status of an end in itself, an end to which people may be freely sacrificed. A typical expression of this altruism-fetishism is the response of Michael Boo, chief strategy officer of the National Marrow Donor Program (NMDP), to the recent legalization of bone marrow sales in the USA: he refuses to list prospective vendors of bone marrow on the NMDP site, asking rhetorically: "Is that what we want people to be motivated by?" (see Satel 2012). Altruism-fetishism has even led some members of the ITC to protest against organizations like LifeSharers for trying to enclose the organs commons by introducing the principle of reciprocity into organ transplants (LifeSharers 2007).

## Crowding-out anxieties and misbehaving markets

A third reason for the ITC's opposition to kidney markets is also based on the assumption that markets would "crowd out" the altruistic motive. The worry here is the practical one that without this motive, we would get even fewer kidneys for transplantation. Granting, again, that the assumption is true, is it plausible that the crowding-out of altruism would reduce the supply of kidneys? If common sense and evidence from analogous phenomena are any guide, there is reason to believe the exact opposite. Blood donations went down after payment (though not all material incentives; Domen 1995) for blood was banned in the USA, whereas plasma, which continues to be paid for, is so abundant that the USA now exports a large amount of the world's plasma stock (Hippen and Satel 2008, 100–101). In the UK, which never allowed payment either for plasma or for blood, there is a constant shortage of both. In both the USA and UK, as in many other countries, organizations constantly appeal for volunteers to donate blood to keep their transfusion stock at a safe level (3 days, in the USA). The only time there is more than enough volunteer blood in the USA is during emergencies. By contrast, Iran eliminated its waiting list for kidneys 11 years after it legalized kidney markets.

If an altruism-only policy fails even for plasma, the donation of which requires less of a sacrifice in terms of time, pain, and risk than a kidney donation, and a largely altruism policy just barely works for blood, what reason is there to think that it will ever work for kidneys? Conversely, if payment produces an abundance of plasma in the USA and eliminates a shortage of kidneys in Iran, what reason is there to believe that payment for kidneys will have the opposite effect here or anywhere else? More strongly, if markets in other goods for which there is a strong demand make those goods more plentiful, why should a market in kidneys make kidneys less plentiful? The idea that this might happen is contrary to the most basic law of economics: the law of supply and demand, and to one of the most basic features of human psychology: the desire for, and expectation of, reciprocity. Ignorance of markets has combined with wishful thinking and altruism-fetishism to perpetrate an ongoing tragedy.

## The USA: community without kidney markets

A final reason for the ITC's opposition to kidney markets is its belief that they would be inevitably unequal and exploitative of the poor, since only the poor would sell their kidneys and only the middle class or rich would buy them. The rich would live off the bodies of the poor, who would be left vulnerable to disease and early death. A society that tolerated such inequality would be a community only in name. While this claim has some merit in developing countries, it has little in the USA or, I expect, other developed countries. I will start with *inter vivos* markets in the USA, since a successful defense of these is also a successful argument for cadaveric markets. The first point to note is that in the USA many poor would-be vendors would be excluded from the market precisely because low socioeconomic status is an independent risk factor for kidney disease (Hossain *et al.* 2009). It is likely, however, that of the healthy candidates, most would be relatively poor, as would most kidney recipients, who would continue to be paid for by Medicare.

But is it such a terrible thing that most kidney vendors would be relatively poor? After all, only relatively poor people take janitorial jobs, house cleaning jobs, or exhausting farm jobs. For many people, selling a kidney would be far preferable to picking blackberries all day in the sun, or cleaning office buildings every day, for a fraction of the sum they would get for a kidney, and not much more of a risk, since laparoscopic nephrectomy, the procedure used in the USA for removing a kidney, is extremely safe (Department of Health & Human Services; cf. Radcliffe-Richards *et al.* 1998). Since a patient on dialysis is far more expensive to maintain than a patient who gets a kidney transplant, the American government and insurance companies would save money even if they paid a kidney vendor up to $90,000 and provided him or her with free medical care for all subsequent problems related to the nephrectomy (Major 2008). In addition to poverty, being African-American is also an independent risk factor for kidney disease, yet African-Americans rarely donate kidneys. If poor but healthy African-Americans could sell their kidneys, they would improve their own lot, and also provide better-matched kidneys for other African-Americans. This last point also applies to members of other minority groups. Far from exacerbating inequality, then, a legal market in kidneys would reduce inequality and strengthen the bonds of community. It would also reduce exploitation in poor countries by reducing black-market "transplant tourism" the practice of well-off people in Western and other countries traveling to poor countries to buy kidneys from living vendors in the black market.

## India: kidney markets without community

Freely chosen, non-exploitative relationships of mutual advantage promote a sense of community by fostering mutual goodwill and trust and undermining social hierarchies. The vegetable vendor on a New Delhi street and his customer deal with each other as independent equals, even if the vendor lives in a shack and his customer in a mansion. This is all the more remarkable because their equality is limited to their relationship as seller and buyer of vegetables: in India there is almost no other social sphere in which poor vendors and non-poor customers can meet as equals. In commuter and long-distance trains, as well as in cinema theaters, the poor sit in third-class coaches or sections, respectively, while the rest sit in the first and second classes. Most marriages are still arranged on the basis of class, caste, and religion. Markets alone cannot wipe out these differences. Indeed, kidney markets, both black and legal, face special problems in India, thanks to a generalized distrust and lack of mutual goodwill between the various classes: the well-off often prey on the not-so-well-off, the not-so-well-off on the poor, and the poor on the very poor. Sometimes, as Katherine Boo (2012) documents in her book on an Indian slum, the very poor also prey on each other. The vast socio-economic differences between the various strata of society, and the struggle for existence on the margins by the poor, serve as a barrier both to the development of a sense of community and to a strong rule of law. And the absence or weakness of a sense of community and the rule of law serves as a barrier to a genuinely free, non-exploitative market in kidneys. The result, all too often, is involuntary or exploitative exchanges. Poor people are promised huge sums of money that dwindle to a fraction of the original sum after the surgery or fail to materialize at all (Goyal *et al.* 2002; Jha 2004; Taylor 2006). This happened in the legal market before 1994 and happens in the black market now. Even when they are not cheated, they are offered paltry sums (between $1,000 and $2,000) for their kidneys, and often undergo badly performed nephrectomies, with little or no post-operative medical care forthcoming. This, in turn, often leads to an inability to work, leaving them worse off financially as well. In short, the poor are treated as a collection of "spare parts" (Scheper-Hughes 2002), mere means to the ends of others. Some studies – although not all – have reported that the vast majority of vendors in India, Pakistan, Egypt, and the Philippines regret their decision to sell their kidneys on account of worsening health and, consequently, worsening financial condition.[2] For their part, desperate to earn some money, vendors sometimes deliberately hide their problems from doctors (or doctors from patients) and pass on their infections to kidney recipients. Thus, kidney markets in India are often involuntary, and even when they are not involuntary, they are often exploitative of kidney vendors in taking unfair advantage of their desperation. In short, exchanges in kidney black markets in India, like exchanges in drug black markets, are often predatory (see, for example, Scheper-Hughes 2011).

Kidney black markets in India also often have adverse third-party effects, such as husbands coercing wives to sell their kidneys or moneylenders pressuring their debtors to sell their own or their wives' kidneys to pay off their debt, or insisting on their kidneys as collateral before making a loan (Satz 2010). Extreme poverty, lack of community bonds, and the demand for kidneys, together suffice for these third-party effects. Yet selling a kidney is sometimes the better alternative: if it weren't for their kidneys, it might be their children that poor people had to sell (Robertson 2009).

Some would reject my claim that a freely entered into, mutually beneficial transaction can be exploitative as mistaken, perhaps even incoherent. And on the Marxist understanding of exploitation, it certainly is incoherent. For on this understanding, the worker is exploited because he is *coerced* by circumstances to work for the capitalist, and his fate is increasing immiseration. The worker does not engage in market transactions voluntarily. If he did, there would be no ground for saying that he was exploited.[3] But a conception of coercion that does away with the distinction between economic pressures and a gun to the head is conceptually and morally indefensible, and the claim of increasing immiseration in capitalist countries is plainly false. So those who state, as Murray Rothbard does, that exploitation does not occur in a free market, do so because they reject Marx's conception of coercion, but agree with his conception of exploitation as necessarily coercive (2008).[4] They maintain that all that is needed for a non-exploitative and thus just exchange is that it be voluntary and give both parties what they expect, *ex ante*, to get from it. Further, they maintain, all that is needed for a voluntary exchange is that it be free of force and fraud.

However, the claim that all exchanges free of force and fraud are equally voluntary equally just rests on very narrow conceptions of voluntariness and justice, conceptions that reflect neither everyday thinking about, nor philosophical analysis of, either notion. Consider, for example, a desperately poor but healthy woman whose family is on the brink of starvation because of a drought. Her circumstances have reduced her options to only bad ones. Hence, when she agrees to sell her kidney in exchange for $100 or a large sack of rice from a well-off man (a payment actually deemed sufficient by a nephrologist in Manila, according to Scheper-Hughes 2004, 58), her choice is made under duress. It is not coerced, but it has a feature in common with coerced choices: it is made unwillingly, in response to unusually constrained external circumstances and an unreasonable offer far below the usual market price. Her action is neither involuntary nor fully voluntary, but mixed, done only to avoid something even worse (see Aristotle 1999 on voluntary, involuntary, and "mixed actions" in *Nicomachean Ethics*, III.1). Likewise, when her well-off buyer drives, as we say, "a hard bargain," he doesn't coerce her, but his action has a feature in common with coercion: it exploits her vulnerability to gain a hugely disproportionate advantage for himself. Like coercion (and fraud), an exploitative exchange shows scant regard for the vulnerable person.

This last might invite the reply that since the exchange in question both respects the kidney vendor's rights and saves her life, it can hardly be described as showing scant regard for her. Nothing I've said so far shows that a *non-coercive, mutually advantageous* exchange can be exploitative. The kidney-for-a-sack-of-rice deal will enable the kidney seller and her family to survive for a month instead of, say, only five days.

The claim that an exchange *must* be harmful to one party to count as exploitative has been disputed. For example, Feinberg argues that exploitation can occur "without harming the exploitee's interests and … despite the exploitee's fully voluntary consent to the exploitative behavior" (1990, 176–179). But whether or not harm is necessary for exploitation, in the case at hand the harsh terms of the exchange *do* make it harmful to the kidney vendor in the long run. For a nephrectomy on a woman about to go on a starvation diet is all but guaranteed to kill her. The kidney recipient saves the desperate woman's life at time $t_1$ at the cost of depriving her of her health and perhaps even life at time $t_2$. Compared to the baseline of no-exchange (and certain death from starvation in five days), she is better off. This is reason enough not to ban kidney sales. As Alan Wertheimer argues, however, the no-exchange baseline is not the only relevant baseline in evaluating an exchange (1996; Wertheimer and Zwolinski 2013; see also Locke 1661). Evaluating the justice of an exchange requires comparing it to the baseline of a just exchange, an exchange that does not take advantage of either party's vulnerability to harm. And by this baseline, the woman is worse off.

The woman's situation is akin to that of a man dying of thirst in a desert, and the buyer's to that of a well-stocked, well-off tourist who agrees to give the dying man water in return for all his property after they reach home. Every philosophical theory of ethics joins commonsense morality in condemning such a deal as unconscionable, and the common law agrees by refusing to uphold it if the thirsty man reneges on it. For an almost costless rescue such as this ought to be done without demanding anything in return (even though, as most of us believe, this ought not to be legally compulsory). Any well-off tourist with water to spare ought to give the thirsty man some water just because the thirsty man is a human being like himself who has been rendered helpless by circumstance. Likewise, any well-off buyer of a kidney ought to give the desperate woman the price she would have commanded had she not been desperate, and ought to do so just because the kidney seller is a human being like himself rendered helpless by circumstance. The tourist and the kidney buyer would see this for themselves if they asked themselves that most familiar of questions: "How would you like it if someone did this to you?" In both the desert and the kidney exchanges, the well-off parties save the desperate individuals from imminent death in exchange for long-term advantage to themselves and long-term grievous harm, perhaps even death, for the desperate individuals. In so doing, they treat the desperate individuals as mere means to their ends, resources to be sucked dry and left to their fate. Their actions and attitudes say, in effect, that the life and well-being of these individuals are of no moment after they have served the interests of the better-off parties. Thus, they both degrade the vulnerable individuals and harm them. The snapshot view of exchanges typical of economics obscures these facts because it omits the details that make them visible. Like force and fraud, benefiting ourselves by imposing a grave cost on others just because we can violates Kant's "humanity principle," the principle that says that people are ends in themselves, not mere means to our ends. And violating this principle is unjust, because it fails to give people their due.

Ironically, it is the attempt to save people from exploitation or coercion by banning kidney markets that has led to the unimaginably high levels of exploitation and coercion that we see in underground kidney deals. Although fewer people in India sell kidneys now than before the 1994 ban, those who do have no possibility of legal redress against those who cheat or coerce them. The ban has also created more rent-seeking opportunities for bureaucrats, who now have the power to harass potential "donors" who need their permission to "donate," but who cannot get it without wading through several yards of red tape, multiple layers of bureaucracy, and absurd last-minute additional requirements (Menon *et al.* 1997; Iyer and Masand 2012).

Legalizing kidney markets in India would not, of course, solve all the problems of coercion, fraud, exploitation, corrupt politicians, or adverse third-party effects, because most of these problems are due to extreme poverty and ignorance combined with a lack of community spirit and the rule of law. But legalizing kidney markets would allow investigative journalism and social media to expose poor-quality transplant centers and cheating or exploitative brokers and doctors more easily, and give some legal recourse to those who are cheated. It would also lead to a healthy competition among transplant centers, brokers, and doctors for vendors and kidney recipients, and create more nephrologists and transplant surgeons like Thiagarajan *et al.* (1990), whose careful selection methods, including extensive counseling of prospective vendors, successful surgeries, and three years' free follow-up medical care, made them the most "popular" team in South India.

Unfortunately, some of the widespread anti-market bias among professionals infects even Thiagarajan *et al.* (1990), who state proudly that when kidney sales were legal, they did not advertise or allow the market to play a role in deciding payment for the vendor. But advertising would incentivize transplant clinics to improve, and spread news of trustworthy clinics to prospective vendors. The market price would be higher than what seemed then, and seems to be still, the going price in India: between $1,000 and $2,000 (Havocscope, http://www.havocscope.com/black-market-prices/organs-kidneys, accessed July 2013). The higher price would enable the prudent vendor to escape his poverty and also have the salutary effect of preventing government hospitals too poor to pay for patients' anti-rejection drugs from performing transplants on people too poor to buy anti-rejection drugs. But far greater improvements would result from a global free trade in kidneys. Global markets would lead Western insurance companies and transplant centers to establish branches in poor countries that would bring higher standards of screening with more sophisticated laboratory facilities, better drugs, better post-operative care, and perhaps life-long free care for any problems connected with the nephrectomy. Under a consistently free-trade regime, people would be free to go anywhere to get transplants or sell kidneys. Consequently, prices would rise in poor countries and fall in wealthy countries, as they do in other products that are allowed to be freely traded. This would also reduce incentives for black markets that, apparently, still exist in Iran, where kidney vendors are not allowed to sell to foreigners (Ghods and Savaj 2006). Moreover, immigrants to the USA and other Western countries who have a smaller potential supply of kidneys from their own ethnic group in their chosen countries, could go to their countries of origin in order to get matter-matched kidneys. Finally, if kidney markets were legalized, charitable organizations would spring up to help people in poor countries who could not afford a kidney transplant or the necessary drugs after the transplant.

Why, then, does the ITC as a body still oppose kidney markets?

## Communal conformity and moral entrapment

Some charge that the medical personnel who oppose markets are motivated by greed: a shortage of kidneys results in a higher price for their services (Barnett *et al.* 2002). Some argue that the real value of a kidney is folded into the fees charged for the removal, storage, transportation, and transplantation of kidneys, and this creates an incentive for people in this business to oppose payment for kidneys (Tabarrok 2002). Radcliffe-Richards *et al.* argue that the opposition is simply an attempt "to justify the deep feelings of repugnance which are the real driving force of prohibition" (1998, 4–5). Whatever the merit of these speculations (and the last one certainly has a lot of truth in it), we must not overlook psychological reasons for the strong objection to kidney markets. One common reason for agreement among members of a community, or for lack of opposition to the dominant view, is fear of disapproval by their peers or their community's authority figures. This pressure to conform or obey is the dark side of communities and communalism. The hostility of most members of the ITC towards markets leaves those who favor markets afraid to speak their minds. The mavericks are thus robbed of – or allow themselves to be robbed of – any practical influence on the issue. Although some who have suffered disapproval for their defense of kidney markets, such as Thiagarajan *et al.*, don't let it silence them, most people are not made of such stern stuff. Cherry (2005) reports that many transplant surgeons in the USA have told him privately that they favor incentives for organ donations, but are loathe to say so publicly. Indeed, fear of disapproval or even ostracism by peers or people in authority, leading to conformity to the former and obedience to the latter, is a potent factor in human behavior, observable in the playground as much as in private and public organizations. It has also been demonstrated in many experiments, including, most famously, the Asch and Milgram experiments (Asch 1955; Milgram 1974, 170–178; I discuss these experiments in Badhwar 2009).

Another everyday, observable phenomenon that has been demonstrated by the Milgram experiments is "moral entrapment."[5] As the name suggests, moral entrapment occurs when, by small innocuous steps, we end up committed to a project of wrongdoing, unable to free ourselves because the cost of doing so seems too high to bear. This might explain why no one in a position of authority in the ITC has come out in favor of markets. If they were to admit now that they were wrong to oppose kidney markets, they would have to admit that they had been wrong all along. Hence they would have to admit their share of the responsibility for the unnecessary suffering and thousands of deaths over the years. And this is far too hard to admit. It should therefore not be surprising that my letter to the NKF in October 2012 asking why it was so adamantly opposed to kidney markets brought the same hackneyed reply: "there are proven, effective ways to increase donation that should be used more widely, instead of paying for organs." When I pointed out that the waiting list had grown, not decreased, since the NKF adopted its "End the Wait!" resolution in January 2009, I got no reply.

## Conclusion

There is no easy remedy for the tragedy created by the ban on kidney markets. One hope is that scientists will soon create an artificial kidney (Ellis 2013). Another is that pro-market individuals will gain positions of authority in the ITC and start to change the climate of opinion. Another is that the Institute for Justice (IJ) or other similar organizations will successfully challenge the ban in court, as IJ has in the bone marrow case (Kramer 2012). Should the USA legalize markets, India and other poor countries will also eventually follow suit. Insurance companies are already paying for certain treatments, including heart surgeries, in centers of excellence in India, Singapore, and other countries where high-quality health care can be had much cheaper (McQueen 2008). Legalization of kidney markets will make it possible for insurance companies to pay for transplants as well.

## Acknowledgments

Thanks to the editors for their helpful comments on an earlier draft. Thanks also to Christopher Freiman, and to Eric Chwang and his students, for their helpful comments. I regret that I was unable to take them into account.

## Notes

1. Fabre (2003) adds, however, that in the present state of public opinion, the government should not enforce this right. Fortunately, the law doesn't even give parents a blanket permission to force their own children to donate their organs or bone marrow to their siblings. (See Beck 1990).
2. Goyal *et al.* (2002) interviewed 305 kidney vendors in 2001 in Chennai, India, an average of six years after the selling of their kidneys. The authors report that the vast majority of vendors were either poorer than before because their health had deteriorated, or were no better off financially than before. On the plus side, only 2 of the 305 reported having been coerced into selling their kidneys. Budiani-Saberi and Delmonico report that many studies done in Pakistan, Egypt, India, and the Philippines show that kidney vendors deteriorated in their health as well as their financial status (2008, 928). The same was true of vendors in Iran, where kidney markets are legal.
3. This is a simplification. Marx's exploitation theory also rests on the labor theory of value and his view that the capitalist's profits are stolen from the worker.
4. Milton Friedman and Rose D. Friedman (1980) suggest a more expansive conception of exploitation when they write, "The consumer is protected from being exploited by one seller by the existence of another seller from whom he can buy and who is eager to sell to him" (Ch. 7). Here exploitation is understood as taking advantage of someone through monopoly pricing.
5. Sabini and Silver (1982) explain the escalating obedience of many in the Milgram experiments, as well as the escalating obedience of many in Nazi Germany, partly in terms of moral entrapment.

## References

Anderson, Elizabeth. 1993. *Value in Ethics and Economics.* Cambridge, MA: Harvard University Press.

Aristotle, 1999. *Nicomachean Ethics.* Translated by Terence Irwin. Indianapolis, IN: Hackett.

Asch, Solomon. 1955. "Opinions and Social Pressure." *Scientific American* 193: 31–35.

Badhwar, Neera K. 2008. "Friendship and Commercial Societies." *Politics, Philosophy & Economics* 7 (3) (August): 301–326.

Badhwar, Neera K. 2009. "The Milgram Experiments, Learned Helplessness, and Character Traits." *The Journal of Ethics* 13 (2/3): 257–289.

Barnett, Andy H., Roger D. Blair, and David L. Kaserman. 2002. "A Market for Organs." In *Entrepreneurial Economics: Bright Ideas from the Dismal Science*, 89–105. New York: Oxford University Press.

Beck, Joan. 1990. "For Court to Compel Marrow 'Gift' Turns Donor Into a Victim." http://articles.chicagotribune.com/1990-09-17/news/9003180116_1_tamas-bosze-monica-reynolds-bosze-and-curran, accessed May 30, 2014.

Boo, Katherine. 2012. *Behind the Beautiful Forevers: Life, Death, and Hope in a Mumbai Undercity*. New York: Random House.

Budiani-Saberi, D. A. and F. L. Delmonico. 2008. "Organ Trafficking and Transplant Tourism: A Commentary on the Global Realities." *American Journal of Transplantation* 8 (5) (May): 925–929. doi:10.1111/j.1600-6143.2008.02200.x.

Cherry, Mark J. 2005. *Kidney for Sale by Owner: Human Organs, Transplantation, and the Market*. Washington. DC: Georgetown University Press.

Danovitch, Gabriel M. and Alan B. Leichtman. 2006. "Kidney Vending: The 'Trojan Horse' of Organ Transplantation." *Clinical Journal of the American Society of Nephrology* I: 1133–35.

Department of Health & Human Services. *Medicare Coverage of Kidney Dialysis and Kidney Transplant Services*. http://www.medicare.gov/Pubs/pdf/10128.pdf.

Domen, Ronald E. 1995. "Paid-Versus-Volunteer Blood Donation in the US: A Historical Review." *Transfusion Medicine Reviews* IX (1): 53–59.

Ellis, Marie. 2013. "Artificial Kidney Could Help Those with Kidney Failure." *Medical News Today*, September 24. http://www.medicalnewstoday.com/articles/266471.php.

Epstein, Richard. 2006. "The Economics of Organ Donation." http://www.econlib.org/library/Columns/y2006/Epsteinkidneys.html.

Fabre, Cécile. 2003. "Justice and the Compulsory Taking of Live Body Parts," Utilitas, V. 15, 2.

Feinberg, Joel. 1990. *Harmless Wrongdoing*, vol. IV of *The Moral Limits of the Criminal Law*. New York: Oxford University Press.

Friedman, Milton. 1962. *Capitalism and Freedom*. 40th anniversary edn. Chicago: University of Chicago Press.

Friedman, Milton and Rose D. Friedman. 1980. *Free to Choose: A Personal Statement*. Orlando: Harcourt Books.

Ghods, Ahad J. and Shekoufeh Savaj. 2006. "Iranian Model of Paid and Regulated Living-Unrelated Kidney Donation." *Clinical Journal of the American Society of Nephrology* 1: 1136–1145.

Goodwin, Michele. 2004. "Altruism's Limits: Law, Capacity, and Organ Commodification." *Rutgers Law Review* 56 (2): 305–407.

Goodwin, Michele. 2007. "The Organ Donor Taboo." *Forbes.com*, September 28.

Goyal, Madhav, Ravindra L. Mehta, Lawrence J. Schneiderman, and Ashwini R. Sehgal. 2002. "Economic and Health Consequences of Selling a Kidney in India." *Journal of the American Medical Association* 288 (13) (October 2): 1589–1593.

Havocscope. Global Black Market Information. http://www.havocscope.com/tag/organ-trafficking/.

Hippen, Benjamin E. 2008. *Organ Sales and Moral Travails: Lessons from the Living Kidney Vendor Program in Iran*. Policy Analysis No. 614. CATO Institute.

Hippen, Benjamin E. and Sally Satel. 2008. "Crowding Out, Crowding In, and Financial Incentives for Organ Procurement." In *When Altruism Isn't Enough: The Case for Compensating Kidney Donors*, 96–110. Washington, DC: AEI Press.

Hossain, Mohammed P., Elizabeth C. Goyder, Jan E. Rigby, and El Nahas Meguid. 2009. "CKD and Poverty: A Growing Global Challenge." *American Journal of Kidney Diseases* 53 (1) (January): 166–174. http://lpd.com/images/Hossain_2009.pdf.

Institute for Justice. http://www.ij.org/.

Iyer, Malathy and Pratibha Masand. 2012. "Red Tape Kills Teenage Kidney Patient." *The Times of India*, August 23. http://articles.timesofindia.indiatimes.com/2012-08-23/mumbai/33341558_1_patient-and-donor-transplant-operation-liver-and-kidney-transplant.

Jacobson, Mark. 2007. "Dharavi: Mumbai's Shadow City." *National Geographic*, May. Accessed July 28, 2013. http://ngm.nationalgeographic.com/2007/05/dharavi-mumbai-slum/jacobson-text/1.

Jha, Vivekanand. 2004. "Paid Transplants in India: The Grim Reality." *Nephrology Dialysis Transplantation* 9 (3): 541–543.

John Paul II. 2000. "Address to the 18th International Congress of the Transplantation Society." Accessed September 13, 2014. http://www.vatican.va/holy_father/john_paul_ii/speeches/2000/jul-sep/documents/hf_jp-ii_spe_20000829_transplants_en.html, August 29.

Kant, Immanuel. 1948. *Groundwork of the Metaphysics of Morals*. Trans. H.J. Paton, *The Moral Law*. London, New York: Hutchinson's University Library.

Kass, Leon R. 2002. *Life, Liberty and the Defense of Dignity: The Challenge for Bioethics*. San Francisco: Encounter Books.

Kramer, John E. 2012. "Final Victory for Cancer Patients In Bone Marrow Donor Case." http://www.ij.org/bone-marrow-release-6-25-2012.

LifeSharers. 2007. "Transplant Smackdown – Organ Bureaucrats Attack Organ Donors." http://www.lifesharers.org/pressrelease20071205.aspx, Dec. 5.

Locke, John. 1661 [2004]. "Venditio." *Locke: Political Writings*, edited by David Wootton, 442–446. Indianapolis, IN: Hackett Publishing.

Logan, Pamela. 1997. "Witness to a Tibetan Sky Burial." http://alumnus.caltech.edu/~pamlogan/skybury.htm.

Loving Donation. http://lovingdonation.com/surrogate-mother-intended-parents/surrogacy-faq.

Major, R. L. 2008. "Paying Kidney Donors: Time to Follow Iran?" *McGill Journal of Medicine* 11 (1) (January): 67–69.

Matas, Arthur J. 2007. *A Gift of Life Deserves Compensation How to Increase Living Kidney Donation with Realistic Incentives*. Policy Analysis No. 604. Washington, DC: CATO Institute.

McCloskey, Deirdre. 2006. *The Bourgeois Virtues: Ethics for an Age of Commerce*. Chicago: University of Chicago Press.

McQueen, M. P. 2008. "Paying Workers to Go Abroad for Health Care." *Wall Street Journal*. http://online.wsj.com/news/articles/SB122273570173688551, accessed July 31, 2013.

Menon, P, A. Krishnakumar, V. Sridhar, R. Sharma, and L. Bavadam. 1997. "Kidneys Still for Sale." *Frontline* December 13. http://www.frontline.in/navigation/?type=static&page=flonnet&rdurl=fl1425/14250640.htm.

Milgram, Stanley. 1974. *Obedience to Authority: An Experimental View.* New York: Harper & Row.
National Kidney Foundation, The. http://www.kidney.org/.
Organ Procurement and Transplantation Network, The. http://optn.transplant.hrsa.gov/.
Radcliffe-Richards, Janet, A. S. Daar, R. D. Guttmann, R. Hoffenberg, I. Kennedy, M. Lock, R.A. Sells, and N. Tilney. 1998. "The Case for Allowing Kidney Sales." *The Lancet* 351 (9120) (June 27): 1950–1952.
Reddy, K.C. 1993. "Should Paid Donation Be Banned? To Buy or Let Die." *The National Medical Journal of India* 6 (3): 137–139.
Robertson, Nic. 2009. "Man Must Choose between Selling Kidney or Child." *CNN.com Asia*, July 16. http://edition.cnn.com/2009/WORLD/asiapcf/07/16/pakistan.organ.selling/index.html?iref=allsearch.
Rose, David C. 2011. *The Moral Foundation of Economic Behavior.* New York: Oxford University Press.
Rothbard, Murray. 2008. "Free Market." In *The Concise Encyclopedia of Economics.* Indianapolis, IN: Liberty Fund. http://www.econlib.org/library/CEE.html.
Sabini, John and Maury Silver. 1982. "On Destroying the Innocent with a Clear Conscience." In *Moralities of Everyday Life*, 55–87. Oxford: Oxford University Press.
Sack, Kevin. 2012. "60 Lives, 30 Kidneys, All Linked." *New York Times*, February 18, Health section.
Sandel, Michael. 2012. "Lead Essay: How Markets Crowd Out Morals." *Boston Review* (May 1).
Satel, Sally. 2012. "An Organ Donor Revolution." *The Wall Street Journal*, July 10, and http://www.aei.org/article/society-and-Culture/an-Organ-Donor-Revolution.
Satz, Debra. 2010. *Why Some Things Should Not Be for Sale: The Moral Limits of Markets.* New York: Oxford University Press.
Scheper-Hughes, Nancy. 2002. "The Ends of the Body: Commodity Fetishism and the Global Trade in Organs." *SAIS Review* XXII (1): 61–80.
Scheper-Hughes, Nancy. 2004. "Parts Unknown: Undercover Ethnography of the Organs-Trafficking Underworld." *Ethnography* 5 (1): 29–73.
Scheper-Hughes, Nancy. 2011. "The Rosenbaum Kidney Trafficking Gang." *Counterpunch*, November 30.
Tabarrok, Alexander. 2002. "The Organ Shortage: A Tragedy of the Commons?" In *Entrepreneurial Economics: Bright Ideas from the Dismal Science*, 107–111. Oxford: Oxford University Press.
Taylor, James Stacey. 2005. *Stakes and Kidneys: Why Markets in Human Body Parts Are Morally Imperative.* Live Questions in Ethics and Moral Philosophy. Burlington, VT: Ashgate.
Taylor, James Stacey. 2006. "Black Markets, Transplant Kidneys and Interpersonal Coercion." *Journal of Medical Ethics* 32: 698–701.
Thiagarajan, C.M., K.C. Reddy, D. Shunmugasundaram, R. Jayachandran, P. Nayar, S. Thomas, and V. Ramachandran. 1990. "The Practice of Unconventional Renal Transplantation (UCRT) at a Single Centre in India." *Transplantation Proceedings* 22 (3): 912–914.

Tracy, Marc. 2009. "Organ Donation's Legality, Jewish and Otherwise." *The Scroll*, July 30.
United Network for Organ Sharing (UNOS). www.unos.org.
Wertheimer, Alan. 1996. *Exploitation*. Princeton, NJ: Princeton University Press.
Wertheimer, Alan and Matt Zwolinski. 2013. "Exploitation." In *The Stanford Encyclopedia of Philosophy*, edited by Edward N. Zalta. Stanford, CA: The Metaphysics Research Lab. http://plato.stanford.edu/entries/exploitation/.

# 19 Banks and trust in Adam Smith

*Maria Pia Paganelli*

## Introduction

One can see banking as a mediating institution based on trust. In a small pre-commercial society, trust is personal and credit markets quite limited and based on personal knowledge. In larger commercial societies, credit markets tend to expand, but this is not possible if they are based only on personal trust. This is because of the difficulties of getting to know every customer in a large and impersonal society. Institutional trust needs to supplement personal trust. One trusts a bank and/or the banking system more than the individual teller in the bank, and the bank trusts credit scoring and the legal system in the face of a lack of personal knowledge of individual clients. Yet personal and impersonal trust act generally as complements for one another rather than substitutes.

Adam Smith's vision of banking may be interpreted as an example of an analysis of this mix of institutional and personal trust. Bankers in Smith's time tended to be prominent public figures, with known reputation and known assets (personal trust), but bankers were also legally bound by unlimited liability (institutional trust). They gave credit to "men of credit" (personal trust), but when it became difficult to verify this credit, Smith argued, regulation was needed (institutional trust).

## Banks and trust in Adam Smith

The lending market is a market based on trust. Trust is difficult to offer because trustworthiness is difficult to judge. How can we generate enough trust and trustworthiness to create and sustain a lending market?

Adam Smith lived in eighteenth-century Scotland, during a time of social and economic change when the economy began to grow significantly. As commercial interactions expanded, the frequency of interactions with individuals whom one did not previously know and with impersonal instruments of exchange expanded, too. The increased commerce brought about, among other things, new needs and new institutions, such as a credit market and a banking system. Adam Smith's description of the banking system in Scotland in the eighteenth century in his *Wealth of Nations* ([1776] 1981) offers us some possible insights into the complex relationship between trust and trustworthiness and their relationship with personal and impersonal relations in a complex, growing commercial society.

The historical "Adam Smith Problem" (for an overview of the problem, see Montes 2003) held that there was a fundamental tension between Smith's two great works, *The Theory of Moral Sentiments* ([1759] 1984) and *The Wealth of Nations* ([1776] 1981). Though most contemporary scholars reject the crude version of this problem (Montes 2004; Otteson 2002; Paganelli 2008), there nonetheless remains a lingering suspicion that Smith's focus on socialization and communal life in his account of moral psychology and his focus on the "self-interest" of actors in an economic setting reveals an inconsistency in his analysis. In what follows, I want to use the example of what Smith has to say about banking to show not only that there is no tension here, but also that Smith's account of a successfully operating banking system integrates communal experience, in the form of personal knowledge and relationships, with economic interaction through institutions in a competitive banking market. The resulting analysis shows that we can infer from Smith's analysis an awareness of the problems that might arise in an extended commercial society where individuals interact with little personal knowledge of each other. But we can also infer that, for Smith, a combination of personal knowledge and interaction with institutional features such as the legal system and the discipline of the market allows for the growth of a stable banking system and a stable society.

Personal trust may be easily achieved with personal knowledge. Yet, in the presence of impersonal relations, personal knowledge may become excessively expensive to achieve. We therefore rely on other sources of knowledge, such as institutions, to generate and maintain trust. Institutional trust plays an important role in supplementing personal trust when personal trust is either weak or too expensive to achieve, such as in large impersonal environments.

Adam Smith realized the complexity of the interactions of personal and impersonal exchanges and of personal and impersonal trust. On the one hand, he is severely critical of personal relations; on the other hand, he is also severely critical of impersonal relations. Smith claims that personal relations are tyrannical in nature as they imply dependency, such as the relations typical of the feudal system. He welcomes the impersonal relations of commercial societies as they bring freedom and dignity to individuals (Paganelli 2013). Indeed, Smith tells us, "Commerce and manufacturers gradually introduced order and good government, and with them the liberty and security of individuals, among the inhabitants of the country, who had before lived [in] servile dependency upon their superior" ([1776] 1981, III.iv.4, 412). Yet too much impersonality may lead us to vices and debauchery (Paganelli 2010). Indeed, in *The Wealth of Nations* we hear that "a man of low condition," moving from his small village to a great city, abandons an environment with close personal ties for an impersonal one in which he "is observed and attended to by nobody" (V.i.g.12, 795–796). So there is no check on his "low profligacy and vice." Smith suggests the reintroduction of personal exchanges to reestablish balance with the guided "study of science and philosophy" (V.i.g.14, 796) and "publick diversions" (V.i.g.15, 796). Smith therefore views society not in terms of either–or but in terms of a complex web of interactions of personal and impersonal relations and exchanges. His description of the banking system is an example of his vision of integrated personal and impersonal trust.

Adam Smith's description of the eighteenth-century Scottish banking system may not be the most accurate available to us (Checkland 1975a). Yet his description may be even more interesting because of this. His knowledge was certainly profound and almost first-hand (e.g., Gherity 1995; Skaggs 1999; Rockoff 2013), given that one of his benefactors (the Duke of Buccleuch) was involved in a major Scottish bank and its subsequent collapse (the Ayr Bank), and given that there are speculations regarding Smith's involvement in the drafting of a banking bill abolishing some small notes and prohibiting the two major banks from creating a monopoly (Checkland 1975a). So if Smith's account is not a perfectly accurate description of reality, as alleged, it may be considered as a description of an idea (see also: Hueckel 2009): banking is (should be?) a delicate game of trust and trustworthiness and the best way to avoid disaster is a delicate balance of competition and regulation.

So here is a problem that emerges with banking. Smith does not explicitly present it in these terms but the argument can be inferred from his words. Why would anyone accept as a form of payment a piece of paper that said that payment will come at a later moment? Why would anyone accept as payment "a shadow without a substance," as Isaac Gervaise ([1720] 1954) would say? For anyone to accept that piece of paper as payment, that person needs to trust that that piece of paper will indeed be transformed into payment at a later date. This can happen in two ways (Frankel 1977). One way is to trust that it is possible to give it to someone else as a form of payment and have this other person accept it without problems. The other way is to trust that, by bringing it to the issuer, the issuer will redeem it for actual payment without problems. In both cases, trust depends either on the individual issuer or receiver, or on the institutions that guarantee that exchange, or on a combination of both. Smith helps us see how individual trust, institutional trust, and their combination generate and sustain a healthy banking system. Bankers in Smith's time tended to be prominent public figures, with good reputations and known assets. The bankers' personal reputation generated trust. Their known assets also contributed to their personal trust; but the fact that they were also legally bound by unlimited liability allowed institutional trust to enhance that personal trust. Individuals were comfortable accepting papers issued by these well-known bankers bounded by unlimited liability because they trusted that their promises to pay would be fulfilled either by their sound banking activities or by the extent of their estate. We can therefore infer from Smith's work that it is not just personal trust or not just institutional trust, but an intertwined relation between personal and institutional trust that allowed this kind of paper money to be widely accepted as intermediary in exchange.

Banks in Smith's time were not initially banks of deposit. They only came to accept deposits later in time when they ran into serious liquidity problems and were looking for ways to increase their cash. Banks would lend money, mostly in the form of paper certificates. And these papers would circulate as money (Munn 1981). As Smith explains, "It is chiefly by discounting bills of exchange, that is, by advancing money upon them before they are due, that the greater part of banks and bankers issue their promissory notes" ([1776] 1981, II.ii.43, 298). The bank advances the amount of the bill minus the legal interest rate until the bill is due. And when the bill is due, it collects it. But the advance that the bank gives is not in gold or silver, but in its own promissory notes, which allows the bank to make a higher profit from a larger sum advanced. It also allows banks to operate with an amount of gold and silver in reserves that is less than the sum of the amount stated in their notes, because it is expected that, under normal circumstances, not all the notes would come back to the bank for redemption at the same time. According to Smith, bankers need only about 20 percent of gold as reserve for immediate demands, the economy running on one-fifth of the gold and silver otherwise required (II.ii.29, 292–293). For Smith, this is one of the major advantages of banking: a country can have a paper money for domestic trade, freeing gold and silver for foreign investment where paper money cannot go.

It is interesting to note why paper money does not have the same reach as gold and silver. While gold and silver are an impersonal means of exchange, paper money is a fiduciary means of exchange. The quality of gold and silver is easily recognizable everywhere in the world. The quality of notes and of note issuers is recognizable only with the knowledge of them. And that knowledge is "personal," in the sense that it is local. Gold and silver are accepted everywhere. Notes are accepted only within the sphere of reputation of the issuer. Indeed, Smith tells us: "paper cannot go abroad; because at a distance from the banks which issue it, and from the country in which payment of it can be extracted by law, it will not be received in common payment" ([1776] 1981, II.ii.32, 294). Corroborating this point, David Hume would call paper money "counterfeit money," exactly because it would not be accepted abroad ([1752] 1985, 284).

But let's go back to Smith's account of banking. In addition to discounting bills of exchange, the Scottish banks

> invented ... another method of issuing their promissory notes; by granting, what they call, cash accounts, that is by giving credit to the extent of a certain sum ... to any individual who could procure two persons of undoubted credit and good landed estate to become surety for him, that whatever money should be advanced to him, within the sum for which the credit had been given, should be repaid upon demand, together with the legal interest.
>
> ([1776] 1981, II.ii.44, 299)

With cash accounts, there is no need to "keep [any] money unemployed to answering such occasional demands. When they actually come upon him, he satisfies them from his cash account with the bank, and gradually replaces the sum borrowed with the money or paper which comes in from the occasional sales of his goods" (II.ii.46, 300).

There was a lot of paper in Scotland during Smith's time. Indeed, as we saw above, most of the circulating money was paper. Smith even claims that the spectacular economic growth of Scotland in the eighteenth century is due to the presence of these papers:

> by the erection of new banking companies in almost every considerable town, and even in some country villages ... the business of the country is almost entirely carried on by means of the paper of those different banking companies, with which purchases and payments of all kinds are commonly made. ... That the trade and industry of Scotland ... have increased considerably during this period, and that the banks have contributed a good deal to this increase, cannot be doubted.
>
> (Smith [1776] 1981, II.ii.41, 297)

But how is it possible to generate enough trust to sustain it?

Again, Smith does not present the problem in these terms but we can infer the answer from his work. He seems to imply that at least the following factors are responsible for the generation of trust in the credit market: the personal wealth and reputation of the bankers combined with the unlimited liability of the banks, and the convertibility of paper money into commodity money. In addition, to further support this trust, it seems to me, Smith supports free competition among issuing banks. But he also advocates two specific regulations while objecting to others. He favors a ban on small bills and on the option clause (a clause that allows temporary suspension of convertibility of notes into specie [precious metal]), while he objects to monopolistic privileges for the two public banks of Scotland, the Bank of Scotland and the Royal Bank of Scotland. The effective signaling of the trustworthiness of individuals remains more complex and problematic. The "men of credit," the guarantees required for the cash accounts, and competition seem to be the mechanisms he describes to signal trustworthiness of the borrowers. Let us analyze each of these factors.

The first two are based on a sort of personal trust, backed by legal guarantees. The unlimited liability of the partners in a bank implies that its partners are personally responsible for all the debt of the bank. If a bank caves to the temptation to over-issue paper in the attempt to increase its profits, and there is a bank run and the bank fails, the partners will have to use their personal wealth to cover all the liabilities of the bank. This liability arrangement implies two things. First, that the bankers tend to be responsible and careful in their lending, as a bad loan, or a series of bad loans, can mean a loss of their family wealth. Having the bankers' personal assets on the line lowers the chances that the bank will become insolvent and increases the trust one has in the bank. Second, that someone who knows that the partners of the banks are very wealthy would be more willing to accept a note from that bank. If the bank runs into problems, the personal wealth of the partners will kick in and cover its losses. This is indeed what happened in the case of the infamous Ayr Bank (Munn 1981). The partners were extremely wealthy and well-known property owners. People were happy to receive their notes because they could trust the extent and the wealth of their property. And when the bank eventually failed, the partners used their family assets to liquidate the obligations of the bank: none of their clients lost a penny, while a vast amount of land was redistributed through this sale. Yet, the popularity and success of the Ayr Bank before its bust and the success of most other provincial banks testifies to the fundamental role of personal trust and the reputation of bankers in a system of unlimited liability. Systems of limited liability, on the other hand, may tend to be less stable. Partners are not personally responsible for the actions of the bank for more than the amount they have originally invested. So their reputation and personal wealth cannot play the same stabilizing role as in the system of unlimited liability (White 1995).

The more complex society becomes, the more impersonal and the less face-to-face it becomes, the more there is need for mechanisms that can supplement personal trust. Personal trust is no longer able to do all the legwork because of the higher information costs in an impersonal society. Personal trust still remains, but where it cannot reach, another trust-generating mechanism needs to step in. Market competition is, for Smith, one of the most important of these mechanisms (see also Seabright 2010). Yet, market competition does not substitute for personal trust; it simply fills in where personal trust cannot reach and may enhance personal trust where it does reach. With the increasing costs of verifying information that characterize impersonal exchange, lenders may attract riskier borrowers and not be able to distinguish them from the more prudent ones. Borrowers tend to overestimate their probability of success and therefore tend to over-borrow (Bentham 1796; Paganelli 2003). They also tend to like promissory notes more than loans in precious metals because promissory notes free idle capital, and because they could be paid back a little at a time. This, all things being equal, would increase the amount of credit given and therefore the amount of paper money in circulation. For Smith, bankers, inexperienced bankers at least, have incentives to over-issue paper money because they gain from the interest on the notes. Since the interest on the notes is revenue to the bank, the more notes issued, the more interest collected, the more revenue generated, and, allegedly, the higher the profits for the bank. And if banks discount bills of exchange with promissory notes rather than with gold and silver, they could make even more profit (Smith [1776] 1981, II.ii.43, 298–299). Creditors, therefore, are tempted to ask for over-issuing of credit, and banks are tempted to over-issue credit.

This is a problem because it increases the risk of holding notes and the probability that a bank may be subject to a run and become not just illiquid but insolvent. The history of Scottish provincial banks includes many of these cases over time, especially in the early expansionary period of the provincial banks. But Smith and history see the benefits of competition over time, especially in terms of building trust in the fiduciary medium, which eventually is reflected in the increased use and acceptance of it (Munn 1981; Checkland 1975b).

If a bank over-issues, for whatever reasons, that bank most likely will not only not increase its profits, but would increase its probability of failure. For Smith, a bank may over-issue, but this does not imply that note holders are willing to hold these extra notes. The note holders would indeed think of these extra notes as extra and would not be willing to hold them. Rather than holding paper money, the merchant has incentives to go to the bank and redeem the paper money for specie and send that specie abroad for a more fruitful investment. The bank is under obligation to pay on demand and it will have to exchange the note for gold and silver, unless it is willing to face the risk of a bank run, which would increase the probability of bankruptcy (WN II.ii.48, p. 301). To pay for the incoming notes, the bank needs specie. But if the bank over-issues, it will not have all that specie readily available. The bank must get gold and silver by borrowing from another nearby bank or, more commonly, from other banks in London. This is expensive, not only because of the transaction and transportation costs (the precious metals have to be physically transported from a bank (say, in London) to the local bank that over-issued), but also because often the rate at which the over-issuing bank can draw from other local banks and/or London banks is higher than the interest it receives from its borrowers. Indeed, "The Scotch banks, no doubt, paid all of them very dearly for their own imprudence and inattention" (Smith [1776] 1981,II.ii.56, 304).

As Smith points out, borrowing precious metals from other banks (and transporting them to the bank in need) to redeem notes can be done on occasions but not regularly. If it is done regularly, the bank will eventually go out of business. To avoid losing profits or generating bank runs, the banks learn to decrease the amount of issuing (II.ii.49–56, 301–304). This means that, at least after the first period of adjustment, it is possible to trust the bank notes and therefore to increase one's willingness to hold and use paper, because the bank is more likely to behave judiciously. In an impersonal banking system, trust can therefore be built via convertibility of paper into commodities and the discipline of the market.

Despite the personal reputation and responsibility of the bankers and the institutional checks of guaranteed convertibility, the development of an expanding banking system may generate a level of impersonality that may breed inefficiencies, crises, and injustice. This is where Smith calls for free competition in issuing as well as for state regulation – to attempt to reduce the effects of the dominance of impersonality. By analyzing his call for regulations, the fundamental role of competition will emerge. So let us look at the banking regulation that Smith favors. Smith calls for two banking regulations: he wants to see a ban on small notes and a ban on the "option clause," a clause that allows temporary suspension of convertibility of notes into specie.

Smith justifies the ban on small notes because he claims that with small notes the competitive checks may not work well due to excessive impersonality. People will be less reluctant to accept a small note of dubious or unknown origins than a big note of dubious or unknown origins, as the stakes are minor and the options are fewer. In Smith's day, small notes were commonly used to pay for the salary of day laborers, in face of an increasingly chronic and severe absence of coins. The impersonality of the notes, in the case of small notes, may prove dangerous as small notes would tend to be over-issued and may cause extreme financial distress to the small-income earners who would most commonly use them. Smith therefore advocates banning notes of less than five pounds. Smith tells us, indeed, that,

> where the issuing of bank notes for very small sums is allowed and commonly practiced, many mean people are both enabled and encouraged to become bankers. A person whose promissory note for five pounds, or even for twenty shillings, would be rejected by everybody, will get it to be received without scruple when it is issued for so small a sum as a sixpence. But the frequent bankruptcies to which such beggarly bankers must be liable, may occasion a very considerable inconveniency, and sometimes even a great calamity to many poor people who had received their notes in payment.
> (Smith [1776] 1981, II.ii.90, 323)

This ban would confine notes to transactions between dealers and dealers, and not extend them to transactions between dealers and consumers (II.ii.92, 323). The number of dealers is significantly smaller than the number of consumers. Limiting the circulation of notes to dealers also increases the chances of increasing personal trust, as dealers tend to know each other.

The role of market checks was already mentioned above: with the exception of small-denomination notes, the temptation of over-issuing notes that a bank may have is constrained by the presence of other banks and the ability of a person to redeem notes on demand. If one person does not want to hold the notes of a bank, he or she can redeem the notes for gold or silver or take his or her business to another bank. This ability to reject unwanted money generates trust in the system. The preservation of this competitive check in the formation and maintenance of the fiduciary means of exchange is so important for Smith that he calls for government intervention to stop a mechanism meant to short-circuit it: the option clause.

If a bank accepts and discounts a note of another bank, it increases the trust in and the circulation of a competitor's notes, thereby strengthening the competitor. At the beginning, provincial and public banks would not accept and discount rival notes. But eventually they did accept and discount rival notes, especially the ones of close competitors. This was because they saw it as a means to damage the rival bank and hopefully put it out of business. A bank would discount a competitor's notes but then would keep them, rather than bring them to the issuing bank for redemption. When a bank had collected enough of a competitor's notes, it would bring them in to ask for their redemption all at once. The issuing bank must have enough reserve to honor the notes. If not, the bank would risk a run and failure. To try to prevent liquidity problems caused by their rivals, banks started to issue notes with an option clause: the option was that the bank would convert the note back to precious metals upon demand, but with a delay of up to six months, while paying interest for those months. The clause, when exercised, would buy the bank time to find the precious metals that it did not have in reserve (Checkland 1975b; Munn 1981; Gherity 1995). For Smith, the option clause ([1776] 1981, II.ii.98, 325), which seems to be an instrument of stability, is only superficially so. In reality, it dilutes the incentive to restrain over-issuing by suspending convertibility. Trust in banks is now threatened and Smith calls for a ban on the option clause to maintain the trust in the institution.

I believe my reading of Smith is also indirectly supported by the severe criticisms that Smith offers of most of the other regulations present in banking. For example, Smith objects to the attempts of the two public banks to monopolize issuing ([1776] 1981, II.ii.41–42, 297–298), and he may even have been one of the forces that blocked the public banks' petition for privileges to the parliament (Checkland 1975b). Additionally, Smith points out that, in North America, paper money does not come from banks but from the government. Government paper is made into legal tender. And legal tender forces people to accept a particular form of money, even if they otherwise would not. Legal tender substitutes, crowds out, and destroys trust (Frankel 1977). Force does not integrate personal and impersonal trust but eliminates it; it substitutes for trust by taking its place. Smith seems to imply that the laws establishing legal tender should be abolished to let natural trust re-emerge. So Smith tells us:

> But allowing the colony security to be perfectly good, a hundred pounds payable fifteen years hence, for example, in a country where interest is at six per cent. is worth little more than fourty pounds of ready money. To oblige a creditor, therefore, to accept of this as full payment for a debt of a hundred pounds actually paid down in ready money, was an act of such violent injustice, as has scarce, perhaps, been attempted by the government of any other country which pretended to be free. It bears the evident marks of having originally been, what the honest and downright Doctor Douglas assures us it was, a scheme of fraudulent debtors to cheat their creditors.
> ([1776] 1981, II.ii.100, 326)

And he continues: "No law, therefore, could be more equitable than the act of parliament, so unjustly complained of in the colonies, which declared that no paper currency to be emitted there in time coming, should be a legal tender of payment" (II.ii.101, 327).

Finally, as mentioned above, Smith's description of the invention of the cash account is telling of the fundamental role of personal trust in the issuing of fiduciary means of exchange. Signaling personal trustworthiness is difficult and costly. Scottish bankers created a way to make the signal effective: "Any individual who could procure two persons of undoubted credit and good landed estate to become surety for him" (II.ii.44, 299). This seems a clever way to reincorporate the personal trust and trustworthiness of the traditional "man of credit" (Baroni 2002) with an expanding banking system that may not as easily verify the personal signaling of trustworthiness. With the expansion of society and of banking, the role of signaling the trustworthiness of the "man of credit" decreases, as it becomes too costly to gather information. Today we substitute this expensive personal knowledge with the cheaper impersonal knowledge of credit scores. But this is an indication of both the importance and the challenges of signaling trustworthiness effectively.

Another aspect of signaling trustworthiness that proves challenging, both for Smith and for us, is linked to the above: What happens when wise banks reject a too risky credit extension? Smith tells us that traders use "shift of drawing and redrawing" to raise the money to use to over-trade ([1776] 1981, II.ii.65). This is an interesting twist on the ability of personal and impersonal circumstances to generate or destroy trust. As we saw above, for Smith the over-issuing of credit is dangerous. Banks have to be ready to fulfill their obligation at all times or they might generate bank runs and the very expensive attempts to replenish their coffers to fulfill their obligations (II.ii.48). Yet, banks may still over-issue (41–87). And one of the reasons for which "the circulation has frequently been overstocked with paper-money" (II.2.56) is the banks' difficulties in gaining knowledge regarding the trustworthiness of their creditors.

Smith explains that banks may not understand what they are doing because projectors fool banks when traders draw and redraw upon one another. If they do it from the same banks, the bank will eventually realize what is going on because personal knowledge can be built. But traders are well aware of the danger of personal knowledge in this case. In the attempt to increase impersonality and anonymity and break down personal knowledge, traders start using different banks, making it increasingly difficult for banks to gain that kind of personal knowledge required to give trust or not. Smith explains this tension by claiming that there are two different kinds of bills: "real bills of exchange" and "fictitious bills of exchange." He tells us that

> When two people, who are continually drawing and re-drawing upon one another, discount their bills always with the same banker, he must immediately discover what they are about, and see clearly that they are trading, not with any capital of their own, but with the capital which he advances to them. But this discovery is not altogether so easy when they discount their bills sometimes with one banker, and sometimes with another, and when the same two persons do not constantly draw and re-draw upon one another, but occasionally run round a great circle of projectors, who find it for their interest to assist one another in this method of raising money, and render it, upon that account, as difficult as possible to distinguish between a real and a fictitious bill of exchange; between a bill drawn by real creditor upon a real debtor, and a bill from which there was properly no real creditor but the bank which discounted it; nor any real debtor but the projector who made use of the money.
>
> ([1776] 1981, II.ii.72, 311–312)

When a banker realizes that he is discounting "fictitious bills," it may be too late. "Real bills" can be trusted because they are based on personal knowledge. "Fictitious bills" are impersonal, and of a constructed impersonality meant to hide the personal details of the bill – they should not be trusted.

Whether Smith was an early promoter of the "Real Bill" doctrine or whether the Real Bill doctrine works or not has been discussed elsewhere (Arnon 1999; Glasner 1992; Santiago-Valiente 1988; Selgin 1989) and it is not relevant here. What matters in this context is to notice how, in Smith's analysis, personal knowledge about the projectors helps maintain a healthy banking system, while the unscrupulous projectors try to dilute personal knowledge by attempting to create anonymity, which would maintain the fictitious facade of personal trustworthiness for them while eroding institutional trust. Yet Smith seems to trust the impersonal system of competition among issuing banks to readjust the circulating notes to an efficient and safe level (Cowen and Kroszner 1989; White 1995).

Smith's analysis of banking may therefore be interpreted as an example of an analysis of this mix of institutional and personal trust. Complex commercial societies cannot thrive on an either–or system of trust. There is no opposition between personal trust and impersonal institutions. There is, on the other hand, a healthy interaction of personal and impersonal situations, where personal and impersonal trust act as complements for each other, not substitutes. The necessary presence of institutional trust does not replace personal trust. On the contrary, it enhances it and it fills in the spaces that personal trust, by its personal nature, cannot fill. Indeed, the banking system that Smith describes as generating prosperity is a system where the impersonal trust of unlimited liability and of banking regulations work together with the personal trust and trustworthiness of the bankers and of the "men of credit" to create a healthy and prosperity-generating banking system. The two forms of trust become integrated in a successful commercial society where bankers and customers are able to merge their reliance on personal and institutional forms of trust to form a more secure basis for banking activity.

We can therefore imply from Smith's works that trust is possible in an extended, anonymous society and that his understanding of community is wider than that seen in small face-to-face societies. Smith was well aware that the sort of experience of trust that exists in a small community is very different from that which exists in a large commercial society. But rather than arguing in favor of a return to a more communal form of life, which he believed would necessarily limit the market and prevent the full exploitation of the division of labor, he instead sought ways to enhance the levels of trust and trustworthiness between individuals. Rousseau argued that mankind had been corrupted by the move from small-scale communities to larger societies. Smith, on the contrary, provides us with an analysis of the development of banking from which we can infer how the personal interactions of a small community can be supplemented by trust-generating institutional features such as the legal system and competition. Institutional bases of trust make up for a weakening of personal knowledge and allow for the enhanced exploitation of the division of labor.

Where Rousseau saw commerce in opposition to community and as a threat to the personal bonds of communal life, Smith instead sees the two as complementary and mutually reinforcing. Rousseau's belief that the development of the impersonal institutions of a commercial society supplanted the genuinely human personal relationships of small-scale communities was comprehensively rejected by Smith. In Smith's view, the two forms of relationship can be integrated in the behavior of commercial actors. His views on banking give one example of how this is the case.

It is indeed possible to infer from Smith's work that, in his view, there is no simple binary opposition between interactions that exist on a personal and an impersonal level.

In Smith's account of banking, he depicts a system of competitive banks that are "kept" honest by the rigors of competition and the correct application of regulation. The result is a banking system where we are able to rely on others, not always because we know them personally as members of the same community, but because the sense of communal experience is extended to all of those whom we come to trust as bound together by the institutions of a commercial society. From Smith's analysis of banking we can extract the point that the success of the economy is based on interdependence, and that this, in turn, is based upon the interaction of personal and institutional trust.

## References

Arnon, Arie. 1999. "Free and Not So Free Banking Theories among the Classical; Or, Classical Forerunners of Free Banking and Why They Have Been Neglected." *History of Political Economy* 31 (1): 79–107.

Baroni, Chiara. 2002. "The Man of Credit: An Aristocratic Ethics for the Middle Class?" Unpublished manuscript.

Bentham, Jeremy. 1796. *Defence of Usury: Shewing the Impolicy of the Present Legal Restraints on the Terms of Pecuniary Bargains. To which is Added, a Letter to Adam Smith, Esq. L.L.D. on the Discouragement of Inventive Industry*. Philadelphia, PA: Lang & Ustick.

Checkland, Sydney George. 1975a. "Adam Smith and the Bankers." In *Essays on Adam Smith*, edited by Andrew Skinner and Thomas Wilson, 504–523. Oxford: Clarendon Press.

Checkland, Sydney George. 1975b. *Scottish Banking: A History, 1695–1973*. Glasgow: Collins.

Cowen, Tyler and Randall Kroszner. 1989. "Scottish Banking before 1845: A Model for Laissez-Faire?" *Journal of Money, Credit and Banking* 21 (2): 221–231.

Frankel, S. Herbert. 1977. *Two Philosophies of Money. The Conflict of Trust and Authority*. New York: Oxford University Press.

Gervaise, Isaac. [1720] 1954. *The System Or Theory of the Trade of the World*. Baltimore, MD: Johns Hopkins University Press.

Gherity, James A. 1995. "The Option Clause in Scottish Banking, 1730–65: A Reappraisal." *Journal of Money, Credit and Banking* 27 (3): 713–726.

Glasner, David. 1992. "The Real-Bills Doctrine in the Light of the Law of Reflux." *History of Political Economy* 24 (2): 867–894.

Hueckel, Glenn. 2009. "'In the Heat of Writing': Polemics and the 'Error of Adam Smith' in the Matter of the Corn Bounty." In *Elgar Companion to Adam Smith*, edited by Jeffrey Young. Cheltenham, UK: Edward Elgar.

Hume, David. [1752] 1985. *Essays, Moral, Political, and Literary*. Indianapolis, IN: Liberty Fund.

Montes, Leonidas. 2003. "Das Adam Smith Problem: Its Origins, the Stages of the Current Debate, and One Implication for our Understanding of Sympathy." *Journal of the History of Economic Thought* 25 (1): 63.

Montes, Leonidas. 2004. *Adam Smith in Context: A Critical Reassessment of Some Central Components of His Thought*. New York: Palgrave Macmillan.

Munn, Charles W. 1981. *The Scottish Provincial Banking Companies, 1747–1864*. Edinburgh: John Donald.

Otteson, James R. 2002. *Adam Smith's Marketplace of Life*. Cambridge: Cambridge University Press.

Paganelli, Maria Pia. 2003. "In Medio Stat Virtus: An Alternative View of Usury in Adam Smith's Thinking." *History of Political Economy* 35 (1): 21–48.

Paganelli, Maria Pia. 2008. "The Adam Smith Problem in Reverse: Self-Interest in *The Wealth of Nations* and *The Theory of Moral Sentiments*." *History of Political Economy* 40 (2): 365–382.

Paganelli, Maria Pia. 2010. "The Moralizing Role of Distance in Adam Smith: The Theory of Moral Sentiments as Possible Praise of Commerce." *History of Political Economy* 42 (3): 425–441.

Paganelli, Maria Pia. 2013. "Commercial Relations: From Adam Smith to Field Experiments." In *The Oxford Handbook of Adam Smith*, edited by Christopher J. Berry, Maria Pia Paganelli and Craig Smith, 333–352. New York: Oxford University Press.

Rockoff, Hugh. 2013. "Adam Smith on Money, Banking, and the Price Level." In *The Oxford Handbook of Adam Smith*, edited by Christopher Berry, Maria Pia Paganelli, Craig Smith, 307–332. Oxford: Oxford University Press.

Santiago-Valiente, Wilfredo. 1988. "Historical Background of the Classical Monetary Theory and the 'Real-Bills' Banking Tradition." *History of Political Economy* 20 (1): 43–63.

Seabright, Paul. 2010. *The Company of Strangers: A Natural History of Economic Life*. 2nd edn. Princeton, NJ: Princeton University Press.

Selgin, George A. 1989. "The Analytical Framework of the Real-Bills Doctrine." *Journal of Institutional and Theoretical Economics* 145 (3): 489–507.

Skaggs, Neil T. 1999. "Adam Smith on Growth and Credit – Too Weak a Connection?" *Journal of Economic Studies* 26 (6): 481–496.

Smith, Adam. [1759] 1984. *The Theory of Moral Sentiments*. Indianapolis, IN: Liberty Classics.

Smith, Adam. [1776] 1981. *An Inquiry into the Nature and Causes of the Wealth of Nations*. Indianapolis, IN: Liberty Classics.

White, Lawrence. 1995. *Free Banking in Britain: Theory, Experience, and Debate, 1800–1845*. London: IEA.

# 20 Comment: Bankers, vampires, and organ sellers

Who can you trust?

*John Thrasher and David Schmidtz*

Critics of market society argue that community is corrupted by commerce. Rousseau, Marx, Dewey – even Rawls – argue that commercial relations lead us to see our fellows in the wrong way, as mere means to our commercial ends rather than as separate and equal sources of value (see Rousseau 1987, 25–110; Gauthier 2006; Rasmussen 2008; Marx and Engels 1976; Cohen 2009; Dewey 2008, 41–53, 383–403, 460–480; Dewey 1997. chap. 4–5; Rawls, 1999, §13; Part III). The history of market societies tells a more complicated story. In pre-modern times, people lived and worked as their parents and grandparents lived and worked. Horizons were limited. That has changed considerably due to the expansion of markets and market institutions. We now learn from and work, exchange, and communicate with vast networks of distant others. The result has not been an erosion of community per se but a proliferation of community in diverse and novel forms.

Whether these changes are on net good or bad is an open question. The greatest early defender of markets, Adam Smith, saw clearly that markets have the ability to liberate us from the dead hand of the past. With this liberation come dangers, however. Market society and commerce can be corrupting. Some of the virtues and habits that limit or even reverse the damage, however, are themselves a direct outgrowth of markets. Commerce disciplines us and teaches us self-command. It directs us into networks of reciprocity and cooperation that have allowed us to prosper far beyond anything our ancestors could have imagined, but that prosperity also tempts (what Smith called) a "poor man's son" to see wealth as its own reward and to focus on baubles rather than on true happiness (Smith 1976, 181–183, IV.i.8; for a discussion, see Hanley 2009, ch. 1). As Smith understood, the success of markets in creating and maintaining communities that allow for true human flourishing depends, in large part, on legal and cultural institutions that frame markets. Some of these institutions secure a framework for reciprocal exchange and mutual understanding that preserves and extends our sense of community and fraternity; others pervert community.

These three essays make this point, each in its own way. They focus on how real markets impact actual communities. There are tensions between intimate community and larger market orders. The question is how those tensions manifest themselves and whether (and if so how) market institutions can create new forms of community that mediate human action in fruitful and cooperative ways.

Maria Paganelli looks at how commercial relationships evolved in response to changing market conditions in the emerging eighteenth-century Scottish banking industry. Neera Badhwar suggests how kidney markets can create new international communities, supplanting existing perverse communities with new market-based associations. Steve Horwitz suggests that communities, at their best, consist of market-like processes of social learning and cooperation. As Steve Horwitz stresses, associational relationships can be mutually advantageous and voluntary with or without currency-mediated commerce. That is, communities of a certain type are not merely compatible with commerce; they *are* commerce.

This highlights an important distinction between thicker communities and what can be called "associations." Badhwar's and Horwitz's essays in particular use the term "community" to refer both to (thick) communities based on shared values, goals, interests, or beliefs and to (thin) communities that do not presuppose any broad sharing of values, goals, interests, and beliefs. Associations form and are sustained by particular shared interests, without members necessarily having to share other beliefs, values, or goals. Firms, professional groups, international institutions, and many other similar networks of people are associational communities. Even if markets undermine thicker communities, they encourage associations. Market societies foster a kind of equality based on the exchange relation. Traders tend not to care about the social status, religious affiliation, or ultimate moral worth of their trading partners so long as trade is beneficial. As such, vertical relations in market societies tend to level and become less important. Tocqueville noted that this leveling and distancing have the paradoxical effect of fostering associations. As he famously observed:

> Americans of all ages, all conditions, all minds constantly unite. Not only do they have commercial and industrial associations in which all take part, but they also have a thousand other kinds: religious, moral, grave, futile, very general and very particular, immense and very small; Americans use associations to give fêtes, to found seminaries, to build inns, to raise churches, to distribute books, to send missionaries to the antipodes ... Everywhere that, at the head of a new undertaking, you see the government in France and a great lord in England, count on it that you will perceive an association in the United States.
> (2011, 489, II.ii.5)

What Tocqueville saw in nineteenth-century Americans can today be seen in market societies across the world. Critics of markets often privilege one form of community, which markets and liberalism disrupt, while ignoring diverse forms of association and enterprise that markets and freedom foster. How those associations develop and the role that they play in a larger society will depend on how those associations and institutions interact with one another and with the thicker communities that precede market associations.

Paganelli illustrates the complex relationship between the personal trust formed in thick, local communities and the operation of largely impersonal lending institutions in eighteenth-century Scotland. This period saw the rise of modern financial institutions in England and Scotland. The development of lending banks was of particular interest to Adam Smith in his inquiry into the wealth of nations. Smith saw that the paper money and credit that banks create were essential to the stunning economic development of the time, but this was puzzling. Banks create loans in the form of pieces of paper (bank notes) that are then exchanged for real goods and are backed by specie. What, Smith wondered, fosters the trust that this system presupposes, absent the traditional networks of local knowledge that maintained earlier lending markets? The answer, Paganelli argues, is that *institutional* assurances, themselves resting on networks of personal trust, could create and extend conditions for impersonal exchange in credit markets. *Personal* trust is hard to earn and costly when misplaced. Crucially, its scope is also inherently limited. Trust in Aberdeen need not extend to London. To limit oneself to networks of personal trust would be to limit the scope of our commercial society to people we know, recognizing that even then we are likely to be wrong some of the time.

The enduring solution to these knowledge problems and credibility/assurance problems is to build extended networks of impersonal, institutional trust. Adam Smith, according to Paganelli, saw three ways of ensuring trust in credit markets. First, banks should have unlimited liability, making their principals personally accountable for losses. This would discipline their lending and introduce a personal stake and personal element of trust into the impersonal banking institution. Second, market competition forces banks to economize. Finally, regulation plays a role in reinforcing trust and allowing the smooth functioning of a community of lenders and borrowers by eliminating practices that tend to undermine cooperation in the lending market. For instance, Smith argued that the practice of issuing "small bills" backstopped by "options clauses" should be banned to prevent destabilizing bank runs by other lending institutions. Extending and institutionalizing impersonal trust is by implication a powerful mechanism for building extended communities.

It is puzzling that people should be as trusting as they are in the face of (sometimes rapidly) evolving institutions. Smith's conjecture was that there is in human nature, quite apart from self-interest, a primordial propensity to truck, barter, and exchange. We are built to make deals, to trade, to be part of relations of mutual benefit; that is how we build a case for self-esteem and for the warranted esteem of others. Ultimately, that is how we build a community. This propensity could – and apparently sometimes does – drive us to trust others on terrain where self-interest fears to tread. As a new kind of association begins to evolve, we observe early adopters taking the plunge. Upon seeing that their propensity to explore unknown territory has not been a disaster, we take the plunge ourselves, often trusting the appearance of a profit opportunity far more than would be objectively warranted. It leads to bubbles, but we are wired not only to seek profit but also to join in the fun.

Badhwar highlights the interplay between personal and impersonal dimensions of trust and reciprocity in the context of organ markets. She argues that thicker forms of community can be perverse. They can hamper rather than benefit. Norms in parts of India, for instance, create exploitative communities that spread in Indian organ markets as currently constituted. She contrasts these perverse communities with the romantic notions of community presupposed by Western critics of organ markets. International open markets in organs may indeed undermine rather than sustain perverse communities, and no one but exploiters and the grossly misinformed would lament the demise of the perverse ones. Some critics fear that international organ markets will destroy what is good about communities of altruistic organ donations that currently exist. This fear is, according to Badhwar, unfounded. In an international organ exchange regime, she believes, people will remain as willing and able as they are now to give organs to friends and family. The difference is that people who are not altruistically motivated will be safely and surely brought into a network of exchange that can save thousands of lives every year.

Communal networks of personal trust and altruism do not extend much beyond friends and family. Altruism and fellow-feeling is real, but not robust enough to support extended networks of cooperation among strangers. Associations, as we described them, do not require much by way of personal trust and local knowledge, and thus are the main form in which cooperation extends beyond the local level. This is not to say personal trust is unnecessary or absent in associational communities, only that it comes in many forms. International organ markets, as Badhwar sees them, are associational communities requiring vast structures of impersonal trust assured through international institutions and norms. Individuals will be able to donate and receive organs reliably and safely, without needing to know much about other individuals involved in the association. Indeed, personal ties would not help much. One may trust a doctor's good will, but if the doctor's hospital is unsanitary or unsafe, the trust is misplaced.

## Conclusion: community *is* commerce

As Horwitz notes, the group of "people we know" can be much larger than our circle of kin. Thus, wider circles of cooperation are often common. Impersonal trust may not be so fundamentally different from personal trust in its effect. A community is essentially a functional unit. It exists in order to be a particular framework of mutual aid, taking shape as a response to the particular problems it exists to solve. Horwitz's discussion of implicit norms of vampire bat communities illustrates this point. Vampire bats occasionally fail to find food, and the consequence of failing two nights in a row is death. Accordingly, it is a matter of life and death for vampire bats to be part of a community where bats with surplus food share with neighbors. And they do. Vampire bats have a knack for understanding the plight of fellow vampire bats and for being ready to help, sometimes even in preference to helping immediate kin. They share not so much with kin per se or neighbors per se as with neighbors who can reasonably be trusted to reciprocate.

It is important that vampire bats don't need to share values or beliefs to form such a community. Shared vulnerability and the ability to benefit through mutual exchange is enough. Although they are not a "thick" community, they literally bet their lives on each other's goodwill, and in so doing build community ties that transcend kinship. They build communities not based on historically specific knowledge out of which individuals build networks of personal trust. Instead, they build communities based on a "tit-for-tat" willingness to cooperate first and continue to cooperate until presented with concrete evidence that a potential partner is a free rider rather than a reciprocator.

Associational communities tend to have attractive features that communities based on shared norms or values tend to lack. First, they are voluntary to the extent that individuals have a right to exit. Second, to the extent that members of the association have means of limiting parasitism, free riding, and commons tragedies, they limit relationships within the community to forms of voluntary cooperation and mutual advantage, and to that extent treat individual members with respect rather than as replacement parts of an organic whole. Where relationships are a matter of one-way charitable transfer, the fact remains that those relationships too are voluntary. Third, the degree to which an association's members are free agents who can walk away when the costs of association outweigh the benefits is an association's way of monitoring itself and of knowing when it is ceasing to be truly functional. Thicker communities, so deeply intertwined that exit comes only at monumental cost, lack this internal discipline. Finally, calling a relationship *impersonal* is not the same as calling it *cold*. Butchers and bakers (and even the world's largest retailers) build up loyal clienteles partly by creating places of business that make customers feel welcome.

Commerce and associational communities as we have described them both involve reciprocal exchange relations. Forming and sustaining a community is an act of trust, but so is an exchange. Commerce requires us to place enormous trust in distant others and, as these essays illustrate in different ways, this trust is possible only in the context of large networks of impersonal associational communities. Given this, we might ask whether communities are a precondition for commerce or whether commerce creates communities. This way of thinking is mistaken. Associational communities and commerce are different aspects of the most tangible manifestation of humanity's propensity to exchange and reciprocate. In this way, it is proper to say that commerce (at its best) is community and community (at its best) is commerce.

## Acknowledgments

Our heartfelt thanks to editors Rob Garnett and Lenore Ealy for their patient, encouraging, and productive editorial assistance.

Work on this chapter was supported by a grant from the John Templeton Foundation, but the views expressed are solely those of the authors and do not necessarily reflect the views of the Templeton Foundation.

## References

Cohen, G. A. 2009. *Why Not Socialism?* Princeton, NJ: Princeton University Press.
Dewey, John. 1997. *Experience And Education.* Reprint edition. New York: Free Press.
Dewey, John. 2008. *The Middle Works of John Dewey,* vol. XIV, 1899–1924: Human Nature and Conduct, 1922. Edited by J. Boydston. Carbondale, IL: Southern Illinois University Press.
Gauthier, David. 2006. *Rousseau: The Sentiment of Existence.* Cambridge: Cambridge University Press.
Hanley, Ryan. 2009. *Adam Smith and the Character of Virtue.* Cambridge: Cambridge University Press.
Marx, Karl and Friedrich Engels. 1976. *Collected Works of Karl Marx and Friedrich Engels, 1845–47,* vol. V: Theses on Feuerbach, The German Ideology and Related Manuscripts. London: International Publishers.
Rasmussen, Dennis Carl. 2008. *The Problems and Promise of Commercial Society: Adam Smith's Response to Rousseau.* University Park, PA: Pennsylvania State University Press.
Rawls, John. 1999. *A Theory of Justice.* Revised. Cambridge, MA: Belknap Press.
Rousseau, Jean-Jacques. 1987. "Discourse on the Origin of Inequality." In *The Basic Political Writings,* edited and translated by D. Cress, 25–110. Indianapolis, IN: Hackett.
Smith, Adam. 1976. *The Theory of Moral Sentiments.* The Glasgow Edition of the Works and Correspondence of Adam Smith. Indianapolis, IN: Liberty Fund.
Tocqueville, Alexis de. 2011. *Democracy in America.* Translated by Harvey C. Mansfield and Delba Winthrop. Chicago: University of Chicago Press.

# Envoi

## *The Apologia of Mercurius*

### Frederick Turner

– One of my names, and it will have to do.
I've had so many names, I can't keep track.
If you're a god, and everywhere at once,
And you have been around a long, long time,
You find it hard remembering events
In their right order, and you often tend
To wander and digress. And one is busy
With being what one is. Right now, for instance,
I'm trying to figure out the price of gold,
Tracking a sweet and viral metaphor,
Checking a Hindu wife's new microloan,
Getting to know an optical computer
With quantum logic, that I'll have to use,
Stalking a loophole in a banking regulation,
And trying to guide this stupid poet's mouse.

Or maybe "Hermes" would be better – sure,
"Hermetic," "hermeneutics" still have traction,
And Trismegistus, though a fiction, lives.
Fictions can live, metabolize, and grow,
Respond to stimuli, and sometimes think.
But Hermod, Lug, Chibchakun, Ayizan,
Yacatecuhtli, Hebrew Metatron,
Or Benzai-ten, or Volos of the Slavs,
Or Ekahau or Eshu, all would work
If you repeat the name; oldest of all
Among the written languages of men
Would be Ningizzida, the lord of light,
The lord of the all-fruited, snake-girt tree,
But I'll stick with "Mercurius" for now.
In every myth I am a latecomer,
And there's a deep injustice in this charge.
I recall dimly, as a larval daemon,

## The Apologia of Mercurius

Coming to consciousness among the lichens.
Only a trade then, a communication
Between the alga and its fungal host,
The phycobiont and the mycobiont,
A sort of contract, offering sugar fuel
For solvent from the fungus water-tank.

But traders always seem new-fangled to
The partner who takes on a middle-man;
As Hermes I was deemed a parvenu,
And had to steal Apollo's kine to get
A voice with the august Olympians,
And pull off one of my most favorite deals,
The herald's karykeion for the lyre.
That karykeion, the caduceus,
Was Jacob's crook, who in a war of cons,
Outsmarted Laban, as he had his brother,
And plied the lever of domestication
To make a profit and to make a prophet,
The father of the tribes of Israel.

I warned you I would wander, but it seems
My story's so connected everywhere
That every thread drags out another braid.
As an old god I know I'm garrulous;
As an old goddess, more garrulous still.
But there's a river-mouth to these meanders:
Follow me from the source and we'll get there.

The lichens surely weren't my beginning
(Now that I think about it). That was late.
I must have been around to be the trade
Of ions between molecules, electrons
Between the nuclei, and waves of light
And gravity between the particles,
Even the glue that fastens quark to quark.
I am the quid pro quo, what Dante called
The love that moves the sun and the other stars.

You want to say that that's not love, I see.
You want a love that's "unconditional,"
Dearer than eyesight, space, and liberty,
Beyond what can be valued, rich or rare.
(Alas that they should wear our colors there
In that chill, Kantian, eternity!)

You have begot me, bred me, loved me; I
Return those duties back as are right fit.
Sure, you must cast your bread upon the waters,
Suffer the risk of magnanimity;
That's not the point. You run more risk, not less,
In hoping that your gift will be repaid.
The greater risk than gift without return
Is trusting that reciprocation will
Bear all the fruits of prodigality.
The unrequited gift is not a bond
But the attempt by one to eat another.
Making the needy one a part of you.
A merchant's doctrine, yes, but that's my name.
If you want something else, then go elsewhere.

Yes, he who paid his life down for your sake,
Said that you could not serve both God and Mammon;
But also, it's as just to give to Caesar
What's Caesar's, as to give to God what's God's.
And you reciprocate by all the glory
Of art and science, wealth and liberty,
That you have piled up prodigally since
He seeded it with his audacious story.

To understand me, you must learn to see
More than one meaning of "eternity."
Plato, who hated me, and took me as
A god for only cities of the pigs,
Despised the common usage of the word
As just a long, a very long, extent of time.
Seeking a final validation, proof
Against the many rotting shams of change,
He took the timeless for eternity.
Who eats no food is surely safe from poison;
Who takes no breath can surely breathe no harm;
To save Good from decay one way might be
To take away the time where rot can grow
(The time where Good can also come to be).
Is good that cannot grow a good at all?
Can music happen where there are no waves?
Timeless is beingless: being is trade,
And time's the money of benevolence.

Suspect eternity you cannot count,
Suspect a numberless infinity.

The only true eternity is time
That you can count but cannot cease to count;
The only true infinity is time,
Blossoming inward always out and on.

What counts is always only who can count:
A counter that records what happens to it,
One who accounts for what he, she, has done.

But there's a third kind of eternity,
The one I count as mine: the branching tree
Of bifurcations, broken symmetries,
Physics' four forces sprouting out of one,
Carbon's unending new vocabularies,
Darwin's wild bush aflame with speciation,
The stemma of the human languages,
Entropy multiplying information,
Matings that propagate the family tree.

The Karykeion is the DNA,
The mating snakes that old Tiresias knew,
Coiled round a staff of bonding hydrogen,
Whose parting makes a four from what was two.
I am that staff of Moses, Metatron,
The branch I plucked out from the tree of life;
I am both angel and the branch he plucked,
The serpent tamed, the dead stick come alive,
The lyre of Orpheus wherewith he sought
To heal the sickness of Eurydice,
The golden bough that offers you safe-passage
Through the strange valley of the shade of death.
I am the herb of immortality
Snaked from the grasp of weary Gilgamesh,
I am the shepherd's staff of Jacob, who
Guided the sheep to mate and breed a stock
Pied with the stigma of domestication,
And won himself an endless progeny
Such that his name became that of a nation.

As Eshu, god of paths, I walk Benin,
Driving hard bargains with the sons of men,
Bringing them messages of what things cost.
I lead them from one state into another,
Even from life into the vale of death.
I wear a hat, red one side, black the other;

The villagers on each side come to blows
About my hat, if it is red or black.
The wise ones know deep truths reverse themselves;
And for the rest, I am the lord of strife.

Even the self itself is generated
Out of the knot of reciprocity:
To trade is to acknowledge as an agent
The one whose interest and will one shares.
How can a being know another mind
Unless it has had dealings with it? More,
How can one know one is a mind at all,
Except another give it recognition?
So here is my apology for who
I am: one who is not good, nor a goodness,
But one who makes all goodness possible.
I am the trickster, the invisible hand;
I am exchange, the love of interest,
The work you do whenever you decide
To choose this dress, this home, this work, this lover,
And so engender value and desire.

# Index

"advergaming" 246
"agency" concept 199
Althusius, Johannes 143
altruism 14–16, 31–3, 102, 199; in animals 282–3; of organ donation 307–9, 339
altruistic hedonism 202
Anderson, Chris 246–8
Anderson, Elizabeth 95, 110
animal behaviour 281–4
Appiah, Kwame Anthony 47
Aquinas, Thomas 40, 196, 202
Arce, M. 206
Aristotle 22, 201, 208, 262–3, 306
Arrow, Kenneth 112, 125, 128, 141, 205
associations and associational life 122–3, 127–43, 151–2, 191, 337–41
assurance game payoff structures 24
Axelrod, Robert 47
Ayr Bank 324, 327

Badhwar, Neera K. xii, 8, 337, 339
Bahamas, the 161
Baier, Annette 204
banking 322–34, 338; regulation of 329
Bartolus of Saxoferrato 265
Batt, Francis 267
Becker, Gary 148, 197–8, 205, 274
beliefs, preferences and constraints approach to individual action 20
Bell, Daniel 45
beneficence 57–60, 67–72, 90; corrective feedback to 70
Benkler, Yochai 72, 243, 245, 275
Bentham, Jeremy 205
Berlin, Isaiah 225, 257
Bewley, Truman 21
Bicchieri, Cristina 47

*Bildung* 128
bills of exchange 325, 328, 332
Bird-David, Nurit 161
Bitcoin 275
Black, Antony 178
black markets 312
Blackstone, William 262
body parts, sale of 305–6; *see also* kidney markets
Boehm, Christopher 28–9
Boettke, Peter J. xii, 6–7, 69–70, 77–9
Böhm, Franz 181–6, 189
Boo, Katherine 311
Boo, Michael 309
Boulding, Kenneth E. 5–6, 59, 101
bourgeois society 162
Bowles, Samuel xii–xiii, 6–7, 77, 79
Brown, David W. 47
Bruni, Luigino xiii, 7, 103–12, 146–52
Buccleuch, Duke of 324
Buchanan, James M. 69, 107, 255, 261–70, 281, 299–300
Buddhism 305–6

Card, Claudia 230–1
catallactic approach: to economics 281; to politics 300
central planning 126, 140
Chamlee-Wright, Emily xiii, 7, 214–16, 227
charity 49
Cherry, Mark J. 316
Chesterton, G.K. 186
Civil Economy theory 85–6, 93–8
civil society 47–50, 90–4, 116
civilizing role of commerce 42–6, 50, 79, 88, 94, 96
Coase, Ronald H. 56, 63, 255, 267
codetermination 183, 261

collective action 19
collective intentionality, theory of 101–10, 113–15, 146
competitive economic systems 18
concerted action 123, 146
Condorcet, Marquis de 43
Confucius 207
Connolly, William 69
consent of the governed 263–5
constitutional citizenship 59
contractarianism 39–40
Cooley, Charles Horton 22
cooperation: altruistic 33; and competition 18–19; definition of 14–15; prevalence and potential benefits of 31; roots of 15–18; theories of 13–14
cooperatives 269
Cornuelle, Richard 3–8, 47, 59, 113, 117, 122–3, 129–35, 140, 143, 221, 224–5, 230–2, 253
corporate personality 130–2, 135–6, 143
Corwin, Edward S. 264
cosmopolitanism 47, 49
cost–benefit analysis 169
Coulson, Charles 201
Cowen, Tyler 254–6
Cox, James Ray 165–8, 217
cultural transmission 26–31
culture: definition of 25; theories of 227

Danby, Colin xiii, 1, 7, 239, 274–5
Davies, John B. 123, 140–1
Daviss, Bennett 206
Dawkins, Richard 26
*de jure* and *de facto* responsibility 267–9
Debreu, Gerard 1
Deming, W. Edwards 256
democracy 188–9
Descartes, René 209
digital communities 239–42
digital gifts 236–45, 275
Dobuzinskis, Laurent xiii–xiv, 7
Dore, Ronald 259
Doria, Paolo Mattia 92
*doux-commerce* thesis 40–1, 44, 46, 49–50, 79, 96
Dow, Sheila 101–3
Dragonetti, Giacinto 94–8
Dumont, Louis 87
Durkheim, Emile 126

Ealy, Leonore T. i, xiv
*Economia Civile* 86
Edgeworth, F.Y. 21
Elder-Vass, Dave xiv, 8, 274–5
Ellerman, David xiv, 8, 255, 274–7
"entangled spheres" 7–8
Epictetus 208
epigenetic transmission 26–7
ethical codes 206
ethnographic research 164
Eucken, Walter 181–2, 186, 189
evolutionary processes 282–4
exchange, theory of 61, 281–5; *see also* market exchange
exchange values 288–9
extended families 292–3

Fabre, Cecile 308
Facebook 240, 249
Fehr, Ernst 19
Feinberg, Joel 313
Ferguson, James 231–2
feudalism 147, 231
Field, Alexander 204–5
Filangieri, Gaetano 93
Fodor, Jerry 200
Follett, Mary Parker 257
Forman-Barzilai, Fonna 64
Founding Fathers of the USA 270–1
Frankfurt, Harry 200–1
"free riding" 14, 18, 22, 31, 217, 283, 296
Freyer, Hans 125
Friedman, Milton 205–6, 224
Fuchs, Christian 245, 248

Garnett, Robert F. i, xiv–xv, 6–7, 78–80, 115–16, 221, 249
*Gemeinschaft–Gesellschaft* distinction 1–4, 126, 157–60, 163, 166–9, 173–4, 177–85, 190, 193, 214–16, 259
gene-culture coevolution 25, 33
genetic transmission 27
Genovesi, Antonio 89–98
Germany 178–93, 261, 276
Gibson-Graham, J.K. 248
Gide, André 204
Gierke, Otto von 126, 130–6, 143, 264–5
Gilligan, Carol 229
Gintis, Herbert xv, 6–7, 77, 79, 195
global financial crisis (2008) 45–6, 77
Google 248–9
Gregg, Samuel xv, 7, 215
Griswold, Charles L. 57

Grosby, Steven xv–xvi, 7, 146–7, 151–2
group membership 107–9
Gudeman, Stephen 161

Haidt, Jonathan 70
Hampshire, Stuart 198
Hanley, Ryan Patrick 58, 193
Hardin, Garrett 18
Hargreaves Heap, Shaun P. xvi, 7, 148
Hayek, F.A. 39, 46, 56–7, 63, 69–73, 79, 101–2, 106–13, 116–17, 125–6, 129, 143, 157–8, 181, 191, 215, 222–4, 230, 257, 281–2, 285–7, 299–300
Hegel, G.W.F. 89
Held, Virginia 198, 210
Henrich, Joseph 47, 150
Herder, Johann Gottfried 224
Hil, Garet and Jan 307
Hirsch, Fred 45
Hirschman, Albert 45, 95, 258, 271
Hobbes, Thomas 18, 22, 39–40, 89, 129, 196, 263–4
holist conception of community and knowledge 223–6
*Homo economicus* 21
*Homo reciprocans* 217
Hooker, Richard 208
Horwitz, Steven xvi, 8, 337–40
household production 289–90
human nature 102
"humanomics" 195
Hume, David 39–43, 222, 325
Hutcheson, Francis 266–7
Huxley, Aldous 209
Huxley, Julian 26

identity and group membership 108
"impartial spectators" 63–7, 70, 217
inalienable rights, theory of 266–8, 271
incentive pay for employees 255–7
India 311–17, 339
individuality 87
inducement gifts 245–9
Institute for Justice (IJ) 316
international transplant community (ITC) 303–6, 309–10, 315–16
intersubjective conceptions of community and knowledge 225–7
"invisible hand" metaphor 18, 40, 44, 57, 67, 88–91, 134
Iran 309

Jacob, Margaret 47
James, William 26

Japan 206–7, 258–61, 276
Jefferson, Thomas 267
Jell-O 246
Jevons, William Stanley 78
Jinsai, Itō 207
Joken, Nishikawa 207
Josselson, Ruthellen 160
Justinian, Institutes of 263–4

Kagono, Tadao 258–9
Kant, Immanuel 97, 107, 198, 206, 222, 307, 314
Kappeler, P.K. 13–14
Kass, Amy 70
Kass, Leon 305–6
Katrina (hurricane) 164–73, 216
Keefer, Philip 148, 150
Keynes, John Maynard 258
kidney markets 303–17, 337
kin selection 283–4, 298–9
Kiyonari, Toko 24
Klein, Daniel B. 57
Klein, Richard 29–30
Klemm, David 196
Knack, Stephen 148, 150
Knight, Frank 45, 126–7, 132, 199
Kobayashi, Takao 258–9
Koehn, Daryl 208–9
Kolm, Serge-Christophe 217–18
Kropotkin, Pyotr 19

language, role of 79–80, 108
Lavoie, Don 227
legal tender 330–1
Lerner, Josh 244
Lessig, Lawrence 248
Lewis, C.S. 196, 202–3, 208
Lewis, Paul i, xvii, 7, 146–52
Lewis, Renee 170–1
*lex regia* 264
Lieblich, Amia 160
"loaded" gifts 248
Loasby, Brian 228
Locke, John 40
love, concepts of 195–205, 208, 214, 217
Luther, Martin 87, 265–6
Lyons, Kate 170

McAdams, Dan P. 160, 162
McClelland, David 210
McCloskey, Deirdre xvii, 7, 47, 158, 162, 214–18, 291
McEntee, Kevin 244
MacIntyre, Alasdair 95, 162, 199

Maine, Henry Sumner 126
Maitland, Frederic William 129–33, 136
Malinovski, Bronislaw 217
Mandeville, Bernard 38
market exchange 86–8, 92–3, 101–16, 146–52, 185–6, 238, 246–7, 254, 288, 337; definition of 1; Hayekian theory of 106–13
marketing gifts 246–7
marriage contracts 262–3
Marsilius of Padua 265
Marx, Karl 44, 49, 312, 336
Mauss, Marcel 89, 217, 240
"memes" 26
Mencken, H.L. 21–2
mental models 161
mercantilism 39–40, 97–8
methodological individualism 123, 125; and social relations 133–41
micro-philanthropy 60
Mill, John Stuart 199, 216
Millet, Randy 172
Mises, Ludwig von 46, 122, 181, 281, 288–90, 299–300
Montes, Leonidas 72
Montesquieu, Baron de 43, 96
Morley, John 265–6
motivation, internal and external 255–8, 270–1
Moynihan Report (1965) 291
Müller-Armack, Alfred 183–4
Murray, Gilbert 208
mutuality 14, 111–16, 148–52

Najita, Tetsuo 206–7
Naples and Neapolitan economists 93–6
narrative scholarship 160–74
Nash equilibrium 24
National Organ Transplant Act (US, 1984) 305
Neanderthals 29
neoliberalism 179, 181, 185–93, 214–15
Netflix 244
new institutional economics 253–5
New Orleans 168–75
niche construction 26–7
North, Douglas C. 161
Nozick, Robert 200–1, 209
Nussbaum, Martha 163, 166–7

*oikeiōsis* 72–3
Olson, Mancur 18–19

open-source software 242–5
option clauses in banking 330
organ donors 308
Ostrom, Elinor 19
Ostrom, Vincent 141
O'Sullivan, Dan 242
Otteson, James R. 63, 113, 134–5, 193

Paganelli, Maria Pia xvii, 8, 337–8
Paine, Thomas 43, 95–6
Pareto inefficiency 22
Parker, Catherine 170
Parker, David 254–6
Parsons, Talcott 124, 127
payoff monotonic dynamic 27
Pearcey, Nancy 201
Peart, Sandra J. xvii, 6–7
Percy, Eustace 269
Peters, R.S. 106
philanthropy 101, 113–17; definition of 113; *see also* micro-philanthropy
Pinker, Steven 200, 202
Plato 38, 209, 262–3, 306
Polanyi, Michael 127, 257
political philosophy 38–41, 44, 214
Pollock, Frederick 131
Popper, Karl 128, 138
post-modern societies 90
praiseworthiness 80
preference functions 20
preferences, self-regarding and other-regarding 22; *see also* social preferences
prices 288–90
prisoner's dilemma 18–19, 22–4, 79
propriety, sense of 128, 139
Protestantism 87

Radiohead 247
rationality 112
Rawls, John 336
reciprocity 67, 92, 98, 103, 107, 115–16, 218, 240, 246–8, 281–4
Red Hat (company) 244
reputational benefits 244–5, 296
resource allocation 290–1
Ricard, Samuel 43
Ridley, Matt 284
Roberts, Russell 209
robust political economy 39, 41, 50
Roman Catholic Church 87, 203, 306
Romily, Samuel 57
Röpke, Wilhelm 185–91, 215
Rothbard, Murray 196, 312

Rousseau, Jean-Jacques 44, 49, 188, 201, 257, 333, 336
Ruddick, Sara 230–1
rule of law 125–9
Rüstow, Alexander 180–6

Sally, Razeen 187–8
Samuelson, Paul 1, 205, 267
Samuelsonian economics 4–5, 195–6, 199–202
Sandel, Michael 45
Scheper-Hughes, Nancy 312
Schervish, Paul 114
Schmalenbach, Herman 124
Schmidtz, David xviii, 8, 199, 208–9
Schumpeter, Joseph 45
Scottish banking 322–8, 331, 337–8
Scottish Enlightenment 40–6, 49–50, 86–8, 177, 193, 265–7
Seabright, Paul 73, 116–17
"self-destruction" thesis of capitalist society 45
self-interest 15, 19, 21, 56, 72, 77, 79, 101–2, 114, 201, 214–18, 323
self-understanding, development of 141–3
Seligman, Martin 70–1
Sen, Amartya 107–10, 199, 203, 209–10
Shaftesbury, Earl of 92
"shaggy" networks 227, 232
Shaw, Eleanor 171–2
Shils, Edward 124, 127, 130, 132
Shirky, Clay 241–2
Shunro, Miyake 206–7
Simon, Herbert 253–5
Sirico, Robert 47
Skidelsky, Edward 45
Skidelsky, Robert 45
Skinner, Quentin 265
slavery 263, 267, 271
Smith, Adam 1, 18, 39–42, 46–9, 56–61, 64–73, 77–80, 86–91, 124, 128, 134, 139, 148–52, 179, 193, 204–8, 216–17, 222, 228, 262, 281–2, 285, 288, 322–34, 336, 338
Smith, Daniel J. xviii, 6–7, 77, 79
Smith, Eric Alden 32
Smith, Vernon 195
social capital 93
social cooperation 6–7, 58, 62–3
Social Darwinism 19
social dilemmas 22
social entrepreneurship 58–9
social learning 25–6

social networking sites 240
social norms 17, 106–9, 115
social preferences 15–18, 22–4, 31–2, 79
sociality 92; thin and thick 3
Socrates 305
solicitation gifts 246–7
Solomon, Robert 208
Solow, Robert 1–2
special-interest communities 303–4
"spontaneous order" concept (Hayek) 285–7
Stack, Carol 282, 291–300
Starr, Martha J. xviii, 8
states, role of 160–4, 178, 184–8, 191–2, 215–16
Stern, Jessica 21
Stigler, George J. 72, 196
Stocker, Michael 196
Stoicism 63–4, 72
Storr, Virgil Henry xviii–xix, 7, 112, 161, 214–16
Sugden, Robert 103–12, 202
sympathy, Adam Smith's moral theory of 62–6

Taylor, Daniel 163
Tennyson, Alfred 19
Thiagarajan, C.M. 314–16
"thin" moral framework of markets 48
"third sector" (Cornuelle) 224
Thrasher, John xix, 8
Tirole, Jean 244
Tocqueville, Alexis de 114, 122, 129, 148, 188–93, 215, 337
Todorov, Tzvetan 85
Tomes, Nigel 197–8
Tönnies, Ferdinand 1, 123–6, 157–8, 177–8, 190, 193, 214–15, 237
Totman, Conrad 207
tradition and traditionalism 140, 223–4
"tragedy of the commons" 18–19, 22, 308
"trickle-down" 151–2
Tronto, Joan 199–200
trust 148–51, 322–34, 339–41
Turner, Frederick xix, 8, 342

Ulpian 263–4
unlimited liability 324–7, 338

vampire bats 283–4, 340
van Schaik, Carel P. 13–14
Veblen, Thorstein 22, 201, 275
Verri, Pietro 89

Viner, Jacob 57, 78
Voltaire 41–2

Walker, Jordan and Irene 173
Wal-Mart 165–8, 217
Walrasian exchange 1
Weber, Max 123–6
"we-intentions" 108–10;
  *see also* collective intentionality
Weintraub, E. Roy 1
welfare states 188–9
Wertheimer, Alan 313
Whitehead, Alfred North 198, 203
Whittaker, Hugh 259
Wieser, Friedrich von 269
Wikipedia 241–3

Wilbur, Richard 203
Wilkinson, Gerald S. 283–4
Wills, Garry 267
Wilson, Bart 195
Winterhalder, Bruce 32

X-efficiency 258

Yeats, William Butler 203
Young, Allyn 228
Yuengert, Andrew 198–9

Zak, Paul 110
Zeno 208
*Zollverein*, the 179
Zoroastrianism 305